1984

FAREWELL TO THE PARTY OF LINCOLN

FAREWELL TO THE PARTY OF LINCOLN

Black Politics in the Age of FDR

Nancy J. Weiss

PRINCETON UNIVERSITY PRESS
PRINCETON, NEW JERSEY

Copyright © 1983 by Princeton University Press
Published by Princeton University Press,
41 William Street, Princeton, New Jersey 08540
In the United Kingdom: Princeton University Press,
Guildford, Surrey

All Rights Reserved

Library of Congress Cataloging in Publication Data
will be found on the last printed page of this book

ISBN cloth: 0-691-04703-0
ISBN paper: 0-691-10151-8

This book has been composed in Linotron Trump

Clothbound editions of Princeton University Press books
are printed on acid-free paper, and binding materials
are chosen for strength and durability.
Paperback editions, while satisfactory for personal
collections, are not usually suitable for library rebinding

Printed in the United States of America by Princeton
University Press, Princeton, New Jersey

For Bonnie and Rob,
Scott and Brad

Contents

Illustrations

Illustrations

Tables

Tables

Preface

Fifty years after Franklin D. Roosevelt first won the presidency, political analysts wrote the obituary for his electoral coalition. By 1980, farmers, blue-collar workers, ethnics, and Southerners had all loosened if not broken the historic ties that had bound them to the Democratic party. The group of voters most firmly committed to the Democrats were black Americans, the last to join the New Deal coalition. This book explains the origins of that commitment in the 1930s.

Most blacks who voted in 1932 were loyal to the Republicans as the party of emancipation. But by 1936, blacks had moved overwhelmingly into the Democratic column. In four years, Roosevelt and the New Deal changed the political habits of black Americans in ways that have lasted to our own time. How and why that happened is the central theme of this study.

The forging of the New Deal coalition, and with it the cementing of the Democratic party's new status as the nation's majority party, have received extensive scholarly analysis. But the political scientists who have produced the most important works on the subject have written very little about black Americans.[1] Two circumstances make the black vote a distinctive and interesting problem. First, black voting behavior differed from that of other ethnic groups, who were quicker to join the Democratic coalition. Immigrant voters, attracted to the party in large numbers in 1928 because of Alfred E. Smith, solidified their Democratic loyalties in 1932 under the pressures of economic distress. Blacks joined the Democratic party at a different time, with a more varied range of inducements to attract them and a stronger set of obstacles to overcome. Second, the problem is essentially paradoxical: the New Deal paid only the most limited attention

[1] The two most notable exceptions are Everett Carll Ladd, Jr., with Charles D. Hadley, *Transformations of the American Party System: Political Coalitions from the New Deal to the 1970s*, 2nd ed. (New York, 1978); and Samuel Lubell, *White and Black: Test of a Nation*, 2nd ed., rev. (New York, 1966).

to blacks, and yet it was in response to the New Deal that blacks moved into the Democratic fold.

Farewell to the Party of Lincoln attempts to account for that paradox. Set against a portrait of the racial climate of the 1930s, it interweaves several important themes: the black electoral response to the New Deal; the extraordinary chemistry between blacks and the Roosevelts; the New Deal's record on race; the central role of economic concerns in shaping black political behavior; the impact of the New Deal in politicizing blacks as a special interest group; and the function of the Roosevelts and the New Deal in determining the continuing loyalty of blacks to the Democratic party.

The main argument of the book—that blacks became Democrats in response to the economic benefits of the New Deal and that they voted for Franklin Roosevelt in spite of the New Deal's lack of a substantive record on race—should come as no surprise to most readers. The vital role of New Deal relief and recovery programs in attracting blacks to the Democratic party is taken for granted by scholars who have written about the 1930s.[2] Although it has been a common theme, however, it has rarely occasioned more than the briefest mention—a few sentences or paragraphs in most general accounts. Specialized studies of black voting at the local level have begun to flesh out the story, but a comprehensive national portrait remains to be drawn.[3] The fullest study of blacks in the 1930s, Harvard Sitkoff's *A New Deal for*

[2] The best and most extensive discussions of the subject can be found in Arthur M. Schlesinger, Jr., *The Politics of Upheaval* (Boston, 1960); John Hope Franklin, *From Slavery to Freedom: A History of Negro Americans*, 5th ed. (New York, 1980); Raymond Wolters, "The New Deal and the Negro," in *The New Deal*, vol. I: *The National Level*, ed. John Braeman, Robert H. Bremner, and David Brody (Columbus, Ohio, 1975).

[3] Among published studies, the following are notable: John M. Allswang, "The Chicago Negro Voter and the Democratic Consensus: A Case Study, 1918-1936," *Journal of the Illinois State Historical Society* LX (Summer 1967):145-75; Ernest M. Collins, "Cincinnati Negroes and Presidential Politics," *Journal of Negro History* XLI (Apr. 1956):131-37; Larry W. Dunn, "Knoxville Negro Voting and the Roosevelt Revolution, 1928-1936," *East Tennessee Historical Society's Publications*, no. 43 (1971); Rita Werner Gordon, "The Change in the Political Alignment of Chicago's Negroes during the New Deal," *Journal of American History* LVI (Dec. 1969):584-603; Elmer W. Henderson, "Political Changes among Negroes in Chicago during the Depression," *Social Forces* XIX (May 1941):538-46; Peirce F. Lewis, "Impact of Negro Migration on the Electoral Geography of Flint, Michigan, 1932-1962: A Cartographic Analysis," *Annals of the Association of American Geographers* LV (Mar. 1965):1-25; Edward H. Litchfield, "A Case Study of Negro Political Behavior in Detroit," *Public Opinion Quarterly* V (June 1941):267-74. In addition, there is a growing body of unpublished studies, cited in the notes to Chapter IX.

Blacks, argues that the New Deal moved affirmatively to embrace the cause of civil rights, and that its positive record on race brought blacks into the Democratic party.[4] That argument is at odds with the one developed in this book.

A rich array of sources makes it possible to study black political attitudes in the 1930s. Black newspapers, the personal papers of the Roosevelts and other members of the administration, the papers of blacks who were in government in the 1930s, and the records of federal agencies form the main body of written sources from which this book has been shaped. More than sixty-five interviews with white New Dealers, black politicians, governmental officials, civil rights leaders, journalists, clergymen, and others supplement the written record.

Black political attitudes, however, are much easier to discover than black political behavior. Polling—the instrument that tries to measure the black vote today—was in its infancy in the 1930s, and pollsters rarely isolated blacks as a distinct political group.[5] Because official voting records are not kept by race, it is impossible to say how black Americans in general voted in any national election.

It is possible, nevertheless, to undertake an analysis of black political behavior, provided some important limitations are understood. The first is that the analysis of black voting in this period means the analysis of black voting in the cities of the North. Two-thirds of blacks of voting age in the 1930s lived in the old Confederacy and in the District of Columbia; for the most part, this meant that they were unable to vote. By 1940, of the 2,400,000 blacks of voting age who lived elsewhere, and usually escaped disfranchisement, two-thirds resided in cities of over 100,000.[6]

Studying black voting in the cities, then, partly reflects where black voters lived. It is also a matter of necessity. In examining black political attitudes, one can draw on expressions of opinion from people in widely scattered locations, urban as well as rural,

[4] Harvard Sitkoff, *A New Deal for Blacks: The Emergence of Civil Rights as a National Issue,* vol. I: *The Depression Decade* (New York, 1978). Leslie H. Fishel, Jr., "The Negro in the New Deal Era," *Wisconsin Magazine of History* XLVIII (Winter 1964):111-26, offers a similar interpretation.

[5] See, for example, George H. Gallup, *The Gallup Poll: Public Opinion, 1935-1971,* 3 vols. (New York, 1972), vol. I.

[6] Derived from U.S. Department of Commerce, Bureau of the Census, *Sixteenth Census of the United States: 1940, Population,* vol. II: *Characteristics of the Population,* pt.1 (Washington, D.C., 1943), pp. 119-51.

northern as well as southern. But analyzing the black vote requires isolating precincts or election divisions whose population was almost entirely black. Such units are extremely difficult to find. They can be located most readily in major cities with relatively large black populations, where blacks were concentrated in narrow geographic areas. Such cities—New York, Philadelphia, Chicago, Cleveland, Detroit, and Pittsburgh—provide the principal quantitative evidence for this study. The numbers involved are small; the election units studied necessarily comprise only a fraction of the black electorate in the respective cities and an even smaller fraction of that electorate nationwide. Still, the quantitative evidence fits into a clear pattern.

Documenting black political behavior in the urban North is appropriate, finally, because urbanization sparked the political transformation that brought blacks into the Democratic party in the 1930s. Migration from the rural South—historically the stronghold of Democratic racism—set the stage for liberation from the party of Lincoln. "The significance of urbanization to the political modernization of Negroes," Martin Kilson has written, "cannot be overemphasized: it afforded them the quality of social organization and institutional differentiation or specialization without which effective political development is impossible."[7] The massing of large numbers of blacks in limited geographical areas made possible the articulation of common political interests. It fostered the development of specialized interest groups with particular political objectives. It created an environment conducive to the emergence of black political leadership. It brought blacks under the sway of local Democratic political machines. And it made the black vote a sufficient force to warrant attention from the national parties.

Blacks in northern cities in the 1930s voted Democratic because the New Deal brought them some relief from the Depression. Despite the willingness of the Roosevelt administration to make some symbolic racial gestures, the race issue never became part of the New Deal agenda. It was Franklin Roosevelt's ability to provide jobs, not his embrace of civil rights, that made him a hero to black Americans.

[7] Martin Kilson, "Political Change in the Negro Ghetto, 1900-1940's" in *Key Issues in the Afro-American Experience*, ed. Nathan I. Huggins, Martin Kilson, and Daniel M. Fox, 2 vols. (New York, 1971), II:168.

Acknowledgments

Like most scholarly enterprises, this book has profited greatly from the generosity and good judgment of many people. I am indebted, first, to the directors and staffs of the libraries that house the main body of materials on which this study is based: the Franklin D. Roosevelt Library, the Library of Congress, the Moorland-Spingarn Research Center at Howard University, the National Archives, and the Schomburg Center for Research in Black Culture. To single them out for special thanks in no way diminishes my gratitude to their counterparts at the many other libraries and institutions in which I worked: the Archives of Labor History and Urban Affairs, Wayne State University; the Trevor Arnett Library, Atlanta University; the Beinecke Library, Yale University; the Board of Elections of Cuyahoga County, Cleveland; the Butler Library, Columbia University; the Center for Political Studies, Institute for Social Research, University of Michigan; the Chicago Board of Election Commissioners; the Chicago Historical Society; the Columbia University Oral History Collection; the Cuyahoga County Archives, Cleveland; the Detroit Election Commission; the Detroit Public Library; the Drew University Library, Madison, N.J.; the Milton S. Eisenhower Library, The Johns Hopkins University; the Firestone Library, Princeton University; the Free Public Library, Philadelphia; the Municipal Reference and Research Center, New York City; the Municipal Reference Library, Chicago; the National Archives for Black Women's History, Washington, D.C.; the New York Public Library; the National Opinion Research Center, Chicago; the Phelps-Stokes Fund Archives; the State Archives and History Bureau, New Jersey State Library, Trenton; the Wayne County Election Commission, Detroit; the Western Historical Collections, Norlin Library, University of Colorado; and the Widener Library, Harvard University. The librarians of the American Baptist Historical Society; the Amistad Research Center, Dillard University; the Carnegie Library, Livingstone College, Salisbury, N.C.; the Commission on Archives and History, the United Methodist

Acknowledgments

Church; the Lawson McGee Library, Knoxville; the Tennessee State Library and Archives; the United Methodist Publishing House; and the University of Pittsburgh Library were good enough to provide information and copies of material which I requested.

A number of individuals graciously shared information and permitted me to use material that would not otherwise have been accessible. Hilton B. Clark allowed me to read the transcripts of his interviews with J. Raymond Jones and to consult clippings and correspondence about Jones which he has collected. Pat A. Mercurio, Ivy Graves, and Odessa Wellesley guided me through the birth records at Harlem Hospital. Harold Rome sent me information about his song, "F.D.R. Jones." Jacqueline Harris, Alice Isom, Eleanor James, A. J. Levin, Roosevelt Thompkins, Joel W. Woodall, Sr., and Frank Albert Young responded to my inquiry about black naming practices. Nancy Grant, Laurence I. Hewes, Jr., Kenneth T. Jackson, Richard T. Meister, Gary C. Ness, Gary W. Reichard, Roy Rosenzweig, Elaine M. Smith, H. Lewis Suggs, and Christopher G. Wye let me consult their unpublished papers. Dorothy Height granted me access to the transcript of her interview with the Schlesinger Library's Black Women's Oral History Project. Clara M. Mitchell allowed me to use the papers of her husband, Arthur W. Mitchell, at the Chicago Historical Society.

The Trustees of Columbia University in the City of New York granted me permission to quote from the following memoirs in the Columbia Oral History Collection: Will Winton Alexander, Samuel J. Battle, Joseph A. Gavagan, and Roy Wilkins, all copyright 1972, and Frances Perkins, copyright 1976. Dr. Bettye Collier-Thomas, Director of the National Archives for Black Women's History and the Mary McLeod Bethune Memorial Museum, permitted me to quote from material in the Records of the National Council of Negro Women. Harold Rome allowed me to quote the lyrics of his song, "F.D.R. Jones." Viking Penguin Inc. gave me permission to quote passages from Walter White, *A Man Called White: The Autobiography of Walter White.* Oxford University Press allowed me to reprint tables originally published in Nancy J. Weiss, *The National Urban League, 1910-1940.* W. W. Norton & Company, Inc., granted permission to reprint a table originally published in Everett Carll Ladd, Jr., with Charles D. Hadley, *Transformations of the American Party System: Political Coalitions from the New Deal to the 1970s.* Albert H. Cantril allowed me to reprint polls from Hadley Cantril, ed., *Public Opin-*

ion, 1935-1946. Harold Ober Associates Incorporated gave permission to reprint Langston Hughes's poem, "Ballad of Roosevelt," originally published in the *New Republic*.

Benjamin D. Berry, Jr., Anthony Broh, Richard D. Challener, Ev Ehrlich, Jean Firstenberg, Christopher H. Foreman, David J. Garrow, Fred Greenstein, David C. Hammack, Suzanne Keller, Stanley Kelley, Jr., Eamon Kelly, Martin Kilson, Kenneth L. Kusmer, David Levin, Richard A. Long, Christine A. Lunardini, Gladys W. McGee, Amanda F. MacKenzie, William McLoughlin, Elaine Tyler May, Lary May, August Meier, Clara M. Mitchell, Nell Irvin Painter, Clement A. Price, Rebecca Scott, Bernard Sternsher, Sidney Verba, and Meyer Weinberg offered ideas, leads, and suggestions about sources. Danny Bradley, Lawrence Hamm, Robert Ray, and Patricia Vaughan provided research assistance at various stages of the project. To all of them, my warmest thanks.

Grants from the Charles Warren Center for Studies in American History at Harvard University, the Eleanor Roosevelt Institute, the Princeton University Committee on Research in the Humanities and Social Sciences, and the Princeton University Department of History helped importantly to facilitate my research and writing, and I am grateful for their support. Isobel Abelson typed the manuscript with great competence and good cheer. At Princeton University Press, my editor, Gail M. Filion, shepherded it from first submission to final publication, and my copyeditor, Marilyn Campbell, added significantly to its precision and style. I thank all of them for their cooperation and their confidence in this book.

Two groups of people made extraordinary contributions to this project, and I want to record my deep appreciation for their efforts. The men and women who consented to be interviewed added immeasurably to the store of information on which this study is based. More than that, they provided an invaluable link to the times in which they lived; to the extent that this book accurately evokes the mood and experiences of the 1930s, it is due in great measure to their recollections. Their names are listed in the Note on Sources; I owe them a great debt.

I owe a different debt, though one no less important, to the friends who read all or parts of the manuscript at various stages in its evolution: Alan Brinkley, William H. Chafe, Robert Curvin, Paul B. Firstenberg, Frank Freidel, Dewey W. Grantham, Jeannette Hopkins, Arthur S. Link, James M. McPherson, Arthur Mann,

Acknowledgments

Arno J. Mayer, James T. Patterson, Ingrid W. Scobie, and W. J. Trent, Jr. Whatever strengths this book has grow directly from their wise counsel and constructive criticisms. Its weaknesses, of course, are my own responsibility.

My family, as always, provided inestimable support of all kinds.

Princeton, New Jersey
September 1982

FAREWELL TO THE PARTY OF LINCOLN

PROLOGUE ▪ *The Election of 1928*

In the summer of 1932, not long after his twenty-first birthday, Clarence Mitchell registered to vote. Had he heeded tradition, Mitchell would have chosen the Republican party. His family were loyal Republicans. In Baltimore, where he grew up, everyone knew that Republicans were "the high-minded, idealistic, God-fearing people," while Democrats dabbled in influence-peddling and vice.[1] The Grand Old Party was the party of Lincoln—a party that had held black allegiance for more than half a century on the strength of its record in the Civil War and Reconstruction.

To Mitchell, such traditions carried limited weight. Newly graduated from Lincoln University in Pennsylvania, he was vitally concerned with public issues—the issues of America in the Depression-ridden 1930s, not the 1870s. Trained to think systematically about social problems, eager to address the pressing concerns of his day, and fired with the independence of youth, he could hardly see Herbert Hoover's Republican party as a panacea for his nation or his race. When he went to register that summer, he recorded his name in the columns of the Democratic party.

Decades later, when Mitchell was nearing the end of a distinguished career as the chief Washington lobbyist for the National Association for the Advancement of Colored People, the memory of the reaction he evoked in 1932 remained sharp in his mind. To some people in his neighborhood, declaring for the Democratic party "was the equivalent of a traitorous act."[2] There was a "gen-

[1] Interview with Clarence M. Mitchell, Jr., Oct. 29, 1976, Washington, D.C.

[2] Clarence Mitchell, Jr., interview, Dec. 6, 1968, p. 17, Civil Rights Documentation Project, Ralph J. Bunche Oral History Collection, Moorland-Spingarn Research Center, Howard University. The same was true in Elizabeth, New Jersey, where Russell Bingham started a black Democratic organization: "The idea of a black being a Democrat was something like treason." Lawrence Hamm interview with Russell Bingham, July 10, 1979, Newark, N.J. In fact, as George L.-P. Weaver summed up, "Black Democrats were looked upon as not quite respectable in most communities." Interview with George L.-P. Weaver, May 23, 1977, Washington, D.C. See also "Call and Convention Manual of the National Colored Democratic Association, 1940," Franklin D. Roosevelt Papers, President's Personal File (PPF) 3634, Franklin D. Roosevelt Library, Hyde Park, N.Y. (hereafter cited as the FDR Papers); Isadore Martin to Walter White, Nov. 12, 1932, National Association for

eral feeling," Mitchell recalled, "that anybody who wasn't a Republican was somehow or other a kind of questionable character." Friends came to his parents in astonishment at the news: "What on earth was happening to this college graduate registering as a Democrat?"[3]

Such a reaction was far from unique. E. Frederic Morrow, who grew up in Hackensack, New Jersey, remembered his community's view of Negro Democrats. They "were as rare as a five-dollar bill in the middle of Broadway!" he wrote. "It was a form of heresy practically unknown and unpracticed. . . . Being a black Democrat was like announcing one had typhoid."[4]

For all of its novelty, Mitchell's act foretold the future political affiliation of most black Americans. When he cast his first vote for Franklin Roosevelt in 1932, Clarence Mitchell stood in the vanguard of a massive political migration that was to dislodge blacks from their traditional Republicanism and enlist them firmly in the Democratic party. In 1932, as a new black Democrat, Clarence Mitchell was something of a renegade; by 1936, the majority of black Americans stood beside him.

For all the magic of the name of Lincoln, there had been plenty of reason for black disenchantment with Republicans well before 1932. No twentieth-century Republican President had measured up to the Lincoln legacy. At first, Theodore Roosevelt had seemed to have the makings of a worthy successor to the Great Emancipator. Roosevelt's willingness to appoint blacks to federal offices, his reliance on the advice of Booker T. Washington, and his strongly stated opposition to lynching seemed to indicate that blacks would have a place in the Square Deal. But black optimism proved to be short-lived. In his second term, Roosevelt alienated many blacks, especially by his summary discharge of three companies of black infantrymen who refused to inform on their fellows who had allegedly shot up the town of Brownsville, Texas. When Roosevelt ran for President in 1912 as a Progressive, he gave blacks further reason for dissatisfaction. With Roosevelt's

---

the Advancement of Colored People Papers, Box C-391, Manuscript Division, Library of Congress (hereafter cited as the NAACP Papers); W.E.B. Du Bois, *Dusk of Dawn: An Essay Toward an Autobiography of a Race Concept* (1940; reprint ed., New York, 1968), p. 17.

[3] Mitchell interview, 1976. The experience was common. "When I told my father I had registered as a Democrat [in Newark], he of course bawled me out." Lawrence Hamm interview with Harry Van Dyke, Aug. 28, 1979, Newark, N.J.

[4] E. Frederic Morrow, *Way Down South Up North* (Philadelphia, 1973), p. 38.

approval, the new party cultivated a lily-white constituency in the South and refused seats at its national convention to black delegates from that region. Nor would the convention consider an equal rights plank drafted by W.E.B. Du Bois.[5]

William Howard Taft proved to be no more attractive. Eager to strengthen southern Republicanism, he paid special attention to the sensitivities of the white South. Particularly offensive to blacks was his policy of not appointing to federal offices anyone whom the local community found objectionable. In practice, that meant the exclusion of blacks from federal posts in the South—a record scarcely offset by some showcase appointments in Washington and in diplomatic and consular positions. Equally troubling was Taft's inattention to problems of segregation, discrimination, disfranchisement, and racial violence.[6]

Disappointed with Roosevelt and Taft and tempted by Woodrow Wilson's campaign promises of justice and fair dealing for the race, significant numbers of influential blacks backed the Democratic party in the election of 1912. Expecting some attention in return for their support, they were rudely disappointed. Patronage proved to be meager, and segregation in the federal departments in Washington, which had begun in the Roosevelt years, spread to the point where it appeared to have official sanction. The result was to kill the Democratic party's chance to capitalize on black disenchantment with Republican policies.[7]

In the 1920s, the Republican party showed more interest in cultivating lily-white Republicanism in the South than in strengthening the party's traditional ties to blacks. The Harding

[5] On Theodore Roosevelt and blacks, see Seth M. Scheiner, "President Theodore Roosevelt and the Negro, 1901-1908," *Journal of Negro History* XLVII (July 1962):169-82; Willard B. Gatewood, Jr., *Theodore Roosevelt and the Art of Controversy: Episodes of the White House Years* (Baton Rouge, 1970); George Sinkler, *The Racial Attitudes of American Presidents: From Abraham Lincoln to Theodore Roosevelt* (Garden City, N.Y., 1971), chaps. 9-10; Arthur S. Link, "Theodore Roosevelt and the South in 1912," in *The Higher Realism of Woodrow Wilson and Other Essays* (Nashville, 1971), pp. 243-55.

[6] On Taft and blacks, see Richard B. Sherman, *The Republican Party and Black America: From McKinley to Hoover, 1896-1933* (Charlottesville, Va., 1973), pp. 83-112.

[7] On Wilson and blacks, see Nancy J. Weiss, "The Negro and the New Freedom: Fighting Wilsonian Segregation," *Political Science Quarterly* LXXXIV (Mar. 1969):61-79; Arthur S. Link, *Wilson: The New Freedom* (Princeton, 1956), pp. 243-54; Kathleen L. Wolgemuth, "Woodrow Wilson and Federal Segregation," *Journal of Negro History* XLIV (Apr. 1959):158-73; Henry Blumenthal, "Woodrow Wilson and the Race Question," *ibid.* XLVIII (Jan. 1963):1-21; Christine A. Lunardini, "Standing Firm: William Monroe Trotter's Meetings with Woodrow Wilson, 1913-1914," *ibid.* LXIV (Summer 1979):244-64.

and Coolidge administrations appointed few blacks to federal posts and failed to reverse the policy of segregation in the civil service. Neither President—nor the Republican Congresses—made any effort to secure the right to vote of black Americans. Although Harding and Coolidge both deplored lynching, the battle of the National Association for the Advancement of Colored People to secure federal antilynching legislation found little support in the White House. And although Harding and Coolidge both spoke favorably of creating an interracial commission to investigate social and economic conditions among blacks, neither chose to establish it by Executive Order when Congress failed to act.[8]

In 1928, as in 1912, years of Republican inattention made black voters ripe for Democratic courting. The Democratic candidate, Alfred E. Smith, seemed to be the right person to do the wooing. The grandson of immigrants from Italy, Germany, and Ireland, who had grown up on New York City's lower East Side, Smith personified the demographic changes that were transforming the Democratic party. Not only was he the new political spokesman for ethnic minorities in the cities of the North; he was also the first Catholic ever to be nominated by a major party for President of the United States. Smith's very candidacy struck a blow against religious prejudice; one could imagine extending it to racial prejudice as well. Although the governor had no particular history of personal concern for racial justice, he was a product of Tammany Hall, which, since 1919, had had a reputation for using patronage to cultivate black support.[9]

Moreover, Smith had the right enemies. Alien to the traditionally Democratic South as a Catholic and a wet, he became the target of a scurrilous whispering campaign which painted him not only as a drunkard and a puppet of the Pope, but also as a foe of white supremacy.[10] Vituperative southern opposition to Smith made him more attractive to northern blacks. At the same time, the vigorous efforts of the Republican candidate, Herbert Hoover, to crack the Solid South made Smith all the more dependent on northern urban votes. Wooing blacks might be to Smith's advan-

[8] Sherman, *The Republican Party and Black America*, chaps. 6-8.

[9] On Smith, see *Dictionary of American Biography*, Supplement Three (New York, 1973), pp. 716-21; Matthew and Hannah Josephson, *Al Smith: Hero of the Cities* (Boston, 1969).

[10] Edmund A. Moore, *A Catholic Runs for President: The Campaign of 1928* (New York, 1956). On the role of religion and Prohibition in the Smith campaign, see also Allan J. Lichtman, *Prejudice and the Old Politics: The Presidential Election of 1928* (Chapel Hill, 1979), chaps. 2-4.

tage. With a low-key campaign, he might win black votes without much risk of losing white supporters, since the whites most likely to be offended already opposed him because of his religion or his stand on Prohibition.[11]

The Smith forces planned a campaign among blacks even before the Democratic national convention met at Houston in July. Working through intermediaries, Smith approached Walter White to direct it. White, a Negro who was blond, blue-eyed, light-skinned, and college-educated, had the contacts and the personal stature to function easily in white society. As the assistant executive secretary of the National Association for the Advancement of Colored People, who carried the prestige and the visibility of the nation's most prominent organization for racial advancement, he was a perfect emissary to blacks.

White was on leave from the NAACP on a Guggenheim fellowship to write a book about lynching and considered the offer at his temporary residence in France. He was strongly tempted to accept. He had "long been convinced" that Smith was "by far the best man available for the Presidency." The New Yorker's enemies were "the Negro's enemies"; his "nomination and election would be the greatest blow at bigotry that has ever been struck." What an "excellent . . . opportunity to appeal to Negroes to end their chronic Republicanism" and break the pernicious habit of "having their votes counted before ever they are cast."[12] White returned to New York in April under the official cover of a research trip in connection with his book to confer with Smith's supporters and learn more about the Smith candidacy, "all keen" about the job that he was to do.[13]

Once Smith won the nomination, the question of enlisting in the campaign became more complicated for White. His personal uncertainty typified the dilemma that confronted black voters in the general election. The Democratic convention had spelled

[11] Neal Lloyd Wolf, "The Negro Voter and the Election of 1928" (Senior thesis, Princeton University, 1970), pp. 72-75.

[12] Charles H. Studin to Walter White, Feb. 21, 1928, and White to Studin, Mar. 7, 1928, NAACP Papers, Box C-96. The quotations are from White to Studin.

[13] Walter White to Charles H. Studin, Mar. 26, 1928; NAACP press release, "Walter White Returns to U.S. to Gather Further Data," Apr. 13, 1928, NAACP Papers, Box C-96. It would appear that White did some careful thinking about the organization of the campaign. A preconvention memorandum in the NAACP Papers outlines in considerable detail the kinds of activities that the director of the campaign among blacks might undertake. Since it is unsigned, however, we cannot be certain that White wrote it. See "Suggested Program of Work," undated typescript, [1928], NAACP Papers, Box C-96.

nothing but trouble for blacks. There were no black delegates and no Negro plank in the platform. As a deliberate sop to the South, the New Yorker chose as his vice-presidential running mate Joseph T. Robinson, senator from Arkansas. The Democrats met in Houston, where a lynching that occurred just before the convention was to open had provided an ominous backdrop for the party's proceedings. The convention fenced off black alternates and spectators behind chicken wire in a separate cagelike enclosure.[14]

But the argument for supporting Smith still seemed more compelling to White. The Republican party was clearly unwilling to do anything for blacks. "The Hoover forces," White thought, had "quite obviously made up their minds to throw the Negro overboard in their efforts to Republicanize the South." Black delegates were also segregated at the Republican convention in Kansas City, and blacks had long since ceased to win significant patronage from the party. A Smith administration might not bring much positive action in behalf of blacks, but it surely would not be any worse than a Republican presidency. Most important, by breaking away from the Republican party, blacks could strike a blow for the political independence of the race. Once they saw that the black vote could no longer be taken for granted, White wrote, the parties might learn "that they must make concessions of importance to the race" if they wished to win black support.[15] And Smith's election would "be a long step towards wresting domination of the Democratic Party from the southern bourbon and vesting it in the hands of the North and East."[16] Most of White's confidants agreed that he could enlist in the campaign without jeopardizing the NAACP. He could always take a leave from the organization; besides, if Smith won, they imagined, the NAACP would be "the power behind the throne."[17]

White decided to join the Smith forces, provided that Smith promised to be guided in his appointments by character and ability instead of race, and that he devote some campaign speeches specifically to racial questions. At first, the alliance looked prom-

[14] Walter White to John Hurst, July 18, 1928, ibid.; Wolf, "The Negro Voter and the Election of 1928," pp. 70-71.

[15] Walter White to John Hurst, July 18, 1928, NAACP Papers, Box C-96. On the Republican convention and blacks, see Wolf, "The Negro Voter and the Election of 1928," pp. 50-58.

[16] Walter White to Moorfield Storey, July 22, 1928, NAACP Papers, Box C-96.

[17] John Hurst to Walter White, July 19, 1928; Moorfield Storey to White, July 25, 1928, both in ibid.; Storey to James Weldon Johnson, July 28, 1928, James Weldon Johnson Papers, Folder 465, Beinecke Library, Yale University. The quotation is from White to Hurst, July 20, 1928, NAACP Papers, Box C-96.

ising. Smith told White that he wanted to show blacks that the Democratic party was changing: the days of southern dominance were past; power had shifted to northern Democrats, who had "a totally different approach to the Negro." Smith asked White's help in planning a program to counteract black distrust and to demonstrate the party's "conversion." White and James Weldon Johnson, the executive secretary of the NAACP, drafted a statement for Smith to issue to make it clear to blacks and whites alike that Smith "would be president of all the people and would not be ruled by the anti-Negro South." The statement was direct enough to appeal to blacks and still sufficiently guarded not to inflame the South. The candidate was to meet privately with black leaders to give them more specific assurances of his intentions toward the race.

But the statement was never issued, and the meeting never took place. The inducement to woo blacks proved less powerful than the pressure from Senator Robinson and other Smith advisers to avoid unnecessarily antagonizing the South. Disappointed, White decided to drop the idea of managing the campaign among blacks and to return to his regular duties at the NAACP.[18]

Despite their failure to consummate the alliance with White, the Smith forces waged a more active campaign among blacks than had been the custom of the Democrats. With White continuing to provide unofficial assistance behind the scenes, the party established a Smith-for-President Colored League under the joint direction of two lawyers from Boston, one white (William Gaston), the other black (Julian D. Rainey). Earl B. Dickerson, a black lawyer in Chicago, directed the campaign in the critical midwestern states; Lester A. Walton, the editor of the black newspaper the *New York Age,* took on the job of director of publicity, and Bishop Reverdy C. Ransom of the African Methodist Episcopal (AME) Church took charge of the speakers' bureau.

The Colored League, in Dickerson's words, "had a considerable budget"—the unprecedented sum of $125,000—and made "an all-out effort" to bring blacks into the Democratic party. The *Chicago Defender, Baltimore Afro-American, Boston Guardian*, and the *Norfolk Journal and Guide* all supported Smith. So, too, did Mar-

[18] Walter White to William H. Lewis, Sept. 18, 1928; White to John Hurst, July 20, 1928; White to Moorfield Storey, July 31, 1928, NAACP Papers, Box C-96; Walter White, *A Man Called White: The Autobiography of Walter White* (New York, 1948), p. 100 (source of the quotations). Copyright 1948 by Walter White. Copyright renewed 1975 by H. Lee Lurie. Reprinted by permission of Viking Penguin Inc.

cus Garvey, recently the messiah of millions of black Americans. The enthusiasm of these black leaders seemed to strike a responsive chord. Smith-for-President Colored Clubs sprang up across the country; black Democratic campaigners found large receptive audiences; and ordinary blacks spoke out in favor of the political emancipation of the race from the Republican party.[19]

A considerable number of blacks were attracted by the Democratic campaign and impressed by Smith's gubernatorial record, and they voted for Smith in the election of 1928. Smith's share of the vote was not large in itself—17 percent in the black precincts of Philadelphia, 27 percent in the black precincts of Cleveland and Chicago, and 28 percent in Harlem.[20] But it was substantially larger than the black Democratic vote in those cities in previous presidential elections. Blacks in Harlem, for instance,

[19] Walter White to Clarence Darrow, Aug. 3, 1928; White to William H. Lewis, Aug. 4, 1928; White to John Hurst, Aug. 9, 1928; Hurst to White, July 21, 1928; "Analysis of Possible Effect of Negro Vote in the 1928 Election," undated typescript, NAACP Papers, Box C-96; *Pittsburgh Courier*, Aug. 25, Sept. 8 (editorial), 1928; editorials, *Chicago Defender*, Oct. 20, 27, Nov. 3, 1928; interview with Earl B. Dickerson, Aug. 16, 1974, Chicago; John G. VanDeusen, "The Negro in Politics," *Journal of Negro History* XXI (July 1936):272; "How Shall We Vote?" *Crisis* XXXV (Nov. 1928):368; David Burner, *The Politics of Provincialism: The Democratic Party in Transition, 1918-1932* (New York, 1968), p. 238; Lichtman, *Prejudice and the Old Politics*, pp. 147-59; William Wayne Giffin, "The Negro in Ohio, 1914-1939" (Ph.D. diss., The Ohio State University, 1968), p. 283; Larry H. Grothaus, "The Negro in Missouri Politics, 1890-1941" (Ph.D. diss., University of Missouri, 1970), p. 121.

[20] The figures for Harlem are drawn from "Official Canvass of the Votes Cast . . . at the Election Held November 6, 1928," *City Record* LVI (Dec. 31, 1928). Map no. 3 in Gilbert Osofsky, *Harlem: The Making of a Ghetto; Negro New York, 1890-1930*, 2nd ed. (New York, 1971), p. xvii, showed those blocks in Harlem which were at least 90 percent black: the appropriate election units were chosen with the assistance of assembly district maps which are available on slides at the Municipal Reference and Research Center, New York City. The figures for Philadelphia are drawn from Registration Commission for the City of Philadelphia, *Twenty-third Annual Report, December 31, 1928* (Philadelphia, 1929); the analysis is based on election divisions where the voter registration was at least 90 percent black. The figures for Chicago are drawn from the Records of the Board of Election Commissioners of the City of Chicago, which are available on microfiche at the Municipal Reference Library in Chicago; the appropriate precincts were chosen by matching census tracts with the heaviest concentration of black population—identified in Ernest W. Burgess and Charles Newcomb, eds., *Census Data of the City of Chicago, 1930* (Chicago, 1933)—with ward maps, which are held by the Board of Election Commissioners. The figures for Cleveland are drawn from the Records of the Board of Elections of Cuyahoga County, which are held at the Board of Elections in Cleveland; the appropriate precincts were chosen by matching census tracts identified in Kenneth L. Kusmer, *A Ghetto Takes Shape: Black Cleveland, 1870-1930* (Urbana, Ill., 1976), p. 284, Table 25, with ward maps and the Board of Elections of Cuyahoga County's *Register of Voters*, both deposited in the Cuyahoga County Archives in Cleveland.

had voted 3 percent Democratic in 1920 and 28 percent in 1924; in Chicago, the figures were 11 percent Democratic in 1920, 10 percent Democratic in 1924.[21]

Still, Smith failed to change the political habits of black Americans. He was intrigued by the prospect of winning black support but unwilling to risk white support in order to get it.[22] The result was a standoff. For every Democratic argument to the effect that blacks had long since repaid their debt to the party of Lincoln, black Republican supporters made the case for a politics based on history: "What little that has been done for us the Republicans gave to us."[23] For every Democratic argument to the effect that a Smith victory promised new opportunities for the race, Republicans responded by sending to black newspapers photographs of the Democratic convention in Houston which showed the Jim Crow section surrounded by chicken wire.[24] For every Democratic avowal of Smith's progressive record as governor of New York, Republicans countered with a case for Hoover's humanitarianism.[25] For every insistence that a vote for Smith was a blow for black political emancipation, there were always some voices to point out that neither party cared a whit about blacks, and that the election was unlikely to change their attitudes. W.E.B. Du Bois put the case succinctly. With neither Smith nor Hoover willing to speak out on key issues such as disfranchisement, discrimination, segregation, economic inequality, and racial violence, "it does not matter a tinker's damn which of these gentlemen succeed."[26]

Under such circumstances, it was hard to make a very persua-

[21] Burner, *The Politics of Provincialism*, p. 237; John M. Allswang, *A House for All Peoples: Ethnic Politics in Chicago, 1890-1936* (Lexington, Ky., 1971), p. 42, Table III.1.

[22] Smith's adviser, Belle Moskowitz, later reported to Walter White that Smith, after his defeat, had told her that he wished he had signed the statement White and James Weldon Johnson had prepared for him and had "made an all-out bid for the Negro vote. He was convinced that he would thereby have won enough votes in pivotal Northern and border states, which he had lost by narrow margins, to elect him." White, *A Man Called White*, p. 101.

[23] Letter to the editor from F. J. Wise, Greenwood, S.C., Oct. 27, 1928, in *Pittsburgh Courier*, Nov. 3, 1928.

[24] R. L. Vann to the Editor, *The Light*, Sept. 28, 1928, Claude A. Barnett Papers, Chicago Historical Society. The same theme made a good subject for radio broadcasts. See *Pittsburgh Courier*, Oct. 20, 1928.

[25] *Pittsburgh Courier*, Oct. 27, Nov. 3, 1928.

[26] W.E.B. Du Bois, "Postscript," *Crisis* XXXV (Oct., Nov. 1928):346, 381 (source of the quotation). For an analysis after the election of how neither party cared about blacks, see James Weldon Johnson, "A Negro Looks at Politics," *American Mercury* XVIII (Sept. 1929):88.

sive case for black political involvement. Which was the more compelling alternative? To stay with the Republicans as the lesser of two evils? (As the Memphis politician, Robert R. Church, put it, "the Republican party offers us little. THE DEMOCRATIC PARTY OFFERS US NOTHING.") Or to vote Democratic as a demonstration of black political independence? Neither was particularly attractive.[27]

The premise of Smith's campaign among blacks was fundamentally defective. Vague assurances and spirited exhortations were not the stuff from which to forge a new black political alignment. With neither party ready to make the fundamental racial commitments that might have changed black voting patterns, blacks remained passively with the Republicans. It would take a crisis of major proportions and an appeal based more on economics than race to move them into the Democratic party.

[27] Open letter from R. R. Church, Memphis, Oct. 26, 1928, in *Chicago Defender*, Nov. 3, 1928. For the argument for a show of political independence, see James Weldon Johnson to Moorfield Storey, July 31, 1928, Johnson Papers, Folder 465; W.E.B. Du Bois, "Postscript," *Crisis* XXXV (July 1928):239; editorial, *Pittsburgh Courier*, Sept. 1, 1928.

CHAPTER I ▪ *The Election of 1932*

Robert L. Vann had had enough of the Republican party by 1932. Vann was the editor of the *Pittsburgh Courier*, one of the most widely-read Negro-owned papers of its day. He had taken a leading role in the "colored division" in every Republican presidential campaign of the 1920s, but his efforts had never been adequately rewarded. As the decade progressed, he had become increasingly disillusioned with Republican racial policies and personally disappointed with the party's failure to grant him the federal appointments to which he aspired.

Vann's loyalty to the Republican party finally broke over the Pennsylvania gubernatorial election of 1930. In the primary, and later in the general election, Vann actively backed Gifford Pinchot, a Republican reform candidate who ran against the regular Republican organization. Although Pinchot lost Philadelphia, the stronghold of the Republican machine, he carried every ward in Pittsburgh and won the governorship by so narrow a margin that Vann could claim that the black vote had tipped the balance of power. But a thank-you note from Pinchot was Vann's only reward; control of black patronage in the state went not to him, but to Judge Edward W. Henry of Philadelphia, which had a black population four times the size of Pittsburgh's.[1]

Vann had little prospect of recognition as a Republican leader on either the state or national level and, by 1932, was ready to defect to the Democratic party. The first indication that the Democrats might welcome him came from Michael L. Benedum, a wealthy white oilman who had contributed generously to Franklin D. Roosevelt's campaign and who saw the conversion of the black vote as a potential means of swinging Pennsylvania into the Roosevelt column. On the advice of his black butler, Benedum met with Vann. Why should blacks stay with a party that never

[1] Andrew Buni, *Robert L. Vann of the Pittsburgh Courier: Politics and Black Journalism* (Pittsburgh, 1974), pp. 174-87.

rewarded their loyalty? Benedum asked. Surely their historic debt had long since been repaid.[2]

At Benedum's suggestion, Vann approached Joseph F. Guffey, a Democratic leader in Pennsylvania and one of the strategists for Roosevelt's presidential campaign. Vann made the contact indirectly. At his request, Eva DeBoe Jones, a black manicurist, told Emma Guffey Miller during a manicure that Vann would like to see her brother Joseph. The two men met at Mrs. Miller's home. Guffey found Vann "bitter against the Republican leadership." He learned from Vann that blacks "were beginning to realize that their vote was connected with their economic condition." To Guffey's way of thinking, "it was an opportunity" to be taken advantage of.[3]

Guffey was impressed by Vann's insistence that he could help the Democrats win the black vote in Pennsylvania and persuaded Roosevelt's top political lieutenants, James A. Farley and Louis McHenry Howe, to organize an active campaign among blacks. The result was the creation of the Democratic National Committee's Colored Advisory Committee, of which Vann was one of four principal leaders.[4] In his first public speech as a Democrat, "The Patriot and the Partisan," Vann exhorted blacks to emancipate themselves from blind allegiance to the Republican party. He delivered the address before a capacity audience at the St. James African Methodist Episcopal Church in Cleveland on Sunday afternoon, September 11. Vann told his listeners that blacks had misread the history of the Republican party. Although the party had been born out of the political issue of slavery, Republicans had never shown any real concern for blacks. They had used the race issue when it had served their advantage, but once the party "had built itself to the point of security," it had turned its back on blacks. In recent years, Republicans had actively discouraged Negro support. Blacks were beginning to see "the difference between blind partisanship and patriotism." They were beginning to select "the party which they believe will guarantee them the privileges to which any patriot is entitled."[5]

[2] Ibid., pp. 190-91; "Elks & Equality," *Time*, Aug. 12, 1935, p. 10; Sam T. Mallison, *The Great Wildcatter* (Charleston, W. Va., 1953), pp. 403-404.

[3] Joseph F. Guffey, *Seventy Years on the Red-Fire Wagon* (n.p., 1952), p. 170. See also Buni, *Robert L. Vann*, p. 191; Joseph Alsop and Robert Kintner, "The Guffey: Biography of a Boss, New Style," *Saturday Evening Post*, Mar. 26, 1938, pp. 5-6.

[4] Buni, *Robert L. Vann*, pp. 192-93; Alsop and Kintner, "The Guffey," p. 6; Guffey, *Seventy Years*, p. 170.

[5] *Pittsburgh Courier*, Sept. 17, 1932.

"I see in the offing a horde of black men and women throwing off the yoke of partisanism practiced for over half a century," Vann declared. "[I see them] casting down the idols of empty promises and moving out into the sunlight of independence. I see hordes and hordes of black men and women, belonging to the army of forgotten men, turning their faces toward a new course and a new party." Then came the dramatic peroration: "I see millions of Negroes turning the pictures of Abraham Lincoln to the wall. This year I see Negroes voting a Democratic ticket."[6]

The Hoover administration gave blacks ample reason to turn their backs on the Grand Old Party. In a nation beset with economic crisis, blacks were disproportionately afflicted. In Baltimore, for example, where Negroes constituted 17 percent of the city's population, they made up 31.5 percent of the unemployed in March 1931. In Chicago, which was only 4 percent black, blacks accounted for 16 percent of those out of work. The same was true in other cities. By 1931, the National Urban League reported, the displacement of Negroes from their jobs "to reduce unemployment among *whites*" seemed to be "an accepted policy." And, as long as whites were out of work, the chances of blacks being rehired by private employers were slim. In the somber assessment of the League's industrial relations director, T. Arnold Hill, "At no time in the history of the Negro since slavery has his economic and social outlook seemed so discouraging."[7]

The economic burden of the Depression was reason enough to question the wisdom of continuing the Hoover leadership. Equally compelling was what many blacks saw as the President's "grossly unsatisfactory" racial policy—a "record of disregard and disrespect for his colored brother."[8] Incident after incident had made

---

[6] Ibid.

[7] National Urban League, Department of Industrial Relations, "How Unemployment Affects Negroes," Mar. 1931, National Urban League Papers, Department of Industrial Relations files, Manuscript Division, Library of Congress; Hill quoted in *New York Times*, Apr. 5, 1931.

[8] Editorial, *Pittsburgh Courier*, May 10, 1930; editorial, *Savannah Journal*, July 6, 1932, clipping in Claude A. Barnett Papers, Box P7, Chicago Historical Society. Other contemporary critiques include W.E.B. Du Bois, "Postscript," *Crisis* XXXIX (Nov. 1932): 362-63; editorial, *Pittsburgh Courier*, Mar. 29, 1930; editorial, *Chicago Defender*, Mar. 30, 1929. For a summary of the black case against Hoover, see *To Colored Voters: Franklin D. Roosevelt, A Leader in Progressive Democracy*, a pamphlet issued in 1932 by the National Colored Citizens Roosevelt Committee, in Arthur W. Mitchell Papers, Chicago Historical Society. For the Republican National Committee's defense of the President, see their 1932 pamphlet, *The Negro and the Republican Party*, also in the Mitchell Papers. On Hoover's role in alienating blacks from the Republican party, see Lawrence Gordon, "A Brief

it clear to black Americans that there was "a fundamental difference between the party of Lincoln and the party of Hoover."[9] Even before Hoover's election in 1928, his reputation had been suspect among many Negroes. As secretary of commerce, he had had charge of the relief efforts following the flood of the Mississippi River in 1927. To no one's surprise, there was discrimination in the administration of flood relief. More serious, Negroes in the refugee camps were treated like prisoners and were usually released only to the landlords on whose plantations they had previously been employed. The NAACP undertook a well-publicized investigation and charged Hoover with indifference to the plight of the black refugees and failure to take corrective action.[10]

The Republican convention in 1928 had made clear Hoover's political objectives, for it was there that he had embarked on a policy of encouraging lily-white Republican organizations in the South. Throughout his administration, the desire to cultivate white Southerners helped to shape his response on racial issues. Black leaders complained that Hoover really had no racial policy. He ignored black concerns such as racial violence and disfranchisement. He had a mediocre record on black appointments, and some of his principal white appointees were known to be anti-Negro.[11] Worse than Hoover's neglect of blacks were the actions that blacks interpreted as deliberate slaps at the race.

One of these actions—primarily symbolic—involved the segregation of the Gold Star Mothers. Congress had authorized the mothers and widows of American servicemen buried in Europe to travel there to visit their graves. In 1930, with the pilgrimage set to begin, the War Department chose to send the black women on separate ships. Despite protests by the NAACP and the black press against the segregation, the policy remained in force, and

---

Look at Blacks in Depression Mississippi, 1929-1934: Eyewitness Accounts," *Journal of Negro History* LXIV (Fall 1979):381, quoting Walthaw Bennett of Jackson, Miss. ("Hoover killed my taste for Republicans"), and Lawrence Hamm interview with Julia Gee, July 31, 1979, East Orange, N.J.: "I regretted the day [in 1928] that I ever went to the polls and voted for Herbert Hoover. I was so glad when his time was up I didn't know what on earth to do. And from that day to this I never voted another Republican ticket." After the election, analysts explained black votes against Hoover in terms of two principal concerns: the effects of the Depression on blacks and Hoover's racial policies. See, e.g., Henry Lee Moon, "How the Negroes Voted," *Nation*, Nov. 25, 1944, p. 640.

[9] Lester A. Walton in *Pittsburgh Courier*, Nov. 5, 1932.

[10] Richard B. Sherman, *The Republican Party and Black America: From McKinley to Hoover, 1896-1933* (Charlottesville, Va., 1973), pp. 225-29.

[11] Ibid., pp. 229-39.

the majority of Negro Gold Star Mothers declined to make the trip.[12]

The action with more significant political repercussions was Hoover's nomination to the United States Supreme Court in 1930 of John J. Parker, a circuit court judge in North Carolina.[13] The American Federation of Labor launched a vigorous campaign to block Parker's confirmation on the grounds of his decision in the case of the *United Mine Workers v. Red Jacket Coal and Coke Company* in 1927, which upheld the use of injunctions against labor unions and recognized the validity of yellow-dog contracts. The NAACP undertook its own campaign against the Parker nomination on the grounds that he was anti-black. In 1920, while running for governor of North Carolina, Parker had reportedly spoken out in favor of the continued disfranchisement of blacks. "The Negro as a class does not desire to enter politics," Parker was quoted as saying. "The Republican party of North Carolina does not desire him to do so. We recognize the fact that he has not yet reached the stage in his development when he can share the burdens and responsibilities of government."[14]

The race issue was one of the factors responsible for the Senate's rejection of the Parker nomination. The NAACP's lobbying could be correlated with important votes against confirmation, and the victory encouraged the Association to mobilize blacks to vote against pro-Parker senators in the elections in 1930. There it was more difficult to find evidence that black opposition was decisive—of the four senators the NAACP targeted, two won reelection, and the two defeats involved other issues. But campaigning against Parker gave blacks a taste of the possibilities of organized political power.[15]

As the election of 1932 approached, even the staunchest black Republicans were prepared to admit disappointment with Hoover. But it was quite another thing to be ready to move into the Democratic camp. "Four more years of [Hoover] as a Republican," the *Chicago Defender* conceded with some reluctance before the election year had begun, "will be better than a possible eight years of any Democrat." It was hard to break free of traditional party

[12] Ibid., pp. 246-48.
[13] The principal account of the fight over the Parker nomination is Richard L. Watson, Jr., "The Defeat of Judge Parker: A Study in Pressure Groups and Politics," *Mississippi Valley Historical Review* L (Sept. 1963):213-34.
[14] Greensboro *Daily News*, Apr. 19, 1920, quoted in ibid., p. 218.
[15] Ibid., pp. 232-33; Sherman, *The Republican Party and Black America*, pp. 244-46.

allegiance. No matter how far short of black expectations Hoover had fallen, his was the party responsible for the Thirteenth, Fourteenth, and Fifteenth Amendments; the Democrats were the party of Jim Crow and disfranchisement. Again and again, publicists, campaigners, and voters recalled the traditional associations. The *California Eagle* told its readers to "register again with the party of Lincoln and Grant and Sumner and Phillips." A black woman in Nashville, accounting for her involvement in the Republican campaign, called it "the party to which we owe our advancement." A black man in Detroit described his loyalty to the Republicans the same way: "Every right that we have and every privilege we enjoy came through the blood of those who stood for Republicanism like Nathan Hale in the days of old."[16]

The Democratic nominees in 1932 offered blacks little inducement to overcome their traditional antipathy to the party. To some blacks, Franklin D. Roosevelt was "the weakest possible candidate."[17] There was no mistaking his patrician heritage. For generations the Roosevelts had been merchants and sugar refiners in New York City. Franklin's great-grandfather, James, bought an estate in Dutchess County, on the Hudson River near Poughkeepsie; thereafter, his branch of the family settled into the life of well-established country gentlemen.[18]

Like most people of his station, Franklin Roosevelt was not concerned about racial equality or racial justice. He was aware that Dutchess County had known slavery well into the nineteenth century, for he later told the story of his great-grandfather manumitting his slaves and pointed out that slave houses remained on the family estate. And he remarked, too, on the former slave

[16] Editorial, *Chicago Defender*, Dec. 19, 1931; editorial, *California Eagle* (Los Angeles), n.d. [1932], clipping in Barnett Papers, Box P7; Nettie Langston Napier telegram to Mary Church Terrell, Oct. 19, 1932, Mary Church Terrell Papers, Box 6, Manuscript Division, Library of Congress; letter to the editor from J. W. Rawlins, *Pittsburgh Courier*, July 18, 1931. See also *Chicago Defender*, Nov. 5, 1932; Mary Church Terrell, "Some Facts for Colored People to Think About," n.d. [1932], Barnett Papers, Box P3.

[17] Robert W. Bagnall to Walter White, stamped July 5, 1932, National Association for the Advancement of Colored People Papers, Box C-63, Manuscript Division, Library of Congress (hereafter cited as the NAACP Papers). See also editorial, *Cleveland Gazette*, Oct. 29, 1932; cartoon, *Lansing Eye Opener*, Oct. 22, 1932, Barnett Papers, Box P7; *Chicago Defender*, July 2, 1932; Charles H. Martin, "Negro Leaders, the Republican Party, and the Election of 1932," *Phylon* XXXII (First Quarter, 1971):88-89.

[18] *Dictionary of American Biography*, Supplement Three (New York, 1973), p. 641.

who had served as sexton of his boyhood church.[19] In terms of immediate, personal experience, however, blacks were virtually absent from his world. As a student at Groton, he had done odd jobs for an elderly black widow, but, growing up in Hyde Park, he had not even known blacks as servants. His mother's household staff had always been English and Irish, and it was not until late in his tenure as assistant secretary of the navy that he and his wife, Eleanor, had blacks in their employ.[20] When, during the White House years, one of Roosevelt's Brain Trusters, Rexford G. Tugwell, twitted him on what he regarded as Roosevelt's "aristocratic inability to see a servant going in and out of the room," Roosevelt laughed and replied that Tugwell would understand such things if he had been reared in the Hudson River Valley. Years later, when Tugwell went to Warm Springs, Georgia, to interview people who had been associated with the President, he found Daisy Bonner, who had cooked for Roosevelt at the Little White House, crippled and penniless, living "in a shack . . . back in the fields, full of weeds, looked as though it was about to tumble down." "This was the Roosevelts," Tugwell said. "They didn't think it was their job at all to look after somebody who had been as loyal as that to them. I've never sort of forgiven the President for that. But he didn't know she existed, really."[21]

The South, too, shaped Roosevelt's racial outlook. He had become deeply involved in the region as a result of his battle to regain the use of his paralyzed legs after his polio attack. He first journeyed to Warm Springs in 1924 to take advantage of its healing mineral waters. By 1927, he had raised the money to establish a national center there to provide therapy for victims of poliomyelitis. When Roosevelt ran for President in 1932, it was well known that he considered himself a Georgian by adoption.

Roosevelt invested in mountain farmland in Warm Springs and, by experimenting with crops and livestock, sought to demonstrate to the impoverished farmers of the region that there were alternatives to the unprofitable business of raising cotton. From his experiences he gained an intimate awareness of the concerns and attitudes of southern rural farmers. Southern politicians, too, be-

[19] See June 19, 1942 diary entry in William D. Hassett, *Off the Record with F.D.R., 1942-1945* (New Brunswick, N.J., 1958), p. 63. On the Roosevelt family background, see Frank Freidel, *Franklin D. Roosevelt: The Apprenticeship* (Boston, 1952), chap. 1.

[20] Kenneth S. Davis, *FDR: The Beckoning of Destiny, 1882-1928* (New York, 1972), p. 121; interview with John A. Roosevelt, Mar. 11, 1977, New York City.

[21] Interview with Rexford G. Tugwell, Feb. 7, 1977, Santa Barbara.

came his friends and neighbors. While he never shared their intense, emotional commitment to white supremacy, he seemed, for all intents and purposes, to be entirely comfortable with the racial folkways of the South.[22]

Roosevelt's political career had shown no sensitivity to the problems of blacks. In 1911, while serving in the New York State Senate, he made a note in the margin of one of his speeches: "story of nigger."[23] In 1916, as assistant secretary of the navy in the Wilson administration, he took a hand in the imposition of segregated toilets in the State, War, and Navy Department Building. "Roosevelt Exposed as Rabid Jim Crower" was the way one campaign headline viewed his role.[24] He strongly supported the occupation of Haiti in 1915—so much so that he later claimed credit for writing the constitution that confirmed the control of the United States over the internal affairs of Haiti. "And if I do say it," he declared, "I think it is a pretty good constitution." In fact, Roosevelt did not draft the document, but his expansive claims to the contrary persuaded later black critics that he had "contempt for the darker races."[25] As governor of New York, Roosevelt paid little, if any attention to his Negro constituents. Indeed, as late as 1929, he found it to be politically advantageous to deny that he had entertained blacks at an official luncheon.[26]

Perhaps most damning to blacks was Roosevelt's choice of a running mate, John Nance Garner of Texas. Garner was just too much a captive of "the Texas spirit," as the *Chicago Defender* put it. Garner's nomination for Vice-President, according to a St. Louis lawyer, "should be enough to cause every Negro to run from the Democratic Party, as though it was a case of smallpox."[27]

As the campaign opened, then, black voters faced a considerable dilemma. Ought they to choose the known quantity, a Republican who had proven sorely disappointing? Or ought they to vote for

[22] Frank Freidel, *F.D.R. and the South* (Baton Rouge, 1965), passim.

[23] Arthur M. Schlesinger, Jr., *The Politics of Upheaval* (Boston, 1960), p. 430.

[24] *Washington Bee*, Aug. 19, 1916, prints an official memorandum from Roosevelt with respect to the new segregation; the campaign headline is in *Chicago Defender*, Oct. 15, 1932.

[25] Roosevelt statement of Aug. 19, 1917, quoted in editorial, *Chicago Defender*, Sept. 10, 1932; criticism voiced in editorial, *New York Age*, Nov. 2, 1940. On Roosevelt's actual role with respect to Haiti, see Freidel, *Franklin D. Roosevelt: The Apprenticeship*, pp. 276-84.

[26] Schlesinger, *The Politics of Upheaval*, p. 431.

[27] Editorial, *Chicago Defender*, Mar. 5, 1932; Joseph P. Harris to Claude A. Barnett, Sept. 7, 1932; Barnett Papers, Box P2. For similar sentiments see B. F. Booth to Barnett, Sept. 16, 1932, ibid.; Emma F. G. Merritt to Mary Church Terrell, Oct. 19, 1932, Terrell Papers, Box 6.

the unknown representative of the party that blacks had long seen as their oppressor? Nothing in the course of the campaign helped substantially to clarify the dilemma. Although the Communists nominated a black man for Vice-President, and both the Communist and Socialist parties forthrightly affirmed racial equality, neither major party did very much to court black votes.

One could hardly have expected them to do otherwise, for blacks comprised only a tiny fraction of the voters whom the parties hoped to attract. Although blacks accounted for close to 10 percent of the population of the United States, disfranchisement in the South made the potential black voting population proportionally much smaller. Two-thirds of all blacks who were twenty-one years of age or older lived in the eleven ex-Confederate states and the District of Columbia; poll taxes, property qualifications, literacy tests, white primaries, intimidation by voting registrars, and a variety of other devices, legal and extralegal, kept the vast majority of southern blacks away from the polls. As late as 1940, out of a potential black electorate of more than 4.2 million in the old Confederacy, only 200,000—less than 5 percent—were even registered to vote. Those blacks who resided elsewhere—2.1 million twenty-one years of age or older in 1930, 2.4 million in 1940—constituted less than 3 percent of the potential national electorate.[28]

Under such circumstances, it would have been surprising if the Republicans or the Democrats had gone out of their way to appeal to blacks. The Democratic platform included a general pledge of equal rights to all, but it failed even to mention blacks.[29] "We fear," the *New York Amsterdam News* wrote, "that equal rights in the national Democratic party mean exactly what they meant in 1913 when the Woodrow Wilson administration came into power—equal rights for the white man but hell and damnation for the colored man."[30] The Republicans rested on loyalty to tra-

---

[28] U.S. Department of Commerce, Bureau of the Census, *Sixteenth Census of the United States: 1940, Population*, vol. II: *Characteristics of the Population* (Washington, D.C., 1943), pt. 1, pp. 31, 209, 391; pt. 2, pp. 17, 189; pt. 3, p. 335; pt. 4, p. 205; pt. 5, p. 269; pt. 6, pp. 349, 563, 765; pt. 7, p. 137; Ralph J. Bunche, *The Political Status of the Negro in the Age of FDR*, ed. Dewey W. Grantham (Chicago, 1973); Monroe N. Work, ed., *Negro Year Book: An Annual Encyclopedia of the Negro, 1931-1932* (Tuskegee, Ala., 1931), pp. 111-12. The District of Columbia, of course, was effectively disfranchised until the adoption of the Twenty-third Amendment in 1961.

[29] Kirk H. Porter and Donald Bruce Johnson, comps., *National Party Platforms, 1840-1960*, 2nd ed. (Urbana, Ill., 1961), pp. 331-33.

[30] Editorial, *New York Amsterdam News*, July 6, 1932, Barnett Papers, Box P7.

dition: "For seventy years," their plank read, "the Republican Party has been the friend of the American Negro. Vindication of the rights of the Negro citizen to enjoy the full benefits of life, liberty and the pursuit of happiness is traditional in the Republican Party, and our party stands pledged to maintain equal opportunity and rights for Negro citizens. We do not propose to depart from that tradition nor to alter the spirit or letter of that pledge."[31]

Black editors scoffed at the statement. "The Republicans resorted to the time-worn method of baiting the proverbial hook to catch the suckers," the *Louisiana Weekly* commented. The plank was a worthless "political sop to members of our Race," agreed the *Chicago Defender*, which had hoped for a "four-square" endorsement of enforcement of the Fourteenth and Fifteenth Amendments.[32] What a lot of "flapdoodle," exclaimed Walter White, who had tried, on behalf of the NAACP, to persuade both parties to adopt substantive planks on race.[33] The NAACP had lobbied among the resolutions committees "with no hope" of getting its proposed planks adopted—its demands, rather, could serve "as a yardstick by which the failures of the Republicans and Democrats would be made more evident." And evident they were. The obvious inconsistency between Hoover's record and the platform's profession of friendship for blacks made the GOP platform "a mere catch-penny device to get votes from the unthinking," which no knowledgeable person could "take . . . seriously." "When we consider what actually was put into the platform," White wrote privately, "I shudder to think of what might have been said had no efforts at all been made."[34]

Throughout the campaign Roosevelt and Hoover clashed over the causes of the Depression and the best means of coping with it—how to deal with the problem of relief; how to stimulate and stabilize economic activity; and how to keep federal expenditures in check. They differed over farm policy and the relationship of

[31] Porter and Johnson, comps., *National Party Platforms*, p. 349.

[32] Editorial, *Louisiana Weekly*, July 9, 1932, Barnett Papers, Box P7; *Chicago Defender*, June 25 (editorial) and June 18, 1932.

[33] White is quoted in an undated NAACP press release, "G.O.P. Plank on Negro 'Flapdoodle' SAYS WALTER WHITE IN COMMENT," NAACP Papers, Box C-399. The NAACP suggestions for the platform planks are in typed draft of press release for June 15, 1932, "NAACP Demands Negro Planks of G.O.P. & Democratic National Conventions," ibid.

[34] Walter White to Edward Levinson, July 1, 1932; White, quoted in NAACP press release, "G.O.P. Plank on Negro 'Flapdoodle' . . ."; White to Claude A. Barnett, June 28, 1932, NAACP Papers, Box C-399.

the federal government to public utilities. They debated the repeal of Prohibition. They worried over the gold standard, the protective tariff, and a balanced budget. But they did not concern themselves about blacks. Both national campaign committees mounted "colored divisions," which cranked out publicity for black newspapers and sent prominent blacks on the campaign trail.[35] But these efforts were limited and late, and they were peripheral to the central business of the campaign. Neither candidate addressed a predominantly black audience. Neither took the initiative to issue statements that appealed specifically to black voters.

It was easy enough for blacks to construe these omissions as evidence of racism, but in light of the relative insignificance of the black vote, it was not realistic to expect more attention. Still, black leaders tried repeatedly to make blacks a larger part of the parties' political agendas. The NAACP sent questionnaires to Roosevelt and Hoover to pin down their positions on racial questions. What steps would they take to remove obstacles to black political participation in the South? To eliminate racial criteria for civil service appointments? To extend patronage to blacks in proportion to their strength in the party? To end segregation in governmental service? To open opportunities for blacks in the armed services? To support Howard University? To back a federal antilynching law? To protect the independence and self-government of Liberia and to restore self-government to Haiti? To bar discrimination on relief and public works projects? To bar discrimination in federal funding for education? To work for full civil rights for blacks?[36] At best, the questionnaires, if answered, might elevate the campaign beyond the generalities and platitudes spewed forth under the auspices of the colored divisions. At least, even if the candidates dodged the inquiry, the questionnaires would "serve as a yardstick by which the shortcomings of the two parties

---

[35] See, for example, *Chicago Defender*, Aug. 20, Sept. 24, 1932; "Politics," *Crisis* XXXIX (Nov. 1932):350; [Claude A. Barnett] to R. R. Moton, Sept. 17, 1932, Barnett Papers, Box P2; Arthur W. Mitchell to Clark H. Foreman, Oct. 14, 1933, Mitchell Papers, Box 1; Eugene A. Hatfield, "The Impact of the New Deal on Black Politics in Pennsylvania, 1928-1936" (Ph.D. diss., University of North Carolina at Chapel Hill, 1979), p. 103. Republican National Committee press releases directed at black voters trumpeted black endorsements of Hoover, presented the case for black support for the Republicans (see, e.g., "Why the Negro Postal Employee Should Support the Republican Party"), and dissected the Roosevelt-Garner record on race (see, e.g., "Garner Advises Negroes to Get Rid of 'Social Equality Idea'" or "When Garner Became Speaker of the House of Representatives Out Went Negro Employees"). Copies of RNC releases can be found in the Barnett Papers.
[36] Walter White to Herbert Hoover, Sept. 14, 1932, NAACP Papers, Box C-399.

may be measured and . . . as a statement of the things which intelligent Negroes and their friends demand."[37]

Neither candidate responded. Making explicit racial commitments was something they understandably wanted to avoid. But saying nothing at all on the subject of race was another matter. Evading questions put by black reporters proved to be harder than ignoring questionnaires sent by the NAACP. Besides, vague professions of sympathy for Afro-Americans, conveyed through the black press, might have some minor political advantages. When the black reporter, E. W. Wilkins, questioned Roosevelt in Topeka about whether blacks were included in plans to assist the nation's forgotten men, Roosevelt responded, "Absolutely and impartially." To an inquiry at a press conference in Detroit about his attitude toward blacks, the candidate answered, "I believe in equal economic and legal opportunity for all groups, regardless of race, color or creed." Later, in Baltimore, in an interview with an *Afro-American* reporter, Roosevelt pledged, "If elected to the Presidency I will accord colored citizens of this country as full a measure of citizenship in every detail of my administrative power, as accorded citizens of any other race or group." Did that mean that he would make appointments to federal offices without regard to race or color, and that he would use his power as chief executive to block discrimination? "I most assuredly will."[38]

When Wilkins interviewed Garner in Topeka, he, too, declared, "I believe in a fair deal for the submerged part of the population and you know that the Negro belongs to that class." But Garner rejected "specific legislation for the Negro"—"no intelligent Negro wants that and it would be wrong."[39] The interview doubtless surprised officials of the Colored Division of the Republican National Committee, who thought that asking Garner to talk with a black reporter would set the perfect trap: if he granted the interview, it would "make one of the most effective documents of the campaign," because Garner would be unable to "give an interview favorable to Negroes." If Garner turned down the request, that in itself would make a good story.[40]

As a Southerner, Garner had a special problem in presenting himself to blacks as a credible candidate. Republican campaigners

---

[37] Walter White to J. E. Spingarn, Aug. 9, 1932, ibid. See also White to Carl Murphy, Aug. 16, 1932, ibid.
[38] *Afro-American*, Sept. 24, Oct. 15, 29, 1932.
[39] Ibid., Sept. 24, 1932.
[40] Memo for Mr. Benjamin, [?] 1932, Barnett Papers, Box P3.

made much of his purported unfriendliness to the race. Mary Church Terrell, director of the Republican campaign among black women in the East, took a typical view: "I do not see how any colored person could vote for John Nance Garner up here in the north, when he knows that . . . Garner and the other leaders of the Democratic party in the State of Texas will not let him vote down there."[41] Accordingly, the vice-presidential candidate took special pains to paint himself in a more favorable light. First, he issued a statement affirming his sympathy for black Americans. In his long political career, he declared, he had never supported "any proposal injurious to the colored race." Indeed, decades earlier, as a judge in Uvalde County, Texas, he had fought for and secured an appropriation to establish a school for black children. "The Negro," he asserted, ". . . is entitled to equality before the law. He should not be discriminated against because of his color." Just before the election, Garner granted an exclusive interview to Manuel R. Roque, a reporter for the *Pittsburgh Courier.* Again, Garner declared his belief in "equal opportunity." As if to prove the point, he produced two letters: a testimonial from the black citizens of his hometown ("We . . . wish to commend him to the colored voters all over our land. . . . We trust him implicitly.") and another from a black man who had known him since childhood ("I love him. . . . He is the Negro's friend.").[42]

Like Roosevelt and Garner, Hoover could not entirely avoid the race issue. He was under strong pressure from black Republicans to do something to shore up the party's declining popularity with the black electorate, and he finally agreed to meet with more than one hundred black leaders on the White House lawn on October 1—the first time during his presidency that he had permitted himself to be photographed with blacks. Hoover had made only one other appearance before a predominantly black audience. Just before the Republican National Convention in June 1932, he spoke for a few minutes at the Howard University commencement exercises. The speech was primarily an apologia: he had only "a hurried moment and a short statement," Hoover said, "for these are times when it is difficult to find the opportunity for preparation of an extended address such as this would warrant."[43] At the October meeting, his message was as vacuous as the Repub-

[41] Mary Church Terrell to Esther M. Bruce, Nov. 1, 1932, Terrell Papers, Box 6.
[42] The statement is printed in *Pittsburgh Courier,* Oct. 29, 1932; the letters are in the Nov. 5 issue.
[43] Ibid., June 18, 1932.

lican platform. "You may be assured," he told the assembled blacks, "that our party will not abandon or depart from its traditional duty toward the American Negro."[44] Republican newspapers inflated the meeting out of all proportion to its merits. "President Hoover Offers New Deal to Colored Race," the *Cleveland Gazette* exclaimed over a six-column, front-page photograph of the gathering.[45] But other blacks appraised the meeting as a calculated campaign gesture undertaken "in the interest of political expediency."[46] The President's "address should be entitled 'Hoover's Hooey,' or 'Apple Sauce for the Suckling Sucker,' " sneered a black Republican politician from New Jersey who saw through Hoover's "innate platitudes."[47] The rhetoric did not match the record of the past four years, and the obvious discrepancy made the President's "belated effort . . . to placate Negroes . . . hard to swallow." "It is indeed strange," the *Carolina Tribune* remarked, "that our Chief Executive suddenly finds his tongue after such a long period of silence."[48]

Given the fact that the black electorate was at best of incidental importance to the major parties in the election of 1932, how were blacks to cast their votes? When the choice was "Between the Devil and the Deep Blue Sea," many blacks understandably argued that it was safer to stay with the Republicans.[49] They used a variety of metaphors to convey that message: "Sensible folk do not swap horses in the middle of a stream"; already well down the road of the Depression, the country should rely on an experienced chauffeur "instead of turning . . . to an untried driver"; it was no time to switch to "a practitioner who has several untried remedies," a "magician and medicine man" of uncertain ability to deal with the economic crisis.[50]

---

[44] *Chicago Defender*, Oct. 8, 1932; *Norfolk Journal and Guide*, Oct. 8, 1932.

[45] *Cleveland Gazette*, Oct. 15, 1932. The *Gazette* copied its account directly from Republican National Committee campaign literature; see the flyer "President Hoover Offers New Deal to Colored Race" in Mitchell Papers, Box 1.

[46] *Savannah Tribune*, Oct. 13, 1932.

[47] W. G. Alexander, quoted in ibid.

[48] *Carolina Tribune*, quoted in ibid.

[49] Editorial, *Chicago Defender*, Aug. 27, 1932. For variations on the theme, see J. Max Barber column in *Pittsburgh Courier*, Dec. 5, 1931, and George S. Schuyler column in ibid., Dec. 12, 1931.

[50] Terrell, "Some Facts for Colored People to Think About"; letter to the editor from T. C. Williams of New York, Aug. 30, 1932, *Chicago Defender*, Sept. 17, 1932; editorial, *Louisville Leader*, n.d., and editorial, *Richmond Planet*, Oct. 22, 1932, Barnett Papers, Box P7. For other expressions of support for Hoover, see editorials, *Dayton Forum*, Oct. 15, 1932; *Oklahoma Eagle*, Nov. 5, 1932; *Lansing Eye Opener*, Nov. 5, 1932, all in ibid.

But increasing numbers of blacks felt differently. With the distinction between the two parties reduced to "the difference between tweedledee and tweedledum," one columnist argued, the black voter had to "take his chances with the unknown." It was "no time for Negroes to get on board a sinking ship," the *Southwestern Christian Advocate* admonished.[51] A protest vote to "turn the rascals out" was a positive way of "register[ing] resentment against the Republican party and . . . Hoover."[52] Blacks had no cause to "expect to be treated to a special bed of roses under a Democratic administration."[53] But even though the Democratic unknown might not have much to commend him, at the very least, proponents of change argued, nothing could be worse than Hoover.[54]

In fact, it was possible to make a more positive case for breaking from the Republican party without succumbing to illusions about what a Democratic victory might bring. When both major parties had so little to offer, it was, as the *Savannah Journal* pointed out, "an opportune time for our group to scatter our votes."[55] So long as blacks were blindly loyal to the Republican party, it was no wonder that neither Republicans nor Democrats paid them any special heed. The only hope for blacks politically was to become "an uncertain factor to be sought and wooed." Once blacks divided their votes, neither party could any longer take them for granted; with both parties forced to bid for black support, their votes would begin to count and their political prestige would start to rise.[56]

Instead of an act of fealty, voting became, from this perspective, "purely a business proposition," in which blacks could trade votes

[51] J. Max Barber column in *Pittsburgh Courier*, Dec. 12, 1931; editorial, "A Sinking Political Ship," *Southwestern Christian Advocate*, Oct. 27, 1932, p. 672.

[52] Letter to the editor from L. Jerome James of Detroit, *Pittsburgh Courier*, Sept. 17, 1932; Lester A. Walton in ibid., Nov. 5, 1932.

[53] Letter to the editor from Joseph J. McClain of New York City, ibid., Nov. 5, 1932.

[54] Editorial, *Kansas City American*, July 14, 1932, Barnett Papers, Box P7; S. W. Green to Carl Murphy, Oct. 11, 1932, ibid., Box P2.

[55] Editorial, *Savannah Journal*, July 6, 1932, ibid., Box P7.

[56] N. J. Frederick to Claude A. Barnett, Sept. 8, 1932, ibid., Box P2 (source of the quotation); [Claude A. Barnett?], Memorandum for Mr. Everett Sanders: The Attitude of Negro Voters, n.d. [1932], ibid., Box P3; editorial, *Pittsburgh Courier*, Apr. 23, 1932. On the necessity and potential of the divided vote, see also Kelly Miller columns in *Pittsburgh Courier*, Nov. 28, Dec. 19, 1931, May 7, Nov. 5, 1932; *St. Louis Argus*, quoted in editorial, *New York Age*, Mar. 5, 1932; editorial, *Savannah Tribune*, Nov. 3, 1932; NAACP press release, " 'Greatest Political Revolt' Predicted by NAACP Secretary," Oct. 17, 1932, NAACP Papers, Box C-391; editorial, *Chicago Whip*, June 28, 1932, Barnett Papers, Box P8.

for "patronage, rights, and privileges." "Pay no attention to the party name," the *Philadelphia Independent* told its readers; vote for the party that gives the most in return. If blacks would begin to vote "on issues rather than worn-out traditions," the historian, Carter G. Woodson, advised, they could make the ballot a tool for advancing the interests of the race.[57]

Splitting the black vote was not only smart politics, it was also a declaration of political independence. Its proponents argued its merits in the imagery of bondage and freedom. Blacks would no longer be the "slaves" or "chattel of any political party"; they had turned instead "toward the sunlight of political freedom." A vote for Roosevelt was "a vote for political emancipation." "An uprising of Negro voters against Mr. Hoover and his party," Bishop Reverdy C. Ransom wrote, "would free our spirits equally as much as Mr. Lincoln's Proclamation freed our bodies."[58]

The Lincoln legacy was one of the toughest obstacles to overcome in converting blacks to the Democratic party. Robert L. Vann's exclamation—"I see millions of Negroes turning the pictures of Abraham Lincoln to the wall"—symbolized the problem of the abandonment of the Republican party. The legacy was still so powerful that Democratic supporters had to square it with a vote for Roosevelt. This they did in several ways. Lincoln had long been dead, one line of argument ran; blacks were therefore free to vote their present best interests.[59] By their previous con-

[57] Editorial, *Philadelphia Independent*, Mar. 6, 1932, quoted in James Erroll Miller, "The Negro in Pennsylvania Politics with Special Reference to Philadelphia since 1932" (Ph.D. diss., University of Pennsylvania, 1945), p. 218; Carter G. Woodson, quoted in *Norfolk Journal and Guide*, Sept. 10, 1932. See also letter to the editor from Raymond Bunn of Washington, D.C., ibid., Nov. 5, 1932; editorial, *New York Age*, July 9, 1932; Kelly Miller column in *Pittsburgh Courier*, Apr. 23, 1932; editorial, ibid., Nov. 5, 1932.

[58] *Buffalo Star*, July 1, 1932, Barnett Papers, Box P7 ("slaves," "sunlight"); NAACP press release, " 'Greatest Political Revolt' Predicted by NAACP Secretary" ("chattel"); letter to the editor from James M. Harrison of Norfolk, *Norfolk Journal and Guide*, Nov. 5, 1932 ("emancipation"); Reverdy C. Ransom, "Why Vote for Roosevelt?" *Crisis* XXXIX (Nov. 1932):343. See also *St. Louis Argus*, quoted in editorial, *New York Age*, Mar. 5, 1932. The language of emancipation was also popular after the election to explain the increase in black Democratic strength. "The Negro is really becomming [sic] emancipated," a black Los Angeles dentist observed. The election was "a Second Emancipation," a Spokane, Washington, correspondent exulted, in which blacks "struck from their limbs the shackles of political bondage." "It shows that their political emancipation is well under way," Walter White declared. See Claude Hudson to Walter White, Nov. 22, 1932, NAACP Papers, Box C-391; letter to the editor from E. H. Holmes, *Pittsburgh Courier*, Nov. 26, 1932; NAACP press release, "Blind Allegiance of Negroes to Republicans Ended Says White," Nov. 9, 1932, NAACP Papers, Box C-391.

[59] See, e.g., Mary McLeod Bethune, quoted in Emma Gelders Sterne, *Mary McLeod*

duct and loyalty, according to another justification, blacks had long ago repaid their debt to Lincoln and the Republicans.[60] Perhaps most compelling of all, Democrats said, the Republican party in its modern incarnation could no longer lay claim to the enduring elements of the Lincoln legacy. The "spirit" of Abraham Lincoln, the *Norfolk Journal and Guide* declared, "does not even dwell in the House of Herbert Hoover."[61] Thus the perceptive voter could see that it was possible, in Kelly Miller's words, to "honor the principles of Lincoln as well by voting for Roosevelt as for Hoover."[62]

Arguments like these had been voiced before. They gained special currency in 1932, however, as a consequence of the Depression and the Hoover record of racial insults. Blacks had good reason to reconsider their Republican allegiance. In such circumstances, arguments for a Democratic vote as the route to political independence and maturity became particularly timely; the Lincoln legacy became, not just a well-worn slogan, but a real issue to be reckoned with in changing longstanding political habits.

When the votes were counted, it became clear that there had been no massive movement of black voters away from the Republican party. Indeed, as the political analyst, Samuel Lubell, has noted, "Negroes defected in smaller numbers in the 1932 election than did any other group of Republican voters."[63] As Table I.1 shows, Hoover ran far ahead of Roosevelt in black election districts in most cities. In some cities, as Table I.2 illustrates,

---

Bethune (New York, 1957), p. 216. For a retrospective analysis along these lines, see Arthur Krock, "Did the Negro Revolt?" *Opportunity* XI (Jan. 1933):19: "The Negro, in brief, voted as a citizen on Hoover and Roosevelt, forgetting Lincoln and Jefferson Davis, who were not running in 1932."

[60] See James E. Stephens to Claude A. Barnett, Sept. 17, 1932, Barnett Papers, Box P2; letter to the editor from Lafalette C. Newby, *Pittsburgh Courier*, Oct. 1, 1932; letter to the editor from Alberta G. Foster, *Chicago Defender*, July 2, 1932.

[61] Editorial, *Norfolk Journal and Guide*, Oct. 8, 1932. On the same theme, see *Chicago Defender*, July 9, 1932; editorial, *New York Age*, Aug. 27, 1932; letter to the editor from C. L. McKenzie of Flint, Mich., Sept. 14, 1932, *Chicago Defender*, Sept. 17, 1932; editorial, *Star of Zion*, Oct. 6, 1932; *Boston Guardian*, quoted in *Savannah Tribune*, Oct. 13, 1932; Bishop J. A. Hamlet of Kansas City, quoted in ibid., Oct. 20, 1932.

[62] *Savannah Tribune*, Sept. 22, 1932. On the same theme, see letter to the editor from Joseph J. McClain of New York, *Pittsburgh Courier*, Nov. 5, 1932. The possibility also of cloaking Roosevelt with the mantle of his Republican forebear was not lost on supporters of his election. The *Houston Informer*, for instance, urged a vote for FDR "to insure the return of the spirit of 'Teddy' Roosevelt to the White House." Editorial, Oct. 15, 1932, Barnett Papers, Box P7.

[63] Samuel Lubell, "The Negro & the Democratic Coalition," *Commentary* XXXVIII (Aug. 1964):20.

TABLE I.1
Presidential Vote in Black Districts, 1932

City	% Republican	% Democratic
Chicago	75.1	21.0
Cincinnati	71.2	28.8
Cleveland	82.0	17.3
Detroit	67.0	31.0
Knoxville	70.2	29.8
New York	46.0	50.8
Philadelphia	70.5	26.7
Pittsburgh	56.2	41.3

SOURCES: The figures for Chicago are drawn from the Records of the Board of Election Commissioners of the City of Chicago, which are available on microfiche at the Municipal Reference Library in Chicago; the appropriate precincts were chosen by matching census tracts with the heaviest concentration of black population—identified in Ernest W. Burgess and Charles Newcomb, eds., *Census Data of the City of Chicago, 1930* (Chicago, 1933)—with ward maps which are held by the Board of Election Commissioners in Chicago. The figures for Cincinnati came from Ernest M. Collins, "Cincinnati Negroes and Presidential Politics," *Journal of Negro History* XLI (Apr. 1956):133. The figures for Cleveland are drawn from the Records of the Board of Elections of Cuyahoga County, which are held at the Board of Elections in Cleveland; the appropriate precincts were chosen by matching census tracts identified in Kenneth L. Kusmer, *A Ghetto Takes Shape: Black Cleveland, 1870-1930* (Urbana, Ill., 1976), p. 284, Table 25, with ward maps and the Board of Elections of Cuyahoga County's *Register of Voters*, both deposited in the Cuyahoga County Archives in Cleveland. The figures for Detroit are drawn from the Board of County Canvassers' Statement of Returns, on microfilm at the Wayne County Election Commission in Detroit; the appropriate precincts were chosen by matching census tracts with the heaviest concentration of black population—identified in Detroit Bureau of Governmental Research, *Population (1930 Census) and Other Social Data for Detroit by Census Tracts* (Schools of Public Affairs and Social Work of Wayne University, Report No. 7 [Detroit, March 1937]), Table 1—with ward maps held at the Detroit Election Commission. The figures for Knoxville come from Larry W. Dunn, "Knoxville Negro Voting and the Roosevelt Revolution, 1928-1936," *East Tennessee Historical Society's Publications*, no. 43 (1971), p. 89. The figures for New York are drawn from "Official Canvass of the Votes Cast . . . at the Election Held November 8, 1932," *City Record*, Dec. 31, 1932. Map no. 3 in Gilbert Osofsky, *Harlem: The Making of a Ghetto; Negro New York, 1890-1930*, 2nd ed. (New York, 1971), p. xvii showed those blocks in Harlem which were at least 90 percent black; the appropriate election units were chosen with the assistance of assembly district maps which are available on slides at the Municipal Reference and Research Center, New York City. The figures for Philadelphia are drawn from Registration Commission for the City of Philadelphia, *Twenty-seventh Annual Report, December 31, 1932* (Philadelphia, 1933); the analysis is based on election divisions where the voter registration was at least 90 percent black. The figures for Pittsburgh are drawn from *The Pennsylvania Manual, 1933* (Harrisburg, 1933), pp. 432-39; the appropriate precincts were chosen by matching census tracts identified in U.S. Department of Commerce, Bureau of the Census, *Sixteenth Census of the United States: 1940, Population and Housing, Statistics for Census Tracts: Pittsburgh, Pa.* (Washington, D.C., 1942), with ward maps provided by the University of Pittsburgh Library.

TABLE I.2
Republican Presidential Vote
in Black Districts, 1928 and 1932

City	% 1928	% 1932
Chicago	71.4	75.1
Cleveland	71.7	82.0
Knoxville	55.9	70.2
New York	66.0	46.0
Philadelphia	82.1	70.5

SOURCES: For 1932, see Table I.1. For 1928, see Prologue, n. 20.

Hoover actually increased his share of the black vote in comparison to his showing in 1928. Contemporary observers remarked on the persistence of Republican loyalties. In Charleston, West Virginia, the president of the local NAACP reported, "we hardly knew there were any Negro Democrats on election day, as they were so few in number and were rather quiet." The same was true in Delaware, where it was "still not quite 'respectable' for a Negro . . . to be anything other than a Republican."[64]

But the general pattern of black support for Hoover was only part of the picture. There was also considerable evidence to show that blacks were "breaking away from old party yokes."[65] Harlem, profiting from more than a decade of local Democratic efforts to court black voters, proved to be the exception to the rule of black Republican majorities. Not every city showed increasing or even steady Hoover strength; observers in Kansas City, St. Louis, and Indianapolis, for example, remarked that Roosevelt did much better in the black districts in 1932 than Smith had done in 1928.[66]

[64] T. G. Nutter to Walter White, Nov. 12, 1932; Louis L. Redding to White, Nov. 11, 1932, NAACP Papers, Box C-391.

[65] Robert W. Bagnall to Daisy E. Lampkin, Nov. 15, 1932, ibid., Box C-63.

[66] NAACP press release, "National Negro Democratic Swing Disclosed in Returns to NAACP," Nov. 17, 1932; N. B. Young, Jr., to Walter White, Nov. 14, 1932; Robert L. Bailey to White, Nov. 11, 1932; F. B. Ransom to White, Nov. 10, 1932, ibid., Box C-391. For other reports of a swing to the Democratic party, see P. B. Young to White, Nov. 10, 1932; Mrs. Charles W. French to NAACP, Nov. 28, 1932; Gordon H. Simpson to White, Nov. 10, 1932; and H. Claude Hudson to White, Nov. 22, 1932, all in ibid.; letter to the editor from Oliver H. Bond of Pennsauken Township, *Philadelphia Tribune*, Dec. 1, 1932; Dewey W. Fox to Eleanor Roosevelt, May 27, 1938, Eleanor Roosevelt Papers, Box 740, Franklin D. Roosevelt Library; Arthur W. Mitchell to Morris Barnett, Nov. 25, 1932, Mitchell Papers, Box 1. See also Larry H. Grothaus, "The Negro in Missouri Politics, 1890-1941" (Ph.D. diss., University of Missouri, 1970), p. 135.

Depending on one's perspective, then, it was possible to draw various conclusions about the black vote in 1932. The black press and the organizations dedicated to racial advancement were justified in reporting a real change in black voting behavior. Although blacks lagged substantially behind other groups in moving into the Democratic fold (see Table I.3), there was still "convincing evidence" in 1932 that the black vote had, for the first time, "broken away from its traditional moorings," that there had been a "remarkable defection from Republican ranks of the hitherto almost 100% loyal Negro." But while it was accurate for the NAACP to advertise a "National Negro Democratic Swing," there was less certain justification for Walter White's claim that the election had demonstrated the end of "the blind allegiance of Negroes to the Republican party."[67] There was no doubt that many blacks had voted *against* Herbert Hoover; but had they also voted *for* Franklin Roosevelt? Given the nature of this protest vote, some analysts doubted that blacks had permanently defected from Republican ranks.[68]

The results of the election of 1932 gave no absolute assurances about the future direction of the black vote. Nor did they guarantee how the new Democratic administration would treat blacks.

TABLE I.3
Democratic Presidential Vote, by Ethnic Group, 1932
(in percentages)

City	Blacks	Germans	Jews	Poles	Irish	Italians
Chicago	21	69	77	80	n.a.	64
New York	51	80	82	n.a.	81	79

SOURCES: For New York, David Burner, *The Politics of Provincialism: The Democratic Party in Transition, 1918-1932* (New York, 1968), pp. 234-41; for Chicago, John M. Allswang, *A House for All Peoples: Ethnic Politics in Chicago, 1890-1936* (Lexington, Ky., 1971), p. 42. The figure for blacks in New York is mine for Harlem; Burner gives a figure of 58 percent for sanitary districts in New York County having a black population of about 95 percent.

[67] "The National Election, 1932," *Opportunity* X (Nov. 1932):336 ("convincing evidence," "traditional moorings"); Herbert J. Seligmann to Arthur Krock, Nov. 16, 1932 ("remarkable defection"); NAACP press releases, "National Negro Democratic Swing Disclosed in Returns to NAACP" and "Blind Allegiance of Negroes to Republicans Ended Says White," NAACP Papers, Box C-391. As the *New York Age* read the election returns, President Hoover had "convinced the Negroes that the time had come for the race to split its vote"; that meant, ironically, that he "should go down into history as the political emancipator of the race." Editorial, Nov. 19, 1932.

[68] Krock, "Did the Negro Revolt?" p. 19.

The victory gave the Democratic party a chance to prove that it had outlived "the tragic era of hate, prejudice and bigotry," a "great opportunity to wipe out the distrust with which it has justly been regarded by many colored people."[69] But there was no way of knowing in 1932 how the party would respond to that opportunity. It remained to be seen whether blacks, by voting Democratic, had, as *World Tomorrow* appraised it, "gone from the frying pan into the fire."[70] Probably the most accurate forecast of the significance for blacks of the Democratic victory came from Walter White: "It is an open question as to whether or not the Democrats *nationally* will do very much for the Negro; I doubt that they will attempt to do very much against him, which will be a vast improvement over the last four years."[71]

Black defections from the Republicans might make the New Dealers marginally more sensitive to race than the Hoover administration had been. But the black vote was still too insignificant, and its behavior too inconclusive, to do much more than that. Blacks were still peripheral to the main business of the new administration: handling the Depression. "It's my guess," White wrote, "that unless things take a turn for the better, . . . within a couple of years we will be talking about the 'good old Hoover days' and . . . Roosevelt will be as unpopular . . . as Hoover is today."[72] Blacks, like other Americans, were going to judge the new administration by the way it met their economic needs.

[69] Editorial, *Chicago Defender*, Nov. 19, 1932; NAACP press release, "Democrats on Trial Before Negro Says NAACP on Election."

[70] "From Frying Pan . . . ," *World Tomorrow*, Dec. 7, 1932, p. 534.

[71] Walter White to Claude A. Barnett, Nov. 11, 1932, NAACP Papers, Box C-391.

[72] Walter White to William Pickens, Nov. 9, 1932, ibid., Box C-77.

CHAPTER II · *New Deal or New Bluff?*

Immediately after the election, the National Association for the Advancement of Colored People set out to establish contact with the President-elect. It had laid out an agenda of racial concerns in the questionnaire it had sent to the presidential candidates that summer, but Roosevelt had never responded. It was important for the Association to know more precisely where he stood on the race question, and for Roosevelt to understand the views of the NAACP. Perhaps it would be possible to influence his opinions. In any event, a visit from officials of the NAACP would bring the Association to his attention. In January 1933, Walter White wrote Roosevelt to ask for an appointment for himself and the board chairman of the NAACP, Joel E. Spingarn. At first White was optimistic that the meeting would be arranged. But his optimism proved to be ill-founded. Seven weeks after he requested the appointment, the answer came: it would be impossible for Roosevelt to see White and Spingarn, "due to pressure of work."[1]

Did the NAACP really expect anything different? Given its dealings with previous administrations, perhaps not. No matter what the results, however, the Association had to try to reach the new President, if for no other reason than to maintain its image as the representative, nationally, of the interests of black Americans.

That even the NAACP could be so easily ignored, however, illustrates how little blacks mattered in the United States in the early 1930s. Roosevelt and his advisers were not especially insensitive or inattentive. But the race issue was not perceived as a matter of pressing national concern, and other, more urgent problems pushed it beyond the administration's field of vision.

Would the rebuff of the NAACP set a pattern? It was too early to be absolutely certain. But for so canny an observer as Walter

---

[1] NAACP board minutes, Nov. 14, 1932, p. 4, National Association for the Advancement of Colored People Papers, Box A-10, Manuscript Division, Library of Congress (hereafter cited as the NAACP Papers); Walter White telegram to Franklin D. Roosevelt, Jan. 4, 1933; White to Joel E. Spingarn, Jan. 13, 1933; M. H. McIntyre telegram to White, Feb. 22, 1933, ibid., Box C-78.

White, it must have carried some revealing portents. Two things were evident already, neither of them particularly surprising. It was going to be difficult for black spokesmen to establish direct contact with Franklin Roosevelt. And, especially in light of the economic emergency, race was going to rank low among the new administration's priorities.

At the outset of the New Deal, in letters, newspaper editorials, and organizational pronouncements, black spokesmen articulated a common racial agenda. They looked to Washington for action. Speak out on racial problems, they counseled the new President. Put an end to segregation and discrimination in governmental departments, the civil service, and the military. Appoint more blacks to diplomatic positions and federal offices. Enforce the Fourteenth and Fifteenth Amendments. Restore the franchise to blacks. Put an end to Jim Crow in interstate travel. Support legislation to make lynching a federal crime. Treat blacks even-handedly in the distribution of federal aid. Count blacks in on programs to bolster the economic security of the American people.[2]

The race question, however, simply was not a part of the dominant New Deal consciousness. When he insisted, years later, that "there *wasn't* any race problem" in the 1930s, Thomas G. Corcoran spoke for the administration. Corcoran was in a position to know what New Dealers were thinking; as an adviser, he had the President's ear. "When Roosevelt came in in 1933," he explained, "there were many more things to worry about than what happened to civil rights. . . . We weren't concerned with civil rights because there was so much more to worry about." Most people in the new administration did not focus on racial justice. "I don't know anybody around the president who was a strong Negrophile," commented Jonathan Daniels, the White House aide most directly responsible for racial matters during the war; "I don't know *anybody*." As Rexford G. Tugwell, perhaps the most advanced social thinker of the New Deal period, described Roosevelt's attitude, "I wouldn't say that he took no interest in the race problem, but he didn't consider it was important politically, never

---

[2] See, for example, editorial, *Pittsburgh Courier*, Nov. 12, 1932; Lionel A. Francis and Julia Clarke telegram to Franklin D. Roosevelt, Mar. 5, 1933; J. Dalmus Steele to Roosevelt, Mar. 8, 1933; Zebedee Green to Roosevelt, Aug. 3, 1933, Franklin D. Roosevelt Papers, Official File (OF) 93, Franklin D. Roosevelt Library (hereafter cited as the FDR Papers).

as far as I knew." Did Tugwell or any of his colleagues worry about a race problem or about ways to aid minorities? "I think the answer is very little." James Roosevelt, the President's eldest son and for several years his secretary in the White House, could not remember "a single discussion" among family members or friends "with respect to, say, voting rights in the South" or other issues of pressing concern to blacks. In the memory of his youngest brother, John, race was never discussed—"I don't think it was a problem" to which anyone paid attention.[3]

Even the watchdogs of the federal establishment, J. Edgar Hoover and the Federal Bureau of Investigation, who later fastened intently on the struggle for racial equality as a vehicle of communist subversion, virtually ignored racial matters before 1941.[4]

This portrait perhaps exaggerates the point. Racial concerns did impinge on the consciousness of some people in government from time to time—as, for example, when lynchings reinforced the NAACP's campaign to make such acts federal crimes. And some New Dealers, such as Eleanor Roosevelt, Secretary of the Interior Harold L. Ickes, or Senator Robert F. Wagner of New York, demonstrated genuine sensitivity to the plight of racial minorities. But on the whole, New Dealers rarely thought about blacks as a distinct group.

There was nothing unusual about the omission of race from the New Deal agenda. If the administration had had a different outlook, it would have been out of the ordinary. Americans perceived the race problem as southern rather than national. Most

[3] Interview with Thomas G. Corcoran, May 23, 1977, Washington, D. C.; Jonathan Daniels interview, Nov. 16, 1979, p. 19, Eleanor Roosevelt Oral History Project, Franklin D. Roosevelt Library; interviews with Rexford G. Tugwell, Feb. 7, 1977, Santa Barbara, James Roosevelt, Feb. 28, 1977, Newport Beach, Calif., John A. Roosevelt, Mar. 11, 1977, New York City. See also interview with Joseph P. Lash, May 5, 1977, New York City.

[4] This conclusion is based on a reading of FBI files which I requested under the Freedom of Information/Privacy Act on the three principal organizations concerned with racial advancement in this period—the National Association for the Advancement of Colored People, the National Urban League, and the National Negro Congress. Of 895 pages of material released to me from the FBI's main file on the NAACP (file number 61-3176) for the period 1933-1945, only 6 pages dealt with the years before 1941. In the case of the National Urban League, 12 of 125 pages in the FBI file captioned "National Urban League" for the years 1933-1945 dealt with the years before 1941; this percentage is considerably higher, but the subjects were completely innocuous. Even the National Negro Congress, which was widely acknowledged to be "radical," if not under communist influence, seemed not to attract any serious attention from Hoover and his colleagues. Of 2,974 pages of material released to me from the FBI's files on the National Negro Congress, 55 concern the period before 1941.

blacks still lived in the South; the fact that the black population of northern cities had grown remarkably since World War I had not yet affected the widespread sense of race as a sectional concern. Indeed, even in years to come, when massive migration made race hard for the North to ignore, perception still lagged behind demography: race remained "their" problem.

Not only was race the business of the South, but its handling was to be left to the discretion of the states. It had been that way for generations. Federal intervention in race relations in the Civil War and Reconstruction had been a brief aberration. More commonly, whether by law or by custom, each southern state prescribed place and behavior for its own blacks.

A number of factors made it unlikely that New Dealers would depart from this pattern to make race a part of a national agenda. One was the genuine conviction on the part of even the most racially enlightened New Dealers that blacks ought not to be singled out for special attention. The problems of black Americans were seen to be primarily economic; their advancement, closely linked to that of white Americans, could best be accomplished through broad-based economic and social reform.[5] Ickes, for example, insisted repeatedly that the "Negro problem merges into and becomes inseparable from the greater problem of American citizens generally, who are at or below the line in decency and comfort from those who are not."[6] Mrs. Roosevelt, although she recognized that blacks suffered acutely from prejudice and discrimination, believed that the Negro problem in the end came down to economic oppression and exploitation. It was because "colored people, not only in the South, but in the North as well have been economically at a low level," she asserted, ". . . that they have been physically and intellectually at a low level."[7] By including blacks in its programs of economic assistance, the New Deal would ameliorate the conditions that fostered racial hostility.

A second factor that kept race off the New Deal agenda was the world view of the President. The racial vision that Roosevelt brought to the presidency would not have motivated him to pay

[5] John B. Kirby, *Black Americans in the Roosevelt Era: Liberalism and Race* (Knoxville, Tenn., 1980), chaps. 2-4. See especially pp. 92-94.

[6] Harold L. Ickes, "To Have Jobs or To Have Not," *Negro Digest* IV (Jan. 1946):73, quoted in Kirby, *Black Americans in the Roosevelt Era*, p. 32.

[7] Eleanor Roosevelt, "The Negro and Social Change," *Opportunity* XIV (Jan. 1936):22, quoted in Kirby, *Black Americans in the Roosevelt Era*, p. 92.

particular attention to race, and he had few personal experiences in office that might have changed his perceptions.

Unlike his wife, he never formed personal friendships with blacks. The ones he knew best were Graham Jackson, an accordionist who often played for him at Warm Springs, and Irvin and Elizabeth McDuffie, his valet and maid. Roosevelt and Jackson never discussed racial issues.[8] Lizzie McDuffie told Roosevelt that she "was going to serve as his 'SASOCPA, self-appointed-secretary-on-colored people's-affairs.' " "How he laughed," she remembered.[9] She claimed that she interested the President in the case of three blacks who had been sent to Leavenworth penitentiary in connection with the Houston race riot, with the result that they were eventually pardoned. It was no idle boast; when one of them was released, Walter White wrote her, "a large part of the credit for this should go to you for your persistent efforts." She also claimed to have interested Roosevelt in cases of discrimination against blacks in the postal service and on WPA and to have acted as an "unofficial liaison" with the President for black leaders in and out of government. In addition, she made suggestions about black artists and glee clubs who might sing at the White House. Blacks sometimes looked to the McDuffies as intermediaries who could supply presidential autographs, communicate requests for aid, and voice concerns about patronage, discrimination, and other matters of concern to the race.[10]

Still, the McDuffies' influence was limited at best, and their occasional successes in bringing racial matters to Roosevelt's attention did not appreciably alter his outlook. Irvin McDuffie probably cast his employer's views about blacks in the most favorable light possible when he commented that Roosevelt "does not think in terms of races but in terms of Americans, and he believes the Negro is an American."[11]

The disinclination to pay particular attention to race was also,

---

[8] Interview with Graham W. Jackson, June 10, 1977, Atlanta.

[9] Elizabeth McDuffie, "FDR Was My Boss," *Ebony* VII (Apr. 1952):65.

[10] Ibid., pp. 65, 76, 81-82; Walter White to Mrs. I. H. McDuffie, Sept. 19, 1936, McDuffie Papers, Box 1, Negro Collection, Trevor Arnett Library, Atlanta University; Millicent Dobbs Jordan, "She Knew Roosevelt," *New Vistas* I (Jan. 1946):8-9, McDuffie Papers, Box 2; Memo for Mac from M. A. L., May 9, 1933, attached to W. A. Murphy to Franklin D. Roosevelt, Apr. 30, 1933, FDR Papers, OF 93; Memorandum for Hon. Harllee Branch, Feb. 21, 1935; Presidential Memorandum for the Postmaster General, Mar. 2, 1936; STE[arly] memorandum for McDuffy [sic], June 12, 1935; M. H. McIntyre confidential memorandum for Harllee Branch, Oct. 25, 1937, all in ibid., President's Personal File (PPF) 6714.

[11] Quoted in unidentified 1933 press clipping in McDuffie Papers, Box 1.

in large part, a matter of priorities. Problems of economic recovery naturally preoccupied the administration. Even some blacks felt that it was inappropriate to ask for consideration of racial concerns when the country faced problems of great moment. It was "silly and inopportune" to seek to see the President about "the grievances and demands of the Negro people" when conditions in general were so "distressing," the African Methodist Episcopal Zion Church's *Star of Zion* editorialized at the outset of the Hundred Days. "The Negro is a part of this great American citizenship and what affects the one affects the other." No group deserved special attention, the paper admonished, "and the sooner the Negro understands this and quits his whining the better it will be for him. All of the people take precedence over any of the people."[12]

Political realities reinforced the low priority of race on the New Deal agenda. Most blacks in the 1930s could not vote. That meant that blacks were not a strong enough political force to warrant attention to racial concerns.

Nor was there yet a politically potent body of liberal public opinion pressuring the administration to act in behalf of blacks. But there *was* a vocal body of reactionary opinion, especially in the South, that constituted an effective counterpressure not to act. Because blacks were not a powerful political constituency, it was unrealistic to expect Roosevelt to respond specifically to their concerns.[13]

By contrast, it was absolutely vital for the President to respond to the concerns of the southern senators and congressmen who could determine the fate of his legislative program. Not only was the new Vice-President a Southerner; so were the majority leaders of the House and Senate and the chairmen of major congressional committees. Roosevelt needed their votes to put through what he regarded as "must" recovery legislation, and he was unwilling to risk alienating them by championing racial causes. Refusing to risk his legislative program by pushing unpopular civil rights

[12] Editorial, *Star of Zion*, Mar. 16, 1933. For a similar view, see statement of Emory B. Smith upon accepting membership on the national committee of the Good Neighbor League, n.d. [1936], Good Neighbor League Papers, Box 1, Franklin D. Roosevelt Library.

[13] Rexford Tugwell, for one, singled out the fact that blacks could not vote to explain why race matters were not of central concern in the New Deal. Tugwell interview. See also interviews with Laurence I. Hewes, Jr., Feb. 7, 1977, Santa Barbara, and Martin Luther King, Sr., June 10, 1977, Atlanta. Earl Brown made the same point in terms of lack of "sophistication" and "understanding of what it takes to move the power structure" as impediments to attention to racial issues. Interview with Earl Brown, June 29, 1977, New York City.

measures was practical politics: it was clearly more important to the administration to keep southern political support than it was to court blacks. "Remember," Tommy Corcoran pointed out, explaining why race figured so little among New Deal concerns, "we were in a difficult situation—we always had to have that southern [support]. All of this trimming and compromising is the price you pay for having democratic government at all."[14]

Had blacks been fully aware of the racial climate that was to prevail in the new administration, they would have had good reason to fear for their fortunes under the New Deal. But it was impossible to know, early in 1933, the extent to which the deck would be stacked against a New Deal for the race.

Black observers evaluated varied evidence to measure the racial atmosphere of the new administration. The inauguration was encouraging: there were more blacks than ever before in the inaugural parade, a black Boy Scout in the honor guard on the White House lawn, well-known blacks readily visible in the audience, and "countless other evidences . . . of honor being paid the Race."[15] Black servants were more prominently represented at the White House. When Mrs. Roosevelt, responding to her husband's insistence on economy, trimmed the size of the domestic staff, she discharged the white employees and kept the Negroes. ("Perhaps," Frank Freidel has speculated, "she thought whites could more easily obtain employment.")[16] The new First Family made the White House a more relaxed, comfortable place to work. Lillian Rogers Parks, a black seamstress and maid who joined the White House staff during the Hoover years, described the difference between the two administrations:

> In the pantry [during the Hoover presidency], you had to whisper so that the Hoovers wouldn't hear you as they ate; and Mrs.

[14] Corcoran interview. Beginning in 1935, the Speaker of the House was also a Southerner.

[15] *Chicago Defender*, Mar. 11, 1933 (source of the quotation); *Afro-American*, Mar. 11, 1933.

[16] Frank Freidel, *Franklin D. Roosevelt: Launching the New Deal* (Boston, 1973), p. 268. The black press made much of the large proportion of black servants in the White House employ. See, for example, *Chicago Defender*, Mar. 11, 1933; *Afro-American*, Sept. 16, 1933, Oct. 12, 1935; *Pittsburgh Courier*, Dec. 23, 1933. The White House clearly noticed that blacks were paying attention; see the typed list of "Negro Employees at the White House, Executive Office, and White House Garage as of March 31, 1933," FDR Papers, OF 93.

Hoover's hand signals told you when to move and when not to move, when to speak and when not to speak.

Under the Roosevelts, doors stood open, and happy voices rang out, and there was no more popping into closets, and no more hiding when the President or the First Lady took the elevator. You were invited to "come in and ride along." We walked freely down the halls, and kept running into members of the big, sprawling Roosevelt family.[17]

Another notable difference was the frequency and the variety of roles in which blacks came to the White House. Individual black artists and black college glee clubs sang for the President in the executive mansion.[18] When Roosevelt entertained his Harvard classmates, black men and their wives were included in the group.[19] The President of Haiti visited the White House as President Roosevelt's guest—the first Haitian official ever to be thus honored—and was treated like any other chief of state.[20]

Somewhat later, Roosevelt even made brief public appearances before black audiences. On a trip to Nashville, he and Eleanor stopped at Fisk University and spent fifteen minutes listening to the glee club sing Negro spirituals. The hall was jammed, and blacks lined the streets for blocks to get a glimpse of the President and the First Lady. One newspaper estimated that 25,000 blacks had come "to pay homage to their national leader." The same was true in Atlanta, where Roosevelt stopped at Atlanta University to inspect a low-cost housing project that was under construction. He spoke briefly to the 20,000 blacks who had assem-

[17] Lillian Rogers Parks, *My Thirty Years Backstairs at the White House* (New York, 1961), p. 235.

[18] White House Usher's Diary, May 17, Dec. 5, 1933, Franklin D. Roosevelt Library; "At the White House," *Crisis* XL (July 1933):160; *Afro-American*, Dec. 2, 1933, Feb. 10, 17, 1934; Lizzie McDuffie, "I Swept the King's Carpet," typed draft chapter, Lizzie McDuffie Memoirs, Franklin D. Roosevelt Memorial Foundation, Record Group 21, Franklin D. Roosevelt Library. When the Tuskegee Choir took time from their scheduled appearance at Radio City to sing at Roosevelt's mother's birthday celebration in January 1933, he told them that he wanted them to sing for him in the White House. The story rated a banner front-page headline in the *Afro-American*, Jan. 21, 1933.

[19] White House Usher's Diary, Apr. 21, 1934; *Afro-American*, Apr. 7, 1934, clipping in Schomburg Center for Research in Black Culture; Claude A. Barnett to John H. Stelle, Oct. 17, 1934, Claude A. Barnett Papers, Box P3, Chicago Historical Society.

[20] White House Usher's Diary, Apr. 17, 1934; *Afro-American*, Mar. 31, Apr. 28, 1934; editorial, *Norfolk Journal and Guide*, Apr. 28, 1934, Roosevelt Administration Scrapbooks, vol. III, microfilm reel 16, Schomburg Center for Research in Black Culture.

bled on the university's athletic field; the crowd "cheered enthusiastically and waved thousands of flags."[21]

Actions like these on the part of the President were a real departure from past practice. Indeed, in the judgment of the *Afro-American*, the Roosevelts were setting "an example of interracial behavior" that was unprecedented in recent memory.[22]

On other counts, however, the evidence was less encouraging. As White had discovered, in the early months of the administration, it was impossible to see Roosevelt about racial matters. One interracial delegation, concerned about persistent violations of black rights, was deflected by Louis Howe, who, as secretary to the President, held the top position in the White House. "The Negro people," Howe told the delegation, "have no special problems; they are American citizens."[23] Julian Rainey, one of the chiefs of the Colored Division in the campaign of 1932, asked for an appointment. It would be good politics, he told Howe; black Americans would take it as "assurance that they were not 'forgotten.' " The President was too busy, Howe responded.[24]

The International Labor Defense sought a meeting with Roosevelt about the Scottsboro case. Nine black youths had been convicted of raping two white girls on a freight train near Scottsboro, Alabama, in 1931, and eight of them had been sentenced to die. The ILD, an organ of the American Communist party, took on the defense of the Scottsboro Boys and turned the case into a *cause célèbre*. Shortly after the election in November 1932, the United States Supreme Court had ordered a new trial on the grounds that the defendants had not had adequate counsel. In April 1933, despite substantial evidence to the contrary, a jury again found the youths guilty. The ILD planned a march on Washington to demand the freedom of the Scottsboro Boys, and it asked Roosevelt to meet with the mothers of the boys and with Ruby Bates, one of the white girls involved in the case, who had subsequently denied the accusations. The ILD sent four telegrams requesting a meeting. All of them were ignored.[25]

---

[21] On the visit to Fisk, see *Louisiana Weekly*, Nov. 24, 1934, clipping in Roosevelt Administration Scrapbooks, vol. II, microfilm reel 16, Schomburg Center for Research in Black Culture; on the visit to Atlanta University, *New York Age*, Dec. 7, 1935.

[22] Editorial, Apr. 7, 1934, clipping in Schomburg Center for Research in Black Culture.

[23] Quoted in editorial, *Chicago Defender*, Apr. 1, 1933.

[24] Julian D. Rainey to Louis M. Howe, Apr. 17, 1933; Howe to Rainey, Apr. 20, 1933, FDR Papers, OF 93.

[25] Dan T. Carter, *Scottsboro: A Tragedy of the American South* (New York, 1969), p. 249; *Afro-American*, May 6, 13, 1933.

The managing editor of the *Baltimore Afro-American* wanted to bring a group of black newspaper editors and economists to the White House to acquaint Roosevelt with "some facts of vital moment" about "the growing spirit of desperation developing among colored citizens." It was impossible to make the appointment, Marvin McIntyre, Roosevelt's appointments secretary, replied. Try again sometime—or better yet, send the information through the mail.[26] The NAACP counsel, Charles H. Houston, and the newspaperman, George B. Murphy, Jr., sought an audience for a delegation concerned about lynching. Howe's secretary said that she would be unable to make the appointment for them; if they returned the next morning, she would take it up with Howe. They returned according to her instructions, and after an hour, the secretary appeared. "What do you BOYS want?" she asked. After another hour's wait, a message came from Roosevelt's press secretary, Stephen Early. The President could not see the delegation. Nor would Early see Houston and Murphy—he was too busy with more important matters.[27]

Even patronage for blacks proved to be difficult to accomplish. Given their defection from Republican ranks in the election of 1932, blacks expected (so they reminded the President) increased attention. Besides, the judicious use of patronage was smart politics; by rewarding blacks who worked for Roosevelt, the Democrats could build party loyalty.[28] At the insistence of Joseph Guffey, Roosevelt appointed Robert L. Vann an assistant attorney general.[29] " 'I ought to tell you he's colored,' " Guffey told Roosevelt when he asked for a job for Vann. " 'Will I have to get him confirmed by the Senate?' " Roosevelt asked. " 'No,' " said Guffey, grinning. " 'The job's yours, Joe.' "[30]

On other major appointments, however, Roosevelt's response was unsettling at best. The minister to Haiti, minister to Liberia, the register of the treasury—to these and other posts that blacks

[26] William N. Jones to Louis M. Howe, June 14, 1932 (actually 1933); M. H. McIntyre to Jones, June 16, 1933, FDR Papers, OF 93.

[27] *Afro-American*, Sept. 2, 1933.

[28] See, for example, William F. Davis to Franklin D. Roosevelt, Feb. 26, 1933; W. A. Allen and G. D. Hammonds to Roosevelt, Mar. 8, 1933; I.J.K. Wells to Louis McHenry Howe, Mar. 18, 1933; C. H. Carter and J. H. Young to Roosevelt, Mar. 21, 1933, FDR Papers, OF 93; Arthur W. Mitchell to Roosevelt, Feb. 27, 1934, Arthur W. Mitchell Papers, Box 1, Chicago Historical Society; Mitchell to J. Hamilton Lewis, Jan. 12, 1935, Mitchell Papers, Box 4.

[29] Joseph F. Guffey, *Seventy Years on the Red-Fire Wagon* (n.p., 1952), p. 171; Joseph F. Guffey to Louis McHenry Howe, Dec. 16, 1932, Democratic National Committee Papers, Box 682, Franklin D. Roosevelt Library.

[30] Joseph Alsop and Robert Kintner, "The Guffey: Biography of a Boss, New Style," *Saturday Evening Post*, March 26, 1938, p. 6.

had once held, Roosevelt appointed whites.[31] The one major "traditional" position to go to a black man was recorder of deeds. William J. Thompkins, editor of the *Kansas City American* and one of the "Big Four" from the Colored Division in 1932, won the post in 1934. The minister to Liberia finally became a black man when Roosevelt named Lester A. Walton to the job in 1935.[32]

When Vann pushed for more political jobs for blacks, the Democrats in charge of patronage became evasive and noncommittal. Vann's own position, impressive as it may have been in title, proved to be a great disappointment. His office accommodations were woefully inadequate; stenographers resisted taking his dictation because of his race; and he could not even get an appointment to see the attorney general. Most important, his work was limited to routine, insignificant tasks. From time to time, the administration gave him minor duties outside the Justice Department, but they, also, were too unimportant to hold his interest. In the fall of 1935, frustrated and disappointed, Vann resigned his position and returned to the *Pittsburgh Courier*.[33]

To black publicists, lobbyists, political leaders, and others, patronage mattered for a number of reasons. As the most familiar medium of political exchange, federal appointments showed who counted in Washington. Groups that had the most influence won the lion's share of the jobs. Since the federal government had long refused to embrace civil rights measures, patronage had been the only form of recognition blacks could expect. Beyond that, self-styled black leaders had a personal stake in patronage, for they were the ones who stood to profit most directly from such appointments.

But most blacks had no hope themselves of benefiting personally from federal patronage, and the symbolic significance of appointing a black man as register of the treasury or minister to Haiti paled against the pressing problems of everyday life. The issue that preoccupied ordinary blacks in 1933 was the economic catastrophe. Within the space of a hundred days, the new administration in Washington created an extraordinary array of programs to restore public confidence, fight the Depression, and put the country on the road to a healthy economic recovery. The

[31] Editorial, *Philadelphia Tribune*, Apr. 6, 1933; *Afro-American*, June 17, Aug. 5, 1933.

[32] *Afro-American*, July 6, 1935.

[33] Andrew Buni, *Robert L. Vann of the Pittsburgh Courier: Politics and Black Journalism* (Pittsburgh, 1974), pp. 205-211, 219, 221.

principal concern for the masses of blacks was easy to identify: what share would they have in the relief and recovery programs of the New Deal?

"If any group needs a 'New Deal,' " the *Philadelphia Tribune* asserted as the Roosevelt administration took office, "it is black Americans."[34] As the census of 1930 had made clear, economic adversity was nothing new for blacks. For decades, they had been stuck at the bottom of the economic ladder. Migration from farm to city had changed the traditional patterns of black employment—agriculture, which had accounted for more than half of all gainfully employed black workers in 1910, claimed just over a third of them two decades later. But the movement away from the land did not appreciably affect the overall economic status of blacks in the United States. There were significant numerical gains in black employment in manufacturing and mechanical industries in the 1920s, but blacks in those fields in 1930 constituted the same percentage of all employed blacks as in 1920. The largest gains in black employment in the 1920s—in terms of both absolute numbers and percentage of employed blacks—came in domestic and personal service (see Table II.1). All in all, as Tables II.2 and II.3 show, blacks in 1930 were still disproportionately concentrated in semiskilled, laboring, and servant jobs. Indeed, the general employment picture for blacks who were working in 1930 looked very much the way it had in 1920.

What *was* new in the early 1930s was the crushing impact of the Depression on this already depressed economic structure. Blacks in the rural South bore the heaviest burden. Cotton prices fell by close to 70 percent between 1929 and the beginning of 1933, and the precipitous decline took the earnings of black farmers down with it. For more than two-thirds of them, cotton farming in the early 1930s yielded no profits. At best, they broke even; at worst, they plunged deeper into debt.[35]

In the cities, those blacks who managed to hold onto their jobs suffered crippling declines in wages. Harlem was probably typical: there the median income of skilled workers was cut in half between 1929 and 1932; among semiskilled and unskilled workers,

[34] Editorial, *Philadelphia Tribune*, Feb. 2, 1933. The *Tribune*'s formulation was certainly not unique. See "A 'New Deal' for the Negro," *Opportunity* XI (May 1933):135.

[35] Harvard Sitkoff, *A New Deal for Blacks: The Emergence of Civil Rights as a National Issue*, vol. I: *The Depression Decade* (New York, 1978), p. 35.

TABLE II.1
Gainfully Employed Workers, Ten Years of Age and Over,
by Occupation, 1910, 1920, 1930
(in percentages)

Occupation	Blacks			All Workers		
	1910	*1920*	*1930*	*1910*	*1920*	*1930*
Agriculture, Forestry, Animal Husbandry	55.7	45.2	36.7	33.2	26.3	21.9
Extraction of Minerals	1.2	1.5	1.4	2.5	2.6	2.0
Manufacturing and Mechanical Industries	12.2	18.4	18.6	27.8	30.8	28.9
Transportation	4.9	6.5	7.2	6.9	7.4	7.9
Trade	2.3	2.9	3.3	9.5	10.2	12.5
Public Service	.4	1.0	.9	1.2	1.9	1.8
Professional Service	1.3	1.7	2.5	4.4	5.2	6.7
Domestic and Personal Service	21.6	22.1	28.6	9.9	8.2	10.1
Clerical Occupations	.4	.8	.7	4.6	7.5	8.2

SOURCES: U.S. Department of Commerce, Bureau of the Census, *Fourteenth Census of the United States Taken in the Year 1920*, vol. IV: *Population, 1920: Occupations* (Washington, D.C., 1923), pp. 340-41; *Fifteenth Census of the United States: 1930*, vol. V: *Population: General Report on Occupations* (Washington, D.C., 1933), p. 74. Originally published in Nancy J. Weiss, *The National Urban League, 1910-1940* (New York, 1974).

median incomes plummeted 43 percent.[36] Black families stood at a substantial disadvantage in comparison to whites; in Cleveland, for example, 53.8 percent of the Negro families surveyed in 1933 had incomes of less than $500, compared to 26.1 percent of the whites. By contrast, 18.3 percent of the white families, but only 1.1 percent of the Negroes, had incomes of $2,000 or more.[37]

Wages aside, employment of any sort for blacks in the cities was increasingly hard to come by. Fierce competition from whites

[36] Clyde V. Kiser, "Diminishing Family Income in Harlem," *Opportunity* XIII (June 1935):172.

[37] Richard Sterner, *The Negro's Share: A Study of Income, Consumption, Housing and Public Assistance* (New York, 1943), p. 373.

TABLE II.2

Employment Distribution of Gainfully Employed Workers, Ten Years of Age and Over,
in Nonagricultural Occupations, 1920 and 1930

(in percentages)

Occupation	1920			1930		
	Native-born Whites	Foreign-born Whites	Blacks	Native-born Whites	Foreign-born Whites	Blacks
Proprietors, Officials, Managers	9.3	10.3	1.9	9.6	11.9	1.9
Clerks and Kindred Workers	23.5	8.4	2.3	25.6	10.8	2.2
Skilled Workers	16.4	19.1	5.5	14.5	19.9	5.0
Semiskilled Workers	21.2	24.6	14.4	22.4	24.7	15.4
Laborers	14.8	25.6	36.2	11.3	17.4	31.2
Servants	3.9	7.2	35.9	4.7	9.4	40.3
Public Officials	.7	.2	<.1	.6	.2	<.1
Semiofficial Public Employees	1.8	1.2	.7	1.6	1.1	.4
Professional Persons	8.4	3.4	2.9	9.7	4.6	3.4

SOURCES: U.S. Department of Commerce, Bureau of the Census, *Fourteenth Census of the United States Taken in the Year 1920,* vol. IV: *Population, 1920: Occupations* (Washington, D.C., 1923), pp. 342-59; *Fifteenth Census of the United States, 1930,* vol. V: *Population: General Report on Occupations* (Washington, D.C., 1933), pp. 76-85; Dean Dutcher, *The Negro in Modern Industrial Society: An Analysis of Changes in the Occupations of Negro Workers, 1910-1920* (Lancaster, Pa., 1930); U.S. Department of Commerce, Bureau of the Census, *A Social-Economic Grouping of the Gainful Workers of the United States* (Washington, D.C., 1938), especially pp. 10, 13, 86-87. Originally published in Nancy J. Weiss, *The National Urban League, 1910-1940* (New York, 1974).

TABLE II.3
Employment Distribution of Gainfully Employed Workers, Ten Years
of Age and Over, in Semiskilled and Unskilled Positions
in Nonagricultural Occupations, 1920 and 1930
(in percentages)

	1920			1930		
	Native-born Whites	*Foreign-born Whites*	*Blacks*	*Native-born Whites*	*Foreign-born Whites*	*Blacks*
Unskilled	18.7	32.8	72.1	16.0	26.8	71.5
Semiskilled	23.0	25.8	15.1	24.0	25.8	15.8
Total	41.7	58.6	87.2	40.0	52.6	87.3

SOURCES: See Table II.2.

meant that even the most menial jobs were no longer reserved
for Negroes. Unemployment had reached a staggering nationwide
level of just under 25 percent by 1933; among blacks, it was
substantially greater. In some of the larger industrial centers, the
black unemployment rate exceeded 50 percent. Although just over
9 percent of the American people were black, blacks accounted
for more than 18 percent of all cases on relief. In the cities, the
disproportion was even more striking: over 26 percent of urban
blacks, but less than 10 percent of urban whites, were on relief
in 1933. Unemployment itself, as the Fisk University sociologist,
Charles S. Johnson, pointed out, was the most prominent index
of black misery, but it had broader implications: overcrowded
housing, the erosion of savings, the loss of homes and household
possessions, the disruption of family life, and, more generally, "a
loss of work habits" and "a loss of the spirit to carry on the
determined struggle" for survival.[38]

At the outset of the new administration, the National Urban
League sent the President a memorandum on the economic and
social condition of black Americans. The memorandum presented
a detailed portrait of the suffering of blacks in the economic crisis
and called on the administration to include blacks in its efforts
to fight the Depression.[39] The administration's response to the

[38] National Urban League memorandum to Franklin D. Roosevelt, "The Negro
Working Population and National Recovery," Jan. 4, 1937, NAACP Papers; Charles
S. Johnson, *The Economic Status of Negroes* (Nashville, 1933), p. 20; Robert W.
Bagnall to Walter White, Apr. 20, Sept. 30, 1932, NAACP Papers, Box C-63.
[39] National Urban League memorandum to Franklin D. Roosevelt, "The Social
Adjustment of Negroes in the United States," Apr. 15, 1933, National Urban
League Papers, Manuscript Division, Library of Congress.

Urban League came, not from the President, but from his secretary of labor. Frances Perkins, like other members of the cabinet, was not especially cognizant of the race issue. As a young social worker in Philadelphia, she had run an agency to protect black girls new to northern cities, and, yet, early in her tenure at the Department of Labor, she expressed amazement, upon arriving in Atlanta to deliver a speech, that she was to address a segregated audience.[40] By her own account, the trip underscored her naiveté about racial issues in other ways as well. She went to tea at Spelman College and was surprised to find that it might be an unusual gesture for an official visitor to the city to make. By the time she dined with the governor, however, she had become sufficiently attuned to the situation to avoid mentioning her visit to Spelman. "I just thought it was better not to if we were trying to become popular with the government and political leaders of Georgia." During her visit to Atlanta University, Perkins met W.E.B. Du Bois. She did not know that she had ever heard of him before. What struck her especially were his non-Negroid features. "I remember . . . recognizing that here was a cross-breed situation, all right. . . . I remember thinking, 'This is one of those interesting types that occurs in the U.S.A.' "[41]

Will W. Alexander, who succeeded Rexford G. Tugwell as head of the Farm Security Administration, later remarked that Perkins "dread[ed] very much to deal with the racial problem in the South."[42] While she appointed black aides in the Department of Labor, she seemed baffled by black demands for additional representation: "Every day brings a group of demands from a group of Negroes to be appointed to something or other. . . . I do not know how we are going to deal with them."[43] When Eleanor Roosevelt consulted her about the possibility of appointing a black woman to the Women's Bureau, Perkins replied that there appeared to be "no real reason for having a negro there"—and besides, "there undoubtedly would be some difficulty" because of prejudice.[44] She

[40] George Martin, *Madam Secretary: Frances Perkins* (Boston, 1976), pp. 65-67; Frances Perkins, *Reminiscences* (Columbia University Oral History Collection, 1955), vol. V, pt. 3, p. 467.

[41] Perkins, *Reminiscences*, vol. V, pt. 4, pp. 469-72.

[42] Will Winton Alexander, *Reminiscences* (Columbia University Oral History Collection, 1952), p. 369.

[43] Meeting of Special Industrial Recovery Board, Sept. 18, 1933, National Negro Congress Papers, Box 1 (microfilm reel 1), Schomburg Center for Research in Black Culture.

[44] Frances Perkins to Eleanor Roosevelt, Apr. 17, 1934; Eleanor Roosevelt's secretary to Perkins, Apr. 26, 1934, Eleanor Roosevelt Papers, Box 627, Franklin D. Roosevelt Library (hereafter cited as the ER Papers).

won from Roosevelt the assignment of responding to the Urban League, then, not because of any special concern on her part for blacks, but probably because the economic and social needs of Negroes seemed to fall most logically in the domain of the secretary of labor.

In a widely-publicized letter in April, Perkins assured the executive secretary of the National Urban League, Eugene Kinckle Jones, that blacks would not "be overlooked" in the administration's "vast reconstruction plans . . . for employment and relief."[45] The President understood the plight of blacks, she said, and then she added her own assurance: "As this Administration undertakes the problems of relief administration, of providing work opportunities, of raising basic wage levels, . . . we shall not forget the special problems of the more than ten million people who belong to your race."[46]

By official pronouncement, the Roosevelt administration forbade discrimination in New Deal programs. But there were wide variations in the way in which those programs actually affected blacks. Each program promised opportunities for blacks; each had plenty of loopholes for discrimination. It was most difficult to win fair treatment for blacks when Congress set explicit guidelines for a program's operation, because other, more powerful interest groups had more influence in the legislative process. It was difficult, too, when fair treatment of blacks would have struck at the conventional arrangement of relations between the races. Blacks had a better chance when a program was administered by an emergency agency under a broad grant of congressional authority, because that gave maximum leeway for influence by a sympathetic agency head or a particularly effective racial adviser. Agencies that were run with "heavy centralized control" made it easier to protect the interests of blacks; "where local control was powerful, there was always a battle."[47] Blacks were more likely to benefit, too, when a program could yield a tangible political payoff—in other words, when the aid extended would be most likely to buy black votes and when the inclusion of blacks could be accomplished without threatening to upset established black-white relations.

In the early years of the Roosevelt administration, most of the programs demonstrated the limits to New Deal assistance for

[45] *Afro-American*, May 13, 1933.
[46] Frances Perkins to Eugene Kinckle Jones, Apr. 27, 1933, published as "A Letter," *Opportunity* XI (June 1933):169.
[47] W. J. Trent, Jr., to Nancy J. Weiss, Jan. 6, 1981.

blacks rather than its reach. The record of one agency—the Public Works Administration—shows how federal power could be used creatively to benefit black Americans. More typically, four major relief and recovery agencies—the Civilian Conservation Corps, the Agricultural Adjustment Administration, the National Recovery Administration, and the Federal Emergency Relief Administration—illustrate the various ways in which the New Deal fell short of evenhanded treatment for blacks.

The Public Works Administration, established to build the public works projects authorized in the National Industrial Recovery Act of June 1933, operated so cautiously that it never had much success in stimulating industrial recovery.[48] For all the limitations of its scope and impact, PWA stood out as one of the agencies where blacks were most likely to find a real New Deal. The principal reason for the PWA's favorable record on race was the public works administrator, Harold L. Ickes. Ickes came to Washington as one of the few New Dealers with credentials in the area of racial advancement. He had served as president of the Chicago branch of the NAACP for a brief period in the early 1920s, and although his presidency had not been especially happy—the Chicago NAACP was weak and disorganized—he often spoke about it to blacks as if to prove the seriousness of his commitment to their welfare. Smug, arrogant, and egotistical, he antagonized many of the people around him. But his self-righteous certainty that he was the only truly honest, moral public servant in Washington gave him the freedom to stand up for what he thought was right, even at the risk of political costs. Ickes was a passionate defender of the underdog, and he cared intensely about individual rights and civil liberties. Fair treatment for black Americans was one of his many causes.[49] He promised blacks "a square deal" in work that came under his jurisdiction, and he described "the prevention of discrimination against the Negro race" as a subject that was "very close" to his heart.[50] Next to Eleanor Roosevelt, he became

[48] William E. Leuchtenburg, *Franklin D. Roosevelt and the New Deal, 1932-1940* (New York, 1963), pp. 70-71.

[49] Kirby, *Black Americans in the Roosevelt Era*, pp. 18-35; M. Judd Harmon, "Some Contributions of Harold L. Ickes," *Western Political Quarterly* VII (June 1954):238-52; Arthur M. Schlesinger, Jr., *The Politics of Upheaval* (Boston, 1960), pp. 358-60.

[50] Harold L. Ickes to Walter White, July 11, 1933, Department of the Interior Papers, Record Group 48, Office Files of Harold L. Ickes, Box 9, National Archives ("a square deal"); Ickes to Butler R. Wilson, Jan. 25, 1934, ibid., Office of the Secretary, Central Classified Files, File 1-280, pt. 1. See also Ickes to White, Mar. 1, 1933, NAACP Papers, Box C-391.

widely regarded as the best friend that blacks had in the new administration.[51]

In September 1933, Ickes issued a general order prohibiting "discrimination on the basis of color or religion in employment for public works"[52] and drafted a nondiscrimination clause for PWA contracts. But in the absence of a precise definition of discrimination, the clause proved difficult to enforce. Contractors and building trades unions were notorious for discriminating against blacks; with employment for public projects determined locally, it was difficult for the PWA to prevent discrimination. When the agency began to build public housing, it shifted the burden of proof to the contractor. Moving beyond a simple prohibition against discrimination, it established a prima facie definition of discrimination: "The failure to pay a minimum percentage of the skilled and of the unskilled payrolls to Negro workers." Percentages were set according to the occupational census of 1930 for each city. Each PWA contract included a specific percentage requirement. If a contractor failed to meet it, he had to prove that he had not discriminated. Despite strong opposition from unions, the PWA succeeded in employing black construction workers on public works projects.[53] The historian of the quota plan explained why it worked: much of the plan's effectiveness, he wrote,

> may be attributed to Ickes. Committed to assisting black workers, he was involved in the program from its formulation to the actual hiring of black workers. . . . Perhaps more important to the success of the PWA's quota plan than the efforts of any

[51] On black attitudes toward Ickes, see, for example, Walter White telegram to Harold L. Ickes, Feb. 23, 1933, NAACP Papers, Box C-391; editorial, *Chicago Defender*, Oct. 13, 1934; White to Ickes, Mar. 11, 1936, and Roy Wilkins to Harry Slattery, Apr. 29, 1936, Harold L. Ickes Papers, Folder 140, Box 281, Manuscript Division, Library of Congress; first draft of introduction by Arthur B. Spingarn of Secretary of the Interior Harold L. Ickes, June 26, 1936, ibid., Folder 140A, Box 281; Edgar G. Brown to Ickes, July 2, 1936, and Simeon B. Osby, Jr., to Ickes, July 11, 1936, ibid., Folder 140, Box 281; S. G. Chamberlain to Ickes, Oct. 12, 1936, Interior Department Papers, File 1-280, pt. 2; interviews with Roy Wilkins, Aug. 17, 1976, New York City, Rayford W. Logan, Nov. 29, 1976, Washington, D.C., E. Frederic Morrow, Apr. 29, 1977, Princeton, N.J., Pauli Murray, July 1, 1977, Alexandria, Va.

[52] Clark Foreman to W. H. Christian, Oct. 12, 1933, Ickes Papers, Box 213.

[53] Harold L. Ickes, Message to NAACP Annual Conference, June 30, 1935, NAACP Papers, Box B-11; Robert C. Weaver, "Racial Policy in Public Housing," *Phylon* I (Second Quarter, 1940):153 (source of the quotation); Robert C. Weaver, *Negro Labor: A National Problem* (New York, 1946), pp. 11-13; Marc W. Kruman, "Quotas for Blacks: The Public Works Administration and the Black Construction Worker," *Labor History* XVI (Winter 1975):37-49.

individual was the centralized nature of the program. The negotiators for the government were Washington-based employees of the Bureau of Labor Statistics, the agreements had to be approved in Washington . . . , and the implementation of the agreements was supervised by the PWA's Inspection Division. Such a centralized organization provided little opportunity for local prejudices and biases to interfere with the program.[54]

The absolute number of workers whom the quota plan benefited may have been small, but, for the families involved, the importance of such public works employment cannot be overstated. Sterling Tucker summed it up in a simple recollection: "When I was a kid, PWA meant, 'Poppa's working again.' "[55]

Other New Deal programs showed more pervasive discrimination. The Civilian Conservation Corps epitomized the wide gap between official pronouncements about nondiscrimination and actual performance. Designed to put young men to work building dams, draining marshlands, fighting forest fires, and planting trees, the CCC was conceived for the conservation of human beings as well as natural resources.[56] Participation in the CCC meant a chance to acquire skills and earn money. Leon Higginbotham remembered what it meant when young blacks in his neighborhood in Trenton went off to CCC camps: "That was as important as going to Princeton University—they had status."[57]

But black participation in the CCC was not easy to accomplish. The language of the legislation creating the agency was clear: there would be no racial discrimination in CCC employment. No matter how plain the intent, implementation was another matter. It was one thing to put such a policy into effect in the North; in the South, the issue was not simply to secure a fair share of the employment for blacks, but also to persuade local selection agents to include blacks at all. Practice varied, but the experience of Georgia was typical of the southern states that were the worst offenders. In counties in Georgia that were more than 60 percent black, the CCC had been in operation for more than a month, and no blacks had been enrolled. It was only when W. Frank Persons, director of CCC selection in Washington, called Gov-

[54] Kruman, "Quotas for Blacks," p. 49.

[55] Interview with Sterling Tucker, Mar. 23, 1977, Washington, D.C.

[56] James MacGregor Burns, *Roosevelt: The Lion and the Fox* (New York, 1956), p. 169.

[57] Interview with A. Leon Higginbotham, Jr., Jan. 21, 1981, Philadelphia. See also interview with Carl B. Stokes, Aug. 22, 1979, New York City.

ernor Eugene Talmadge and threatened to block *all* CCC enrollment in Georgia unless blacks were included that things began
to change. But progress in the South was painfully slow. Mississippi, the worst case of all, a state that was over 50 percent black,
enrolled only forty-six blacks, or 1.7 percent of the total enrollment, by the middle of June. In the North, enrollment went more
smoothly, but by the year's end, slightly more than 5 percent of
CCC enrollees nationwide were black—hardly the fair share which
the legislation had promised.[58]

Enrollment itself was only part of the problem. When the number of black enrollees was too small to justify the creation of a
separate black company, blacks were assigned to integrated work
camps, which raised problems of racial friction. When, as was
most often the case, blacks were assigned to camps of their own,
local communities, North as well as South, often resisted the
location of the campsites in their vicinity.[59] Black spokesmen
protested strongly against the administration's policy of excluding
blacks from employment in the camps as officers and supervisory
personnel—a protest that finally bore fruit in 1936 when Roosevelt decided that a few blacks might be hired for such positions.[60]

Pressure from local communities; the latitude given local authorities; the division of authority for the CCC between the army,
which strongly supported segregation, and the Labor Department,
which tried to enforce the law against discrimination; and the
personal predilections of the agency's chief made black participation in the CCC a continuing problem. Contrary to the intent
of the legislation creating the Corps, the director of the CCC,
Robert Fechner, himself a conservative Southerner, pushed increasingly for rigid segregation and explicit limitations on black
enrollment—a decision in which President Roosevelt concurred.

[58] John A. Salmond, *The Civilian Conservation Corps, 1933-1942: A New Deal
Case Study* (Durham, N.C., 1967), pp. 88-91; Allen Francis Kifer, "The Negro
under the New Deal, 1933-1941" (Ph.D. diss., University of Wisconsin, 1961), pp.
4-13, 67.
[59] Salmond, *The Civilian Conservation Corps*, pp. 91-93; Kifer, "The Negro
under the New Deal," pp. 13-16, 26-38.
[60] Salmond, *The Civilian Conservation Corps*, pp. 95, 189-90; Kifer, "The Negro
under the New Deal," pp. 50-66; Calvin W. Gower, "The Struggle of Blacks for
Leadership Positions in the Civilian Conservation Corps: 1933-1942," *Journal of
Negro History* LXI (Apr. 1976):127-31; Charles Johnson, "The Army, the Negro
and the Civilian Conservation Corps: 1933-1942," *Military Affairs* XXXVI (Oct.
1972):84-86; Franklin D. Roosevelt memoranda for Robert Fechner, Jan. 15, 1936,
Mar. 13, 1937, FDR Papers, OF 93.

By 1936, black participation had reached 10 percent, a share technically equitable insofar as it corresponded to the black percentage of the national population, but less than adequate when measured against the disproportionate relief needs of blacks.[61]

Some New Deal programs were organized in such a way as to invite discrimination. The Agricultural Adjustment Administration was the classic case. In its simplest terms, the farm problem involved farm surpluses that were too large and farm incomes that were too low. The government's solution was to prop up prices at a level of parity and pay farmers not to produce. The spectacle of crops plowed under and baby pigs led to slaughter was hard to square with a starving nation, but administration economists agreed that it was the best way to save the farmer.

Saving the farmer, however, meant saving some farmers at the expense of others. The government sent crop reduction payments to farm owners and managers. In theory, they were to pass along a proportionate share to the sharecroppers and tenant farmers in their employ. But there was no enforcement machinery and no federal official to whom one had to account, and the temptation for owners to keep the money themselves was often too strong to resist. And since they were cutting back on production, planters no longer needed so many croppers and tenants on the land. Not only did the owners fail to pass along the share of the federal payments to which their employees were entitled, but—again in violation of federal regulations—they simply let the croppers and tenants go.[62]

Nearly two million black people worked in agriculture in 1930; of those, roughly 306,000 were tenant farmers and 393,000 were sharecroppers. The AAA was single-handedly responsible for a drastic curtailment in their numbers—over the decade of the 1930s, the number of black tenants was cut by nearly a third and the number of croppers by just under a quarter. By comparison, the number of white tenants actually grew between 1930 and 1935, but then leveled off by 1940 to a number virtually identical to that of 1930. The number of white sharecroppers, however, fell by 37 percent.[63] "It was galling to see this going on and not be

[61] Salmond, *The Civilian Conservation Corps*, pp. 95-99; Kifer, "The Negro under the New Deal," pp. 16-26, 67, 74-75.

[62] For a detailed account of blacks and the AAA, see Raymond Wolters, *Negroes and the Great Depression: The Problem of Economic Recovery* (Westport, Conn., 1970), chaps. 1 and 2.

[63] Sterner, *The Negro's Share*, p. 13; Gunnar Myrdal, *An American Dilemma*, 2 vols. (1944; 20th anniv. ed., New York, 1964), I:251-53.

able to do anything about it," recalled Rexford G. Tugwell, who was undersecretary of agriculture in the first Roosevelt administration. But both the President and the secretary of agriculture, Henry Wallace, believed in "the trickle-down theory"—"if the larger farmers improved their own situation they would take care of their tenants and laborers."[64] And Wallace was certainly no friend of blacks. The secretary, who, by his own admission, enjoyed "darky" jokes, was, in Will Alexander's description, "terribly afraid" of the race issue—he "just wouldn't stand up under it." Years later, as the second Roosevelt term drew to a close and Alexander left his post in the Farm Security Administration, he bade Wallace farewell. " 'Will,' " Wallace said to him, " 'don't you think the New Deal is undertaking to do too much for negroes?' "[65] In such a climate, it is not surprising that Tugwell's protests about the plight of croppers and tenants under the AAA were "simply ignored."[66]

Of all the New Deal agencies, none was so frequently vilified by blacks as the National Recovery Administration. To many Americans the NRA, with its codes of fair competition and standards for wages and hours, was an important stride toward economic recovery. But to most blacks, the Blue Eagle was no symbol of hope; it seemed more like "a black hawk, a predatory bird."[67] Blacks translated the acronym in terms descriptive of their own experience: "Negro Rights Abused," "Negro Rights Assassinated," "Negro Removal Act," and "Negroes Ruined Again."[68] "How's things since the NRA?" one angry black man asked rhetorically. "Less work and no pay."[69] "Before the Blue Eagle we was just one-half living," another commented, "but now we is only one-third living."[70]

No matter how blacks looked at the NRA, there was plenty to complain about. Some codes—such as the one for the cotton tex-

[64] Rexford G. Tugwell, *Roosevelt's Revolution: The First Year—A Personal Perspective* (New York, 1977), pp. 218, 260. See also p. 126.

[65] Henry Agard Wallace, *Reminiscences* (Columbia University Oral History Collection, 1963), vol. VI, pp. 1150-52; Alexander, *Reminiscences*, pp. 607, 608.

[66] Tugwell, *Roosevelt's Revolution*, p. 218.

[67] John P. Davis, "Blue Eagles and Black Workers," *New Republic*, Nov. 14, 1934, p. 9.

[68] Letters to the editor from Ridgley Miller and Harold C. Newsome, *Philadelphia Tribune*, Oct. 12, Sept. 14, 1933; William Pickens, "NRA—'Negro Removal Act'?" *World Tomorrow*, Sept. 28, 1933, pp. 539-40; Davis, "Blue Eagles and Black Workers," p. 9.

[69] Letter to the editor from Ridgley Miller, *Philadelphia Tribune*, Oct. 12, 1933.

[70] Quoted in Davis, "Blue Eagles and Black Workers," p. 9.

tile industry—simply left out the categories of employment where blacks were most heavily concentrated. Some—such as lumber—set the minimum wage for the South, where the work force was heavily black, far below that of the North, where most workers in the industry were white. When code wages were set high, employers sometimes fired their black workers instead of paying them what the codes demanded; or they disregarded the codes altogether and paid blacks what they thought they ought to receive. In such cases, blacks often had trouble securing justice from the NRA compliance boards. Filing a complaint might be reason enough to lose a job, and a compliance board made up of employers was not disposed to look too favorably on black appeals.[71] The NRA, one persistent critic summed up, was "a weapon of calamity for Negro workers," "a hopeless shambles so far as Negroes are concerned."[72]

It seemed briefly that NRA officials meant to look into problems of discrimination. In September 1933, the agency hired Mabel Byrd, a young black graduate of the University of Chicago. Her duties, the *Afro-American* reported enthusiastically, would be "to ferret out" code violators who wanted separate wage codes for blacks and "whip them into line."[73] But her tenure was short-lived. The administrator of the NRA, Hugh S. Johnson, refused to let her go south to investigate wage discrimination against blacks on the grounds that it was "crazy"—entirely too dangerous to turn a northern-trained black investigator loose to interrogate white southern employers.[74] Within four months of her employment, Byrd's job had ended, and the unit to which she had been assigned in the NRA had been disbanded. To the *Afro-American*, the Byrd incident was proof positive of the NRA's "indifference to the problems of the Negro workers in the South."[75]

Even the agency designed to deal most directly with the immediate relief needs of suffering Americans was dogged by prob-

[71] See, e.g., John P. Davis, "What Price National Recovery?" *Crisis* XL (Dec. 1933):271-72; "Negro Complaints Against Codes," *Christian Century*, Mar. 28, 1934, p. 434; John P. Davis, "The Maid-Well Garment Case," *Crisis* XLI (Dec. 1934):356-57. For a scholarly account of blacks and the NRA, see Wolters, *Negroes and the Great Depression*, pt. II. For a case study of the experience in one southern state, consult Michael S. Holmes, "The Blue Eagle as 'Jim Crow Bird': The NRA and Georgia's Black Workers," *Journal of Negro History* LVII (July 1972):276-83.

[72] John P. Davis, "NRA Codifies Wage Slavery," *Crisis* XLI (Oct. 1934):298, 304.

[73] *Afro-American*, Oct. 7, 1933.

[74] Meeting of Special Industrial Recovery Board, Sept. 18, 1933, National Negro Congress Papers, Box 1 (reel 1).

[75] *Afro-American*, Dec. 9, 30 (editorial), 1933.

lems of discrimination. The Federal Emergency Relief Administration was established to make outright grants to the states for
direct unemployment relief.[76] Forrester B. Washington, the social
work educator who served as the agency's first racial adviser,
called the FERA "a godsend to the Negro of the masses."[77] Governmental aid meant an improvement in black living standards.
Those standards may still have been "wretchedly low," as one
local caseworker put it, but they were better under the FERA than
they had been before. "It is a curious commentary on industrial
conditions in the South," Washington wrote, "that at the height
of prosperity many Negroes never earned as much or ate as well
as is the case under relief." The relief agencies brought food,
clothing, and employment. Along with this tangible aid came
basic education—schools to teach illiterate adults to read and
write, classes ranging from typing and stenography to art and
music, and instruction in home management and effective methods of planting vegetables, raising livestock, and canning food.
"The adult school here in Jackson," one teacher wrote the President, "is the grandest thing ever happen since the Birth of our
Lord and Savior Jesus Christ. There have been many old white
haired grown up colored people made proud after learning to read
and write."[78]

But there were large inequities in the way in which FERA relief
was distributed. Blacks were paid lower wages than whites, hired
only after whites had been taken care of, employed only as unskilled laborers, and excluded altogether from gainful employment—these and other complaints poured into the offices of federal relief administrators in Washington.[79] Despite an official policy

[76] Burns, *Roosevelt: The Lion and the Fox*, p. 169.

[77] Forrester B. Washington, "The Negro and Relief," *Proceedings of the National Conference of Social Work* (1934):190.

[78] For the caseworker's report, see Esther Morris Douty, "FERA and the Rural Negro," *Survey* LXX (July 1934):215; Washington is quoted in "The Negro and Relief," p. 190; the letter from the teacher is K. Robinson to Franklin D. Roosevelt, Apr. 29, 1934, Works Progress Administration Papers, Box 1, Manuscript Division, Moorland-Spingarn Research Center, Howard University. See also Melvin Reuben Maskin, "Black Education and the New Deal: The Urban Experience" (Ph.D. diss., New York University, 1973), pp. 65-66, 81-82.

[79] See, for example, the following correspondence in the Records of the Civil Works Administration, Box 83, Record Group 69, National Archives: unsigned letter to Franklin D. Roosevelt from a committee of blacks in Jackson, Miss., Dec. 2, 1933; Clark Foreman to William Zimmerman, Dec. 4, 1933; H. T. Johnson to Harold Ickes, Dec. 7, 1933; William Zimmerman, Jr., to Harry L. Hopkins, Dec. 8, 1933; John R. Perkins, "A Hint to the Wise" [Dec. 1933]; Jesse O. Thomas to Eugene Kinckle Jones, Dec. 16, 1933; U.S. Government Subjects, Lincoln County, Oklahoma, to Clark Foreman, Jan. 6, 1934; Mary E. Cheney to Thad Holt, Feb.

of nondiscrimination, relief administration was in the hands of state and local officials, whose attitudes and prejudices governed the treatment of blacks.[80] Some people in Washington agreed with them. Lorena Hickok, who toured the country for Harry Hopkins, had considerable sympathy for the point of view of the local administrators. Her observations in the South and West convinced her of the merits of a double standard which would permit them to apply racial classifications in the distribution of relief.[81] Given such views, it was not surprising to find, especially in the South, that discrimination in relief administration was more often the rule than the exception. "In some sections," a black critic summed up, "the administration of relief . . . could just as well be handled by the K.K.K."[82]

As the relief and recovery programs carried out their work, black observers concluded dispiritedly that the race was too often left out of the promised New Deal.[83] Was the Democratic administration going to deliver "a new deal or a NEW BLUFF?"[84] It remained to be seen.

20, 1934; Harry Green to William [sic] Hopkins, Apr. 20, 1934. In the Records of the Federal Emergency Relief Administration, Box 19, Record Group 69, National Archives, see: Walter White to Eleanor Roosevelt, Nov. 13, 1934; Katherine Bethea to Mr. President Franklin Roosevelt, May 8, 1934; Pickens Brooks to President Rosivelt, May 8, 1934; Charles Bryant to Franklin D. Roosevelt, May 9, 1934. In the WPA Papers, Box 1, see: John Johnson to Harry Hopkins, Dec. 11, 1934; Grace Eliza Taylor to Franklin D. Roosevelt, Dec. 31, 1934; J. E. Perkins to Franklin D. Roosevelt, Mar. 21, 1935. See also letter to the editor from Kermit Hockenhull, *Pittsburgh Courier*, Aug. 4, 1934. For an assessment which confirms the complaints, see Washington, "The Negro and Relief," pp. 188-89.

[80] Relief officials in Washington were entirely candid about the fact. See, e.g., Mr. [Robert T.] Lansdale memorandum to Harry Hopkins, Nov. 27, 1934, FERA Papers, Box 19.

[81] See Lorena Hickok to Harry L. Hopkins, Apr. 13, 17, May 4, 1934, Lorena Hickok Papers, Box 11, Franklin D. Roosevelt Library.

[82] Jesse O. Thomas, "The Negro Looks at the Alphabet," *Opportunity* XII (Jan. 1934):12.

[83] See, for example, *Afro-American*, June 17, 24, 1933; letter to the editor from Willie Jones of Augusta, Ga., June 14, 1933, *Chicago Defender*, June 24, 1933; "The Week," ibid., July 1, 1933; editorial and cartoon, ibid., Aug. 5, 1933.

[84] Letter to the editor from William Feinsinger, *Philadelphia Tribune*, June 15, 1933.

The pot was empty,
The cupboard was bare.
I said, Papa,
What's the matter here?
   I'm waitin' on Roosevelt, son,
   Roosevelt, Roosevelt,
   Waitin' on Roosevelt, son.

The rent was due,
And the lights was out.
I said, Tell me, Mama,
What's it all about?
   We're waitin' on Roosevelt, son,
   Roosevelt, Roosevelt,
   Just waitin' on Roosevelt.

Sister got sick
And the doctor wouldn't come
Cause we couldn't pay him
The proper sum—
   A-waitin' on Roosevelt,
   Roosevelt, Roosevelt,
   A-waitin' on Roosevelt.

Then one day
They put us out o' the house.
Ma and Pa was
Meek as a mouse
   Still waitin' on Roosevelt,
   Roosevelt, Roosevelt.

But when they felt those
Cold winds blow
And didn't have no
Place to go
   Pa said, I'm tired
   O' waitin' on Roosevelt,
   Roosevelt, Roosevelt.
   Damn tired o' waitin' on Roosevelt.

I can't git a job
And I can't git no grub.
Backbone and navel's
Doin' the belly-rub—
   A-waitin' on Roosevelt,
   Roosevelt, Roosevelt.

And a lot o' other folks
What's hungry and cold
Done stopped believin'
What they had been told
　　By Roosevelt,
　　Roosevelt, Roosevelt—

Cause the pot's still empty,
And the cupboard's still bare,
And you can't build a bungalow
Out o' air—
　　Mr. Roosevelt, listen!
　　What's the matter here?
　　　　　　　—Langston Hughes,
　　　　　　"Ballad of Roosevelt"[85]

[85] *New Republic*, Nov. 14, 1934, p. 9.

CHAPTER III ▪ *Organizing a Special Interest Group*

The problem of discrimination in the relief and recovery programs posed a special challenge for blacks. What vehicles could they use to convey their outrage? What leverage did they have? What means might they employ to get the administration to listen?

This was an administration that responded most quickly to organized pressure. It played broker politics—something for labor, something for business, and something for the farmer. The groups most likely to benefit were those that were well organized, well financed, familiar with the levers of power, knowledgeable about who counted in Washington, capable of generating an outpouring of correspondence to the right people, and capable of delivering— or withholding—a substantial vote.

Blacks were not one of those groups. There were comparatively few black voters. If a million went to the polls in 1932, they were but a fraction of the farm vote or the labor vote. They had no obvious champion in Washington. Farmers could count on Henry A. Wallace in the cabinet and John H. Bankhead in the Senate; labor could turn to Frances Perkins and Robert F. Wagner. The few strong contacts blacks had in the Senate were a legacy of the NAACP's fight against the nomination of John J. Parker to the Supreme Court, and none of those friends would have counted racial issues as their principal preoccupation.

More than that, blacks were not a very well organized pressure group. They had an active press, but who in the administration gave a second thought to the opinions of the *Courier*, the *Defender*, or the *Afro-American*? Compared to the labor or the farm bloc, what kind of money could blacks muster? Through what kind of organized apparatus could they convey their point of view?

The New Deal transformed the methods of the two oldest national organizations for racial advancement, the National Association for the Advancement of Colored People and the National Urban League. It prompted the creation of new ones—the Joint Committee on National Recovery in 1933 and the National Negro Congress in 1936. However, despite the increasing sophistication of the organizational apparatus that blacks could employ, they remained far behind other groups in the political power that they could muster.

The most influential organization for racial advancement was clearly the NAACP. It had led the fight for civil and political equality for black Americans for nearly a quarter of a century. The New Deal was tailor-made for the NAACP's traditional tactics of agitation and protest. Investigation, publicity, lobbying in Washington, and the rallying of public protest—such methods were the NAACP's stock in trade, and they were readily adaptable to the urgent task of securing fair treatment for blacks in the new relief and recovery programs. Within the constraints of small staffs and desperately limited funds, both the national office and the branches engaged in vigorous lobbying against discrimination in federal relief efforts. At the same time, the Association revived its campaign against lynching. Later, it scored some notable victories in state and federal courts in its newly invigorated battle against disfranchisement and discrimination in education.[1]

The ferment of national politics and the new immediacy of the government to the lives of ordinary citizens created an environment conducive to the NAACP's emphasis on the importance of political action to secure black rights. In past years, rallying blacks for political action had been difficult, because what happened in the political sphere had so little relevance to most black people. Since neither major party took any interest in racial issues, politics carried no particular attraction as a route to secure black rights. Nor had the federal government previously functioned as an agent of social welfare. When debates in Washington centered on taxes and tariffs, it was no wonder that most black people failed to pay attention. But with the advent of the New Deal, the federal government daily made decisions that directly affected the well-being of individual black Americans. Here was a basis for

[1] B. Joyce Ross, *J. E. Spingarn and the Rise of the NAACP, 1911-1939* (New York, 1972), pp. 152-53, 158-59; Raymond Wolters, *Negroes and the Great Depression: The Problem of Economic Recovery* (Westport, Conn., 1970), p. 44; Richard Kluger, *Simple Justice: The History of Brown v. Board of Education and Black America's Struggle for Equality* (New York, 1975), chaps. 6-9; Steven F. Lawson, *Black Ballots: Voting Rights in the South, 1944-1969* (New York, 1976), chap. 2; Darlene Clark Hine, "Blacks and the Destruction of the Democratic White Primary, 1935-1944," *Journal of Negro History* LXII (Jan. 1977):43-59.

engaging blacks more directly in the political process, and the NAACP took advantage of the circumstances.

Officially nonpartisan, the NAACP nonetheless functioned as a significant agent of politicization. It polled candidates for the presidency and Congress for their views on issues of racial importance, such as antilynching legislation, equal treatment for blacks in relief and federal employment, and nondiscrimination in the civil service. By publicizing the commitments it was able to obtain, the Association sought to educate black voters to hold candidates accountable when they went to the polls. This tactic, in modified form, had worked effectively when the NAACP had campaigned in 1930 to defeat senators who had voted to confirm Parker as a justice of the Supreme Court.[2] The organization also urged the importance of voter registration and encouraged blacks to qualify to exercise their franchise, even in the Deep South. As the NAACP's membership secretary summed up, "We . . . began to try to build the image of the Negro as a voting personality, as a person who would influence his government by his vote."[3]

Younger, more militant blacks challenged the appropriateness of the NAACP's focus on civil and political rights in the midst of the economic emergency. They identified the economic problems of black Americans as paramount and tried to push the Association to foster interracial working solidarity as the principal avenue to black advancement. For many reasons, the NAACP's board and national staff resisted pressures to redirect the organization's traditional emphases. But the tension between the NAACP's longtime political and legal concerns and the new urgency of economic issues bore fruit in a number of ways. Branches offered adult education classes in subjects ranging from black history to contemporary economic problems and experimented with "Don't Buy Where You Can't Work" campaigns which or-

[2] See, for example, NAACP press release, "Congressional Candidates Polled by N.A.A.C.P. on Lynching, Jobs, Relief and Civil Service," Sept. 4, 1936, National Association for the Advancement of Colored People Papers, Box C-392, Manuscript Division, Library of Congress (hereafter cited as the NAACP Papers). On the Parker fight, see Langston Hughes, *Fight for Freedom: The Story of the NAACP* (New York, 1962), pp. 74-75.

[3] See, e.g., Walter White, quoted in *Richmond Times Dispatch*, June 30, 1939, clipping in Aubrey Williams Papers, Box 5, Franklin D. Roosevelt Library; Lucille Black interview, Nov. 1, 1967, p. 8, Civil Rights Documentation Project, Ralph J. Bunche Oral History Collection, Moorland-Spingarn Research Center, Howard University.

ganized blacks to boycott businesses that refused to hire Negro workers.[4]

The same kinds of influences that led young blacks to advocate a reorientation for the NAACP also affected the National Urban League, and there they had more immediate results. Unlike the NAACP, the Urban League had traditionally made economic opportunities for blacks one of its primary emphases. The League had lobbied among the American Federation of Labor to end discrimination in the ranks of organized labor. It had entreated private employers to make jobs available to blacks. Its approach had been quiet but firm: marshal the facts, rely on reason, deal politely, one on one, and count on persuasion rather than protest.

The New Deal brought the National Urban League into a new relationship with the federal government. While the NAACP had long been accustomed to lobbying in Washington, it was a new experience for the League. With the federal government emerging as the nation's chief employer, the League needed a new approach. The organization would have to cope with Congress as well as with a broad range of federal departments and agencies that had autonomous state and local subsidiaries. Quiet, confidential entreaties would never be heard. To plead an unpopular cause with a government that responded to organized pressure, the Urban League had to go public with its protest. And to deal with a proliferation of federal agencies, instead of a handful of private employers, it needed additional vehicles to carry its message.

The League still undertook the detailed factual investigations of black economic conditions that had been its hallmark. But quiet, sober studies had to be supplemented with somewhat more aggressive techniques. The organization began for the first time to encourage public protest. "Write Harry Hopkins," "write Frances Perkins," "write Secretary Ickes"—all these became familiar refrains in intra-League correspondence. The League undertook limited lobbying in federal agencies and on Capitol Hill. In letters, telegrams, and meetings with Washington officials, it sought to make the administration aware of inequities in New Deal programs and to accomplish some ameliorative action.

Even more than the NAACP, the Urban League felt the constraints of a small staff and dwindling financial resources. Insofar as possible, it relied on its affiliates, which were funded locally,

[4] Ross, *J. E. Spingarn*, pp. 145, 152; Hughes, *Fight for Freedom*, pp. 81-82; Wolters, *Negroes and the Great Depression*, pt. III.

to provide the ammunition it needed for its campaign. The national office looked to them to provide evidence to substantiate charges of racial discrimination, and it enlisted their aid in pressing for the appointment of qualified blacks to staffs, boards, and committees of New Deal agencies and employment services on the federal, state, and local levels. The affiliates, however, had their hands full with local projects; and even if their staffs had been able to devote full time to insuring equity in the relief and recovery programs, there were scarcely enough Urban Leagues to cover the field. The New Deal's administrative decisions that affected blacks most directly were made on the state and local level; with fewer than fifty affiliates, and almost none of those in the South, the Urban League did not have enough manpower to oversee critical local operations.

To fill this gap, the League began, in September 1933, to organize a network of Emergency Advisory Councils to investigate complaints of racial discrimination under the NRA, to lobby for black representation on compliance boards, to educate blacks about the workings of the various relief and recovery acts, codes, and agencies, and to teach them how to secure the benefits that New Deal legislation had promised. For a short time the idea caught fire: 200 councils were organized, most of them in cities without Urban League affiliates or other organizations concerned with the welfare of blacks. They supplied manpower and influence to supplement the League's own efforts to see that the New Deal offered a fair deal for blacks. Still, it was hard to win clear-cut victories; the successes were modest at best. Keeping a far-flung network of councils going without funds or other means of organizational support proved to be impossible; by the fall of 1935, the EACs were out of business.[5]

By then, however, the Urban League had launched yet another new venture which reflected the impact of the New Deal on the organization's traditional emphases. The Depression had awakened the League to the realization that "ordinary 'old-fashioned' diplomacy [would] get Negroes nowhere in their fight for jobs." For too long, black workers had been relying, with less-than-satisfactory results, on the efforts of others to secure concessions in their behalf. Now, through a network of Workers Councils, the Urban League set out to prepare black workers to speak effectively for themselves. The councils offered classes in workers' education

[5] Nancy J. Weiss, *The National Urban League, 1910-1940* (New York, 1974), chap. 17.

and practical assistance in organizing. "You must organize to compel the breakdown of discriminatory barriers that keep you out of unions," the League's industrial relations director, T. Arnold Hill, told black workers. "You must organize to demand, with other workers, a new deal for labor."[6]

Just as discrimination under the NRA had been the catalyst for the formation of the Urban League's Emergency Advisory Councils, so it prompted the creation of a new independent agency, the Joint Committee on National Recovery. The committee had its roots in a small group of black graduate students at New England universities who began to meet informally to discuss social and economic problems. In the summer of 1933, when the hearings began on the proposed NRA codes, the young men observed that "there seemed to be no Negro organization [in Washington] ready to represent the interests of the race in these new economic arrangements." So the Negro Industrial League, as they named their group, "decided it should desert the realms of discussion and theory and enter into the sphere of practical measures." The league defined an ambitious program: "Whenever the Federal Government lends its hand to aid recovery in the nation," the league would "seek to insure the protection of the interests of the race."[7]

In fact the league was hardly an organization at all. It consisted of a twenty-eight-year-old executive secretary, John P. Davis, a graduate of the Harvard Law School, and a twenty-six-year-old research director, Robert C. Weaver, who had a Ph.D. in economics from Harvard. Davis and Weaver made up in energy and intelligence what they lacked in money, organizational backing, and experience. They turned up at the early NRA code hearings to demand fair treatment for blacks and to point out potentially discriminatory code provisions. Their efforts captured the attention of Walter White of the NAACP and George Edmund Haynes of the Federal Council of Churches, who, in turn, acquainted other black leaders with their work. In September 1933, fifteen organ-

[6] Ibid., chap. 18; quotations from Emergency Advisory Council, *Bulletin*, June 11, 1935, p. 4, in Workers' Bureau Report, Oct. 25, 1935, National Urban League Papers, Manuscript Division, Library of Congress, and T. Arnold Hill, "Workers to Lead the Way Out," *Opportunity* XII (June 1934):183.

[7] "The Negro Industrial League," n.d., National Negro Congress Papers, Box 1 (microfilm reel 1), Schomburg Center for Research in Black Culture. See also Robert Weaver oral history interview, Nov. 30, 1973, p. 1, Labor-Management Documentation Center, New York State School of Industrial and Labor Relations, Cornell University.

izations joined with the Negro Industrial League to form a new Washington lobby against discrimination in the NRA, which they called the Joint Committee on National Recovery.[8] Davis and Weaver (until he left to join the government in November 1933) handled the work: analysis of the proposed NRA codes for provisions detrimental to blacks; the collection of data on employment patterns and wage levels; meetings with governmental officials; the preparation of written briefs; appearances at hearings to testify; and publicity for their activities.[9]

The Joint Committee claimed at least one important victory: the NRA refused officially to sanction lower standards for wages and hours for black workers in the South. Beyond that, however, it was difficult to make much headway. With meager resources—it ran on an annual budget of $5,000—and weak organizational backing, the Joint Committee was no match for the businesses and trade unions which worked aggressively to shape the codes in their own best interests. Still, by keeping the issue of discrimination before the public, the committee served an important educative function. Without its vigilance, it seems likely that NRA discrimination against blacks would have been even more severe.[10]

Racial lobbies outside the government were only one way to influence policy. Another was to have someone inside the government to speak on behalf of blacks. The idea that there ought to be someone in Washington specifically charged with looking out for the interests of black Americans originated with two white Southerners long committed to the cause of racial advancement— Will W. Alexander, director of the Commission on Interracial

[8] Wolters, *Negroes and the Great Depression*, pp. 110-11.

[9] "The Work of the Negro Industrial League and the Joint Committee on National Recovery up to Sept. 12, 1933"; "Statement of the Negro Industrial League Concerning the Code of Fair Competition for the Cotton Textile Industry," [July 1, 1933?]; "Statement of the Joint Committee on National Recovery Concerning the Code of Fair Competition for the Shipping Industry," n.d.; "Statement of the Negro Industrial League Concerning the Code of Fair Competition Proposed by the Structural Clay Products Industry," n.d.; "Statement of the Negro Industrial League Concerning the Code of Fair Competition for the Lumber and Timber Products Industry," July 21, 1933; "Statement of the Negro Industrial League Concerning the Codes of Fair Competition Submitted for the Coal Industry," Aug. 11, 1933, all in National Negro Congress Papers, Box 1 (reel 1). There is extensive correspondence documenting Weaver's work for the Joint Committee on National Recovery in the Robert C. Weaver Papers, Box 6, Schomburg Center for Research in Black Culture.

[10] Wolters, *Negroes and the Great Depression*, pp. 112-13; Charles Radford Lawrence, "Negro Organizations in Crisis: Depression, New Deal, World War II" (Ph.D. diss., Columbia University, 1952), pp. 250-51.

Cooperation, and Edwin R. Embree, president of the Julius Rosenwald Fund.

A Methodist minister by training, Will Alexander had resigned his pastorate in Nashville during World War I to commit himself to the promotion of racial harmony. He had conceived the notion of the Commission on Interracial Cooperation and had directed the organization since its founding in 1919. Based in Atlanta, with committees in each southern state, the commission stood out as a unique embodiment of racial liberalism in the South. Preventing racial violence was its chief practical preoccupation. It established the Southern Commission on the Study of Lynching, whose findings—published in 1933 as Arthur F. Raper's *Tragedy of Lynching*—helped importantly to educate a wide audience about the causes and frequency of lynchings and about the way that southern communities handled them. The Interracial Commission also sponsored the Association of Southern Women for the Prevention of Lynching, a lobby that demonstrated that the best people of the South refused to condone mob violence. More broadly, the commission worked to encourage better understanding between the races and to achieve better treatment for blacks in the South, though without challenging segregation.[11]

Embree, too, had devoted his professional career to promoting the welfare of Negroes, though from a different vantage point. The great-grandson of the abolitionist preacher who founded Berea College in Kentucky, Embree grew up in Berea and imbibed from his earliest years the school's commitment to racial integration. He worked for a decade on the staff of the Rockefeller Foundation. In 1928, Julius Rosenwald, the president of Sears, Roebuck and Company, hired Embree to head the Julius Rosenwald Fund. Under Embree's direction, the Fund made important contributions in the areas of health and education, with special emphasis on black Americans and social conditions in the South. Among its other activities, the Fund built rural schools and libraries for blacks, gave money to Negro colleges, supported black artists and scholars, and provided training for black physicians. In the 1930s, at Embree's instigation, the Fund undertook research on farm tenancy which provided the stimulus for the creation of the Farm Security Administration.[12]

---

[11] Morton Sosna, *In Search of the Silent South: Southern Liberals and the Race Issue* (New York, 1977), pp. 20-41.

[12] *Dictionary of American Biography*, Supplement Four (New York, 1974), pp. 250-52; Edwin R. Embree and Julia Waxman, *Investment in People: The Story of the Julius Rosenwald Fund* (New York, 1949).

The advent of the New Deal gave Alexander and Embree a new outlet for their activities. Now Washington was to be the focus for people interested in promoting social change. Alexander sensed the possibilities immediately. As he reported to Embree, who had been abroad during the inauguration and the early part of the Hundred Days, there was "something unusual" about the man in the White House, "a sort of messiah" who seemed likely to exert vigorous leadership. If, as Alexander imagined, Roosevelt succeeded in making Washington "the center" of the country, it seemed probable that "the next stage" in the advancement of race relations would also arise from what happened there. Alexander told Embree that they ought to "go down" to the capital "and see somebody."[13]

The two men visited Washington and confirmed Alexander's hunch. "There was every evidence," they found, "that there was yeast in the place—that something was going to happen, good or bad. You could just feel it all around the place." The question was how best to take advantage of the ferment to benefit blacks. They debated the issue with Charles S. Johnson, the black sociologist who headed the department of social sciences at Fisk University. They decided that the best strategy was to place someone in Washington "who could be watching all [the] activity [there] for its effect on American race relations . . . interpret it, and maybe do a little about it."[14] What they had in mind, as Embree phrased it, "was a 'generalissimo of Negro welfare' who would 'look after the Negro's interests in all phases of the recovery.' "[15] With such a man in place, federal officials would have to face up to the issue of fair treatment for blacks in relief and governmental employment. To be most effective, such a person should be rooted in one of the major federal departments and should possess a broad mandate to work across departmental lines to represent the interests of blacks. The proposal went to the White House and came back with presidential approval.[16]

The Rosenwald Fund agreed to pay the salary, and the authors

[13] The quotations are from Will Winton Alexander, *Reminiscences* (Columbia University Oral History Collection, 1952), vol. II, p. 368. See also Wilma Dykeman and James Stokely, *Seeds of Southern Change: The Life of Will Alexander* (Chicago, 1962), p. 193.

[14] Alexander, *Reminiscences*, vol. II, p. 368.

[15] John B. Kirby, *Black Americans in the Roosevelt Era: Liberalism and Race* (Knoxville, Tenn., 1980), p. 16, quoting Edwin R. Embree to Clark Foreman, June 19, 1933, Rosenwald Fund Archives, Box 412.

[16] Dykeman and Stokely, *Seeds of Southern Change*, pp. 194-95.

of the plan next considered where to locate their man. The Department of Labor seemed a logical choice, but Secretary Perkins had already hired a young black man, Lawrence A. Oxley, to work on her staff, and he seemed ill-equipped for the responsibilities that Alexander, Embree, and Johnson envisioned. So they decided to approach Harold Ickes, whom Embree had known personally and who had a reputation of fair-mindedness and concern for blacks. Ickes considered the plan "a grand idea" and agreed to appoint the man as his special assistant, "back him up" within the Department of the Interior, and facilitate his contacts throughout the government.[17] The men never attempted to identify Negro candidates for the position; given the racial climate, they believed that a white man could do more to advance the interests of blacks than a Negro could.[18] From a short list of candidates proposed by Alexander, Embree, and Johnson, Ickes chose Clark Foreman, a native of Atlanta who had studied at the London School of Economics and had recently earned a Ph.D. in political science at Columbia University. Tough, persistent, in Will Alexander's words "a young man of great charm" with "a very keen mind" who "leaned over backwards to be on the liberal side," Foreman carried impressive credentials in the field of racial advancement. His master's thesis focused on the interracial struggle in the South; his dissertation had just been published under the title *The Environmental Factors in Negro Elementary Education.* He had worked for three years for the Commission on Interracial Cooperation and, since 1928, had been a staff member at the Rosenwald Fund.[19]

Foreman at first resisted the appointment. "This is one job in the Administration which a Negro could hold," he told Ickes. But Ickes rejoined that if Foreman refused the position, he would find a white person to fill it, "as he did not know any Negro to whom he would be willing to offer it." The two men settled the issue

[17] Ibid., p. 195; Alexander, *Reminiscences*, vol. II, pp. 368-70. The quotations are from p. 370.

[18] Ickes's views on the advantages of a white racial adviser can be found in *Afro-American*, Sept. 9, 1933, and Meeting of Special Industrial Recovery Board, Sept. 18, 1933, National Negro Congress Papers, Box 1 (reel 1). On Embree and Alexander's views, see Kirby, *Black Americans in the Roosevelt Era*, p. 17.

[19] Alexander, *Reminiscences*, vol. II, pp. 370-71; Dykeman and Stokely, *Seeds of Southern Change*, pp. 195-96; Kirby, *Black Americans in the Roosevelt Era*, p. 36. Embree went to see Ickes about the Foreman appointment "as a dollar a year man" in August 1933. See Edwin R. Embree to Harold L. Ickes, Aug. 11, 1933, Harold L. Ickes Papers, Box 169, Manuscript Division, Library of Congress.

with the understanding that Foreman would resign the post when he found a qualified black man to replace him.[20]

Foreman's reluctance to take the post of racial adviser proved prescient. His appointment, announced in August to take effect as of September 1, 1933, raised angry protests from black spokesmen. While more moderate voices like the National Urban League acknowledged the appointment as a gratifying indication of "a recognition of the importance of including the Negro in the plans of the Administration," even it joined the consensus that the particular selection was "a great mistake."[21] How could blacks expect "fair and impartial treatment" from a white Georgian? the *Chicago Defender* wondered. The real issue, however, as the Urban League made clear, lay not with Foreman personally but with the choice of a white man "as an interpreter of the needs and aspirations of the Negro." Forcing white leadership on blacks, the *Afro-American* declared, was "the most insidious insult" that could be thought of. W.E.B. Du Bois called the arrangement "an outrage," notwithstanding that it had been made "through the efforts of some of our best friends." "The age of paternalism in relations of the races is past so far as Negroes are concerned," the NAACP objected in a telegram to Ickes.[22] It was time for blacks "to be represented by members of their own Race," who really could know and understand, as whites could not, the needs and aspirations of blacks in the economic emergency.[23]

Foreman's efforts soon laid to rest the suspicion that a white Southerner could not be trusted, indeed, to the point where the black press began to write approvingly of him as "a real, bighearted, true American in his relationships with Negroes."[24] He chose as his chief assistant the young black economist from the

[20] The Foreman-Ickes exchange is reported in Clark Foreman to Allen Kifer, Feb. 13, 1962, quoted in Jane R. Motz, "The Black Cabinet: Negroes in the Administration of Franklin D. Roosevelt" (Master's thesis, University of Delaware, 1964), p. 88, n. 7.

[21] "Negro Leadership?" *Opportunity* XI (Sept. 1933):263; editorial, *Pittsburgh Courier*, Sept. 9, 1933 ("a great mistake").

[22] Editorial, *Chicago Defender*, Sept. 16, 1933; "Negro Leadership?" p. 263; editorial, *Afro-American*, Sept. 9, 1933; W.E.B. Du Bois, "N.R.A. and Appointments," *Crisis* XL (Oct. 1933):237; NAACP quoted in *Afro-American*, Aug. 26, 1933.

[23] Editorial, *Chicago Defender*, Sept. 16, 1933. See also editorial, *Pittsburgh Courier*, Sept. 9, 1933; Alphonzo J. Harris to Louis McHenry Howe, Aug. 31, 1933, Franklin D. Roosevelt Papers, Official File (OF) 93, Franklin D. Roosevelt Library (hereafter cited as the FDR Papers).

[24] *Pittsburgh Courier*, Oct. 13, 1934. See also editorial, *Chicago Defender*, Nov. 25, 1933.

Joint Committee on National Recovery, Robert Weaver, and he employed a black secretary. In carrying out his duties, he received the backing that Ickes had promised. Ickes gave Foreman a letter of introduction to cabinet members and agency heads which described his functions and requested their cooperation. When Foreman discovered situations where New Deal agencies were paying insufficient heed to the concerns of blacks, Ickes was the man to whom he turned for influence to remedy the problem.[25]

Even with a supportive secretary at the head of his own department, Foreman could make little headway in working across departmental lines. Ickes, to whom he reported instances of probable discrimination, could do little more than ask the agencies involved for further information and suggest that ameliorative action be taken.[26] Part of the problem was the inhospitality of some agencies to intervention from outsiders; Foreman "got kicked out of the War Department when he went over to find out what they were doing," and the same thing happened when he visited Harry Hopkins at the FERA.[27] Part was the difficulty of making several agencies move in concert when a problem fell within multiple jurisdictions, as was the case with regard to the appointment of black supervisory officers in black CCC camps. The CCC Advisory Board found itself stalemated when the Interior Department was willing to allow such appointments in camps run by the National Park Service and the War Department refused to consider them in camps supervised by the army.[28]

One man alone was clearly inadequate to keep the government honest when it came to race. Foreman, in consultation with Ickes, sought to deal with these obstacles in two ways. The answer to the inhospitality to outsiders was to press for the appointment of a racial adviser within each agency or department. The solution to the problem of multiple jurisdictions was to bring these advisers, or other representatives of the various federal offices, together on a regular basis to examine the way in which New Deal policies were affecting blacks.[29]

[25] See, e.g., Harold L. Ickes to the Secretary of Labor, or Ickes to Henry Morgenthau, Jr., Aug. 22, 1933, Ickes Papers, Box 180; Clark Foreman to Harold L. Ickes, Dec. 13, 1933, Department of the Interior Papers, Record Group 48, Office Files of Harold L. Ickes, Box 9, National Archives.

[26] Motz, "Black Cabinet," p. 12.

[27] Alexander, *Reminiscences*, vol. II, p. 371.

[28] Clark Foreman to Harold L. Ickes, Sept. 8, Nov. 7, 9, 1933; Ickes memoranda to Foreman, Sept. 9, Nov. 24, 1933; Arno B. Cammerer memorandum to Ickes, Nov. 23, 1933, Interior Department Papers, Office Files of Harold L. Ickes, Box 9.

[29] Harold L. Ickes memorandum to Clark Foreman, Jan. 2, 1934, ibid.

The first strategy worked well, with the appointment of such capable men and women as Eugene Kinckle Jones, executive secretary of the National Urban League, as adviser on Negro affairs in the Department of Commerce; Forrester B. Washington, dean of the Atlanta University School of Social Work, as racial adviser in the Federal Emergency Relief Administration; and Mary McLeod Bethune, the founder-president of Bethune-Cookman College and of the National Council of Negro Women, as director of Negro affairs for the National Youth Administration. The second strategy—that of coordination—failed in its official incarnation when the Interdepartmental Group on the Special Problems of the Negro foundered not long after its creation in 1934. However, it proved more viable in its unofficial form with the emergence of a Black Cabinet in the summer of 1936.

Pressure to appoint racial advisers came from various quarters. From the outset of the administration, black newspapers counseled the President on the importance of seeking advice on racial needs from a new type of racial adviser—well-educated, perceptive, disinterested spokesmen for the race, distinguished by their expert qualifications from the "purely politically minded" blacks who were out for their own personal preferment.[30] Organizations like the NAACP and the Urban League supported the idea, pressed for appointments, and hailed those that were made for bolstering "the Negro's faith in the sincerity of the Administration's attitude toward his status."[31] Clark Foreman urged the appointment of racial advisers, as did his assistant, Robert Weaver.[32]

Their efforts met with mixed responses from cabinet officials and agency heads. At one extreme were people like Ickes or Aubrey Williams, who later welcomed Mary McLeod Bethune to the National Youth Administration. Others took some persuading. Harry Hopkins, for example, saw no need for a special racial adviser in the FERA—if the relief programs under his direction were administered fairly, everyone would be taken care of.[33] But his chief aide, Williams, was sensitive to the reality that without special vigilance, discrimination would be difficult to stop. Wil-

---

[30] See, e.g., editorials, *Chicago Defender*, July 8 (source of the quotation), Nov. 25, 1933.

[31] "A Federal Appointment," *Opportunity* XI (Nov. 1933):327. The suggestions came from individual blacks as well. See, e.g., F. B. Ransom to Louis Ludlow, May 12, 1933; Rienzi B. Lemus to Louis McH. Howe, Aug. 14, 1933, FDR Papers, OF 93.

[32] Interview with Robert C. Weaver, Nov. 12, 1976, New York City.

[33] Interview with Alfred Edgar Smith, May 24, 1977, Washington, D.C.

liams conferred with Will Alexander about the "best method [of] meeting problems arising [in the] relief program among Negroes" and found that Alexander agreed with him that it was desirable to secure for the staff of the relief administration the "services [of an] able and experienced Negro social worker with demonstrated ability for executive responsibility."[34] Alexander's intercession, combined with black pressure, did the trick, and Hopkins agreed to hire the man he recommended—Forrester Washington—as the "person to handle Negro Affairs in our Organization."[35] When Washington resigned after a short time to return to Atlanta, he was succeeded by his black research assistant, Alfred Edgar Smith, a native of Hot Springs, Arkansas, who had recently earned bachelor's and master's degrees at Howard University. Smith remained as racial adviser in the FERA and WPA until 1944.[36]

Still other agencies refused to single out blacks for special representation. The Department of Agriculture, resisting appeals to set up a bureau to aid black farmers or to appoint an assistant to the secretary in charge of contacts with blacks, argued that such arrangements would "seem to be patronizing and discriminatory" and thus "not the most advantageous thing for the negroes, themselves."[37] The argument was legitimate: designating blacks for special representation gave them a peculiar status and set them apart from the rest of the population. But the theoretical cogency of Henry Wallace and Rexford Tugwell's reservations needs to be matched against the practical reality: not to have someone looking out for the interests of blacks might mean a license to continue the ordinary practice of treating them in a discriminatory fashion.

As a rule, it was easiest to place black advisers where bureaucracy and traditions were least strongly entrenched. The State, Treasury, Post Office, and Navy Departments never hired racial

[34] Telegram, Will W. Alexander to Harry L. Hopkins, Jan. 15, 1934, Civil Works Administration Papers, Box 83, Record Group 69, National Archives.

[35] Will W. Alexander to Aubrey Williams, Jan. 16, 1934; Williams memorandum to Harry Hopkins, Jan. 16, 1934; Hopkins memorandum to Williams, Jan. 23, 1934, CWA Papers, Box 83. The quotation is from Williams's memo.

[36] *Who's Who in Colored America,* 6th ed. (Brooklyn, N.Y., 1942), p. 468; "A Pioneer's Pioneer: Al Smith," *Oracle* LVII (Summer 1974):1-11.

[37] Travis B. Howard to Henry A. Wallace, July 17, 1933; W. F. Reden to Wallace, July 25, 1933; Benjamin F. Hubert to Wallace, Sept. 27, 1933; Rexford G. Tugwell to Reden, July 7, 1933; Wallace to Hubert, Oct. 2, 1933, Records of the Department of Agriculture, Correspondence Files of the Office of the Secretary of Agriculture, "Negroes," Record Group 16, National Archives. The quotations come from the latter two documents.

advisers; the War Department did so only in the final months before Pearl Harbor. Justice had a political appointee rather than the usual racial adviser. Of the regular departments, only Interior, Agriculture, Commerce, and Labor made such appointments during the 1930s. The record in the special agencies was markedly better.[38] The ability of the racial adviser to maneuver effectively also varied according to the type of agency. "In the traditional agencies," as W. J. Trent, Jr., who served in the Public Works Administration, reflected, "not that much was done." In the emergency agencies, it was easier to get things accomplished.[39]

Coordinating the work of the racial advisers was first attempted on an official basis through the Interdepartmental Group on the Special Problems of the Negro. The Interdepartmental Group convened initially in February 1934, at the call of Clark Foreman. Foreman had written to agency heads in January, at Ickes's suggestion, and asked them to designate a representative to the group. It ought to be someone "who is charged with the responsibility of seeing that fair consideration is given Negroes," he explained. The problems confronting Negro Americans were "complicated," and an interdepartmental review would be the best means of formulating "general principles of action" to deal with them.[40]

The group met four times between February and June, each time at a different department, with attendance varying between twelve and twenty. It was useful for the representatives to meet their counterparts in other agencies and to learn about the work of the different agencies as it affected blacks. But it was hard for the group to see clearly what it might do. Subcommittees were appointed "to get facts on what is happening to Negro labor under the recovery program" or "to find out what is happening in the rural field." Subsequent meetings discussed the subcommittee reports and considered the implications for blacks of official New Deal policies, pending legislation, and the like. But was it sufficient to prepare factual reports? Or should the group propose solutions to the problems that its studies pinpointed? The last documented meeting of the group, held June 1, dissolved in a debate over its functions. The apparent consensus was that the group "had no powers to do anything but present facts, each mem-

[38] Motz, "Black Cabinet," p. 19.

[39] Interview with W. J. Trent, Jr., Dec. 8, 1976, New York City.

[40] See, e.g., Clark Foreman to Harry L. Hopkins, Jan. 2, 1934, CWA Papers, Box 83. For further confirmation that the Group was Ickes's idea, see Clark Foreman to Harold L. Ickes, Apr. 28, 1934, Interior Department Papers, Office of the Secretary, Central Classified Files, File 1-280, pt. 1.

ber, however, backing them up with personal conversation with and suggestions to his chief whenever possible." It would be up to each department to work out remedies on the basis of the facts presented in the group's studies.[41]

The dilemma of the Interdepartmental Group made clear the difficulty of advancing the cause of the Negro in the New Deal. Even if they could have agreed on the best strategy, the racial advisers confronted formidable odds. Their ability to affect racial practices certainly depended on the disposition of the person for whom they worked, but even with a well-intentioned agency head, the room for maneuvering was limited. In so many respects, the mission of the racial advisers was out of step with the world in which they operated. These talented blacks, many of them professionals, were working for a federal government which was accustomed to seeing its black employees in custodial positions;[42] equally difficult, they were trying to function effectively in what was, for all intents and purposes, a segregated southern city. The national political and social climate, far from supporting their concern for racial equity, militated against it. And the bureaucratic confusion of New Deal Washington, with agency responsibilities vaguely defined and often overlapping, made making any headway all the more complicated.

Will Alexander's hunch had been well founded. Without someone to speak up for blacks in Washington, the black cause would surely have gone unnoticed amid the clamor of competing interests in the early New Deal. But finding black spokesmen was clearly no solution in itself. Virtually powerless to make a difference on their own authority, Foreman and his colleagues looked on a little helplessly as the racial patterns of the New Deal began to take shape.

[41] Minutes of the first meeting of the inter-departmental group concerned with the special problems of the Negro population, Feb. 7, 1934, Interior Department Papers, File 1-280, pt. 1; Minutes of the second meeting of the inter-departmental group concerned with the special problems of Negroes, Mar. 2, 1934, ibid., Office Files of Harold L. Ickes, Box 9 (source of the quotations); Minutes of the third meeting of the inter-departmental group concerned with the special problems of Negroes, Mar. 30, 1934, ibid.; Minutes of the fourth meeting of the inter-departmental group concerned with the special problems of Negroes, June 1, 1934, ibid., File 1-280, pt. 1; also in that file, Report on Negro Labor of the Inter-departmental Group, Apr. 18, 1934; Report of the Agriculture Committee, Inter-Departmental Group concerned with the special problems of Negroes . . . , June 1, 1934.

[42] On black employment in Washington, see Laurence J. W. Hayes, *The Negro Federal Government Worker: A Study of His Classification Status in the District of Columbia, 1883-1938* (Washington, D.C., 1941), pp. 73ff.

CHAPTER IV ▪ *The Rise of Black*
Democratic Politicians

The redirection of the tactics and concerns of the established organizations for racial advancement, the creation of new pressure groups, and the entry of racial advisers into federal agencies provide important evidence of the New Deal's role in stimulating new kinds of politicization and involvement with government on the part of black Americans. The New Deal also stimulated the emergence at the local level of a new group of black politicians. Ambitious and impatient with the entrenched black Republican leadership, they saw a chance for personal advancement in the concurrent rise of the national Democratic party and local Democratic political machines. Dismayed at the record of the Hoover administration, they saw in the ferment of the New Deal an opportunity to advance the interests of their race. Once in office, these politicians, in turn, became one of the reasons why black Americans took a more sympathetic view of the Democratic party.

The Democrats offered aspiring black political leaders opportunities that seemed to be closed off in the Republican party. Younger blacks especially spoke with some disdain of their elders who were firmly established in the Republican political hierarchy. They painted an unflattering portrait: "handkerchief heads," they called them—old party warhorses, self-interested, self-satisfied, feeding off the patronage of white political machines, and insensitive to the broader concerns of the race. While such criticism was directed mainly at black Republican politicians, those few older, established black Democratic politicians evoked much the same reaction from younger blacks trying to break into politics.[1]

"Handkerchief heads" typified the dominant mode of black politics. Urban political machines commonly singled out an influential black to function as what Martin Kilson has called the

[1] Tammany Hall leader J. Raymond Jones's view of Ferdinand Q. Morton, the leader of the United Colored Democracy in New York, is a case in point. Jones wanted to topple Morton—"an old, handkerchief head"—and supplant the United Colored Democracy—an "extraterritorial organization" under the control of white Democrats—with regularly elected black district leaders. See Hilton B. Clark interview with J. Raymond Jones, pt. 10, July 13, 1974, pp. 4-6.

"agent of . . . neoclientage politics"—that is, as a link between the machine and the black community. The role of these agents "was to guarantee the Negro vote for Republicans and when necessary discourage Negro voting altogether rather than allow Negro voting power to grow and diversify." Sometimes the agents were professionals or businessmen; more often, they were "gamblers, successful hustlers, flophouse keepers, and occupants of other antisocial roles."[2]

E. Frederic Morrow recalled his early impression of black politicians:

> The term politician in Negro life was a sinister and degrading one, and indicated that the individual was a crafty schemer and a "fixer." He had little power of his own, but was often the liaison between the white straw boss assigned to "oversee" Negro activities and the Negro voters.[3]

Ralph J. Bunche, the Howard University political scientist, who made a careful study of black leadership in 1940, described the typical black political leader as "the self-made, not too well educated man who has pushed his way up from the ranks." "In most cases," Bunche continued, "the big Negro politician has some white backer, some influential white person who has one motive or another in keeping check on Negroes—most frequently it is to control the Negro's voting." As for black Republicans, Bunche reported,

> This professional Negro leadership, by and large, has been socially unintelligent, inept and self-seeking. . . . This leadership has reaped individual rewards for delivering the Negro vote to the Republican Party, but the Negro voters have gained nothing. . . . The Negro knows that this leadership has never been willing to risk its own precarious position in the favor of the higher councils of the party in order boldly to represent the interests of the Negro. Throughout the country it is regarded as pussy-footing, cowardly and stupid.[4]

[2] Martin Kilson, "Political Change in the Negro Ghetto, 1900-1940's," in *Key Issues in the Afro-American Experience*, ed. Nathan I. Huggins, Martin Kilson, and Daniel M. Fox, 2 vols. (New York, 1971), II:183.

[3] E. Frederic Morrow, *Way Down South Up North* (Philadelphia, 1973), p. 36.

[4] Ralph J. Bunche, "A Brief and Tentative Analysis of Negro Leadership" (research memorandum prepared for Carnegie-Myrdal study, Sept. 1940), p. 113, Schomburg Center for Research in Black Culture; Ralph J. Bunche, "Report on the Needs of the Negro (for the Republican Program Committee)," July 1, 1939, pp. 10-11, Schomburg Center for Research in Black Culture.

Not only did these Republican politicians fail to represent the interests of the race, but they stood in the way of younger blacks who aspired to political careers. To these younger men, the Democratic party offered new opportunities. Earl B. Dickerson, a major figure in Democratic politics in Chicago in this period, reflected on the motivation of aspiring politicians who cast their lot with the Democrats: "I would say that, with few exceptions, they went into the party to improve themselves, get better options politically. They were ambitious politically and they wanted an opportunity. And they never had seen the opportunity with the Republicans. The Republicans were going down anyway; why stay in the Republican party when the new party was seeking new blood and offering opportunities to blacks?"[5]

The concurrence between personal political ambition and the advantageous circumstances of the New Deal shows up most vividly in the case of Arthur W. Mitchell, a black man who was elected to Congress on the Democratic ticket in Chicago in 1934.

Mitchell had long fancied himself a politician. He had not trained for a political career, of course—no black man in late nineteenth-century Alabama could do that. At first his field had been education. As a student at Tuskegee Institute, he had worked as an office boy for Booker T. Washington. He continued his education at Talladega College and at Snow Hill Normal and Industrial Institute, earned his teacher's certification, and subsequently taught in various institutions in rural Alabama. In 1908, following Washington's example, he founded his own school, Armstrong Agricultural College.

But Mitchell had other aspirations. After service in the army during World War I, he gave up his work as an educator and moved to Washington. He entered the real estate business to support himself, soon began to read law, and was practicing by the mid-1920s.[6]

Law may have become Mitchell's new vocation, but it was politics that fascinated him. Now that he was in Washington, he

[5] Interview with Earl B. Dickerson, Aug. 16, 1974, Chicago. On the generational difference between black Republican and black Democratic politicians, see also Howard F. Fisher, "The Negro in St. Louis Politics, 1932-1948" (Master's thesis, St. Louis University, 1951), pp. 36-37.

[6] J. Winston Harrigan, "Ten Dollar Bill Given Him by Mother and Tutelage of Booker Washington Credited by Mitchell for Success," *Chicago Defender*, July 16, 1938; Perry R. Duis, "Arthur W. Mitchell: New Deal Negro in Congress" (Master's thesis, University of Chicago, 1966), pp. 21-23.

enlisted in the Hoover campaign in 1928 as a paid Republican speaker. When the party sent him to speak in Chicago, he had a chance to observe the campaign of Oscar DePriest, a Republican who would shortly become the nation's lone black congressman. Mitchell came away convinced that he could do better himself. He moved to Chicago the following year to try to win the congressional seat away from DePriest.[7]

Mitchell faced a formidable task. DePriest, the first black elected to Congress since the departure of George H. White of North Carolina in 1901, immediately attracted national attention. In part his celebrity reflected the novelty of having a black man in a high governmental position in Washington.[8] In part it grew out of the awkwardness of dealing with a black congressman in a capital where segregation ordinarily prevailed.[9] Sometimes the attempt to draw a color line failed quickly, as in the case of an effort to bar Mrs. DePriest from membership in the Congressional Women's Club. Sometimes it succeeded; when DePriest's secretary tried to take some constituents to lunch in the House restaurant, they were denied service, and the committee that was set up at DePriest's insistence to investigate the discrimination voted to uphold the racial exclusion.[10] Always the incidents attracted public attention—and none of them more than the appearance of Mrs. DePriest at a White House tea for congressional wives, an event that sparked the "wildest storm of protest" from southern whites.[11]

The sensational aspects of DePriest's arrival in Congress made him a familiar figure to most black Americans. Equally important

---

[7] "Memorandum on Mr. Mitchell," 1939, Dawson folder, Claude A. Barnett Papers, Chicago Historical Society; Duis, "Arthur W. Mitchell," pp. 23-24; typescript, "The Papers of Arthur Wengs [sic] Mitchell," reporting interview with Mitchell in connection with the deposit of his papers, July 24, 1967, Arthur W. Mitchell folder, Chicago Historical Society.

[8] See, for example, *New York Times*, Apr. 16, 1929; *Chicago Defender*, Mar. 9, Apr. 20, 1929.

[9] The awkwardness extended even to the point of one Southerner refusing to serve on the same committee with DePriest and another refusing to have DePriest's office located next to his own. See Morris Lewis to Walter White, Dec. 14, 1929, National Association for the Advancement of Colored People Papers, Box C-69, Manuscript Division, Library of Congress (hereafter cited as the NAACP Papers); *Chicago Defender*, Apr. 13, 1929.

[10] *Chicago Defender*, Jan. 19, Feb. 9, May 18, 1929, Jan. 27, Feb. 3, Mar. 3, 10, 24, 31, Apr. 14, 28, June 16, 1934; *New York Times*, Apr. 26, 1934; Kenneth Eugene Mann, "Oscar Stanton DePriest: Persuasive Agent for the Black Masses," *Negro History Bulletin* XXXV (Oct. 1972):136-37.

[11] *Chicago Defender*, June 29, 1929. See also ibid., June 22, 1929, and *New York Times*, June 14, 18, 26, 28, July 3, 4, 7, 1929.

in establishing his popularity among blacks was the role he played as a spokesman for his race. He styled himself as the representative in Congress of all black Americans and made a point of undertaking efforts of particular benefit to blacks.[12] He nominated blacks to West Point and to Annapolis. Although his candidates fared poorly, they were the first such appointments at the Military Academy since the graduation of Charles Young in 1889 and at the Naval Academy since the enrollment of three southern blacks during Reconstruction. He mailed copies of the Declaration of Independence and the Constitution to blacks around the country to teach them "their rights." He supported a variety of legislation in the interests of the race—amendments to guard against discrimination in the relief program; additional appropriations for Howard University; a proposal to make Lincoln's birthday a national holiday; pensions for former slaves; and civil government for the Virgin Islands. He rallied senatorial votes against the confirmation of John J. Parker. He worried about lynching and denial of the franchise, and he spoke from the floor of the House about the discrimination suffered by blacks.[13]

By his own evaluation, DePriest tried "to teach Negroes race pride and how to fight for themselves." In speeches to black audiences, he preached the importance of organizing in order to gain civil and political rights. He was threatened by the Ku Klux Klan, burned in effigy, and barred by Birmingham authorities from speaking in the city auditorium, but he persisted in taking his message to the South as well as to the North.[14] Everywhere, he emphasized the importance of the ballot, for political action gave blacks the means to seek their own salvation. Usually he urged support for the Republican party, but he was more of an oppor-

[12] *Chicago Defender*, Nov. 17, 1928, Feb. 23, 1929, Apr. 16, 1932.

[13] *New York Times*, May 7, 1929, Dec. 12, 1931; *Chicago Defender*, Apr. 6, May 11, 18, June 1, 8, Aug. 24, Dec. 28, 1929; Jan. 18, Mar. 8, Apr. 19, 26, Sept. 6 (editorial), 1930; Feb. 21, Dec. 12, 1931; Mar. 12, Dec. 24, 31, 1932; Mar. 11, 25 (editorial), May 20 (editorial), 1933; Morris Lewis to James Weldon Johnson, May 3, 1929, NAACP Papers, Box C-390; Oscar DePriest to Walter White, Sept. 11, 16, 1930, Dec. 29, 1932, Mar. 30, Apr. 4, 11, 1933, ibid., Box C-64; White to DePriest, Dec. 28, 1932, ibid., Box C-77; Lewis to Richetta Randolph, Feb. 2, 1931, ibid., Box C-69.

[14] Oscar DePriest, "Today's Negroes Have No Guts," *Negro Digest* VIII (Mar. 1950):84 (source of the quotation), 88; *New York Times*, June 25, July 22, 1929, June 12, 1930; *St. Louis Argus*, Aug. 9, 1929; *Boston Chronicle*, July 12, 1930; *Pittsburgh Courier*, Oct. 24, 1931; *New York Sun*, Dec. 16(?), 1933, clippings in Schomburg Center for Research in Black Culture; *Chicago Defender*, June 28, 1930, Aug. 22, 1931, Apr. 9, 1932, Dec. 23, 1933; Oscar DePriest to Walter White, July 13, 1929, NAACP Papers, Box C-64.

tunist than a strict party man, and he advised blacks to vote Democratic "where the Democrats had the most to offer them."[15] Where possible, as in Harlem, he urged them to elect members of the race to positions of political leadership.[16]

Oscar DePriest's message and record made him an important figure to black Americans. The black press trumpeted his accomplishments and hailed him with the most flowery adjectives they could muster.[17] Black correspondents from all parts of the country joined enthusiastically in the litany of praise. A man from Omaha described DePriest as "the greatest asset to the Negro race since the days of Frederick Douglass."[18] The columnist Kelly Miller thought him the best candidate for "spokesman of his Race."[19]

Such acclaim made DePriest a formidable political force. He won reelection in 1930, when he again defeated Harry Baker, the white Democrat who had opposed him in 1928. It was unusual to be a victorious Republican in Illinois that November, as dissatisfied voters used the off-year election to register their frustration with the Hoover administration. Democratic upsets across the state added up to "the worst slaughter" that the Republicans had suffered in Illinois in many years. DePriest not only withstood the Democratic landslide in Cook County, he also substantially enlarged his margin of victory over what it had been in 1928.[20]

[15] *New York Times*, June 25, July 28, 1929; *Chicago Defender*, Sept. 7, 1929; Harold F. Gosnell, *Negro Politicians: The Rise of Negro Politics in Chicago* (1935; reprint ed., Chicago, 1969), p. 194 (source of the quotation). DePriest's advice to blacks to vote Democratic in the South is reported in *Chicago Defender*, Jan. 9, June 25, 1932, and criticized in a *Defender* editorial, July 2, 1932.

[16] See, for example, *Chicago Defender*, Aug. 31, 1929; *New York Times*, Aug. 22, 1929.

[17] Undated *Washington Tribune* editorial, reprinted in *Chicago Whip*, July 6, 1929; editorial, ibid., July 27, 1929; Associated Negro Press column, ibid., Feb. 22, 1930; editorial, *New York Age*, Oct. 25, 1930; editorial, *Philadelphia Tribune*, Dec. 28, 1933, clippings in Schomburg Center for Research in Black Culture; *Chicago Defender*, Aug. 24, 1929; William Lee, "DePriest Shows Real Leader's Qualities," ibid., Feb. 13, 1932; "The Twilight of Two Eras," *Ebony* VI (Aug. 1951):102.

[18] Letter to the editor from Andrew Stuart of Omaha, *Chicago Defender*, Oct. 24, 1931. See also Murrell Rather to Oscar DePriest, May 14, 1929; M. Clarence Mitchell to DePriest, May 18, 1929, NAACP Papers, Box C-64; letter to the editor from Henry C. Davis, *Norfolk Journal and Guide*, July 27, 1929, clipping in Schomburg Center for Research in Black Culture; letter to the editor from Margaret Barnes of Oberlin, Ohio, *Chicago Defender*, Jan. 16, 1932.

[19] Kelly Miller, "Oscar DePriest Nominated as Race Spokesman," *Chicago Defender*, July 6, 1929.

[20] DePriest won in 1928 by 24,549 to 20,203; in 1930 by 23,805 to 16,422. *Chicago Defender*, Nov. 10, 1928, Nov. 8, 1930 (source of the quotation); *New York Times*, Nov. 6, 1930.

In 1932, despite intraparty wrangling, DePriest turned back a primary challenge from the black lawyer and city councilman, Louis B. Anderson, and won renomination.[21] The *Defender* argued the case for his reelection in terms of race. Any black voter who supported DePriest's white opponent, Harry Baker, was "an enemy of the Race"; DePriest's defeat would be a "personal defeat" for every black. "Will we be so thoughtless," the *Defender* asked, "as to rob ourselves of the respect that his very presence gives us as a Race?"[22]

Such arguments made compelling sense, and the voters of the First Congressional District defied the Roosevelt tide and returned DePriest to the House, even if by a slightly narrower margin than in his previous victory over Baker.[23]

DePriest looked virtually invulnerable. Three strong showings at the polls; two of his victories in defiance of the national political tide; a national reputation as symbol and spokesman of his race—surely it was wishful thinking to imagine unseating him. But to Arthur Mitchell, DePriest's record proved not the folly of challenging him, but the need to do it from a different tack. At first, Mitchell had intended to make the challenge within the Republican party, and he joined the Second Ward Regular Republican Organization when he moved to Chicago. But once he observed at close range DePriest's firm control of the city's black Republicans, Mitchell quickly realized that it would be very difficult to break that control through the Republican party. Accordingly, he became a Democrat.[24]

Not surprisingly, Mitchell's public account of his party switch ignored the factor of his own political aspirations. In a much publicized speech in 1936, "The Negro and the Democratic Party," he gave his version of his political transformation. It came about, he said, because he perceived a shifting political climate, and he wanted his race to be on the side of the emerging power. "I could see that the political situation was changing and that the Democratic Party was marching to power," he said; "dumb and unacquainted as I was with politics, I could see the stupendous blunders the Republican Party was making, and that the American citizens would not stand for it." Disillusioned by the Hoover

[21] *Chicago Defender*, July 25, Aug. 1, 8, 15, 22, 29, Sept. 5, 12, 19, 26, Oct. 10, 1931, Feb. 6, 20, 27, Mar. 5, 12, 19, 26, Apr. 9 (and editorial), 16, 23 (editorial), Sept. 10, 1932.

[22] Editorial, ibid., Oct. 15, 1932. See also Oct. 1.

[23] Ibid., Nov. 12, 1932. The vote was 33,069 to 25,303.

[24] Duis, "Arthur W. Mitchell," p. 24.

1. Oscar DePriest, the black Republican elected to Congress from Chicago in 1928

2. Arthur W. Mitchell, the black Democrat who defeated DePriest in 1934 and served in Congress until 1943

administration's lack of interest in its black supporters, he approached a Democratic leader in Washington and asked him what the Democrats' attitude toward blacks would be in 1932. The leader told him that the Republican party would not pay attention to blacks as long as it had the black vote in its pocket. To expect any consideration from the Democrats, however, blacks would have to work for and join the Democratic party. "That opened my eyes," as Mitchell told the story, "and I immediately began to work for the Democratic Party and to bring into the Democratic Party as many of my people as I could."[25]

While Mitchell's version of his own political odyssey may have been deficient, his account of his labors in behalf of his new party was accurate. He worked faithfully to establish his Democratic credentials. In 1932, he stumped for Roosevelt in black neighborhoods under the aegis of the Democratic National Committee. He logged thousands of miles, especially in the Midwest and West, reportedly at his own expense.[26]

After the election, Mitchell made plans for what was billed in the press as a "nonpartisan conference" to consider the part blacks might play in the new administration.[27] In fact, for all the insistence that the January gathering was not political, it consisted mainly of Democrats, and it focused primarily on "the necessity of making the Democratic party a party whose vision will not be clouded with racial proscription." And it served, not accidentally, to publicize the name of Arthur W. Mitchell.[28]

In March, Mitchell went to Washington to confer with party leaders and attend the inauguration. He drew on his old Alabama ties to make himself known to national party leaders. "I do not know any colored man in the country who is a more active and loyal Democrat," Congressman John McDuffie wrote to James A. Farley in September. There was "a probability," McDuffie con-

[25] Arthur W. Mitchell, "The Democratic Party and the Negro," *Congressional Record*, 47th Cong., 2nd sess., Apr. 22, 1936, reprint in Mitchell folder, Associated Negro Press files, Barnett Papers. Mrs. Mitchell described the party shift this way: "When Hoover was settled in the White House Mr. Mitchell and some other Blacks tried to reach Mr. Hoover and they were told to go to the back. After that Mr. Mitchell went with the Democratic Party." Clara M. Mitchell to Nancy J. Weiss, Aug. 24, 1974.

[26] Duis, "Arthur W. Mitchell," p. 26; *Chicago Defender*, Nov. 19, 1932; Arthur W. Mitchell to Clark H. Foreman, Oct. 14, 1933, Arthur W. Mitchell Papers, Box 1, Chicago Historical Society.

[27] *Chicago Defender*, Jan. 14, 1933; Arthur W. Mitchell to R. Bentley Strather, Nov. 25, 1932; Mitchell to "Friend Watkins," Nov. 25, 1932, Mitchell Papers, Box 1.

[28] *Chicago Defender*, Jan. 14, 21 (source of the quotation), 28, 1933.

fided, of Mitchell's "succeeding Oscar DePriest." At that point the probability was still a private dream, but Mitchell moved deliberately to make it a reality. In January 1934, he touted his qualifications and made known his availability as a congressional candidate in a letter to Joseph F. Tittinger, leader of Chicago's Second Ward Regular Democratic Organization. The *Chicago Defender*, which prematurely reported Mitchell's designation as the Democratic candidate, described him in early February as "the most formidable opponent possible" for DePriest.[29] But the Democratic organization in the First Congressional District was not quick to embrace the eager candidate. Instead, they turned again to their three-time nominee, Harry Baker. It was not easy to make the leap to a black candidate. Baker was a proven campaigner who would very likely win on the momentum of the New Deal; why turn instead to an inexperienced newcomer? With the organization's backing, Baker defeated Mitchell in the Democratic primary.[30]

Mitchell's break came when Baker died unexpectedly in the middle of the summer. Now the Democratic county central committee turned to him to fill the vacancy on the November ticket.[31]

The New Deal connection made the critical difference in the election. DePriest had an identifiable public record and enjoyed the backing of major black newspapers.[32] But he was weakened by a split in the local Republican party. During the previous year, Louis B. Anderson, DePriest's opponent in the primary of 1932, had retired from his post as Second Ward alderman, and William L. Dawson, a lawyer and acknowledged "DePriest lieutenant," had run successfully to succeed him.[33] Dawson's election to the City Council, accomplished with DePriest's strong backing, had been interpreted as a further indication of DePriest's growing influence.[34]

In 1934, DePriest and Dawson tried to consolidate their control of the First District by taking over the Second Ward organization.

[29] Ibid., Mar. 4, 1933; John McDuffie to James A. Farley, Sept. 13, 1933; Arthur W. Mitchell to Joseph F. Tittinger, Jan. 12, 1934, Mitchell Papers, Box 1; *Chicago Defender*, Feb. 3, 1934.

[30] Duis, "Arthur W. Mitchell," p. 26; Gosnell, *Negro Politicians*, p. 90.

[31] *Chicago Defender*, Aug. 11, 1934.

[32] See, e.g., editorials, ibid., Nov. 3, 1934; *Norfolk Journal and Guide*, Nov. 17, 1934, clipping in Schomburg Center for Research in Black Culture.

[33] *Chicago Defender*, Jan. 7, Feb. 11, 25, Mar. 4, 1933. The quotation comes from the issue of Sept. 3, 1932.

[34] Ibid., Mar. 4, 1933.

With DePriest's backing, Dawson ran for ward committeeman, but he lost a tight race to William King, a state senator.[35]

Factionalism within the Republican party would have been debilitating no matter what the outcome, but when it ended in a de facto defeat for DePriest, it left him particularly vulnerable on the eve of what commentators predicted was to be his toughest congressional race. Had it been another time, DePriest might still have prevailed. But Arthur Mitchell came to the 1934 campaign wrapped in the already magical mantle of Franklin Roosevelt and the New Deal.

Nationally, the election of 1934 was atypical for an off-year contest, for, instead of losing strength, as the President's party usually did, the Democrats actually picked up nine seats in the House and ten in the Senate. The currents that affected the nation also touched Chicago's First Congressional District, where Mitchell defeated DePriest by a vote of 27,963 to 24,820.[36]

Mitchell had run "with the New Deal as his platform," and he called his election "a desire fully expressed . . . for new leadership under the New Deal." He pledged that he was "100 per cent in agreement with the President's program."[37] "I was elected partly on the achievement of your administration . . . and partly on the promise that I would stand back of your administration," he wrote Roosevelt.[38] Although the national Democratic party apparently did little to help Mitchell—his requests to the Democratic National Committee for campaign funds seemed to fall on deaf ears[39]—Democrats were not unwilling to take credit for his victory. The majority whip declared Mitchell's election "a pronounced endorsement of the constructive program of the Democrat Administration," and an Oklahoma congressman called it "a tremendous tribute to President Roosevelt, the Democratic Party, and the New Deal."[40]

[35] Ibid., Jan. 13, Apr. 7, 14, 1934. One account held DePriest "largely responsible" for the "intra-party squabble." See *Southern Broadcast*, Nov. 17, 1934, clipping in Schomburg Center for Research in Black Culture.

[36] James MacGregor Burns, *Roosevelt: The Lion and the Fox* (New York, 1956), p. 202; Gosnell, *Negro Politicians*, p. 90, n. 76.

[37] *Crisis* (Dec. 1934), and *St. Louis Argus*, Nov. 16, 1934, clippings in Schomburg Center for Research in Black Culture.

[38] Arthur W. Mitchell to Franklin D. Roosevelt, Mar. 4, 1935, Franklin D. Roosevelt Papers, President's Personal File 2289, Franklin D. Roosevelt Library.

[39] See, for example, Arthur W. Mitchell to Emil Hurja, Oct. 31, 1934, Mitchell Papers, Box 2.

[40] Arthur H. Greenwood to Arthur W. Mitchell, Nov. 19, 1934; Wesley E. Disney to Arthur W. Mitchell, Nov. 19, 1934, ibid.

The press and the public saw it the same way: Mitchell won his seat as a consequence of national rather than local political currents. The New Deal rolled into Chicago and toppled the Old Guard Republicans "like tenpins"; Mitchell's success should be understood as "a part of the New Deal."[41]

As the first black Democrat to hold elective office in Washington, Mitchell stood out as the most prominent example of blacks who built political careers on the popularity of the New Deal. As a lone black congressman, his experience was unique. But insofar as his embrace of the Democratic party reflected both his personal desire for political advancement and his positive assessment of New Deal liberalism, his experience in many ways encapsulated that of other black politicians at the state and local level.

The political odyssey of another Chicagoan, William L. Dawson, demonstrates the congruence between ambition on the part of the aspiring political leader and self-interest on the part of a Democratic machine eager to build political strength among blacks. Dawson was born in Albany, Georgia, in 1886, and was graduated *magna cum laude* from Fisk University in 1909. In 1912 he moved to Chicago, where he studied law, first at a night school, Kent College, and then at Northwestern University. He enlisted in the army in World War I and saw action overseas as a first lieutenant. Dawson was admitted to the Illinois bar in 1920. While he was practicing law in Chicago, he launched his political career as a precinct worker for the Republican Thompson machine.

Elected to the City Council in 1933 as an ally of Oscar DePriest, Dawson won reelection to a four-year term in 1935—this time with the backing of Chicago's Democratic mayor, Ed Kelly. Dawson twice attempted to win election to Congress as a Republican—in 1928, when he lost the nomination to DePriest's predecessor, Martin Madden, and in 1938, when he ran unsuccessfully against Arthur Mitchell. In 1939, in an intraparty battle with his old nemesis, William King, he lost the primary for the Republican aldermanic nomination; in the general election, he joined forces with the Democratic aldermanic candidate, Earl Dickerson, who defeated King, and he also backed the bid for reelection of Mayor

[41] *Chicago World*, Nov. 10, 1934, clipping in Mitchell Papers, Box 2; editorial, *St. Louis Argus*, Nov. 9, 1934, clipping in Schomburg Center for Research in Black Culture. See also *Afro-American*, Nov. 10, 1934; Lawrence C. Jones to Arthur W. Mitchell, Nov. 26, 1934, Mitchell Papers, Box 3; "Memorandum on Mr. Mitchell," 1939, Dawson folder, Barnett Papers; Dickerson interview.

Kelly. Some months later, Dawson achieved his earlier objective—Second Ward committeeman—but this time as a Democrat. In 1942, when Mitchell retired from the House of Representatives, Dawson—a Democrat—was elected to succeed him.[42]

As Dawson later told the story, he switched from the Republican to the Democratic party "because of the liberalism of Roosevelt."[43] He "felt 'free,' " he sometimes elaborated, " 'to choose any party label that best advances the cause of Negroes.' "[44] What he declined to state was that the party shift best advanced the political career of William L. Dawson. Mayor Kelly, eager to build black Democratic strength in Chicago, offered Dawson control of Democratic patronage in the Second Ward. Dawson had been unsuccessful in his bids for higher office, at odds with the machine that controlled his ward, and unable to realize his ambitions for party leadership. He understandably saw the Democratic party as a promising vehicle through which to gain the power and influence that eluded him as a Republican.[45]

Just as Kelly's willingness to use patronage to build black Democratic strength helped to lure Dawson into the party, so the reluctance of some Republican bosses to acknowledge black demands for political recognition served to push black politicians out of the GOP. Again and again, black Republicans, dismayed at the local party organization's unwillingness to give blacks a share of the patronage, deserted the GOP in hopes of finding better opportunities and a more receptive attitude in the rising Democratic party.[46] Two examples illustrate the point.

[42] *Chicago Defender*, Feb. 11, Mar. 4, 1933, Mar. 2, 1935, Apr. 16, 1938, Mar. 25, 1939, Nov. 25, 1939, Nov. 7, 1942; Edgar A. Toppin, *A Biographical History of Blacks in America since 1528* (New York, 1971), pp. 277-78; John Madigan, "The Durable Mr. Dawson of Cook County, Illinois," *Reporter*, Aug. 9, 1956, p. 40.

[43] Quoted in "Negro America's Top Politician," *Ebony* X (Jan. 1955):24. See also *PM*, Apr. 25, 1943, and Fletcher Martin, "The Boss of Bronzeville," *Chicago* (June 1955):25, clippings in Schomburg Center for Research in Black Culture.

[44] Robert Gruenberg, "Dawson of Illinois: What Price Moderation?" *Nation*, Sept. 8, 1956, p. 196, clipping in Schomburg Center for Research in Black Culture. See also Clayton, "How to Get Ahead in Politics," p. 5; *Newsweek*, Jan. 10, 1949, clipping in Schomburg Center for Research in Black Culture.

[45] Interview with Ralph H. Metcalfe, Mar. 24, 1977, Washington, D.C.; Dickerson interview; Madigan, "The Durable Mr. Dawson," p. 40; *New York Times*, Nov. 10, 1970, clipping in Schomburg Center for Research for Black Culture.

[46] For examples, see Eugene A. Hatfield, "The Impact of the New Deal on Black Politics in Pennsylvania, 1928-1936" (Ph.D. diss., University of North Carolina at Chapel Hill, 1979), pp. 64, 177-78; Bruce M. Stave, *The New Deal and the Last Hurrah: Pittsburgh Machine Politics* (Pittsburgh, 1970), p. 60; William Wayne Giffin, "The Negro in Ohio, 1914-1939" (Ph.D. diss., The Ohio State University,

In St. Louis, a solidly Republican black vote had consistently provided the margin of victory for Republican mayoralty candidates for more than two decades. Marking a Republican ballot was a reflexive act; it was "an emotional vote—a freedom vote," conditioned by the legacy of Lincoln and emancipation.[47] So certain were white Republicans of their captive black constituency that they "made sport of the Black vote . . . claiming to hold it in their vest pockets . . . and even announcing willingness to spot democrats 25,000 votes and still defeat them with returns from Black precincts."[48] "If you're black, you were born a Republican," GOP campaigners commonly declared. Content to boast of automatic black support, the party neither courted nor rewarded its black backers. Patronage was meager—an occasional appointment as justice of the peace or constable—and any black man with a desk job "had to go out and do yard work for city officials." Nor did the party pay any attention to the needs of blacks for municipal services.[49]

Republican callousness pushed young blacks into the Democratic party. David M. Grant, who became the chief patronage dispenser for the Democrats in St. Louis, explained his political transformation this way:

> When I finished law school in 1930, and came home to St. Louis . . . I intended to line up with the Republicans like my father. But I found a lot of "hat in the hand darkies" fighting one another for personal gain at the expense of the race. Moreover, the white Republicans listened only to these men, who had no power among the race voters. They didn't fight for or control a vote. They were relics of Reconstruction politics, the same as Bob Church, Roscoe Conkling Simmons and Perry Howard. So—I joined the Democrats.[50]

It made him "damn mad" to see how little blacks had to show for keeping the Republicans in power, Grant recalled. Accord-

---

1968), pp. 412-15; James Braddie Morris, Jr., "Voting Behavior in Four Negro Precincts in Iowa Since 1924" (Master's thesis, University of Iowa, 1946), p. 53. Insofar as small numbers of black politicians had entered the Democratic party in the North before the New Deal, their motivation had been similar. See, e.g., J. Joseph Huthmacher, *Massachusetts People and Politics, 1919-1933* (1959; reprint ed., New York, 1969), pp. 121-22.

[47] Telephone interview with David M. Grant, June 22, 1977.

[48] "Of Political Parties and Black Voters," I, *St. Louis Argus*, n.d., newspaper clipping sent by David M. Grant to Nancy J. Weiss.

[49] Grant interview.

[50] Quoted in *New York Herald Tribune*, Aug. 7, 1936, p. 7.

ingly, he and some other young blacks launched a campaign to win blacks to the Democratic party in the 1933 mayoral election.[51]

Delicately skirting the powerful symbolism of Lincoln and emancipation—the Lincoln legacy was so strong that they would have been "tarred and feathered" for impugning the Republicans' historic ties to blacks—Grant and his colleagues campaigned against present-day Republican indifference to blacks in St. Louis. "We preached the folly of giving all of your votes to one party that knows about it before the election." Two circumstances made blacks willing to listen to that message. The Depression fostered a "natural resentment" against the party in power. And the Democratic candidate, Bernard F. Dickmann, promised to build a hospital for black indigents, a project that Republican administrations had postponed for a decade. When Grant and his fellow campaigners showed slides of conditions in the existing black hospital at political meetings, it provided convincing proof of Republican negligence.[52]

Dickmann won the mayoralty, the first Democrat to hold that office since 1909. He recognized his indebtedness to black voters and set out to conduct himself as mayor in such a way that the Democrats would never lose the black vote.[53] As a "quid pro quo" for black support, he compiled a record of performance, remembered as "legendary," which included the immediate construction of the hospital and the appointment of blacks as building inspectors, draftsmen, and lawyers in city agencies.[54]

The power of patronage to change the political affiliation of black politicians was also demonstrated in Philadelphia. In 1933, the Republican machine of William Scott Vare slated only one black candidate for municipal office, despite the urgings of blacks for more recognition for the race. And the office that they selected—that of magistrate—was a post that blacks had held since 1921. Marshall L. Shepard, pastor of Mt. Olivet Tabernacle Baptist Church, had tried for some time to make the machine take notice of the political concerns of its black constituents. Shepard was born in 1899 in Oxford, North Carolina, the son of a Baptist minister. He had been educated at Virginia Union University,

[51] Grant interview.

[52] Ibid. See also Larry H. Grothaus, "The Negro in Missouri Politics, 1890-1941" (Ph.D. diss., University of Missouri, 1970), p. 136.

[53] Grant interview.

[54] "Of Political Parties and Black Voters."

City College, and Union Theological Seminary. He held his first pastorates in New York and moved to Philadelphia in 1926.[55] In the summer of 1933, Shepard took a delegation of blacks to call on Vare to ask him to endorse a black man for municipal court judge. While Vare had been evasive about the endorsement, his disregard for black voters had been all too apparent. Philadelphia blacks, he told the delegation, would never desert the Republican party. At a mass meeting to protest the Republican slate, Shepard challenged blacks to respond to the party's condescension and indifference. "Mr. Vare thinks Negroes in this city don't have enough sense to switch parties and now is the time to show him that he is mistaken." The black press took up Shepard's theme: if the Republicans failed to give adequate political recognition, blacks would vote Democratic. Shepard himself led the way: in 1934, he won election to the Pennsylvania legislature as a Democrat.[56]

Perhaps ironically, the entry of blacks into elected and appointed positions in state and local Democratic politics also brought greater political opportunities for black Republicans. The GOP finally awakened to the reality that blacks would in fact desert the party of Lincoln and, in a number of northern states, began to slate black candidates for office in the hope of wooing black voters back into the Republican fold. The invigoration of black politics showed up in the election results. Between 1925 and 1929, twenty-seven blacks served in state legislatures; between 1932 and 1936, the number increased to thirty-eight. In the election of 1932, ten black Republicans and three Democrats won seats in the legislatures of eight states. In 1936, twelve black Democrats and five Republicans were elected to nine state legislatures. Four years later, twenty-three blacks—fourteen of them Democrats—won election to ten legislatures. Blacks made slow but steady inroads into local offices as well—city councilmen, judges, constables, and other such positions.[57]

[55] *Who's Who in Colored America*, 3rd ed. (Brooklyn, N.Y., 1933), p. 384.

[56] Shepard is quoted in *Philadelphia Tribune*, Aug. 10, 1933. On the reactions of the *Tribune* and the *Afro-American*, see ibid., Aug. 17, 1933. For a scholarly account in the larger context of the evolution of black politics in the city, see Hatfield, "The Impact of the New Deal on Black Politics in Pennsylvania," pp. 161-62.

[57] Monroe N. Work, ed., *Negro Year Book: An Annual Encyclopedia of the Negro*, 8th ed., *1931-1932* (Tuskegee, Ala., 1931), p. 84; 9th ed., *1937-1938* (Tuskegee, Ala., 1937), pp. 96-97; undated typed sheet entitled "Negroes Elected November 1932," attached to Walter White to Frederic J. Haskin, Nov. 30, 1932, NAACP Papers, Box C-391; Earl Brown, "How the Negro Voted in the Presidential

Democrats eager to win black votes used patronage to build a political following. In New York, Tammany Hall began giving patronage to blacks as early as 1919, and black voters, in turn, supported Democrats in state and local contests before they first cast a majority of their votes for a Democratic presidential candidate in 1932. By 1936, the roster of black political jobs included a Tammany Hall district leader in Harlem, two municipal court judges, two aldermen, two assemblymen, an assistant state attorney general, three assistant district attorneys, a civil service commissioner, and many lesser city and state employees, including court clerks, deputy sheriffs, secretaries, and marshals.[58] In Pennsylvania, George H. Earle won the governorship in 1934, the first time since the 1890s that the state government had come under Democratic control. "In less than two years," a political reporter observed in the summer of 1936, "the Democrats have given the Negro political leaders more jobs ... than the Republicans gave them in forty-two." Earle appointed blacks to a variety of posts: a state compensation referee, state boxing commissioner, two state deputy attorneys general, two parole officers, a revenue collector, and numerous clerks, stenographers, janitors, and other lesser jobholders. Through his intercession and that of Pennsylvania Senator Joseph F. Guffey, blacks in Philadelphia and Pittsburgh won significant federal patronage appointments: an assistant United States attorney general, two United States attorneys, two attorneys in the Home Owners Loan Corporation, and three post office superintendents.[59]

In Illinois, too, the state Democratic organization and the Kelly-Nash machine in Chicago cut blacks in on Democratic patronage. Mayor Kelly's black appointments included three assistant corporation counsels, two deputy coroners, an assistant attorney for the election commission, and an assistant city prosecutor. Democratic Governor Henry Horner appointed blacks as assistant commerce commissioner and assistant state's attorney; a black man became an assistant United States attorney as well.[60] In St.

Election," *Opportunity* XIV (Dec. 1936):360; *Pittsburgh Courier,* Nov. 26, 1936; *Afro-American,* Sept. 12, 1936, Dec. 17, 1938; Jessie Parkhurst Guzman, ed., *Negro Year Book: A Review of Events Affecting Negro Life, 1941-1946* (Tuskegee, Ala., 1947), p. 286; Grothaus, "The Negro in Missouri Politics," p. 163.

[58] Earl Brown, "The Negro Vote," *Opportunity* XIV (Oct. 1936):303; Ferdinand Q. Morton, "The Colored Voter," ibid. XV (Mar. 1937):85-86; Edwin R. Lewinson, *Black Politics in New York City* (New York, 1974), chap. 4.

[59] *New York Herald Tribune,* July 15, 1936, p. 11.

[60] Ibid., Aug. 5, 1936, p. 7.

Louis it was the same story. David Grant put it this way: "The Democratic party . . . opened the doors of opportunity to Negroes" by appointing them to positions that they had "never held before," including an assistant in the city's free legal aid bureau, an assistant counselor, a chemist, a draftsman, a building inspector, an assistant superintendent of refuse collection, city clerks, a medical director at a city hospital, and a supervisor of Negro playgrounds.[61]

Patronage of this kind meant important symbolic recognition for black Americans; it meant significant posts for a handful of blacks who saw their own careers—and, by association, the furtherance of the interests of their race—as inextricably dependent on the Democratic organization. Not surprisingly, that translated into black votes for the Democratic party.[62]

When the Democrats became the nation's majority party in the 1930s, party leaders at every level found an incentive to woo blacks. Building the Democratic party meant broadening and deepening the party's base; blacks—a constituency that the party had never previously cultivated—were one of the groups that could help to build a powerful new Democratic coalition. Republican callousness loosened the bonds that had tied black politicians to the Grand Old Party. Personal ambition impelled them to look in new directions for avenues of political advancement. The new ascendancy of the Democratic party provided these aspiring politicians with the perfect opportunity; the willingness of the party to include blacks in patronage and the aggressive approach of the Democrats to the economic crisis gave them the perfect rationale for a shift in party allegiance. The New Deal provided the setting for the emergence of black Democratic politicians; their enlistment in the party, in turn, helped to cement black loyalties to the New Deal.

[61] Ibid., Aug. 8, 1936, p. 2. The same was true in Ohio; see Giffin, "The Negro in Ohio," pp. 415-19, 426-42.

[62] On the role of patronage in swinging black support to the Democrats, see also *New York Herald Tribune*, Aug. 28, 1936, p. 4; *New York Times*, Oct. 26, 1936, p. 2; Richard J. Meister, "The Black Man in the City: Gary, Indiana, 1906-1940" (Paper presented at Association for the Study of Negro Life and History Convention, 1969), pp. 11-15; Lawrence Hamm interview with Russell Bingham, July 10, 1979, Newark, N.J.

CHAPTER V ▪ *The Battle for*
Antilynching Legislation

The New Deal gave black leaders renewed hopes that racial issues might be resolved within the political process. Among the main objectives they might have chosen—attacking segregation, discrimination, or disfranchisement, for example—they chose to focus on one: the effort to make lynching a federal crime. The battle for antilynching legislation came to symbolize the cause of racial advancement in the 1930s. It stood out as the most visible and dramatic manifestation of the continuing struggle for racial justice. The fact that the battle went forward when it did showed how the New Deal helped to politicize black Americans. The fact that it fell short of victory demonstrated the limits of black political power in the 1930s.

In part, antilynching legislation became such a central focus of racial advancement efforts because of the stark nature of the act. Blacks might survive, even transcend, discrimination, denial, and indignity—but brutal murder? Whites might rationalize racial separation and differential treatment, but it was another matter to defend the capricious snuffing out of a black man's life. How could any decent person differ with the judgment of the *Catholic World* that lynching was a "monstrous" act, evidence "that we Americans have not yet quite outgrown savagery"?[1]

The second reason for the emphasis on lynching was a calculated decision about priorities on the part of the NAACP. The Association was fresh from the fight against the nomination of John J. Parker and the ensuing effort to defeat senators who had supported his confirmation. It was also recently triumphant in pressing for a Senate investigation of the exploitation of blacks employed in work camps on the federal government's Mississippi River flood-control project. Now it needed a new cause. Moreover, it needed some way to counter the challenge from the left. The NAACP had been overshadowed by the International Labor Defense in the Scottsboro case, and it was alarmed by the Com-

---

[1] "Mobs, Governors, Citizens," *Catholic World* CXXXVIII (Jan. 1934):385.

munist party's aggressive efforts to appeal to blacks. There were challenges inside the organization as well. Young militants were pushing the NAACP to embrace an economic agenda, and the board of directors welcomed an alternative in the more familiar terrain of civil and political rights. A new campaign for antilynching legislation met all these needs.[2]

It also served the interests of Walter White. White had been named executive secretary of the NAACP in 1931. His administrative style generated friction within the organization, for he was tough, arrogant, ambitious, and prone to vanity and egotism, and he often behaved in an autocratic manner. His colleagues found a variety of grounds on which to attack him, including the charge that White had done poorly in managing the Association's money. The most celebrated conflict pitted White against the editor of the *Crisis*, W.E.B. Du Bois. Du Bois used the NAACP's magazine to advocate economic self-sufficiency through racial separation—ideas that were anathema to White, who believed firmly in full equality and integration and who refused any compromise with segregation. Besides resenting the NAACP's failure to allow the *Crisis* the autonomy he believed it deserved, Du Bois chafed especially at direction from White, whom he accused of confusing his personal interests with the interests of all blacks and of being unable to understand the race problem, since he was not dark-skinned. The conflict came to a head in 1934 with Du Bois's resignation from the Association and the consequent strengthening of White's position. But while it was in progress, White needed to define an issue that would give him visibility as an effective leader.[3]

Lynching was the issue with which he was most familiar. As assistant secretary of the NAACP, beginning in 1918, he had investigated more than forty lynchings and eight race riots, often at the risk of his life. His color had proved to be an advantage: posing as a white reporter for the *New York Evening Post* or the *Chicago Daily News*, he could move freely in southern towns and persuade local whites to speak openly about racial tensions. These investigations had made White an authority on lynching, and he had publicized its brutality in magazine articles, in a moving novel, *The Fire in the Flint* (1924), and in the book he wrote

[2] Robert L. Zangrando, *The NAACP Crusade Against Lynching, 1909-1950* (Philadelphia, 1980), chap. 5.
[3] Ibid., pp. 106-108; *Dictionary of American Biography*, Supplement Five (New York, 1977), p. 741.

3. Walter White, executive secretary of the NAACP; in the background, a graphic portrayal of a lynching victim

during his Guggenheim Fellowship year, *Rope and Faggot: A Biography of Judge Lynch* (1929).[4]

Lynching had been a major concern of the NAACP since the time of its founding. The Association's first intensive campaign for a federal antilynching law took shape in 1919 in response to the outburst of racial violence that followed World War I. With the NAACP as chief lobbyist, a bill sponsored by Congressman Leonidas C. Dyer, a Republican from St. Louis, finally passed the House in 1922. The Dyer bill called the murder of any citizen of the United States by a "mob or riotous assemblage" of three or more people a denial of "the equal protection of the laws." Any state or municipal officer who failed "to make all reasonable efforts" to protect a prisoner from being lynched, or to apprehend and prosecute participants in a lynching, was guilty of a felony and subject to a prison term of up to five years and/or a fine of up to $5,000. Any such officer who aided or conspired in a lynching was to be imprisoned for five years to life. If a state failed to prosecute lynchers, the federal government was to be allowed to do so, and jurisdiction was to be vested in the United States District Court in the area. A county in which a lynching occurred and went unpunished by the state was to forfeit $10,000 for the family of the victim. In the event that a victim was seized in one county and put to death in another, both would be liable for the fine.

In the Senate, the Dyer bill fell victim to a filibuster on the part of southern Democrats. The case against the bill was partly racial, for the prospect of a federal law raised the specter of northern interference with racial arrangements in the South. But the argument against the bill was also constitutional and political. The rallying cry of the filibusterers was state rights. Opponents of the bill argued that law enforcement was the responsibility of the states; to bring the federal government into a matter involving punishment of murderers was to upset the traditional balance between state and federal jurisdictions. The state rights argument gave the opposition to the bill such formidable strength and staying power that after 1922, the antilynching bill never got beyond committee.[5] While the NAACP did not abandon the fight, during the next decade, it redirected its energies toward other objectives.

[4] *DAB*, p. 740.
[5] Zangrando, *The NAACP Crusade*, chap. 3; Richard B. Sherman, *The Republican Party and Black America: From McKinley to Hoover, 1896-1933* (Charlottesville, Va., 1973), chap. 7. The text of the Dyer bill is reprinted in ibid., Appendix B, pp. 264-66.

For a number of reasons, the early months of the New Deal seemed to be an opportune time to revive the drive for antilynching legislation. The need was acute: lynchings of blacks, which had increased from thirty-six in 1917 to seventy-six in 1919, had leveled off after 1922 to an average of seventeen for each of the remaining years of the 1920s. But the Depression aggravated the impulse to violence; in 1930, there were twenty lynchings of blacks, and in 1933, in what the *New York Times* described as "a wave of mob killings," the number jumped to twenty-four.[6] There seemed to be a better chance of getting a law passed. There was a new administration in Washington, one disposed to extend the government's reach into so many facets of the national life. The protest against mob violence was growing even in the South, where churches, women's groups, universities, and the press, among others, were speaking out forcefully in behalf of a federal law. Some respected southern organizations—the Commission on Interracial Cooperation and its offshoots, the Southern Commission on the Study of Lynching and the Association of Southern Women for the Prevention of Lynching—made the campaign against lynching their principal concern. The old southern argument that lynching was a local problem and that state law was adequate to handle it seemed blatantly untenable in light of the fact that lynchers were scarcely ever brought to justice by any southern state.[7]

While black spokesmen expressed the hope that lynching might come within the scope of New Deal concerns,[8] there seemed to be little immediate evidence of administration sensitivity to racial violence. How, the *Philadelphia Tribune* wondered in October 1933, could Roosevelt, in Chestertown, Maryland, to receive an honorary degree from Washington College, fail to deplore a lynching a few hours earlier at Princess Anne on the Eastern Shore?[9] Perhaps he did deplore it, but he kept his own counsel. Asked repeatedly at his press conferences to say something about lynching, he declined to comment.[10] When Roosevelt finally broke

[6] U. S. Department of Commerce, Bureau of the Census, *Historical Statistics of the United States, Colonial Times to 1957* (Washington, D.C., 1960), p. 218; *New York Times*, Dec. 3, 1933, section VIII, p. 2.

[7] Zangrando, *The NAACP Crusade*, pp. 101-103, 115.

[8] See, e.g., editorial and cartoon in *Chicago Defender*, Aug. 12, 1933.

[9] Editorial, *Philadelphia Tribune*, Oct. 26, 1933.

[10] Press conferences no. 73, Nov. 29, 1933, no. 74, Dec. 2, 1933, no. 75, Dec. 6, 1933, in *Complete Presidential Press Conferences of Franklin D. Roosevelt*, 25 vols. (New York, 1972), 2:491, 509, 513, 517.

his silence to speak out against lynching, it was not in a racial context. In November 1933, a mob broke into the county jail in San Jose, California, seized the white men who had confessed to the kidnap-murder of a San Jose youth, and hanged them. "This is the best lesson that California has ever given the country," her governor declared. "We show the country that the state is not going to tolerate kidnapping."[11] With such provocation, Roosevelt could no longer remain silent. "Lynch law," he told the Federal Council of Churches on December 6, was a "vile form of collective murder" which could not be condoned.[12]

The President's public condemnation of lynch law, the *New York Times* wrote, "gives a timely lead to all Americans who are ready to unite to proscribe and put down the abhorrent thing."[13] To blacks eager for some leadership in the fight against lynching, Roosevelt's pronouncement was the first encouraging sign in so long that it was easy to exaggerate its significance. The *Chicago Defender* thought that the statement would "do more than any other single factor to bring the nation to a deep and abiding sense of its responsibility to preserve our form of government and perpetuate our ideals of civilization."[14] Soberer commentators made an important distinction; the President had finally spoken out against lynching—but what did he intend to *do* about lynching? Would he, as so many hoped and urged, ask Congress to pass an antilynching law?[15] Roosevelt's message to the new session of the Seventy-third Congress, in January 1934, dashed the hopes that the December speech had raised. While he cited lynching, together with "organized banditry, cold-blooded shooting," and kidnapping, as crimes that "call on the strong arm of government for their immediate suppression," he offered no proposal to make such suppression a matter of federal law.[16]

[11] *New York Times*, Nov. 27, 1933, pp. 1, 3. Governor James Rolph is quoted on p. 3.

[12] Quoted in ibid., Dec. 7, 1933, p. 2.

[13] Editorial, ibid., Dec. 8, 1933, p. 24.

[14] Editorial, *Chicago Defender*, Dec. 9, 1933.

[15] *Philadelphia Tribune*, Dec. 14, 1933; editorials, *Pittsburgh Courier*, Dec. 16, 1933, *Chicago Defender*, Dec. 23, 1933; "Deep Down Under Lynching," *World Tomorrow*, Dec. 21, 1933, p. 678; *New York Times*, Dec. 1, 1933, p. 4, Dec. 17, 1933, section II, p. 1.

[16] Franklin D. Roosevelt, Message of the President to the Congress of the United States, Jan. 3, 1934, p. 4, mimeographed copy in National Association for the Advancement of Colored People Papers, Box C-73, Manuscript Division, Library of Congress (hereafter cited as the NAACP Papers). Some black newspapers took heart from the President's mention of lynching and seemed to excuse the fact that he did not ask for antilynching legislation by noting that he did not ask for

The NAACP, however, was ready with a bill of its own. In nearly every respect, the bill followed the outlines of the earlier Dyer proposal. It brought federal sanctions to bear on law officers who permitted lynchings to occur and who failed to prosecute lynchers, and on counties where lynchings took place. Unlike the Dyer bill, however, it said nothing about federal prosecution of the lynchers themselves. That provision had been dropped after 1922 in response to objections from constitutional conservatives who argued that punishing murderers was the business of the states.[17]

In November 1933, Walter White recruited two Democratic senators, Edward P. Costigan of Colorado and Robert F. Wagner of New York, to sponsor the new bill in the forthcoming session of Congress.[18] Neither man had much of a record of involvement in civil rights, but that criterion would have made it virtually impossible to find a sponsor in Congress in the 1930s. Costigan and Wagner both offered impeccable credentials as liberal reformers. Costigan, a Denver lawyer, had secured the acquittal of the miners accused of conspiring to murder a member of the state militia in the Ludlow massacre in the southern Colorado coal fields in 1914. He was a longtime supporter of progressive political goals such as the direct primary and reform of the civil service, and he helped to found the Progressive party in Colorado in 1912. In 1917, President Wilson appointed him to the Federal Tariff Commission, where, for a decade, he battled for reduced, scientifically established rates. Elected to the Senate in 1930, he pushed the Hoover administration toward more active federal involvement in combating unemployment. With the advent of the New Deal, he emerged as a principal supporter of the Roosevelt legislative program.[19]

Wagner, elected to the Senate in 1926 after more than a decade

---

any specific legislation in the message. See, e.g., editorials, *Philadelphia Tribune*, Jan. 11, 1934, and *New York Amsterdam News*, Jan. 10, 1934, clippings in Roosevelt Administration Scrapbooks, vol. I, microfilm reel 16, Schomburg Center for Research in Black Culture.

[17] For the terms of the Costigan-Wagner bill, see Zangrando, *The NAACP Crusade*, pp. 114-15. On the dropping of the provision for federal prosecution of lynchers, see p. 115. The only other significant difference from the Dyer bill was the stipulation that the federal district court could enter the case if, after thirty days, state and local law enforcement agents had failed to act.

[18] Walter White to Edward P. Costigan, Nov. 27, 1933, Edward P. Costigan Papers, Box 42, FF 16, Western Historical Collections, Norlin Library, University of Colorado.

[19] Zangrando, *The NAACP Crusade*, pp. 111-12; *Dictionary of American Biography*, Supplement Two (New York, 1958), pp. 123-25.

of public service in behalf of working men and women in New York State, quickly established himself as one of the most influential reformers in Washington. Even before the Depression began, he was introducing legislation to give the federal government an active role in fighting unemployment. In 1932, he was chiefly responsible for the passage of the Emergency Relief and Construction Act, which, despite the opposition of the Hoover administration, committed the federal government to providing direct relief for the unemployed and, in a limited way, to financing a public works program. During the Roosevelt years, he sponsored and had a major role in drafting the National Industrial Recovery Act, the Social Security Act, and the Railroad Retirement Act, among others. He gave his name to two pieces of legislation that were to stand out among the New Deal's most significant legacies: in 1935, the National Labor Relations Act, and in 1937, the Public Housing Act. Although Negro rights was never his principal preoccupation, the NAACP had found him to be a staunch and faithful ally. In 1930, during the Senate debate over the Parker nomination, Wagner had been the only senator to raise the issue of Parker's alleged racial bias. The next year, the NAACP had invited him to be the principal speaker at its annual convention in New York City. In 1932, he had sponsored a bill calling for a Senate investigation of the working conditions of black laborers on the Mississippi River flood-control project.[20]

After the Costigan-Wagner bill was introduced in the Senate in January 1934, the NAACP opened a concerted campaign to secure its passage. White went to Washington to coordinate the lobbying. On February 20, a Senate Judiciary subcommittee, with Frederick Van Nuys of Indiana as chairman, opened two days of hearings on the bill. In late March the Judiciary Committee reported the bill favorably with minor amendments.[21]

The campaign for the bill's passage involved rallying public support—on the part of the NAACP, securing influential endorsements; on the part of the black press, encouraging "a mountain of mail" in favor of the legislation.[22] But while the public pressure

[20] J. Joseph Huthmacher, *Senator Robert F. Wagner and the Rise of Urban Liberalism* (New York, 1968); *Dictionary of American Biography*, Supplement Five (New York, 1977), pp. 717-19.

[21] NAACP board minutes, Jan. 8, 1934, p. 3, NAACP Papers, Box A-10; NAACP, *25th Annual Report* (1934), pp. 23-24; Zangrando, *The NAACP Crusade*, pp. 117-18.

[22] Editorials, *Pittsburgh Courier*, Mar. 31 (source of the quotation), May 12, 1934.

was important, perhaps more important were the quieter efforts to win Roosevelt's support for bringing the bill to a vote in the Senate.

Reaching Roosevelt was difficult at best. His aides were always disposed to put Walter White off, to refuse his requests for appointments, and to keep him at arm's length. One way into the White House that circumvented the staff was through the President's valet and maid, Irvin and Elizabeth McDuffie, and White sometimes used them as intermediaries to reach Roosevelt with his concerns.[23]

But the McDuffies' influence was limited. White needed a more direct route. Employing a strategy that he would use repeatedly during the New Deal, he approached Roosevelt through his wife. Just when or why White chose to try such a tack remains unclear. Although he often wrote about the ways in which Mrs. Roosevelt helped him, he never recorded his decision to make the initial approach. In any event, the antilynching fight set the pattern for a close working relationship that lasted until White's death. White corresponded with Mrs. Roosevelt regularly, kept her informed about the progress of the bill, and sent information which she might pass along to her husband.[24] In April 1934, in the first of many such discussions, he met privately with her for forty minutes at the White House.[25] Mrs. Roosevelt told White that she was talking with him "both in her own behalf and at the request of the President." For her own part, she was "very deeply interested and anxious to see the bill passed." But to Roosevelt, who was eager for an early adjournment of Congress, a bill that threatened to provoke a protracted debate posed an obvious "quandary."[26]

Could the adjournment not come *after* a vote on the Costigan-Wagner bill? White wondered. He was confident of enough votes

[23] Elizabeth McDuffie, "FDR Was My Boss," *Ebony* VII (Apr. 1952):81; Frank Harriott, "Three Who Saw FDR Die," *Negro Digest* IX (May 1951):25; "Black's White," *Time*, Jan. 24, 1938, p. 10; Walter White to Mrs. I. H. McDuffie, Sept. 19, 1936, McDuffie Papers, Box 1, Negro Collection, Trevor Arnett Library, Atlanta University; interview with Clarence M. Mitchell, Jr., Oct. 29, 1976, Washington, D.C.

[24] See, e.g., Walter White to Eleanor Roosevelt, Apr. 14, 1934, Eleanor Roosevelt Papers, Box 637, Franklin D. Roosevelt Library (hereafter cited as the ER Papers).

[25] White House Usher's Diary, Apr. 18, 1934, Franklin D. Roosevelt Library. The longest meeting—an hour and a half—came on Sept. 28, 1934; others ranged from twelve to fifty minutes. See ibid., Sept. 28, 1934, Apr. 13, July 23, 1935, Jan. 17, 1936, May 20, 1937.

[26] Walter White to Edward P. Costigan and Robert F. Wagner, Apr. 21, 1934, Costigan Papers, Box 42, FF 16.

to pass it if it could actually be brought to a vote. But the opposition was counting on blocking consideration of the bill, and it was certain to be brought up only if the White House insisted.[27]

When Marvin McIntyre wired White that Roosevelt would be unable to see him, White telephoned Mrs. Roosevelt for help.[28] She again took up his request with her husband, and she reported back to White. "The President talked to me rather at length today about the lynching bill," she wrote. "As I do not think you will either like or agree with everything that he thinks, I would like an opportunity of telling you about it, and would also like you to talk to the President if you feel you want to."[29]

Indeed he did want to, and through Mrs. Roosevelt's good offices, the appointment was arranged for the following Sunday. When White arrived at the White House, Roosevelt had not yet returned from his afternoon cruise on the Potomac River, so White took tea with the First Lady and the President's mother on the south portico. While they waited, Eleanor briefed White about arguments that were being made against the bill. Roosevelt arrived, in good spirits and disposed, as usual, to tell anecdotes on any subject but the business at hand. Finally, Eleanor and White turned the conversation to the antilynching bill.[30]

Years later, White published his recollection of their conversation:

" 'But Joe Robinson . . . tells me the bill is unconstitutional,' the President remarked.

"Having heard from Mrs. Roosevelt some of the arguments on this point which had been presented to the President by the bill's opponents, I was ready with the opinions of prominent lawyers who had declared the bill constitutional.

"The President then told me of another argument which one of the filibusterers had made and I was able to present facts in refutation. When this had happened three or four times, the President turned sharply and declared, 'Somebody's been priming you. Was it my wife?'

"I smiled and suggested that we stick to our discussion of the bill.

"The President then asked Mrs. Roosevelt if she had coached

[27] Walter White to Eleanor Roosevelt, Apr. 20, 1934, ER Papers, Box 1325.
[28] Joseph P. Lash, *Eleanor and Franklin* (New York, 1971), p. 515.
[29] Eleanor Roosevelt to Walter White, May 2, 1934, NAACP Papers, Box C-73.
[30] Lash, *Eleanor and Franklin*, pp. 515-16; White House Usher's Diary, May 6, 1934.

me, and she too smiled and suggested that the President stick to the subject.

"Laughing, the President turned to his mother to say, 'Well, at least I know you'll be on my side.'

"The President's mother shook her head and expressed the opinion that she agreed with Mr. White.

"Being a good loser, the President roared with laughter and confessed defeat."

But for all the good-natured banter, White's only gain from his visit was "a moral victory, because the President was frankly unwilling to challenge the Southern leadership of his party." Roosevelt explained his dilemma candidly, as White recalled: " 'I did not choose the tools with which I must work,' he told me. 'Had I been permitted to choose them I would have selected quite different ones. But I've got to get legislation passed by Congress to save America. The Southerners by reason of the seniority rule in Congress are chairmen or occupy strategic places on most of the Senate and House committees. If I come out for the antilynching bill now, they will block every bill I ask Congress to pass to keep America from collapsing. I just can't take that risk.' "[31]

The southern leadership in Congress: here was the explanation Roosevelt always resorted to whenever he needed to account to blacks for his unwillingness to back antilynching legislation. He especially meant the Southerners who controlled the Senate: John Nance Garner, his crusty Vice-President; Joseph T. Robinson of Arkansas, the majority leader, a man who wrote of himself, "I think I am what the public generally terms conservative, although I regard myself as liberal," a vigorous proponent of administration measures whom a Washington newsman described as "a veritable slave driver, keeping the Senate's nose to the grindstone"; Byron ("Pat") Harrison of Mississippi, chairman of the Finance Committee, who guided critical administration bills to passage, and who was voted by a panel of Washington reporters as the most influential figure in the Senate; and James F. Byrnes of South Carolina, the reporters' choice as a close second in influence, the person who was Roosevelt's chief liaison man in the upper house.[32]

[31] Walter White, *A Man Called White: The Autobiography of Walter White* (New York, 1948), pp. 169-70. Quoted by permission of Viking Penguin Inc. White mistakenly dates the visit in 1935. A brief contemporary account can be found in Walter White to Edward P. Costigan, May 8, 1934, Costigan Papers, Box 42, FF 16.

[32] George B. Tindall, *The Emergence of the New South, 1913-1945* (Baton Rouge, 1967), pp. 609-610. The quotations, cited there, are from Joseph T. Robinson to

These men actively supported the economic and social initiatives of the New Deal. Some of their more conservative southern colleagues—Harry F. Byrd and Carter Glass of Virginia, Josiah W. Bailey of North Carolina, for instance—were much more skeptical of Roosevelt's innovative approaches. Together, these Southerners had the power to block or to move to passage the major legislative proposals of the New Deal.

Roosevelt spoke accurately, then, when he claimed that he needed the support of influential Southerners in the Senate. He was also correct in his assumption that a federal antilynching bill would be abhorrent to most of these men. Their intransigent opposition to antilynching legislation came not from their approval of lynching—none of them ever condoned the practice—but rather from what a federal antilynching law seemed to them to symbolize. Above all, they cared deeply about state rights; a federal antilynching law, which encroached on the responsibility of the states for law enforcement, struck them as an entering wedge of broader federal incursion on the powers of the states.

The threat of a protracted filibuster by southern senators kept the Costigan-Wagner bill off the floor in the spring of 1934. Walter White applied as much pressure as he could muster. It was important to flood the White House with telegrams, he wrote to James Weldon Johnson; "the more telegrams, the surer we are of a vote and passage."[33] White also kept Mrs. Roosevelt informed about developments in Congress. Support for the bill was growing stronger, he wrote at the end of May; it would surely pass if it could be brought to a vote. "To have a small, recalcitrant group of senators prevent a vote" was "almost heart-breaking." White tried, as best he could, to prevail upon the President. When the *New York Times* reported Roosevelt's continuing "doubts regarding the constitutionality of the bill"—doubts White thought he had assuaged weeks earlier at the White House—he sent Mrs. Roosevelt a "brief . . . on the constitutionality of the measure" to give to her husband.[34]

---

unknown addressee, n.d. [Spring, 1937], and Franklyn Waltham, Jr., *Washington Post*, Apr. 19, 1934, both in Nevin Emil Neal, "A Biography of Joseph T. Robinson" (Ph.D. diss., University of Oklahoma, 1958), pp. 390, 472.

[33] Walter White to James Weldon Johnson, May 8, 1934, James Weldon Johnson Papers, Folder 543, Beinecke Library, Yale University.

[34] Walter White to Eleanor Roosevelt, May 29, 1934, ER Papers, Box 1325. For the President's account of his uncertainty about the constitutionality of the bill, see press conference no. 125, May 25, 1934, in *Complete Presidential Press Conferences of Franklin D. Roosevelt*, 3:375.

But try as White might to win some support from Roosevelt, the response from the White House was disappointing. Mrs. Roosevelt had done her best, but it was hard to find much encouragement in the message she conveyed: "If the sponsors of the bill will go at once to Senator Robinson and say to him that, if, in a lull, the anti-lynching bill can be brought up for a vote, . . . the President will be glad to see the bill pass and wishes it passes."[35] The sponsors conveyed the message, but Robinson never replied, and the Senate adjourned without bringing the bill to the floor.[36]

While the Costigan-Wagner bill was pending in Congress, lynchings had ceased—"held in check," or so White told Roosevelt, "by fear of federal legislation." In making such a causal connection, White may well have been stretching the point. But there was no contesting the "recrudescence of mob violence" that followed the adjournment. Lynchings began to occur again at the rate of one a week, for a total of sixteen by the time the year had ended.[37]

A lynching in Marianna, Florida, in October epitomized the savagery and brutality that proponents of antilynching legislation wanted so fervently to restrain. Not long after midnight on October 26, "an armed mob of approximately 100 men stormed the county jail at Brewton, Alabama," and seized Claude Neal, a black man imprisoned for the murder of a white woman. According to an NAACP investigator, the mob took Neal back to Florida, where the murder had been committed, and subjected him to "the most brutal and savage torture imaginable"—"the greatest possible humiliation and agony." They sliced him with knives, severed parts of his body, and made him eat his penis and testicles. Then they branded him with "red hot irons," choked him several times with a rope, tied him to the back of a car, and dragged him to the home of the dead woman, where a member of her family drove a butcher knife through his heart. A crowd of thousands assembled; the body was repeatedly trampled, and "little children . . . wait[ing] with sharpened sticks . . . drove their weapons deep into the flesh of the dead man." The mutilated body was hung on a tree in the courthouse square; hawkers sold photographs for fifty cents apiece.[38]

[35] Walter White to Edward P. Costigan, June 8, 1934, Costigan Papers, Box 42, FF 16.

[36] Edward P. Costigan to Joseph T. Robinson, June 11, 1934, ibid.

[37] Walter White to Franklin D. Roosevelt, June 13, 1934, ER Papers, Box 1325 (source of the quotations); NAACP, *25th Annual Report*, pp. 23-24.

[38] "The Marianna, Florida Lynching: A Report of an Investigation Made for the National Association for the Advancement of Colored People . . . ," Nov. 20, 1934, Costigan Papers, Box 42, FF 16.

A few days later, doubtless prompted by the brutal spectacle, a reporter asked Roosevelt whether he would recommend passage of the antilynching bill. Roosevelt dodged the issue by asking for some time "to check up and see what I did last year. I have forgotten."[39]

Walter White wrote to the President and Mrs. Roosevelt about "the sadistic torture" that Claude Neal had been forced to endure.[40] The NAACP was organizing a protest meeting at Carnegie Hall, and White wanted the First Lady to speak. She was distressed by the Neal incident, committed to the passage of antilynching legislation, and eager to accept. She forwarded the invitation to the President with a penciled note in the margin: "F.D.R. I w[ou]ld like to do it of course talking over the speech but will do whatever you say." White's letter came back, with a handwritten note from Roosevelt's secretary, Missy LeHand: "President says this is dynamite." Careful not to reveal her own inclinations, the First Lady diplomatically declined to attend. "I do not feel it is wise to speak on pending legislation," she wrote White, "but I will talk to the President and see what can be done in some other way on this."[41] White sent her newspaper comments on the need for antilynching legislation and a copy of the NAACP report on the Neal murder. Since the mob had taken Neal across state lines, could not the Justice Department intervene under the Lindbergh Kidnapping Act? "I talked with the President yesterday about your letter and he said that he hoped very much to get the Costigan-Wagner Bill passed in the coming session," Mrs. Roosevelt wrote White. "The Marianna lynching was a horrible thing. I wish very much the Department of Justice might come to a different point of view and I think possibly they will."[42]

But the Justice Department did not intervene in the Neal case, and for all the President's privately expressed hopes that an antilynching bill might be passed, he said nothing publicly in support of that goal. The NAACP kept up the pressure—in December, for instance, it sent Roosevelt a memorial signed by more than 250 prominent public officials, lawyers, jurists, clergymen, aca-

[39] Press conference no. 154, Oct. 31, 1934, in *Complete Presidential Press Conferences of Franklin D. Roosevelt*, 4:156-57.

[40] Walter White to Franklin D. Roosevelt, Nov. 20, 1934; White to Eleanor Roosevelt, Nov. 20, 1934 (source of the quotation), Costigan Papers, Box 42, FF 16.

[41] Lash, *Eleanor and Franklin*, p. 516; Walter White to Eleanor Roosevelt, Nov. 8, 1934; Eleanor Roosevelt to White, Nov. 20, 1934, ER Papers, Box 1325.

[42] Walter White to Eleanor Roosevelt, Nov. 14, 20, 1934, ER Papers, Box 1325; Lash, *Eleanor and Franklin*, p. 517; Zangrando, *The NAACP Crusade*, p. 123; Eleanor Roosevelt to White, Nov. 23, 1934, NAACP Papers, Box C-73.

demics, editors, and writers, which urged him to make the Costigan-Wagner bill "must" legislation in the forthcoming session of Congress. White would have preferred to have an NAACP delegation deliver the memorial in person, but the White House had said that there would be no time for such a meeting before the congressional session began.[43] By the end of the year, the Association reported that organizations with a combined membership of over 42,000,000 had gone on record in support of the bill.[44]

Neither the public temper nor the overwhelmingly Democratic complexion of the new Congress moved Roosevelt to stronger action. Now, unlike 1934, he had a major legislative program to put through Congress. Social security was on the agenda; so were tax reform, regulation of holding companies, and a vast new work relief program. Such measures were controversial enough in their own right without the special complications an antilynching bill was sure to bring. Accordingly, Roosevelt remained impervious to the NAACP's persistent lobbying. The State of the Union address in January 1935 made no mention of lynching at all. White tried his best to put a positive light on Roosevelt's silence. Perhaps the President intended to make lynching the subject of a special message to Congress? Or to urge passage of the antilynching bill in his address to Congress on crime? "I wonder," he asked Mrs. Roosevelt, "if you could advise me if my optimism is well founded."[45]

White was in a difficult position. He trusted Mrs. Roosevelt and her assurances, and he wanted to believe that Roosevelt would do what he could to expedite the legislation. But the larger black community neither shared White's close ties to the First Lady nor was privy to her assurances that Roosevelt intended to deal with the antilynching bill through the private political channels at his command.[46] When Roosevelt let pass a public opportunity to affirm his concern about lynching, other blacks understandably doubted the NAACP's confidence in his good intentions. What was the Association doing dragging its feet, critics wondered, "waiting for action by the President" when no action seemed to be forthcoming? The continuing occurrence of terrible lynchings

[43] Memorial to Franklin D. Roosevelt, and Walter White to Franklin D. Roosevelt, both Dec. 27, 1934; White to Edward P. Costigan, Dec. 21, 27, 1934, Costigan Papers, Box 42, FF 16.

[44] NAACP, *25th Annual Report*, p. 24.

[45] Walter White to Eleanor Roosevelt, Jan. 10, 1935, ER Papers, Box 1362.

[46] She had, for example, written White that the President would "take up the subject of the Costigan-Wagner Bill in his next conference with the leaders." Eleanor Roosevelt to Walter White, Jan. 8, 1935, NAACP Papers, Box C-73.

made Roosevelt's inaction all the more intolerable.[47] White was having "to take it on the chin" and in "other portions of my anatomy" because of his faith in the President, he told the First Lady.[48] What could she do to help?

Typically, Mrs. Roosevelt took White's concerns to her husband. The President "wants me to say," she reported to White, "that he has talked to the leaders on the lynching question and his sentence on crime in his address to Congress touched on that because lynching is a crime." White could expect a letter directly from Roosevelt. Mrs. Roosevelt's report had "done a great deal to revive my somewhat flagging spirit," White wrote gratefully, and he would "look forward eagerly" to hearing from the President. "Show FDR," Eleanor penciled on the letter.[49]

But for every letter that brought some reassurance from the First Lady, there were others in which skeptics challenged the very foundations of the NAACP's public posture. "You are too smart and you have had too much experience with this subject to believe that the present Democratic Congress will enact any legislation of this kind," wrote Leonidas C. Dyer, the Missouri congressman who had been the NAACP's faithful ally in the antilynching efforts of the 1920s. Why delude blacks into thinking that pressure would make a difference? They were "wasting their time and postage in even writing to members of the Congress," and the NAACP ought to be candid and tell them so. Surely the Association itself had "not been deceived in this matter"?[50] Such criticism was hard to counter. White always turned to Mrs. Roosevelt. A lot of thoughtful people were despairing of effective congressional action against lynching, he wrote to her after he read Dyer's letter. But not White: "I . . . still cling to my belief that you and the President will be able through vigorous action to secure a vote on the bill during the present session of Congress."[51]

White tried again to see Roosevelt to learn what he was willing

---

[47] Walter White to Eleanor Roosevelt, Jan. 12, 1935, ER Papers, Box 1362. White to Franklin D. Roosevelt, Jan. 12, 1935, ibid., conveys the details of a Jan. 11 lynching in Franklinton, Louisiana. "Mr. President," he wrote, "we submit that the body of Jerome Wilson cries out to you to demand of Congress without delay that it pass the Costigan-Wagner Bill and throw the full weight of the Federal Government behind the fight to wipe out this bestial crime."

[48] White's account of what he told Mrs. Roosevelt is in Walter White to Lee F. Johnson, Jan. 25, 1935, Costigan Papers, Box 42, FF 17.

[49] Eleanor Roosevelt to Walter White, Jan. 22, 1935, NAACP Papers, Box C-73; White to Eleanor Roosevelt, Jan. 24, 1935, ER Papers, Box 1362.

[50] L. C. Dyer to Walter White, Jan. 28, 1935, ER Papers, Box 1362.

[51] Walter White to Eleanor Roosevelt, Feb. 1, 1935, ibid.

to do to help move the bill through the Senate. He was losing patience with Roosevelt's pattern of sympathy unsupported by political muscle. "I want to find out if I can," White confided to Charles Houston, "if he is giving us the run-around."[52] (Houston clearly thought Roosevelt was. "All along I've been telling you that your President had no real courage and that he would chisel in a pinch," he later wrote to White.)[53] White asked Mrs. Roosevelt to arrange the appointment; "it seems to me wiser," he wrote her, "not to seek this interview through the regular channels." But not even the First Lady could breach the barriers around the President when his aides were determined to shelter him from a sticky problem. Marvin McIntyre, a Southerner who was obviously unsympathetic to the antilynching drive, refused to make the appointment White sought. The President was too busy, McIntyre explained to Mrs. Roosevelt's secretary. Besides, he was not talking to anyone about legislation pending in committee. Both of those were stock excuses that covered up the real reason for McIntyre's reluctance. "Confidentially," he added, ". . . this is a very delicate situation and it does not seem advisable to draw the President into any more than we have to."[54]

White persisted. It was important to see the President, he wrote to Mrs. Roosevelt, "to discuss means of achieving a vote" so that the antilynching bill would not again languish until the end of the session and "be swamped in the usual confusion and press of legislation." Mrs. Roosevelt tried a more direct appeal. "F.D.R.," she penciled on White's letter, "I do think you could see him *here* and help him on tactics with advice. This ought to go through."[55] But Roosevelt held firm; he would not see White before he went on vacation, as White had requested.[56]

When Costigan announced in mid-April that he intended to bring the bill up for immediate consideration, he threw the Senate into an uproar. The storm that broke over Costigan's intention, as Arthur Krock observed, was "a mere gust" in comparison to "the tornado" that would attend any serious effort to pass the

[52] Walter White to Charles H. Houston, Mar. 12, 1935, NAACP Papers, Box C-78.

[53] Charles H. Houston to Walter White, July 3, 1935, NAACP Papers, quoted in Harvard Sitkoff, *A New Deal for Blacks: The Emergence of Civil Rights as a National Issue*, vol. I: *The Depression Decade* (New York, 1978), p. 288.

[54] Walter White to Eleanor Roosevelt, Mar. 8, 1935; M.H.M. [Marvin H. McIntyre] memorandum for Mrs. Scheider, Mar. 14, 1935, ER Papers, Box 1362.

[55] Walter White to Eleanor Roosevelt, Mar. 14, 1935, ibid.

[56] G.G.T. memorandum for Mrs. Scheider, Mar. 20, 1935, ibid. Mrs. Roosevelt, however, saw White on Apr. 13. See White House Usher's Diary, Apr. 13, 1935.

bill. Roosevelt had told White a year earlier that his support for the antilynching bill might scuttle the entire economic recovery program. In the spring of 1935, that political analysis seemed prophetic. Costigan's intent to bring the antilynching bill before the Senate, Krock wrote, "hangs over the calendar and the President's program like a poised avalanche, with destruction its promise." Angry Southerners were ready to "tie up the Senate for months, if need be, to prevent its passage." It was already clear that a filibuster would "play havoc" with "matters of real pith and moment."[57] The social security bill had just been passed overwhelmingly by the House, and Senate leaders had hoped to use that victory to break open "the legislative jam" that had been impeding action on their side of Capitol Hill. But now, as Turner Catledge reported, "instead of going sliding through on the momentum" of the House vote, the social security bill went to the Senate Finance Committee to wait its turn "behind bills for extending the NRA and settling the veterans' bonus."[58]

With central components of Roosevelt's program clearly in jeopardy, Senate leaders moved to sidetrack the antilynching bill by substituting consideration of other legislation. The tactic worked; in a "sudden surrender . . . to the Southern filibusters," the *New York Times* reported, the Senate on May 1 vacated the motion to take up the Costigan-Wagner bill and substituted consideration of the bonus bill. No matter that there was a clear majority ready to vote for the antilynching bill; the determined band of southern antagonists held sway. The surrender to the filibusterers, one observer commented, looked like "Appomattox in reverse."[59]

Typically, Roosevelt had dodged the chance to become publicly involved. "Care to comment on the anti-lynching bill?" a reporter asked him at a news conference while the Senate maneuvering was in progress. "No."[60]

Roosevelt's unwillingness to intercede against the filibuster was too much for Walter White to tolerate. To Mrs. Roosevelt, he wrote privately of his gratitude for her "deep personal interest in the bill." To the President, in protest, he sent his resignation from the Virgin Islands Advisory Council. "It is my belief that the utterly shameless filibuster could not have withstood the

[57] *New York Times*, Apr. 17, 1935, p. 22.
[58] Ibid., Apr. 22, 1935, p. 1.
[59] Ibid., Apr. 26, 1935, p. 1; Apr. 27, 1935, p. 2; Apr. 28, 1935, p. 20; Apr. 29, 1935, p. 4; May 2, 1935, p. 1 (source of the quotations).
[60] Press conference no. 198, Apr. 24, 1935, in *Complete Presidential Press Conferences of Franklin D. Roosevelt*, 5:243.

pressure of public opinion had you spoken out against it," he said. "In justice to the cause I serve I cannot continue to remain even a small part of your official family."[61]

Mrs. Roosevelt sympathized with White's frustration. "I am so sorry about the bill," she wrote in consolation. "Of course, all of us are going on fighting and the only thing we can do is to hope we have better luck next time."[62] From the President's offices came not sympathy but exasperation. Marvin McIntyre had done his best to keep the lynching issue at a distance, but White had persisted in his attempts to be heard. Stephen Early, a Virginian who was the grandson of the Confederate General, Jubal A. Early, thought that White had gone too far.[63] The NAACP secretary was a troublemaker who had made a nuisance of himself by "bombarding the President with telegrams and letters demanding passage of the Costigan-Wagner ... Bill," Early complained to Eleanor's secretary; White's letter of resignation, like others of his all-too-frequent messages to Roosevelt, was "decidedly insulting." Ever the loyal defender, the First Lady tried to account for White's conduct. "I do not think he means to be rude or insulting," she explained to Early. "He is really a very fine person with the sorrows of his people close to his heart." She knew that White's persistence was hard for Early to accept; "I realize perfectly that he has an obsession on the lynching question," she conceded. But, she added, "if I were colored, I think I should have about the same obsession that he has."[64]

The difficulty of dealing with the White House was discouraging, but it served to reinforce Walter White's determination to press for antilynching legislation. On January 2, 1936, he spent thirty-five minutes with the President. Roosevelt made his position plain at the outset: he frankly saw "no chance of getting the Costigan-Wagner bill passed" in the new session of the Seventy-fourth Congress. He suggested trying "two other approaches": a Senate investigation of "lawlessness in general, which would include lynching," and legislation to empower the De-

---

[61] Walter White to Eleanor Roosevelt, May 3, 1935, ER Papers, Box 1362; White to Franklin D. Roosevelt, May 6, 1935, NAACP Papers, Box C-78.

[62] Eleanor Roosevelt to Walter White, May 8, 1935, quoted in Lash, *Eleanor and Franklin*, p. 518.

[63] For Early's biography, see *New York Times*, Aug. 12, 1951, p. 77.

[64] Stephen Early, personal and confidential memorandum to Malvina Scheider, Aug. 5, 1935, ER Papers, Box 1362; Eleanor Roosevelt to Steve [Early], Aug. 8, 1935, FDR Papers, PPF 1336. The First Lady had had another long session with White only two weeks earlier. White House Usher's Diary, July 23, 1935.

partment of Justice to investigate "all instances of improper interference with the courts," including "newspaper and community pressure" and "mob intimidation." White pointed out the loopholes in the latter plan and argued again for the greater effectiveness of the approaches embodied in the Costigan-Wagner bill, but Roosevelt remained unmoved.[65]

White took the opportunity to speak candidly to Roosevelt about the political implications of the administration's policies on racial matters. The South was so much in favor of the New Deal that it would remain Democratic no matter what the administration did on race, he argued. Besides, the southern states had nowhere to go politically; where else could they find the political influence, power, and prestige, not to mention the share of federal monies, that came their way under the Democrats? By contrast, there were seventeen states outside the South, with a total electoral vote of 281, which had a black voting population "sufficient to determine a close election."[66]

" 'Yes, I know how powerful that Negro vote is,' " Roosevelt "readily stated." White told him that the Republicans were making "very vigorous efforts . . . to get the Negro back into the Republican party." He recounted a report that a prominent Republican had offered $25,000 to induce an important black newspaper to support Republican candidates. "The President smiled and stated: 'We are all talking about sharing the wealth—my advice is to take the money and to vote for the administration.' "[67]

White drew the most positive conclusion possible from the interview: Roosevelt wanted some kind of legislation from the new session of Congress to "act as a deterrent" to lynching and "for political effect" upon those voters, black as well as white, who opposed lynching and favored the Costigan-Wagner bill. White could just as easily have reached a less optimistic appraisal. Roosevelt, unwilling actively to support antilynching legislation at

[65] White's account of the meeting can be found in "Memorandum on Interview of the Secretary of the N.A.A.C.P. with the President at the White House on January 2, 1936 . . . ," Jan. 3, 1936, Costigan Papers, Box 42, FF 17.

[66] Ibid. White gave the President a long memorandum setting forth the issues of greatest concern to blacks—lynching, of course, discrimination in relief and public works, discrimination in the postal service, disfranchisement, and the lack of opportunities for blacks in the army and navy. Among the attachments were tables laying out the political arithmetic which White explained to Roosevelt. See Walter White, Memorandum to the Honorable Franklin D. Roosevelt, Jan. 2, 1936, Costigan Papers, Box 42, FF 17.

[67] "Memorandum on Interview of the Secretary of the N.A.A.C.P. . . . ," Jan. 3, 1936, ibid.

any time, would surely not have wanted to associate the Democratic party with so controversial an issue in an election year. Nor, however, did he want to alienate Walter White and the constituency he represented. So he conveyed the impression that he wanted action by endorsing two approaches which he knew the NAACP itself had already considered as temporary alternative strategies to the Costigan-Wagner bill—approaches which, if his political instincts served him accurately, would doubtless make little headway in Congress.[68]

On January 6, Senator Frederick Van Nuys of Indiana introduced a resolution calling for a Senate investigation of the fourteen lynchings which had occurred since May 1, 1935, when the filibuster killed the Costigan-Wagner bill. The idea was to make clear the failure of the states to take action against the lynchers, and thus to disprove the argument of the filibusterers that federal legislation was unnecessary, since the states would prevent lynchings and punish lynchers. At least, such an investigation would have important public relations value, for it could dramatize the lynching problem and its findings could be disseminated to a national audience. At best, it might break the power of the filibusterers and open the way for Senate action on an antilynching bill.[69]

With the Van Nuys resolution pending in the Senate, White followed Roosevelt's second suggestion and went to see Attorney General Homer Cummings about the possibility of legislation to enlarge the authority of the Department of Justice to intervene in certain kinds of lynchings. White found Cummings evasive and unresponsive. There was clearly nothing to be gained from pursuing this tack. White resorted to his usual method of communicating with the White House. Since the conversation with Cummings had proven unproductive, the NAACP would concentrate on Roosevelt's suggestion of a Senate investigation of lynching, White wrote Eleanor Roosevelt. Would she "talk this over with the President and let me have your and his opinion?" She did so immediately: "He thinks it is better to do just what you are doing."[70]

[68] Ibid.; Zangrando, *The NAACP Crusade*, p. 132.
[69] NAACP, *27th Annual Report* (1936), p. 4; Walter White, Memorandum to the Honorable Franklin D. Roosevelt, Jan. 2, 1936, Costigan Papers, Box 42, FF 17; Zangrando, *The NAACP Crusade*, pp. 132-33.
[70] Zangrando, *The NAACP Crusade*, p. 133; Walter White to Eleanor Roosevelt, Jan. 28, 1936; Eleanor Roosevelt to White, Jan. 29, 1936, ER Papers, Box 1411.

The Van Nuys resolution proved to be no easier to move through the Senate than the Costigan-Wagner bill. The Judiciary Committee reported it favorably on February 13, although it recommended only $7,500 to fund the investigation. The resolution went next to the Audit and Control Committee, where two southern Democrats, James F. Byrnes of South Carolina and Nathan L. Bachman of Tennessee, delayed consideration for weeks and thus blocked the appropriation of even the paltry sum set by the Judiciary Committee.[71] In great distress, Walter White turned, once again, to Mrs. Roosevelt. Now there was no prospect of any action on lynching, he wrote her on February 28. The Costigan-Wagner bill could not be brought to the floor; the Van Nuys resolution would either be killed in committee or "held up so long and the amount of money for the investigation cut so drastically as to make it useless"; and he had talked again with the attorney general about the possibility of the Justice Department intervening in the Claude Neal case, but to no avail. The ordinary obstacles to federal action against lynching seemed to be compounded by election-year politics; White had heard disturbing rumors in Washington "that an order had gone out . . . from the Democratic National Committee advising Democratic senators and congressmen to avoid all controversial issues." All of that left White "more discouraged than ever before," he told Mrs. Roosevelt. "I think it is a very serious mistake to assume that it will be safer politically to pass the buck and dodge the issue simply because this is an election year. Such a course may conceivably cost in November far more than will be gained by letting the Costigan-Wagner bill and the Van Nuys Resolution be strangled to death."[72]

As White requested, the First Lady shared his concerns with her husband. "F.D.R.," she penciled on the February 28 letter, "What do I answer?" The President, who had left White with the impression in January that he wanted some action against lynching, told her what to say. He had said repeatedly to the Senate and House leaders "that the White House asks only three things of this Congress (appropriations, a tax bill and a relief bill), and that all other legislation is in the discretion of the Congress." If he made an exception for legislation concerning lynching, he would have to do the same thing in many other cases as well. The better

---

[71] Zangrando, *The NAACP Crusade*, p. 133; Walter White to Franklin D. Roosevelt, Mar. 14, 1936, Costigan Papers, Box 42, FF 17.
[72] Walter White to Eleanor Roosevelt, Feb. 28, 1936, ER Papers, Box 1411.

rule was to make no exceptions at all. Eleanor conveyed the message to White with her own addition, perhaps designed to cushion the blow: "Of course" Roosevelt was "quite willing" that the Costigan-Wagner bill "should be pushed by Congress itself"; "I feel quite sure he will give it any help he can."[73]

At the same time, Mrs. Roosevelt herself went back to the President once more. She told him "that it seemed rather terrible that one could get nothing done" about lynching, and that she "did not blame [White] in the least for feeling there was no interest in this very serious question." To White, Roosevelt's reaction must have been even more discouraging than his unwillingness to press Congress for legislation, for he resorted to the old objection that it was probably unconstitutional for the federal government "to step in in the lynching situation"—the very objection that White had tried so hard to overcome the previous year. (It was one of Roosevelt's stock excuses; as Eleanor reflected years later to Rexford G. Tugwell, if he had "really . . . wanted to push [antilynching legislation,] that fact would not have stood in his way.") "The President feels that lynching is a question of education in the states, rallying good citizens, and creating public opinion so that the localities themselves will wipe it out," the First Lady reported to White. If it were done by a Northerner, however (meaning the President?), it would "have an antagonistic effect." She herself was "deeply troubled about the whole situation," for it seemed to be "a terrible thing to stand by and let it continue and feel that one cannot speak out as to his feeling."[74]

During the remainder of the congressional session, the NAACP persisted in doing what it could to keep the lynching issue alive: lobbying among senators and congressmen, with repeated reminders of the political consequences of inaction on lynching; trying to dislodge the Van Nuys resolution from the Senate Audit and Control Committee; and pressing for a meeting of the House Democratic Caucus to endorse antilynching legislation, as a way of circumventing the determination of the chairman of the House Judiciary Committee, Hatton W. Sumners of Texas, to prevent House action on the matter. But none of these efforts bore fruit,

[73] Penciled note, on ibid.; F.D.R. memorandum for E.R., Mar. 9, 1936; Eleanor Roosevelt to Walter White, Mar. 16, 1936, ER Papers, Box 1411.

[74] Eleanor Roosevelt to Walter White, Mar. 19, 1936, NAACP Papers, Box C-73; Rexford G. Tugwell interview with Eleanor Roosevelt, June 24, 1957, Hyde Park, N.Y., p. 16, transcript lent by Frank Freidel.

and when Congress adjourned on June 20 for the national political conventions, the lynching issue remained "unresolved."[75]

Shortly thereafter, Interior Secretary Harold Ickes addressed the annual conference of the NAACP. In one part of the speech, he decried mob violence, and he had wanted to include a sentence that spoke to the question of antilynching legislation. "It seems to me," the sentence had read, "that the time has arrived when, if local and State Governments are unable or unwilling to deal with this greatest of enemies to constituted authority, the Federal Government should see to it that the fundamental law of the land is respected." But Steve Early considered such a statement politically unwise, and the sentence was eliminated when the speech was delivered.[76]

The antilynching battle showed the futility of committing the administration to the cause of racial justice. It was not that the New Dealers were insensitive to the horrors of lynching—"Oh, once in a while that [a lynching] would happen, and you'd be outraged because it was a breach of the law," Tommy Corcoran said. But a political calculus took precedence over moral outrage, and the need to mollify Congress always won the day. If lynching had turned simply on a question of the morality of murder by mob, it might have been easier to push national leaders to deal with it by executive or legislative action. But the matter of federal action against lynching was so intimately connected in the political mind with state rights and northern interference in the southern way of life that it proved too explosive to be resolved within the political process. Symbol of racial justice or not, antilynching legislation was too hot for Franklin Roosevelt to touch. Corcoran put the issue clearly: given administration priorities and political realities, civil rights was simply "not to be a primary consideration of the guy at the top. He does his best with it, but he ain't gonna lose his votes for it."[77]

[75] Walter White to Edward P. Costigan, Mar. 26, 1936, Costigan Papers, Box 42, FF 17; White, Confidential Memorandum for Senator Costigan, Apr. 2, 1936; White to James A. Farley, Apr. 3, 1936; ibid., FF 18; Zangrando, *The NAACP Crusade*, pp. 133-35 ("unresolved" is on p. 135).

[76] "The Negro as a Citizen," Ickes speech to NAACP annual conference, June 29, 1936, speech #113, Harold L. Ickes Papers, Box 281, Manuscript Division, Library of Congress; Aubrey E. Taylor memorandum to Harold L. Ickes, June 23, 1936, ibid., Folder 140A, Box 281.

[77] Interview with Thomas G. Corcoran, May 23, 1977, Washington, D.C.

CHAPTER VI • *Eleanor Roosevelt*

To one important New Dealer, civil rights *was* a primary consideration. In an administration where race ranked low on the list of priorities, the First Lady stood out as a staunch ally of black Americans. As a result, she played a crucial role in winning black political support for Franklin Roosevelt and the New Deal.

Eleanor Roosevelt grew to maturity in a world far removed from any concern for racial justice. On her father's side, she, too, was a Roosevelt—President Theodore Roosevelt was her uncle. Her mother's family, the Halls, were descendants of the Livingstons and Ludlows, leading landed gentry of colonial New York. Eleanor's parents, Elliott and Anna, were among the gayest, liveliest members of New York society. Their world consisted chiefly of sports and parties; social issues rarely intruded. Prejudice—against immigrants in general, and especially against Jews—was simply taken for granted.[1]

From her paternal grandmother, Martha Bulloch Roosevelt, and her beloved great-aunt, Anna Bulloch Gracie, Eleanor imbibed the traditions and values of the antebellum South. The Bulloch sisters had grown up on a plantation in Georgia, and their passionate southern loyalties made the Confederacy a cause of real moment in the Roosevelt household.[2]

It was from this southern background that Eleanor gained her earliest awareness of race. Her own account of her first acquaintances with blacks, published in *Ebony* in 1953, is striking in its ingenuousness, especially in light of her audience. It deserves to be quoted at length:

> From my earliest childhood I had literary contacts with Negroes, but no personal contacts with them.
>
> Reading about Negroes came about this way: On Saturdays we visited my great aunt Mrs. James King Gracie, who had been born and brought up on a Georgia plantation. She would read

[1] Joseph P. Lash, *Eleanor and Franklin* (New York, 1971), pp. 3-33, 135, 214.
[2] Ibid., pp. 4, 522.

to us from the Brer Rabbit books and tell us about life on the plantation. This was my very first introduction to Negroes in any way.

It was a rather happy way to meet the people with whom I was later to make many friends because all the stories our aunt told us were about delightful people.[3]

Eleanor first met blacks as a teen-ager on a trip to Europe, but, as she explained in the article in *Ebony*, she "never dreamed they had a special problem of any kind."[4] Her awareness of racial matters grew when, in March 1919, the fifteenth year of her marriage to Franklin, she dismissed her white help and restaffed her household with Negro servants. "Well, all my servants are gone and all the darkies are here and heaven knows how it will all turn out!" she wrote to her mother-in-law. When Eleanor gave her first dinner party with the new staff, she expressed some curiosity at how "my darkies [will] manage." That summer, when the butler fell ill with pleurisy, she commented to Sara, "With darkies, one is always suspicious even of a death in the family."[5]

As Eleanor told the story in *Ebony*, hiring black servants helped her to begin "to understand their problem." "Millie and Frances came to work for us," she wrote, "and I learned a great deal from them. I think Millie and Frances were the first Negroes I ever shook hands with. But that is just customary. I always shake hands with older people."[6]

Eleanor's capacity to learn from people and experiences and her willingness to expose herself to different points of view set her apart from most of her contemporaries. In the 1920s, through her involvement in the League of Women Voters, the Women's Trade Union League, and the Democratic party, she emerged as an articulate supporter of progressive social and labor legislation. From the campaign of bigotry waged against Al Smith in 1928, she gained a pointed lesson in the nastiness of intolerance. From her broad social and ethical commitments, she fashioned a personal concern for the welfare of others that called for service in their

[3] Eleanor Roosevelt, "Some of My Best Friends Are Negro," *Ebony* VIII (Feb. 1953):17.
[4] Ibid., p. 18.
[5] Eleanor Roosevelt to Sara Delano Roosevelt, Mar. 4, 13, and Summer, 1919, quoted in Lash, *Eleanor and Franklin*, pp. 238-39.
[6] Roosevelt, "Some of My Best Friends Are Negro," p. 18.

behalf. From her personal acquaintances grew, slowly, a realization of the dimensions of racial prejudice.[7]

In the 1930s and afterward, Negro rights became one of Eleanor Roosevelt's major concerns. She overcame the ignorance of her youth, grew into a staunch defender of black rights, and came to deal with black friends and associates with apparent ease.[8] By her personal conduct as First Lady, the *Pittsburgh Courier* wrote at the time of her death, she set "a living example of what interracial relations should be, without mawkish sentimentality or condescension."[9] The result, in the words of the historian Rayford W. Logan, was that "Negroes almost worshipped Eleanor Roosevelt."[10]

Racial justice was just one among many causes that the new First Lady championed. She went about it with characteristic fervor. She quickly gained a reputation for turning up in unexpected places, and her visits to black churches, colleges, CCC camps, and PWA housing projects surprised and delighted black Americans.[11] The manager of University Homes described Mrs. Roosevelt's tour of the Atlanta housing project: "She was very much impressed with it—asked the usual multitude of questions and made everyone feel at ease."[12] Mrs. Roosevelt invited black leaders and women's and student groups to receptions at the White House—a striking departure in the eyes of whites and blacks alike.[13] The rumor that a proper white Washingtonian had "spot-

---

[7] James R. Kearney, *Anna Eleanor Roosevelt: The Evolution of a Reformer* (Boston, 1968), pp. 62-69; Lash, *Eleanor and Franklin*, passim; Roosevelt, "Some of My Best Friends Are Negro," p. 18; *Notable American Women: The Modern Period* (Cambridge, Mass., 1980), pp. 596-97.

[8] "A personal experience with Mrs. Bethune taught [Mrs. Roosevelt] how deeply inbred racial feelings were among whites. She liked to kiss people whom she knew well when greeting them and when saying good-by, but it took some time and a conscious effort for Eleanor to give Mrs. Bethune a peck on the cheek, and it was not until she kissed Mrs. Bethune without thinking of it that she felt she had at last overcome the racial prejudice within herself." Lash, *Eleanor and Franklin*, p. 523.

[9] Editorial, *Pittsburgh Courier*, Nov. 24, 1962.

[10] Interview with Rayford W. Logan, Nov. 29, 1976, Washington, D.C.

[11] *Afro-American*, Mar. 17, 1934, Apr. 20, Sept. 14, 1935; White House Usher's Diary, Jan. 9, 1934, Franklin D. Roosevelt Library; *New York Herald Tribune*, Oct. 23, 1937, clipping in Roosevelt Administration Scrapbooks, vol. II, microfilm reel 16, Schomburg Center for Research in Black Culture; Nathan Straus to Eleanor Roosevelt, Mar. 3, 1938, Eleanor Roosevelt Papers, Box 738, Franklin D. Roosevelt Library (hereafter cited as the ER Papers); Rackham Holt, *Mary McLeod Bethune: A Biography* (Garden City, N.Y., 1964), p. 221.

[12] Alonzo G. Moron to Robert C. Weaver, Mar. 5, 1937, Robert C. Weaver Papers, Box 6, Schomburg Center for Research in Black Culture.

[13] On blacks at the White House, see, e.g., *Afro-American*, Feb. 10, 17, Apr. 28,

ted her own maid in the receiving line ahead of her" may or may not have been true, but it accurately captured the worst fears of many whites about the unaccustomed mixing going on in the Executive Mansion.[14] "I was over at the White House one night," C. R. Smith, then president of American Airlines, recalled, "and the place was running over with blacks—you never saw so many blacks in your life. And I said to Mrs. Eleanor, I said, 'Looks like we're entertaining most of the blacks in the country tonight.' She said, 'Well, C. R., you must remember that the President is their President also.' "[15]

Mrs. Roosevelt's gestures of interest and concern made an impact on blacks who were unaccustomed to any recognition from the White House. Protecting the jobs of black servants impressed the editor of *Opportunity* as evidence that Mrs. Roosevelt was "sympathetic and interested in the well-being of [the Negro] race."[16] The First Lady's appearances at interracial gatherings and her willingness to pose for pictures with blacks, even in the face of public criticism, prompted praise from the *Afro-American*: "In our day there has never been a mistress of the White House so energetic, so brave, and so fired with the enthusiasm of service to the common people."[17] Were these responses out of proportion to the significance of the acts? One has to remember the racial climate: the unyielding patterns of segregation and discrimination and the persistent assumptions of black inferiority. Any public person who "would either speak out or act in any way" that broke from those patterns understandably evoked "devotion" from black Americans.[18]

Mrs. Roosevelt readily contributed her name or her money where they might do some good. When the Washington branch of the NAACP launched a membership campaign, the First Lady addressed a mass meeting to give it a boost. "The precedent-breaking Roosevelt family scored again," the *Afro-American* marveled. Mrs. Roosevelt "seemed as much at ease . . . as in her own home.

1934, Mar. 23, Apr. 27, May 11, 1935; White House Usher's Diary, Apr. 19, 1935, May 16, 1936.

[14] Lillian Rogers Parks, *My Thirty Years Backstairs at the White House* (New York, 1961), p. 264.

[15] C. R. Smith interview, Feb. 6, 1978, Eleanor Roosevelt Oral History Project, Franklin D. Roosevelt Library.

[16] Elmer A. Carter to Eleanor Roosevelt, Sept. 21, 1933, Franklin D. Roosevelt Papers, President's Personal File (PPF) 902 (hereafter cited as the FDR Papers).

[17] Editorial, *Afro-American*, May 23, 1936.

[18] Interview with Pauli Murray, July 1, 1977, Alexandria, Va.

4. In a widely noted departure from past practice, Eleanor Roosevelt was frequently photographed with black people. Here she visits the Vernon Nursery School in Los Angeles

Among the humble people she appeared as one of them."[19] When the Washington Urban League was first getting organized, she "was the first white person in Washington to give her check."[20] When the New York Urban League planned a theater benefit, she agreed to have her name included on the honorary committee.[21] Invariably, the simple fact of her involvement drew public attention to the cause.

Mrs. Roosevelt often addressed interracial audiences on the importance of racial progress.[22] The interdependence of the races was a recurrent theme: "one group cannot prosper while another is downtrodden." She stressed cooperation between whites and blacks: "The day of really working together has come . . . we must learn to work together regardless of race, creed or color." She held out a clear objective: "to wipe out [the] inequalities and injustices" that "handicapped" black Americans.[23] "Never before has a First Lady made a plea in behalf of fair play and equal opportunity for Negro citizens," *Opportunity* exulted after her address to the National Urban League's twenty-fifth anniversary conference in 1935. "The cause of the Negro is not a popular cause. And those who fight the Negroes' battles have always been the 'chosen few.' Mrs. Roosevelt's entry into the lists gives courage and hope to both black and white at a time when racial intolerance seems to be on the increase all over the world."[24]

The First Lady worked closely with black leaders. She met with

[19] *Afro-American*, Apr. 20, 27 (editorial), 1935.

[20] George W. Goodman to Harold Ickes, July 19, 1940, Department of the Interior Papers, Office Files of Harold L. Ickes, Box 9, Record Group 48, National Archives.

[21] Eleanor Roosevelt's secretary to Milton A. Smith, Nov. 29, 1939, ER Papers, Box 27.

[22] See, e.g., Mrs. Franklin D. Roosevelt, "The National Conference on the Education of Negroes," *Journal of Negro Education* III (Oct. 1934):573-75; Eleanor Roosevelt speech to the Urban League, Dec. 12, [1935], ER Papers, Box 3033 (should be in 3031 if FDR Library refiled properly); Mary McLeod Bethune to Eleanor Roosevelt, Dec. 1, 8, 1936, and Roosevelt to Bethune, Dec. 3, 1936, ibid., Box 1366, and Bethune to Roosevelt, Jan. 13, 1937, ibid., Box 1415, all in reference to the First Lady's appearance at the National Conference on the Problems of the Negro and Negro Youth in 1937; Walter White to Eleanor Roosevelt, Oct. 21, 1938, and [Malvina T. Scheider] to White, Oct. 27, 1938, ibid., Box 1482, and editorial, *Chicago Defender*, July 8, 1939, all in reference to her appearance at the NAACP's annual conference in 1939.

[23] Speech at Metropolitan AME Church in Washington, D.C., quoted in *Afro-American*, Apr. 20, 1935; speech to National Conference on the Education of Negroes, quoted in editorial, ibid., May 19, 1934; speech to National Urban League, printed as "The Negro and Social Change," *Opportunity* XIV (Jan. 1936):22.

[24] "First Lady," *Opportunity* XIV (Jan. 1936):5. For similar enthusiastic praise, see editorial, *Afro-American*, Dec. 21, 1935.

them at the White House,[25] learned from them, assisted them whenever possible by making speeches, inquired about their complaints, and interpreted their concerns to her husband. "The way we used to get things to the President," recalled E. Frederic Morrow, then a member of the NAACP staff, "was for [Walter] White to see if he could see Mrs. Roosevelt. . . . And she in turn would try to get her husband to do something about it."[26] Eleanor conferred with T. Arnold Hill on a number of occasions about Urban League projects and other matters relating to the welfare of blacks. Describing the "flagrant exploitation" of black domestic workers in the South, Hill explained on one occasion, "I write you because I feel certain that you will be moved to exert your influence to correct such practices."[27] White, one of the few people to address Mrs. Roosevelt by her first name,[28] broadened her racial horizons through gifts of such books as W.E.B. Du Bois's *Black Reconstruction* and Arthur Raper's *Preface to Peasantry* and regularly sent her clippings and letters on matters of mutual concern.[29] "She liked to talk things over with him," Joseph Lash has written; "—he clarified situations for her and helped her to see them more objectively."[30] She, in turn, provided him with inestimable support, so that at his worst moments, when he was overcome with hatred for white people, the thought of Mrs. Roosevelt was one of the few things that kept him from giving way entirely to bitterness and despair.[31]

The First Lady sometimes sought White's assistance in dealing

[25] Mrs. Roosevelt's first official appointment to discuss racial matters seems to have been a long evening meeting with a group of blacks concerned about black participation in the Arthurdale homestead project (White House Usher's Diary, Jan. 26, 1934; Lash, *Eleanor and Franklin*, p. 513). The White House Usher's Diary records private appointments with Walter White on Apr. 18, 1934, Sept. 28, 1934, Apr. 13, 1935, July 23, 1935, Jan. 17, 1936, May 20, 1937. There are also records of appointments with Crystal Bird Fauset, Ambrose Caliver, Benjamin E. Mays, Ralph J. Bunche, and Mary McLeod Bethune. See ibid., May 15, 1934, Oct. 16, 1934, Jan. 11, 1937, Apr. 22, 1937, May 15, 1940, June 5, 1940, Dec. 16, 1940.

[26] Interview with E. Frederic Morrow, Apr. 29, 1977, Princeton, N.J.

[27] T. Arnold Hill to Eleanor Roosevelt, Apr. 22, 1935, ER Papers, Box 68. See also Hill to Roosevelt, July 22, 1938, ibid., Box 1462.

[28] Roosevelt, "Some of My Best Friends Are Negro," p. 19. She spoke publicly of her friendship for White. See *Afro-American*, Apr. 20, 1935.

[29] Walter White to W.E.B. Du Bois, Sept. 13, 1935, in *The Correspondence of W.E.B. Du Bois*, vol. II, *Selections, 1934-1944*, ed. Herbert Aptheker (Amherst, Mass., 1976), p. 25; White to Eleanor Roosevelt, Jan. 13, 1937, ER Papers, Box 1446, Jan. 10, Feb. 4, 10, 1936, ibid., Box 1411.

[30] Lash, *Eleanor and Franklin*, p. 522.

[31] Poppy Cannon, *A Gentle Knight: My Husband, Walter White* (New York, 1956), p. 9.

with requests for aid from blacks. "Would you be good enough to see the man and advise Mrs. Roosevelt what should be done?" her secretary wrote on one occasion.[32] Before Mrs. Roosevelt responded to a black correspondent, she might ask White to "look . . . him up and find . . . out all you can about him."[33]

She was an important advocate. When she learned of complaints about discrimination in New Deal programs, or when blacks asked for her assistance in securing federal aid, she wrote to the administrator in charge of the appropriate agency to ask if something could be done. When White asked her to look into the problem of discrimination in relief, she forwarded his letter to Harry Hopkins and added her own message: "I wonder if you will watch the colored situation quite closely and let me know from time to time how things are going for these people?"[34] To Aubrey Williams, accompanying a request for federal aid for a new black high school in Morgantown, West Virginia, she wrote: "I realize it may not be possible to do anything of this kind. However, it does seem to me a very necessary thing—especially as there is so much feeling amongst the negroes that nothing has been done for them and that there has been great discrimination shown."[35]

To black leaders, the First Lady was the New Dealer most likely to intercede for racial justice.[36] Ordinary blacks, too, perceived her as the person most likely to expedite their requests. "If you can't help me," a woman told FDR, "write and let me know, so I can write Mrs. Roosevelt, for I am sure she can help me." "I read a Bout you doin so many things for the Pore so please help me and my children," a "poor colored woman" from Memphis wrote the First Lady. "Please write them here and let them give me work and something to eat." Blacks personalized the New

[32] Malvina T. Scheider to Walter White, July 15, 1935, National Association for the Advancement of Colored People Papers, Box C-418, Manuscript Division, Library of Congress (hereafter cited as the NAACP Papers).

[33] Malvina T. Scheider to Walter White, Dec. 30, 1935, ER Papers, Box 1362. See also Scheider to White, Oct. 16, 1934, and White to Scheider, Oct. 25, 1934, ibid., Box 1325.

[34] Walter White to Eleanor Roosevelt, Nov. 13, 1934; Eleanor Roosevelt to Harry Hopkins, Nov. 22, 1934, Records of the Federal Emergency Relief Administration, Box 19, Record Group 69, National Archives.

[35] Eleanor Roosevelt to Aubrey Williams, July 2, 1935, ER Papers, Box 671.

[36] Even so outspoken a New Deal critic as John P. Davis, executive secretary of the Joint Committee on National Recovery and later of the National Negro Congress, perceived the advantages of her intercession. See Report of the Executive Secretary, Joint Committee on National Recovery, Feb. 9, 1935, National Negro Congress Papers, Box 3 (microfilm reel 2), Schomburg Center for Research in Black Culture.

Deal, so that the First Lady was perceived as the dispenser of New Deal benefits. "An old colored widow" in Philadelphia, who could "neither read nor write" herself, instructed her granddaughter to write Mrs. Roosevelt to ask for her assistance: "Should the old folks pertion [pension] go into effect I would appreciate your putting my name on the list."[37] Each request for employment or assistance was forwarded to the appropriate agency for action.[38] The message that the President's wife was "referring it to the proper authority for investigation" could have been a polite evasion.[39] In Mrs. Roosevelt's case, it was a promise that she would use her influence in the interests of achieving racial justice.

The First Lady also put a great deal of pressure on her husband. "She took it to be her moral duty to . . . argue their [blacks'] causes with Father," her son Elliott has written.[40] Her efforts in the antilynching fight were the best known of her many intercessions in behalf of blacks, but they were by no means unique. Howard University and Freedmen's Hospital in Washington were among her special concerns. Appropriations for both institutions were made by Congress, and Mrs. Roosevelt never missed an opportunity to remind the President of the urgency of their needs.[41] When the NAACP or the Urban League asked Roosevelt for a word of support, their requests were often accompanied by a handwritten note from his wife. "This is a great chance to say some wise things to the Negro & to the rest of the nation!" she once advised; or, on another occasion, "I think this might be a chance for you to do something valuable for the colored people. It w[ou]ld be appreciated too."[42]

[37] G. James Fleming, "Some Reminiscences of Mrs. Roosevelt," *Crisis* LXX (Jan. 1963):17; Cleo Moultry to Eleanor Roosevelt, May 9, 1934, FERA Papers, Box 19; Hattie Phillips to Eleanor Roosevelt, May 6, 1934, ER Papers, Box 627.

[38] See, e.g., Ellen S. Woodward to Eleanor Roosevelt, Mar. 22, 1934, ER Papers, Box 639; Eleanor Roosevelt's secretary to Frances Perkins, Apr. 26, 1934, ibid., Box 627; Eleanor Roosevelt's secretary to Mrs. Henrietta Klotz, Oct. 25, 1934, ibid., Box 619; Owen A. Malady to Ellen S. Woodward, Aug. 16, 1935, and Ellen S. Woodward to Malvina Scheider, Aug. 19, 1935, ibid., Box 672.

[39] Eleanor Roosevelt's secretary to T. Arnold Hill, Sept. 9, 193[5?], ibid., Box 68.

[40] Elliott Roosevelt and James Brough, *A Rendezvous with Destiny: The Roosevelts of the White House* (1975; reprint ed., New York, 1976), p. 145.

[41] Tamara K. Hareven, *Eleanor Roosevelt: An American Conscience* (Chicago, 1968), p. 117.

[42] Handwritten note from Eleanor Roosevelt to Franklin D. Roosevelt on envelope addressed to FDR from NAACP but not postmarked or dated (typed version of her note is sent as a memorandum for the President, June 1, 1940), FDR Papers, PPF 1336; Memorandum re Vocational Opportunity Campaign, Mar. 20-27, 1938, attached to T. Arnold Hill to Eleanor Roosevelt, Jan. 20, 1938, ER Papers, Box 1462. She also sent Roosevelt literature about racial issues when it came across

Free from official responsibilities, and thus able to be "more unswervingly moral than Franklin,"[43] Eleanor could argue for action on the grounds that it was right, but she came up constantly against his more constrained sense of what was possible politically.[44] "While I often felt strongly on various subjects," she later wrote, "Franklin frequently refrained from supporting causes in which he believed, because of political realities."[45] Publicly she defended his decision about what he could and could not do.[46] Privately she sometimes agonized over his choices. Rexford Tugwell, who often commiserated with her over her inability to make much headway on the race problem, later wrote:

> Eleanor ... understood the necessities of politics, but she had many moments of doubt whether Franklin's compromises were worth the price. Sometimes she was seized with the conviction that they were wicked, and then she protested to him. He met her objections sometimes with explanation. Their long-common background made elaboration unnecessary and he could usually convince her—when he himself was convinced. When he was less sure that he had done the right and essential thing, he retreated into evasions. Even Eleanor had to grant a President some leeway. She had done her duty by protesting. She let it go at that. There were no high words. She was a quiet woman whose indignations, however sharp, were still understanding.[47]

Mrs. Roosevelt's behavior stirred up criticism, especially in the South. There was a familiar litany of complaints: "She goes around telling the Negroes they are as good as anyone else." "Wherever she has spoken the Negroes always act like they are white folks." "She preaches and practices social equality."[48] Her actions and

---

her desk—see, e.g., the Commission on Interracial Cooperation's pamphlet, *The Mob Still Rides: A Review of the Lynching Record, 1931-1935,* in FDR Papers, PPF 1820.

[43] Rexford G. Tugwell, *The Democratic Roosevelt: A Biography of Franklin D. Roosevelt* (Garden City, N.Y., 1957), p. 303.

[44] The distinction is drawn repeatedly between Mrs. Roosevelt's concern for morality, justice, and ideals, and the President's preoccupation with politics. See interviews with Earl Brown, June 29, 1977, New York City; George L.-P. Weaver, May 23, 1977, Washington, D.C.; Lawrence Hamm interview with Charles Matthews, July 17, 1979, Newark, N.J.

[45] Eleanor Roosevelt, *This I Remember* (New York, 1949), p. 161.

[46] See, for example, Roosevelt, "Some of My Best Friends Are Negro," p. 26.

[47] Interview with Rexford G. Tugwell, Feb. 7, 1977, Santa Barbara; Tugwell, *The Democratic Roosevelt,* p. 303.

[48] Quoted in Howard W. Odum, *Race and Rumors of Race: Challenge to American Crisis* (Chapel Hill, 1943), p. 81.

her reputation distressed the President's more conservative aides, a fact that she recognized. "They were afraid," she wrote, "that I would hurt my husband politically and socially. . . . There was no use in my trying to explain, because our basic values were very different, and since I was fond of them, I thought it better to preserve the amenities in our daily contacts."[49] Roosevelt himself was more relaxed about what she did and said. Sometimes he even joked about it. A southern governor once told him: "We don't really have any Negro issue in the South, Mr. President. It's white agitators from the Nawth who make all the trouble." The President smiled and said, "You mean Eleanor, don't you?" The governor nodded his assent.[50] The First Lady was usually free to speak her mind. When she would ask her husband, "Do you mind if I say what I think?" he would reply: "No, certainly not. You can say anything you want. I can always say, 'Well, that is my wife; I can't do anything about her.' " "I always used to think," Eleanor mused years later in an interview with Rexford Tugwell, that on sensitive issues like race, "Franklin used me so much as a trial balloon."[51]

Mrs. Roosevelt took the public position that her husband had never prevented her from following her conscience on racial matters. While often "he could not take a stand that would upset the South," he "never said that I could not take a stand." "Sometimes," she continued,

> after talks with my Negro friends and with their white friends too, I used to ask Franklin, "Do you mind if I do so and so." And he would answer: "I shall stand or fall on what I have been able to accomplish. You have a right to do what you think is right." . . . I was never asked by him not to do anything I wanted to do with [my Negro friends] or for them. Franklin had such a deep sense of justice and an over-riding wish to see all Americans treated as equals that he never prevented me from taking any stand even though I sometimes worried if my actions in regards to my friends would harm his campaigns.[52]

Franklin's stance on Eleanor's racial involvements was more complex than the picture she presented. Jonathan Daniels, who

---

[49] Roosevelt, *This I Remember*, p. 164.

[50] Quoted in Alfred Steinberg, *Mrs. R: The Life of Eleanor Roosevelt* (New York, 1958), p. 251.

[51] Rexford G. Tugwell interview with Eleanor Roosevelt, June 24, 1957, Hyde Park, N.Y., p. 16, transcript lent by Frank Freidel.

[52] Roosevelt, "Some of My Best Friends Are Negro," p. 26.

had ample opportunity to observe both of them, commented later that Mrs. Roosevelt "sometimes embarrassed the president . . . by some action she took which he couldn't quite repudiate but which he would've preferred had not arisen."[53] When Roosevelt felt it necessary, he exercised some restraint on his wife's public activities in the cause of racial advancement. The counsel to avoid the mass meeting against lynching as "political dynamite" is one example. On another occasion, at her husband's insistence, the First Lady declined Walter White's request that she be one of the sponsors of a report that he wanted to publish on an investigation of two lynchings.[54] Twice Mrs. Roosevelt turned down invitations to address the NAACP's annual conference after consulting with the President or one of his aides.[55] In none of these cases did she ever reveal publicly that her husband had restrained her from participating.

Other limits on the First Lady's racial stands came from her own personal racial vision. In the context of the 1930s, Mrs. Roosevelt was very much a racial liberal. However, although she was "strong for equal rights" during her early years in the White House, as Robert Weaver described her, she was "not at all fighting the issue of segregation."[56] Her reluctance to take on segregation stemmed, in part, from her unwillingness to challenge local laws and customs. When she entertained delinquents from the National Training School for Girls at a White House garden party, for example, the races were segregated while refreshments were served, following the practice at the school.[57] To critics, white and black alike, Mrs. Roosevelt's acquiescence in segregation was a "regrettable" example of "bad taste," an act of "utter unmorality."[58] "Social changes come gradually," she gently repri-

[53] Jonathan Daniels interview, Nov. 16, 1979, p. 12, Eleanor Roosevelt Oral History Project, Franklin D. Roosevelt Library.

[54] Joseph P. Lash, *Eleanor Roosevelt: A Friend's Memoir* (Garden City, N.Y., 1964), p. 133, n. 1.

[55] Roy Wilkins to Eleanor Roosevelt, May 20, 1935; G.G.T. memorandum for Mrs. Scheider, May 28, 1935; Walter White to Eleanor Roosevelt, June 10, 1935, ER Papers, Box 1362; White to Eleanor Roosevelt, Feb. 4, 1936; Clarence E. Pickett to Eleanor Roosevelt, Feb. 14, 1936; Eleanor Roosevelt to White, Feb. 19, 1936, ibid., Box 1411.

[56] Interview with Robert C. Weaver, Nov. 12, 1976, New York City.

[57] *New York Sunday News*, May 17, 1936, clipping in Roosevelt Administration Scrapbooks, vol. II, microfilm reel 16, Schomburg Center for Research in Black Culture.

[58] Editorials, *Philadelphia Tribune*, May 21, 1936, *New York Age*, May 23, 1936, clippings in Roosevelt Administration Scrapbooks, vol. II; Lisle Greenidge to Eleanor Roosevelt, May 23, 1936, ER Papers, Box 1381.

manded a Presbyterian churchman in New York. "As long as there are certain customs and laws you cannot overthrow even prejudices over night. While I live in the White House I must conform to the laws of the District of Columbia," under which the National Training School practiced segregation. "Therefore, I conformed to their rules and customs. . . . I am obliged to conform at least to the letter of the law and it would not seem right to do otherwise."[59]

In part, too, Mrs. Roosevelt's views on segregation reflected her sense of priorities. As she asserted on several occasions in the mid-1930s, the first objective of blacks should be equal opportunity; from that would follow equal rights.[60] Such matters as social relationships ought to "wait until certain people were given time to think them through and decide as individuals what they wished to do."[61] By the time that she left the White House, however, her racial liberalism had grown still further; steadfastly opposed to discrimination, she had become "strong against segregation" as well.[62]

The nature of Mrs. Roosevelt's racial vision also shows up in the advice that she gave to blacks. If she were a Negro, she wrote in *Negro Digest* in 1943, she "would not do too much demanding." "I would take every chance that came my way to prove my quality and my ability," she continued, "and if recognition was slow, I would continue to prove myself, knowing that in the end good performance has to be acknowledged." She always counseled patience and persistence. "I would try to remember that unfair and unkind treatment will not harm me if I do not let it touch my spirit. Evil emotions injure the man or woman who harbors them so I would try to fight down resentment, the desire for revenge and bitterness."[63] She took the optimistic view that, "if only different races knew each other better, they could live peaceably together,"[64] and she counseled that blacks and whites had to "learn to work together," for it was impossible for whites to move forward if blacks were oppressed: "We go ahead together or we go

---

[59] Eleanor Roosevelt to Lisle Greenidge, June 3, 1936, ER Papers, Box 1381.

[60] Roosevelt, "The National Conference on the Education of Negroes," p. 573; "First Lady Speaks," *Crisis* XLII (June 1935):184; Eleanor Roosevelt, "If You Ask Me," *Negro Digest* VII (July 1949):20.

[61] Eleanor Roosevelt, "Freedom: Promise or Fact," *Negro Digest* I (Oct. 1943):9.

[62] Weaver interview.

[63] Roosevelt, "Freedom: Promise or Fact," p. 9.

[64] Eleanor Roosevelt speech to the Urban League, Dec. 12, [1935], ER Papers, Box 3033 (should be in 3031).

down together."[65] "Even with her sympathies, she could not really understand . . . the depth of the fire that was motivating the protest against humiliation and degradation," reflected Pauli Murray, a severe critic who became her friend. That she could admonish blacks not to push too hard or too fast, "that she could still be cautious, was some indication of her own limitations."[66]

Occasional slips betrayed that even Mrs. Roosevelt was susceptible to racial slurs or stereotypes. She commented on more than one occasion that blacks were "by nature" endowed with "certain gifts," among them "an appreciation of art and of music and of rhythm."[67] When she acknowledged a picture of triplets named Franklin, Delano, and Roosevelt, she picked up the phrase of the emergency relief administrator who had sent it and described the children as "little pickaninnies."[68] The reference drew a banner, front-page headline in the *Afro-American*, which was dismayed at her "bad taste."[69] "Darky," too, was still part of her vocabulary; as she explained to a young black woman who had written of her distress at Mrs. Roosevelt's use of "the 'hated' and humiliating term," " 'Darky' was used by my Georgia great aunt as a term of affection and I have always considered it in that light. I am sorry if it hurt you. What do you prefer?"[70] When the *Afro-American* took Mrs. Roosevelt to task over the use of the term in a magazine article, she apologized and said she would not use it again. But even as late as 1940, she told some of her favorite "darky" stories in public speeches.[71]

The First Lady was, after all, influenced by her background. As Kenneth Clark, who came to know her later, put it, she was "pretty much a product of her class—she was sensitive, she believed in justice and decency, etc. I always felt, though, that she believed in gratitude. She believed that blacks should be grateful. I never had the feeling, as much as I liked her, that she really

[65] Roosevelt, "The National Conference on the Education of Negroes," p. 575.
[66] Murray interview.
[67] Roosevelt, "The National Conference on the Education of Negroes," p. 574. See also a similar statement to Lizzie McDuffie quoted in *Afro-American*, Oct. 31, 1936, clipping in McDuffie Papers, Box 1, Negro Collection, Trevor Arnett Library, Atlanta University.
[68] Ellen S. Woodward to Malvina T. Scheider, Dec. 18, 1934; Eleanor Roosevelt to Woodward, Dec. 20, 1934, ER Papers, Box 672.
[69] *Afro-American*, Jan. 19, 26 (editorial), 1935.
[70] Lash, *Eleanor and Franklin*, p. 522. The quoted exchange is with Esther Cary, Apr. 13, 1937.
[71] *Afro-American*, May 1 (editorial), 8, 1937; Lash, *Eleanor Roosevelt*, p. 198. In later years, she avoided the expression.

understood the fundamental social, ethical, moral aspects of the problem. I think she was much more sentimental about it. She was doing good for blacks and other deprived people."[72] Pauli Murray expressed it this way: "Mrs. Roosevelt was basically . . . a Victorian woman. She came out of, she grew to maturity in, the late nineteenth century . . . at the very time when racism as a developing kind of systematic sociology was . . . rising to its height. . . . Considering where she came from, she moved . . . to the very outer limits of her capacity." While "she [n]ever gave up a very well-embedded sense of her own racial identity, . . . her sense of justice and her sense of compassion, and her capacity to make individual friendships . . . helped her . . . transcend [the] rather sharp sense of race that she had."[73]

However, when all is said and done, the First Lady's record in general amply justifies the nearly universal judgment, as the editor of the Urban League's magazine put it, that "the Negroes in America have a feeling that you can be numbered among their friends."[74] She was "the different person of her time," Basil Paterson remarked, "the outstanding, open-minded, unfettered, thoughtful person," distinguished by her humanitarianism, willingness to fight for the rights of the less privileged, courage to speak forthrightly in behalf of blacks, and empathy for ordinary people.[75] By her conduct, she gave hope to people who found in her an unusual responsiveness in official circles. "Even though I may never have word of any sort from you," wrote a young black woman in Atlanta who appealed to her for aid, "I wish to thank you for showing those of us who are coming along the way in these bewildering times, how fine a woman can be."[76] "Never before in the history of this country has there been in the White House a nobler, a fairer and a more courageous First Lady than Mrs. Franklin D. Roosevelt," the *Chicago Defender* said. "She has been consistently uncompromising and fearless on broad humanitarian questions. She has stood like the Rock of Gibraltar against pernicious encroachments on the rights of helpless mi-

[72] Interview with Kenneth B. Clark, May 17, 1977, New York City.

[73] Murray interview.

[74] Elmer A. Carter to Eleanor Roosevelt, Sept. 21, 1933, FDR Papers, PPF 902.

[75] Interview with Basil Paterson, Dec. 1, 1976, New York City; Walter White, *How Far the Promised Land?* (New York, 1955), p. 180; "In Memoriam: Anna Eleanor Roosevelt, 1884-1962," *Negro Digest* XII (Dec. 1962):34; *New York Times*, Nov. 8, 1962, p. 38; editorial, *Norfolk Journal and Guide*, Nov. 17, 1962.

[76] Typed "Report on the Handling of Mrs. Roosevelt's Mail," attached to Florence Kerr to Eleanor Roosevelt, Apr. 13, 1939, ER Papers, Box 754.

norities."[77] Or, as a woman in Chicago commented at the time of Mrs. Roosevelt's death, "I considered her an engineer who built bridges over which all men could walk with dignity."[78]

Having someone in official circles in Washington whom they could trust was a unique experience for black Americans in the twentieth century. Whether or not Eleanor Roosevelt was able to affect policy, she projected a sense of genuine concern that had a real impact on the way black Americans perceived the New Deal. In fact her function was more symbolic than substantive; on fundamental issues such as lynching and disfranchisement, she was unable to change the way in which the New Deal dealt with blacks.[79] But at a time when there had previously been neither positive symbol nor substance, the First Lady helped significantly to shape the black response to the New Deal.

[77] Editorial, *Chicago Defender*, Mar. 4, 1939.
[78] Quoted in ibid., Nov. 10, 1962.
[79] Nevertheless, Carl T. Rowan has observed, "Millions view Eleanor Roosevelt as one of the major reasons for the change in status of colored people, particularly American Negroes, in the last quarter century." Rowan, "The Life of Eleanor Roosevelt," *New York Post*, Mar. 20, 1958, clipping in Eleanor Roosevelt folder, vertical file, Schomburg Center for Research in Black Culture.

CHAPTER VII · *The Black Cabinet*

Perhaps the most important racial symbol of the New Deal years was the Black Cabinet. The Cabinet was a loosely coordinated group of racial advisers on the staffs of various New Deal agencies and regular departments of government. It served two substantive functions: it brought into government service a larger group of talented black men and women at significantly higher positions than ever before; and it positioned black people for the first time to work from within the government to influence federal policies as they affected members of the race. More important, probably, was the Black Cabinet's symbolic function: it signified to black Americans that the Roosevelt administration cared about their lot.

Such a description conveys the impression that the administration deliberately created the Black Cabinet to appeal to black Americans. That was not the case. The administration had made possible the appointment of racial advisers. There its direct responsibility for the Cabinet ended. It had once tried to coordinate the work of racial advisers through the Interdepartmental Group on the Special Problems of the Negro, but the group had foundered not long after its creation in 1934. The Cabinet resembled the group in one significant respect: both assumed that it was useful to share ideas and develop common strategies to improve the New Deal's treatment of blacks. But the differences between the Cabinet and the group were more striking. The Cabinet was neither formally constituted nor recognized as an arm of the administration. It consisted not of officially designated representatives of the various departments and agencies, but of an informal network of blacks in government who came together at their own initiative in the belief that they could help each other advance the interests of the race. The Cabinet met informally and irregularly. It perceived its function to be much more to develop strategies to influence policy than to ascertain facts. And it met a different fate:

whereas the group had sunk quietly into inactivity, the Cabinet enjoyed prestige and at least symbolic importance.[1]

The Black Cabinet—or, as its members sometimes called it, the "Federal Council on Negro Affairs"[2]—does not lend itself to systematic analysis. Documenting its history is difficult at best, for it left virtually no minutes of its meetings or records of its collective actions. There is not even agreement about the identity of its members.[3] According to the best recollections of some of those most involved in its deliberations, the Cabinet functioned on two levels. The group that was publicly identified as the Black Cabinet consisted of the various racial advisers as well as prominent black officeholders—such as William H. Hastie, assistant solicitor in the Department of the Interior—whose government jobs were not defined in terms of racial functions. This group, assembled and led by Mary McLeod Bethune, began to meet in August 1936, usually at Mrs. Bethune's office or in her apartment. "Let us forget the particular office each one of us holds," she exhorted her young colleagues at the first session, "and think how we might, in a cooperative way, get over to the masses the things that are being done and the things that need to be done. We must think in terms as a 'whole' for the greatest service of our people."[4] A second group, younger, smaller in number, and more selective,

[1] Jane R. Motz, "The Black Cabinet: Negroes in the Administration of Franklin D. Roosevelt" (Master's thesis, University of Delaware, 1964), p. 21.

[2] Alfred Edgar Smith, "Educational Programs for the Improvement of Race Relations: Government Agencies," *Journal of Negro Education* XIII (Summer 1944):364. Mrs. Bethune referred to it as the Federal Council of Negro Affairs. See National Council of Negro Women minutes, Nov. 26, 1938, National Council of Negro Women Papers, Series 2, Box 1, Folder 4, National Archives for Black Women's History, Washington, D.C. (hereafter cited as the NCNW Papers).

[3] See, for instance, *Pittsburgh Courier*, Apr. 7, 1934; William A. H. Birnie, "Black Brain Trust," *American Magazine* CXXXV (Jan. 1943):37; Motz, "Black Cabinet," pp. 23-25. The most complete list of high-level black federal employees during the New Deal is the typescript, "Negroes Appointed to Federal Positions, 1933-1941," lent by W. J. Trent, Jr.

[4] Interview with Robert C. Weaver, Nov. 12, 1976, New York City; Debra Newman interview with Lawrence A. Oxley, Apr. 23, 1973, Lawrence A. Oxley Papers, Box 1385, Records of the United States Employment Service, Record Group 183, National Archives; Frank Smith Horne interview, Sept. 4, 1968, p. 20, Civil Rights Documentation Project, Ralph J. Bunche Oral History Collection, Moorland-Spingarn Research Center, Howard University; Motz, "Black Cabinet," pp. 22, 26. The date of the first meeting is established from minutes of Aug. 7, 1936, cited in Elaine M. Smith, "Mary McLeod Bethune and the National Youth Administration" (Paper delivered at the National Archives Conference on Women's History, Washington, D.C., Apr. 23, 1976), p. 19, and n. 58, p. 43. Mrs. Bethune is quoted in the same minutes. Although the group began meeting in 1936, the black press started using the term "black cabinet" to describe the racial advisers in 1934. See, for example, *Afro-American* and *Pittsburgh Courier*, both Apr. 7.

was convened by Robert Weaver and met on an irregular basis, usually at Weaver's house. Mrs. Bethune was kept informed of the government matters discussed, but she did not attend, mainly because her presence would have inhibited the drinking and poker-playing that comprised the social life of the group.[5]

The Black Cabinet, in Hastie's words, "was a council to which we could turn with our own problems." Each member shared common concerns—as Weaver put it: "getting jobs," "getting better breaks," "getting administrative changes," and securing "equitable participation of blacks in the programs with which we were associated." The group provided a forum to discuss problems, share experiences, and pool brain power. It functioned in an ad hoc fashion. When an issue came up, Lawrence A. Oxley recalled, "We would call up and say let's have a little meeting. . . . We knew we'd come up with some kind of an answer."[6]

The "answer," Weaver said, might take the form of a "united front," wherein various of the racial advisers would take the same proposal to the heads of their agencies. It might call for preparation by other members of the Black Cabinet of background materials which Mrs. Bethune could use on a mission to the White House.[7] It might involve plotting strategy to affect legislation in Congress. It might involve leaking information about discriminatory practices or pending policy decisions to the black press and black organizations, who could "turn on the political heat when ordered."[8]

The Black Cabinet regularly alerted their friends in the press to any development "where there was a black angle," Louis Martin, then editor of the *Michigan Chronicle*, recalled. They would "always give us a line" on what they wanted, and the newspapermen would respond with editorials and news articles helpful to the black cause. Funneling ideas to church groups and labor organizations served the same function. The result—the appearance of substantial, spontaneous public concern—helped members of the Cabinet to get things done.[9] The chain reaction was

[5] Weaver interview; Motz, "Black Cabinet," p. 27.

[6] Hastie quoted in Motz, "Black Cabinet," p. 71: Weaver interview; Oxley interview with Debra Newman.

[7] Weaver interview.

[8] Birnie, "Black Brain Trust," p. 37 (source of the quotation); Smith, "Educational Programs for the Improvement of Race Relations," pp. 364-65.

[9] Interviews with Louis E. Martin, May 13, 1977, Chicago; George L.-P. Weaver, May 23, 1977, Washington, D.C.; Robert Weaver; W. J. Trent, Jr., Dec. 8, 1976, New York City; Motz, "Black Cabinet," p. 54.

really the result of careful planning, but it looked deceptively simple. In the WPA, for example, the racial adviser, Alfred Edgar Smith, would report what he knew about discrimination in relief programs to the NAACP and the National Urban League, who would use their "inside information" to "raise hell with the President." The response to the resulting furor? Smith, previously unable to make headway in countering the discrimination that he had covertly publicized, would now be told by his superiors in the WPA "to do something about it."[10] Such inside information, selectively disseminated, served, too, as "complaint ammunition" for black spokesmen to use when they went to the White House.[11]

The Black Cabinet as such had no traceable impact on policy. Smith maintained that it "never accomplished anything" as a collective entity; whatever it achieved "was done individually" by its members.[12] Such an evaluation may overlook the intangible assets that are harder to measure—the value, for example, of systematic sharing of ideas and experiences with people in similar circumstances. But it is certainly true that the tangible accomplishments of the Black Cabinet need to be assessed by looking at the way that the individual racial advisers functioned in their own domains. Here the results varied, depending on the imagination and skill of the racial adviser and the receptivity of the agency head for whom he worked.[13]

The most important member of the Black Cabinet, in terms of visibility and influence, was Mary McLeod Bethune. She presented a dramatically different figure from her young colleagues. She was three decades older than Weaver and Hastie, for instance. She was very dark skinned, with pronounced Negroid features, in stark contrast to the light skins and "white" features of most of the others. She was the daughter of a poor southern sharecropper, the only one of seventeen brothers and sisters to secure an education, while her young colleagues were the sons of civil servants, ministers, lawyers, and educators. Her higher education consisted

[10] Interview with Alfred Edgar Smith, May 24, 1977, Washington, D.C.

[11] Smith, "Educational Programs for the Improvement of Race Relations," p. 365.

[12] Smith interview.

[13] Another important ingredient in the effective functioning of the racial adviser was the existence of established procedures for checking up on the use of federal funds. Whether such procedures existed depended on the agency head. Trent interview.

5. Mary McLeod Bethune

6. The Black Cabinet. In the front row, Robert C. Weaver is third from the left; Mrs. Bethune stands between Frank Horne and Lawrence A. Oxley. William J. Thompkins, who, as recorder of deeds, was one of the few blacks to hold a political appointment in the Roosevelt administration, is next to Oxley. In the back row, Alfred Edgar Smith is fourth from the right

of two years at the Moody Bible Institute in Chicago; all of her principal associates in the Black Cabinet were college graduates, and all had done at least some graduate work. Robert Weaver and his associate, Booker T. McGraw, who later became the race relations adviser in the United States Housing Authority, both held doctorates in economics from Harvard. William Hastie had graduated from the Harvard Law School. Frank Horne, who came into government as an assistant to Mrs. Bethune and who also later became the race relations adviser in the United States Housing Authority, had earned the degree of doctor of optometry from the Northern Illinois College of Ophthalmology. William J. Trent, Jr., who replaced Robert Weaver as the race relations adviser in the Public Works Administration and served in the same capacity in its successor agency, the Federal Works Administration, held an MBA from the Wharton School of Finance. Alfred Edgar Smith held a master's degree from Howard University, where Campbell C. Johnson, who in 1940 became the adviser to the head of Selective Service, had earned a law degree.[14] While many of the younger men perceived themselves as Democrats or independents

[14] Motz, "Black Cabinet," pp. 14-18, 28-29.

from the start, Mrs. Bethune was a Republican who changed her party allegiance because of Franklin Roosevelt.[15]

There were striking differences, too, in personal style and perceptions of one's role. Mrs. Bethune, a perceptive historian of the Black Cabinet has written, "had an almost mystical sense of identity with the Negro masses. She spoke as a prophet rather than as a trained leader. She was serenely confident that she represented the real will of her people as well as their best interests." The other members of the Black Cabinet, in contrast,

> saw themselves as part of an elite because of their positions, which they felt made them responsible for making decisions on behalf of the Negro public. . . . Their educational and professional experience trained them to analyze and evaluate matters of racial policy. They had the advantage of governmental status and access to other privileged members of the Negro governmental, academic and organizational elite. Therefore they did not hesitate to make decisions based on their own judgments of the best interests of their race. Even when Negroes seemed to prefer other or lesser goals, the Black Cabineteers were sure of their ability to decide for them what was to be sought.[16]

Mrs. Bethune was an imperious, matriarchal figure, "mother confessor to the whole group."[17] Her younger male associates called her "Ma Bethune" and described themselves as her "boys." But there was nothing gentle about her maternal style. One of the members of the Cabinet characterized her as "a dictator, a potentate."[18] She exercised power with obvious relish. Clarence Mitchell recalled an occasion in Washington when Mrs. Bethune summoned churchmen, governmental officials, representatives of the organizations for racial advancement, and "political operators of one sort or another." She "started her speech by saying, 'A lot of people have asked, why are we here?' And she said, 'You are here because I called you to come. And whenever I want you to come I will call you, and I expect you to come whether I want anything important or not.'" "I was stunned," Mitchell said,

[15] Rackham Holt, *Mary McLeod Bethune: A Biography* (Garden City, N.Y., 1964), p. 201.

[16] Motz, "Black Cabinet," pp. 72-73.

[17] Birnie, "Black Brain Trust," p. 95.

[18] Motz, "Black Cabinet," p. 22. The characterizations come from her interviews with members of the Black Cabinet; the quotation is from James C. Evans. See p. 90, n. 4.

"because I couldn't imagine anyone being able to get away with that sort of thing, but she did."[19]

She could get away with it because of her personal force and her unique access to the White House. Alone among members of the Black Cabinet, she was able to command an audience with the President or Mrs. Roosevelt on request, and she enjoyed their respect and—in the case of the First Lady—personal friendship. Her relationship with Mrs. Roosevelt began in 1927, when she met the future First Lady at a luncheon at the Roosevelts' home in New York for leaders of the National Council of Women of the U.S.A.[20] When she entered the room, as Mrs. Bethune later told the story, she hesitated: the other women were white; a number of them were from the South. Sara Delano Roosevelt came to her rescue. "That grand old lady," Mrs. Bethune wrote,

. . . took my arm and seated me to the right of Eleanor Roosevelt, in the seat of honor! I can remember, too, how the faces of the Negro servants lit up with pride when they saw me seated at the center of that imposing gathering. . . . From that moment my heart went out to Mrs. James Roosevelt. I visited her at her home many times subsequently, and our friendship became one of the most treasured relationships of my life. As a result of my affection for her mother-in-law, my friendship with Eleanor Roosevelt soon ripened into a close and understanding mutual feeling.[21]

Mrs. Bethune's formal relationship with the President began in late April 1936, when, as a member of the National Advisory Committee of the National Youth Administration, she went to the White House with Aubrey Williams and other committee members to report on the impact of the NYA on minority groups. She departed from her formal report and lectured Roosevelt passionately on the situation of blacks in the Depression. She implored him to do better and to use his influence to open more opportunities for her people.[22] "We have been taking the crumbs for a long time," she exclaimed. "We have been eating the feet

---

[19] Interview with Clarence M. Mitchell, Jr., Oct. 29, 1976, Washington, D.C.

[20] Holt, *Mary McLeod Bethune*, p. 178.

[21] Mary McLeod Bethune, "My Secret Talks With FDR," *Ebony* IV (Apr. 1949), in *The Negro in Depression and War: Prelude to Revolution, 1930-1945*, ed. Bernard Sternsher (Chicago, 1969), p. 57.

[22] The meeting occurred on Apr. 28. See Smith, "Mary McLeod Bethune," p. 8. See also Holt, *Mary McLeod Bethune*, pp. 192-93; Emma Gelders Sterne, *Mary McLeod Bethune* (New York, 1957), pp. 227-28.

and head of the chicken long enough. The time has come when we want some white meat."[23] The President, by Mrs. Bethune's account so moved that he had tears in his eyes, was so impressed that he decided soon afterwards to ask her to head a newly created Division of Negro Affairs in the National Youth Administration. "Aubrey," FDR said to the NYA administrator when he brought Mrs. Bethune back to the White House to discuss her appointment, "Mrs. Bethune is a great woman. I believe in her because she has her feet on the ground; not only on the ground, but deep down in the ploughed soil."[24]

As Mrs. Bethune told the story, she and the President developed a warm and candid working relationship. Her own accounts provide the only direct evidence of it, and they doubtless contain a measure of the hyperbole to which she was given. Still, to the extent that Roosevelt paid attention to her, the two seem to have gotten on well. Shortly after Roosevelt's death, Mrs. Bethune described one of their early private meetings: "I can see him now as he stretched forth his gracious hand in greeting," she wrote. "I can hear the pathos of his voice as he said: 'Hello, Mrs. Bethune. Come in and sit down and tell me how your people are doing.'

"I poured out of my heart and mind and into his ears the needs—the desires and aspirations of my people. Since that visit, we have seen the path of our opportunities broadened into a wide thoroughfare. He believed truly that all men should have equality of opportunity regardless of race, creed or color."[25]

Mrs. Bethune enthusiastically supported Roosevelt. He, in turn, apparently admired her directness and fervor and respected her judgment. He sometimes asked her for advice about the best way to deal with race-related problems. Where he could, he used his influence to further the causes that she championed.[26] Mrs. Beth-

---

[23] Quoted in Holt, *Mary McLeod Bethune*, p. 193. For Mrs. Bethune's version of the conversation, see Bethune, "My Secret Talks With FDR," pp. 57-58.

[24] Bethune, "My Secret Talks With FDR," pp. 58-59. The President is quoted on p. 59.

[25] Mary McLeod Bethune, "A Tribute to Franklin Delano Roosevelt," *Aframerican Woman's Journal* (June 1945):8, 23, NCNW Papers, Series 13, Box 1, Folder 17.

[26] Holt, *Mary McLeod Bethune*, pp. 201, 203; Edwin R. Embree, *13 Against the Odds* (New York, 1944), p. 19. Mrs. Bethune estimated that she saw the President "six or seven times each year." See Bethune, "My Secret Talks With FDR," p. 63. While her estimate may have been true for the war years, the recorded appointments were less frequent in the 1930s. For some of them, see White House Usher's Diary, Feb. 11, 1937, Jan. 12, 1940, Franklin D. Roosevelt Library; *Afro-American*, Feb. 20, 1937, Jan. 21, 1939; and Mrs. Bethune's card in the index file kept by the White House Social Entertainments Office, Records of the Chief of Social Entertainments, Franklin D. Roosevelt Library.

une recounted an occasion in 1937 when she went to the White House to implore Roosevelt to stop Congress from cutting $100,000 earmarked for higher education from the NYA appropriation: "I became so excited that I shook my finger in the President's face. 'Think what a terrible tragedy it would be for America,' I cried, 'if by this action by a committee of Congress, Negroes would be deprived of the leadership of skilled and trained members of their race!' Suddenly I realized what I was doing, and stopped, staring embarrassedly at my finger now pointing at the President's nose. . . . 'Oh, Mr. President,' I said, 'I did not mean to become so emotional.' FDR smiled quietly. 'I understand thoroughly, Mrs. Bethune,' he said. 'My heart is with you.' " Roosevelt promised to see what he could do, and Congress subsequently voted to continue the full appropriation.[27]

Not all of Mrs. Bethune's requests were that simple, however. She also asked Roosevelt to do things that he regarded as politically unfeasible—as, for example, to act on antilynching legislation and voting rights, or to appoint more blacks to federal positions. Not surprisingly, he demurred.[28]

Mrs. Bethune's relationship with the First Lady was closer, more personal, and less complicated by political pressures. They helped each other in important ways. For Eleanor Roosevelt, Mary McLeod Bethune was a source of information and contacts in worlds—race and education, for instance—where she was a comparative stranger. For Mrs. Bethune, the First Lady was an influential source of support and a means of access to circles of power.[29]

Mrs. Bethune "was practically hand and glove with Mrs. Roosevelt," her NYA associate, Frank Horne, recalled; she "was in the White House as often as need be." "You tell me what needs to be done," she would tell him, "and I'll see that it gets in touch with Mrs. Roosevelt."[30] A housing project which had been promised for blacks in Mrs. Bethune's own city of Daytona Beach illustrates the point. The plans were on the books—167 units were to be built, and $500,000 had been allocated. But nothing happened. In 1939, Mrs. Bethune called Mrs. Roosevelt. The First Lady's intercession with the administrator of the Federal Housing Administration, Nathan Straus, finally got the project moving.[31] To blacks in the 1930s, it appeared—and probably with little

[27] Bethune, "My Secret Talks With FDR," p. 60.
[28] Smith, "Mary McLeod Bethune," pp. 21-23.
[29] Ibid., pp. 15, 24; Holt, *Mary McLeod Bethune*, p. 219.
[30] Horne interview, pp. 20, 16.
[31] Smith, "Mary McLeod Bethune," p. 24.

exaggeration—that when something needed to be done for them, "Mary McLeod would tell Eleanor, and Eleanor would get somebody to get it done."[32]

Because of her access to the White House, Mrs. Bethune had the influence to convene two National Conferences on the Problems of the Negro and Negro Youth and to recruit Eleanor Roosevelt to address both gatherings. The first conference met at the Labor Department in January 1937. It brought together governmental officials and representatives from civic, fraternal, and professional organizations, religious groups, educational institutions, and the press. They offered recommendations for specific federal action to meet the chief needs of the black Americans: "increased opportunity for employment and employment security, adequate educational and recreational facilities, improved health and housing conditions and security of life and equal protection under the law."[33] The second conference, held in 1939 and much larger than the first, assessed developments in the intervening two years and offered similar recommendations. In both instances, Mrs. Bethune herself presented the conference reports to Roosevelt, and her office distributed thousands of copies within the government and to the public.[34]

Between these two conferences, Mrs. Bethune brought the National Council of Negro Women to the White House for a Conference on the Participation of Negro Women and Children in Federal Programs. She told the assemblage how the plans came about:

> I went in and I saw Mrs. Roosevelt.... I asked her to sponsor and to back a conference of this type that we might come, not to put on . . . a meeting at the Odd Fellows Hall, or meet over here or there, or at one of our Methodist or Baptist Churches, but that we might come under the roof of the Government as real citizens to share whatever it has to offer and to study our own situation and have a chance to present our findings to Mrs.

[32] Interview with William Holmes Borders, June 10, 1977, Atlanta.

[33] "Recommendations of the National Conference on the Problems of the Negro and Negro Youth," Jan. 18, 1937, Franklin D. Roosevelt Papers, President's Personal File (PPF) 4266, Franklin D. Roosevelt Library (hereafter cited as the FDR Papers); Smith, "Mary McLeod Bethune," pp. 20-21. For Mrs. Roosevelt's participation, see White House Usher's Diary, Jan. 6, 1937.

[34] Smith, "Mary McLeod Bethune," p. 20; "Second National Conference on the Problems of the Negro and Negro Youth," Jan. 12, 1939, NCNW Papers, Series 4, Box 2, Folders 27 and 28; *New York Times*, Jan. 13, 1939, p. 6. For Mrs. Roosevelt's participation, see White House Usher's Diary, Jan. 12, 1939.

Roosevelt . . . and to the heads of the departments of the Government representing the work particularly among women and children.

The First Lady "saw the importance of such a function."[35]

Mrs. Bethune's "tremendous" influence in the Roosevelt administration depended not only—indeed, perhaps not so much—on what she could persuade the President and the First Lady to do; nor did it extend only to the White House. Equally important was the way that others perceived her relationship with the Roosevelts. "Often it wasn't so much of what you had in the way of authorization by the President, but to some extent it was what people *thought* you had by way of authorization," Clarence Mitchell explained. "And she was very good at that. She had a way of moving into almost every part of the federal establishment and talking with the top people, who, because they knew that she and Mrs. Roosevelt were friends and more or less assumed that, well, maybe she could also get to the boss, . . . would cooperate with her."[36] The Tammany Hall leader, J. Raymond Jones, called her "one of the best" black politicians he knew.[37]

Even if Mrs. Bethune could not cause substantial progress on racial matters, her very presence was a forceful and visible reminder that blacks were part of the New Deal constituency. She was "a symbol of Negroes' aspirations," the president of Howard University, Mordecai Johnson, said.[38] Young blacks idolized her; even those who had trouble identifying other outstanding members of the race knew about the lady who "was head of a government agency that helped poor Negro children to go through school."[39] She, in turn, perceived herself as an ambassador of her people. After one occasion at the White House, she wrote, "It is for me a sacred trust so to touch these fine people as to interpret to them the dreams and the hopes and the problems of my long-suffering people." It was a lonely role to be the only black, as she

[35] "White House Conference of the National Council of Negro Women," Apr. 4, 1938, NCNW Papers, Series 4, Box 1, Folder 4. On Mrs. Roosevelt's attendance, see White House Usher's Diary, Apr. 4, 1938. Two years later, the First Lady hosted a White House tea for the National Council. See ibid., Oct. 25, 1940.

[36] Mitchell interview.

[37] Hilton B. Clark interview with J. Raymond Jones, pt. 3, Mar. 29, 1974, p. 12.

[38] Quoted in B. Joyce Ross, "Mary McLeod Bethune and the National Youth Administration: A Case Study of Power Relationships in the Black Cabinet of Franklin D. Roosevelt," *Journal of Negro History* LX (Jan. 1975):28.

[39] E. Franklin Frazier, *Negro Youth at the Crossways: Their Personality Development in the Middle States* (Washington, D.C., 1940), pp. 177-78 (quotation is on p.178). The description is that of one of the young people Frazier interviewed.

confided to her diary after a tea at the White House for women government workers. But "then I thought how vitally important it was that I be here, to help these others get used to seeing us in high places." "I know so well why I *must* be here, *must* go to tea at the White House," she continued. "To remind them always that we belong here, we are a part of this America."[40]

Mrs. Bethune's visibility and connections entitled her to preside over the Black Cabinet and to represent them in entreaties to the White House. Within the Cabinet, in spite of her imperiousness, she recognized her limitations, and she turned to her young associates to analyze problems and to develop proposals which she could then articulate.[41] While she remained the most important public figure in the group, Robert Weaver increasingly became the most influential person in their internal dealings.[42] And, in her absence, he took charge of Cabinet meetings. As he explained the division of labor, "Mrs. Bethune, as time went on, was the spokesman, I was the secretariat. I got the guys together and prepared the policy memorandums." But she was the front, the figurehead, and the public spokesman. "She had the contacts; she was a dramatic person. It would have been foolish for somebody to have attempted to displace her."[43]

Carrying out the functions of a racial adviser meant waging "war on many fronts." The adviser was concerned, first, with "influencing agency policy" in the interests of blacks.[44] In the main, that meant seeking maximum participation for blacks in federal programs. While most of the racial advisers abhorred segregation, their efforts were focused primarily on ending discrimination in government assistance. The average black American in the 1930s

---

[40] *Pittsburgh Courier*, June 5, 1937, quoted in Smith, "Mary McLeod Bethune," p. 16; diary entry of Dec. 9, 1937, quoted in Holt, *Mary McLeod Bethune*, p. 205.
[41] Motz, "Black Cabinet," p. 22.
[42] See, e.g., Mary McLeod Bethune to Robert C. Weaver, Apr. 24, 1940, Robert C. Weaver Papers, Box 6, Schomburg Center for Research in Black Culture.
[43] Robert Weaver interview. See also Horne interview, p. 16.
[44] Smith, "Educational Programs for the Improvement of Race Relations," p. 365. See also Horne interview, p. 16; Pauline Redmond Coggs, "Race Relations Advisers—Quislings or Messiahs?" *Opportunity* XXI (July 1943):112-14; typescript, "A Statement as of December 1935"; typescript, "The Function of the Office of Adviser on Negro Affairs," n.d.; untitled typescript re activities of Adviser on Negro Affairs (1937?), all in William J. Trent, Jr. Papers, Box 1, Manuscript Division, Moorland-Spingarn Research Center, Howard University. Robert Weaver left his teaching job to go to work for the Interior Department precisely because he expected to be able "to influence the operation of the recovery program as it affects Negroes," and thus "to better the economic status of colored Americans." Robert C. Weaver to John P. Davis, Nov. 6, 1933, Weaver Papers, Box 6.

was more concerned with getting a job than with segregation. "If you went too far out on the segregation issue," Weaver explained, "you were apt to lose your followership." Therefore, although the racial advisers felt strongly that "the federal government should not be a party" to segregated patterns, they recognized that in reality, "you weren't going to get much done along that line. And we didn't get much done."[45]

The racial advisers affected agency practices in a variety of ways. The process of desegregating governmental cafeterias began when Weaver and William Hastie entered the Interior Department cafeteria and were served lunch.[46] Weaver cracked the problem of insuring the employment of skilled blacks on federally financed housing projects by devising the formula whereby federal housing required building contractors "to pay Negro skilled workers . . . a minimum percentage of the skilled payroll."[47] Mrs. Bethune influenced the NYA to ban discrimination in student aid; she saw to it that blacks became eligible for NYA-funded training programs in aviation, library science, and commercial dietetics; and she administered a special fund for support for black college and graduate students that tripled black students' share of NYA aid to higher education. Her success was so striking that some young blacks believed "that NYA stood for Negro Youth Administration."[48] Lawrence Oxley worked with the United States Employment Service in placing black workers; he set up state employment service offices in black neighborhoods; and he taught job interviewers how to deal most effectively with blacks who were unemployed.[49]

The racial adviser's office functioned, too, as "An Adjustment Bureau" by handling complaints, suggestions, and inquiries from blacks addressed to the particular agency or forwarded from the White House.[50] Their range was as varied as the imaginations and needs of their writers. A man in Natchez lost his emergency relief

[45] Robert Weaver interview.

[46] Motz, "Black Cabinet," pp. 35-36. Frances Perkins allowed black employees to use Labor Department eating facilities.

[47] Robert C. Weaver, *Negro Labor: A National Problem* (New York, 1946), p. 11.

[48] Smith, "Mary McLeod Bethune," pp. 29-31; Frazier, *Negro Youth at the Crossways*, p. 178 (source of the quotation).

[49] Debra L. Newman, "Urban Policy of Lawrence A. Oxley, Chief, Division of Negro Labor of the Department of Labor with a Case Study of Chicago, 1934-1939" (typescript, May 9, 1973, xerox copy in Oxley Papers, Box 1385), pp. 3, 10.

[50] Forrester B. Washington, "Accomplishment Report, Feb. 1, 1934 to July 31, 1934," Records of the Federal Emergency Relief Administration, Box 19, Record Group 69, National Archives; Smith interview.

employment for reporting a verbal attack on another black worker. "The job is JIM CROWED, the Office is JIM CROWED, the commodities are JIM CROWED, the very air you breathe under the Adams County Mississippi ERA is contaminated with the parasite of JIM CROWISM," he wrote to Oxley.[51] A black woman in Little Rock appealed for a set of false teeth in addition to the food and clothing already forthcoming from the relief agencies.[52] "An experienced tunnel worker" from Chicago lamented, "It seems though they are putting every nationality on P.W.A. works but the 'Negro People.' All I get is promises."[53]

During his first six months as director of Negro work in the FERA, Forrester Washington handled more than 6,000 such letters, some 1,600 of which complained of discrimination in New Deal programs.[54] When the complaints came in, Washington or his successor, Alfred Edgar Smith, might advise the complainant of the proper steps to take; they might correspond with local and state relief administrators, remind them of federal policy against discrimination, and ask them to investigate the complaint; or, when necessary, they would visit the locality to adjust the problem.[55] Such visits carried some political risks in the South, where the idea of a black man from Washington coming to tell white Southerners how to behave was inflammatory at best.[56] Whether in person or not, the intercession usually worked. The threat that funds would be cut off if discrimination continued proved to be an effective weapon. More often than not, they were able to straighten things out.[57]

[51] W. H. Hyatt to Lawence Oxley, Apr. 17, 1935, Oxley Papers, Box 1390.
[52] *New York Times*, June 24, 1935, p. 36.
[53] Harry Green to William [sic] Hopkins, Apr. 20, 1934, Records of the Civil Works Administration, Box 83, Record Group 69, National Archives.
[54] Washington, "Accomplishment Report, Feb. 1, 1934 to July 31, 1934." In 1936 the WPA race relations office handled 6,525 communications; in 1937, 6,774, in 1938, 8,502. But these communications never exceeded 1 percent of the total WPA incoming correspondence. Alfred Edgar Smith, "Negro Project Workers: 1936 Annual Report," Jan. 1937; "1937 Annual Report," Jan. 1938; "1938 Annual Report," Jan. 1939, Works Progress Administration Papers, Box 10, Manuscript Division, Moorland-Spingarn Research Center, Howard University.
[55] See, e.g., Mary E. Cheney to Thad Holt, Feb. 20, 1934, CWA Papers, Box 83.
[56] See, for example, Walter F. George to James A. Farley, Aug. 3, 1936, Democratic National Committee Papers, Box 1093, Franklin D. Roosevelt Library.
[57] Smith interview; Alfred Edgar Smith, "1935 Report—Summary: Negro Clients of Federal Unemployment Relief," Dec. 31, 1935, FERA Papers, Box 116, and the 1937 report cited above, n. 54. Oxley adjusted complaints from black workers as Commissioner of Conciliation and sat on the NRA's Labor Advisory Board "to advise on cases relating to black workers which were on appeal to that board." Newman, "Urban Policy of Lawrence A. Oxley," p. 3.

Sometimes the adjustment took the form of a straightforward end to a discriminatory practice. Sometimes it called for compromise. Both William Trent and William Hastie were involved in the Interior Department's investigation of a complaint about racial segregation in the Shenandoah National Park in 1938. The result was a moderate solution: desegregation of the largest picnic area as a pilot demonstration and removal of racial labels from National Park Service literature about the park, but the retention of segregation for the time being in the other picnic areas and in campgrounds and concessions. Two years later, the remaining picnic grounds were opened to blacks.[58]

Another function of the racial adviser was to increase the number of blacks on the federal payroll. This meant encouraging blacks, through public meetings, pamphlets, and announcements in the black press, to take civil service examinations; it meant finding people with special talents to fit the needs of administrators who were willing to hire blacks; and it meant increasing the numbers of jobs open to blacks.[59] One way for the racial advisers to do this was to appoint blacks to their own staffs, some of whom might later become racial advisers in their own right. Come to Washington, Mrs. Bethune cajoled when Frank Horne was reluctant to leave his job as acting principal of the Fort Valley Normal and Industrial School; "There is a big job to be done. . . . There are twelve million Negroes in America depending upon the kind of program we shall send out. . . . Your service to the race and the nation will be greatly enlarged. . . . The program of the National Youth Administration is a challenge to the best that there is in us at this time."[60] Horne signed on as her principal assistant—the first step in a public service career that would span three decades.

Mrs. Bethune got blacks named to NYA advisory committees in each southern state; she was primarily responsible for the hiring of black administrative assistants in the offices of NYA state youth directors; and she had some success in pushing the NYA

[58] Motz, "Black Cabinet," pp. 34-35; Phineas Indritz memorandum to Solicitor Margold, Jan. 12, 1939; Nathan R. Margold memorandum to Secretary Ickes, Jan. 17, 1939; W. J. Trent, Jr., memorandum to Secretary Ickes, Feb. 24, 1940; Theodore T. Smith memorandum to the Director [National Park Service], Feb. 28, 1940; Harold L. Ickes to W. J. Trent, Jr., Mar. 6, 1940, Trent Papers, Box 1.

[59] Motz, "Black Cabinet," p. 37.

[60] Mary McLeod Bethune to Frank Horne, July 20, 1936, Frank S. Horne Papers, Amistad Research Center, Dillard University.

to place blacks in professional positions outside her division.[61] Robert Weaver, who gained a reputation as "the chief recruiter" of blacks for federal employment, not only hired able people for his own staff; he also managed to extend his influence so that he "had a rather strong impact in getting a group of new-type black government officials" in other departments and agencies, "people who were primarily technicians and able and competent in the fields in which they were working."[62] While the percentage of blacks in the civil service did not change appreciably—it was 9.59 in 1928 and 9.85 in 1938—the absolute numbers of blacks grew significantly as the New Deal swelled the ranks of federal employees.[63] Not only were more blacks hired, but they filled a wider range of positions than had previously been the case.

The racial adviser served, too, as a collector and disseminator of data about blacks: for example, Ambrose Caliver's studies on black education; Alfred Edgar Smith's statistics on the black share of unemployment relief; and Lawrence Oxley's surveys of blacks in organized labor and black white-collar workers on relief.[64]

Finally—and, in political terms, perhaps most importantly— the racial adviser was a booster for the New Deal. He served a two-way public relations function: he interpreted the needs of blacks to white governmental officials, and he interpreted the program of his own agency to black Americans.[65] One model was that of Weaver, who, although he shrank from the personal publicity attached to a public figure, spoke effectively to an audience of educated blacks, mainly professionals, through a steady stream of scholarly magazine articles published primarily in journals di-

[61] Smith, "Mary McLeod Bethune," p. 24. B. Joyce Ross calls "her constant pressure in regard to the appointment of increasing numbers of black NYA officials on the state and local levels . . . perhaps her most outstanding administrative accomplishment." See Ross, "Mary McLeod Bethune," p. 7. For examples of similar activities in the FERA, see Forrester B. Washington, "Accomplishment Report, Feb. 1, 1934 to July 31, 1934," FERA Papers, Box 19.

[62] Robert Weaver interview.

[63] Laurence J. W. Hayes, *The Negro Federal Government Worker: A Study of His Classification Status in the District of Columbia, 1883-1938* (Washington, D.C., 1941), pp. 73, 153.

[64] Smith, "Educational Programs for the Improvement of Race Relations," p. 365; Newman, "Urban Policy of Lawrence A. Oxley," pp. 4, 7. On Eugene Kinckle Jones's work along these lines in the Division of Negro Affairs of the Bureau of Foreign and Domestic Commerce, see U. S. Commerce Department, Division of Negro Affairs, press release, "Secretary Roper of Commerce Department Includes Work for Negroes in Report," Jan. 9, 1936, Division of Negro Affairs folder, vertical file, Moorland-Spingarn Research Center.

[65] Forrester B. Washington, "Accomplishment Report, Feb. 1, 1934 to July 31, 1934," FERA Papers, Box 19; Robert Weaver interview.

rected at black readers, such as *Opportunity, Phylon,* or the *Journal of Negro Education.*[66] A second model was that of public relations geared toward the masses and depending more on dramatic personal style. Here Mrs. Bethune was a master of the art. She used personal contacts, news releases, public speeches, letters, NYA publications, magazine articles, and newspaper columns to publicize the NYA and to encourage blacks to become involved in its programs. She traveled widely—in her first year as director of Negro affairs, she logged 40,000 miles in twenty-one states.[67] She not only sold the NYA; she also touted the New Deal. In *Opportunity,* she recounted the benefits to blacks under the Democratic administration. It represented, she said, "the dawn of a new day" for Negroes. In the *Pittsburgh Courier,* she defended Roosevelt as "fair at heart in his attitude toward the Negro"—he "regularly inquires of the New Deal agencies as to what is being done for the Negro."[68] She was, in sum, a real "evangelist" for the Democratic party.[69]

Such activities paid obvious political dividends. It is probably an exaggeration to say, as Alfred Edgar Smith did, that the Black Cabinet "had the means to control" the black vote, but they certainly had a political impact.[70] The fact that blacks held such positions was in itself a political selling point for the Democratic party, both because it bespoke the party's concern for the race, and because it helped to dispel the traditional assumption that better-class blacks only associated with Republicans.[71] Every time that a racial adviser successfully countered New Deal discrimination or secured special projects for blacks, it affected the black vote. While the principal members of the Black Cabinet were not political appointees, they played a part in furthering the political interests of the Democratic party. They advised party leaders on the best means of appealing to black voters. They supplied the

[66] Motz, "Black Cabinet," pp. 53-54.

[67] Smith, "Mary McLeod Bethune," pp. 27, 28. On Henry A. Hunt's work in publicizing the services of the Farm Credit Administration to black Americans, see Donnie D. Bellamy, "Henry A. Hunt and Black Agricultural Leadership in the New South," *Journal of Negro History* LX (Oct. 1975):475-76.

[68] Mary McLeod Bethune, " 'I'll Never Turn Back No More!' " *Opportunity* XVI (Nov. 1938):326; *Pittsburgh Courier,* June 22, 1939, quoted in Smith, "Mary McLeod Bethune," p. 15.

[69] Interview with Bryant George, Sept. 24, 1976, New York City.

[70] Smith, "Educational Programs for the Improvement of Race Relations," p. 364.

[71] George R. Brawley to Lawrence A. Oxley, Oct. 2, 1934, Oxley Papers, Box 1396; Motz, "Black Cabinet," pp. 82-83.

Democratic National Committee with materials about the participation of blacks in New Deal programs. They contributed to the preparation of publications like the glossy pamphlet *WPA and the Negro*, or the summary of *Interesting Facts About the Negro and the WPA*, distributed—not coincidentally—just in time for the 1936 election.[72] While individual members of the Black Cabinet campaigned for Roosevelt—Weaver, for example, said that he "did a little campaigning for Roosevelt, not a whole lot," but that he "did work with local politicians to get things done"[73]— the Democratic National Committee does not appear to have made any systematic efforts to send them out on the stump. W. J. Trent, Jr., said that there was no explicit pressure to campaign, but even a nonpolitical speech under the auspices of an organization like the Urban League, touting the administration's accomplishments, could not help but influence the votes of black audiences.[74]

By their very existence, the Black Cabinet made New Dealers more aware than they would otherwise have been of the problems of black Americans. Everywhere that he traveled as chief of the Division of Negro Labor, Lawrence Oxley reiterated a constant refrain, "colored, colored, colored," in an effort "to bring an awareness" of blacks to the officials he encountered. The awareness grew out of small achievements: persuading governmental agencies to subscribe to black newspapers or educating white officials in acceptable modes of addressing blacks. Such achievements were all part of a bigger victory—as Smith put it, "getting Negroes and the government to know each other."[75]

This educative, interpretive function was central to the significance of the Black Cabinet. They made white New Dealers marginally more sensitive to the needs of blacks; and they made the federal government seem more comprehensible and relevant to blacks. In some instances, they affected policy, so that the New

[72] Robert Weaver interview; Lawrence A. Oxley memorandum to the Secretary [Frances Perkins], Mar. 23, 1936, Oxley Papers, Box 1392; *WPA and the Negro*, n.d., received Oct. 30, 1936, Department of the Interior Papers, Office of the Secretary, Central Classified Files, File 1-280, pt. 2, Record Group 48, National Archives; *Interesting Facts About the Negro and the WPA*, n.d., Records of the Works Progress Administration, Division of Information, Box 89, Record Group 69, National Archives.

[73] Robert Weaver interview.

[74] Trent interview. For an example, see *Norfolk Journal and Guide*, Oct. 24, 1936.

[75] Oxley interview with Debra Newman; Smith interview.

Deal treated blacks more fairly than it might have had they not been in government.

Contemporaries disagree over the impact of the Black Cabinet. Were they, as Clarence Mitchell perceived them, "able to get a lot done"? Or were they, in the judgment of the political reporter, Earl Brown, "only window-dressers," "a symbol without any real power"?[76] These judgments are not inconsistent. The symbolism of the Black Cabinet may have been its most important substantive achievement. Whether or not the racial advisers were on the periphery of power, it was "the first time blacks were brought even that close."[77] Many of the members of the Cabinet may not have been much beyond the level of "higher clerical" employees or "lower junior executive[s]." But the point, Roy Wilkins explained, is that such a group "had never existed before." "The Negro had never before had this penetration into the government that he had under Roosevelt," Wilkins continued, "and he'd never had access to this many or this variety of government jobs . . . , nor had that many so-called talented or prepared or white collar or educated Negroes . . . ever been in Washington before."[78] Thanks to the Black Cabinet, "blacks felt," as they never had, "that they were getting through to the man."[79]

In political terms, this sense on the part of blacks that they had some access to official circles, this symbolic recognition that their interests counted, weighed much more heavily than any of the Black Cabinet's concrete accomplishments. No matter whether the access bore significant fruit, nor whether the interests were taken less seriously by the administration than those of many other groups. The Black Cabinet was important to black people because it signified that the government was paying attention to them in ways that had never been the case before. They, in turn, found in the Cabinet a reason to look more favorably on the

[76] Mitchell interview; interview with Earl Brown, June 29, 1977, New York City. Not surprisingly, Mrs. Bethune thought that their efforts really paid off. "Every time you take up the papers," she told the National Council of Negro Women, "we find that some of the things we have been pleading for and working for are happening." NCNW minutes, Nov. 26, 1938, NCNW Papers, Series 2, Box 1, Folder 4.

[77] Interview with Kenneth B. Clark, May 17, 1977, New York City.

[78] Roy Wilkins, *Reminiscences* (Columbia University Oral History Collection, 1960), p. 68. For corroborating views, see interviews with Franklin H. Williams, Oct. 25, 1976, New York City, and E. Frederic Morrow, Apr. 29, 1977, Princeton, N.J.

[79] Interview with Roy Wilkins, Aug. 17, 1976, New York City.

Democratic party. To interpret the Cabinet as evidence of a genuine commitment by the New Deal to racial progress would be to overstate the case. Rather, it shows, once again, the skill of Franklin D. Roosevelt in turning limited departures from past racial practices to his own political advantage.

CHAPTER VIII ▪ *A Climate of*
Racial Conservatism

Although the New Deal's symbolic racial gestures may seem tentative and restrained in retrospect, they need to be evaluated in the context of their times. Blacks in the 1930s found them impressive because there had been nothing like them in anyone's memory. These symbolic gestures broke the prevailing pattern of racial conservatism in notable ways. But they did not betoken any growing commitment by the administration to the cause of civil rights. They were the exceptional gestures, not the bellwethers of change in the making. As the record of the Roosevelt administration in 1935 and 1936 makes clear, caution and conservatism were still the main determinants of the New Deal's record on race.

That record continued to be shaped, as it had in the earliest months of the administration, by the personal conservatism and political caution of White House aides and Democratic party officials, the inability of blacks to command much power as a special interest group, and the inflammatory potential of race as a political issue.

There was no question but that White House aides and Democratic party officials wanted no part of major racial issues, like lynching and disfranchisement. Not only that, they regarded as inappropriate, even offensive, efforts on the part of the NAACP to bring such matters into the political arena. Steve Early's anger at Walter White's aggressive lobbying on lynching was not an isolated incident. When the NAACP tried to persuade the Democratic National Committee to use its influence to stop Democratic state committees in the South from barring qualified blacks from voting in state primaries, it ran up against a stone wall. Over a period of four months, the best that the Association could get out of the National Committee's offices were vague acknowledgments of its letters. Finally Chairman Farley's assistant, Emil Hurja, spoke to the issue: "There is nothing I can do in this Committee in a matter affecting a State primary." When White sent copies of their correspondence to several Democratic senators to protest against the National Committee's inaction, Hurja exploded: "Your act in sending these letters around in this fashion constitutes an act of discourtesy."[1]

Even less momentous matters evoked resistance from the White House. Why not admit a black reporter to the First Lady's press conferences, for example? It seemed a reasonable enough request, and Mrs. Roosevelt had her secretary send it over to Early. But Early had, since the beginning of the administration, denied black reporters access to the President's press conferences on the grounds that only daily newspapers were permitted to send reporters; the black weeklies did not qualify. (Later, when the *Atlanta Daily World* asked for accreditation for its Washington correspondent, Early had to develop a more complicated justification.)[2] "I have taken care of the Negro requests for the President's press conferences," Early answered, "and if Mrs. Roosevelt opens hers it just makes the President more vulnerable. I think it is far the best thing to ignore the letter."[3] There was to be no black reporter at Mrs. Roosevelt's press conferences.

Where possible, avoidance of racial issues was the rule. "Don't you think the best thing to do is just to forget to ack[nowledge] this?" Marvin McIntyre noted on an inquiry from White about Roosevelt's position on a bill to create a Negro Industrial Commission.[4] Otherwise, caution governed. Every time that Ickes gave

[1] Walter White to Edward P. Costigan, July 25, 1934; Emil Hurja to White, Aug. 1, 18, 1934; White to Hurja, Aug. 6, 23, 1934, Edward P. Costigan Papers, Box 42, FF 16, Western Historical Collections, Norlin Library, University of Colorado; *Afro-American*, Sept. 1, 1934. The quotations are from Hurja's letters to White.

[2] Frederick S. Weaver to Franklin D. Roosevelt, Nov. 6, 1933; Stephen Early to Weaver, Nov. 15, 1933, Franklin D. Roosevelt Papers, Official File (OF) 36, Box 1, Franklin D. Roosevelt Library (hereafter cited as the FDR Papers); S. T. E.[arly] memorandum for Mr. McIntyre, Feb. 12, 1936, ibid., OF 93; Weaver to George Durno, Nov. 23, 1940; Early to Eustace Gay, Dec. 7, 1940; Paul Wooten to A. S. Scott, May 28, 1941; Early memorandum to William D. Hassett, May 31, 1941; telegram, John H. Sengstacke to Early, Nov. 2, 1943; mb [sic] memorandum to Ruthjane Rumelt, Nov. 12, 1943; Sengstacke to Early, Dec. 1, 1943; Claude A. Barnett to Early, Dec. 10, 1943, ibid., OF 36, Box 6. Finally, in 1944, a black reporter, Harry McAlpin, was admitted to the President's press conferences as the representative of the Negro Newspaper Publishers Association and the *Atlanta Daily World*. See Ruthjane Rumelt file memorandum, Feb. 7, 1944; Sengstacke to Franklin D. Roosevelt, Feb. 9, 1944; and Sengstacke to Early, Feb. 9, 1944, ibid. For a scholar's account, consult Graham J. White, "Franklin D. Roosevelt and the American Press" (Ph.D. diss., University of Sydney, 1977), pp. 66-69.

[3] Stephen Early to Malvina Thompson Scheider, Sept. 11, 1935, quoted in Joseph P. Lash, *Eleanor and Franklin* (New York, 1971), p. 519.

[4] M.H.M. memorandum to Mr. Foster, attached to Walter White to Franklin D. Roosevelt, Aug. 16, 1935, FDR Papers, OF 93.

a speech to blacks, he had to send the text to the White House to be vetted for inopportune remarks.[5] The White House edited with a remarkably conservative pen: the initial draft of Ickes's much-publicized speech, "The Negro as a Citizen," exhorted blacks, "In spite of the wrongs that have been and still are being committed against you, do not become bitter," but the speech as delivered to the NAACP's annual conference in 1936 omitted "and still are being" at the insistence of Early.[6] The political antennae were always on the alert. Blacks might praise Ickes, but how many whites agreed with the irate Baltimorean who declared that such an appearance was a sure way for the Democratic party to lose the white vote?[7]

Political caution also governed the response when the NAACP, like countless other organizations, asked the White House for a brief message of encouragement to be read at a special meeting or annual convention. Before he was willing to release a perfunctory letter to the Association in 1935, Early sent it to the Democratic National Committee to be "checked carefully, considering the possible political reaction from the standpoint of the South."[8] The committee's publicity director, Charles Michelson, counseled against the inclusion of the final paragraph of the draft letter, in which the President would have said, "I also hope that your organization may receive support and cooperation and that it may continue its constructive program of helping the Nation recognize its obligation to all citizens, and of encouraging public institutions to function justly and without discrimination in their relationship to the colored people."[9] It was not so clear to him, Michelson suggested to Early, that the NAACP's program was entirely constructive: "I am a little hazy about the Association for the Ad-

[5] See, e.g., Michael W. Straus memorandum to Harold L. Ickes, Feb. 21, 1936, Harold L. Ickes Papers, Folder 127A, Box 279, Manuscript Division, Library of Congress; Aubrey E. Taylor memorandum to Ickes, June 23, 1936, ibid., Folder 140A, Box 281; Taylor memorandum to Ickes, Mar. 1, 1938, ibid., Folder 206, Box 302; Straus memorandum to the Secretary, Mar. 7, 1939, ibid., Folder 249D, Box 315.

[6] "The Negro as a Citizen," Ickes speech to NAACP annual conference, Baltimore, June 29, 1936, speech #113, ibid., Box 281; Aubrey E. Taylor memorandum to Harold L. Ickes, June 23, 1936, ibid., Folder 140A, Box 281.

[7] On the views of blacks, see, e.g., Edgar G. Brown to Harold L. Ickes, July 2, 1936; Simeon B. Osby, Jr. to Ickes, July 11, 1936, ibid., Folder 140, Box 281. The objection by a white man is in John F. Heath telegram to James Farley, June 29, 1936, ibid., Folder 140, Box 281.

[8] Stephen Early to Charles Michelson, June 21, 1935, FDR Papers, President's Personal File (PPF) 1336.

[9] Draft, Franklin D. Roosevelt to Walter White, June 22, 1935, ibid.

vancement of Colored People. It runs in my mind that while they have a lot of fine names on their stationery, that there have been some uncomfortable instances concerning intermarriage between races, etc., that concern some of the extremists in the organization." But since it would "probably cause more comment to omit the greeting than to send it," Michelson suggested sending the letter without the too-effusive final paragraph.[10]

Roosevelt's staff were racial conservatives, to be sure, but they were also acutely sensitive to the political context of the times. Race relations was such a highly charged issue in the 1930s that *any* act that seemed to depart from accepted patterns of racial separation or any glimmer of fairness and decency was capable of eliciting a public outcry. A man in Dearborn, Michigan, put the case succinctly: any white who worked "for the betterment of negroe races," the President included, was a traitor.[11]

Angry charges of upsetting proper racial hierarchies accompanied practically every gesture that the New Deal made to black Americans. It was easy to distort what was actually happening. Hiring blacks to work in the White House was translated, in the columns of the *Tampa Tribune*, into a hostile act by the President, who "shoved white men out" to make places for them. If what she read in the *Tribune* was true, a woman wrote Roosevelt from Miami, "you have lost a vote. I think you will lose a great many through the South. And I will do my best to help you do so."[12] When Mrs. Roosevelt was photographed speaking before integrated audiences or walking with black student escorts at Howard University, or the President was reported appointing blacks to federal offices or receiving a delegation of Negro Elks at the Executive Mansion, racial reactionaries screamed angry recriminations about the "nigger-lovers" in the White House.[13] A popular jingle which circulated during the campaign of 1936 summed up the rage that many people felt. It purported to convey an exchange between Franklin and Eleanor:

[10] Charles Michelson to Stephen Early, June 22, 1935, ibid.

[11] Copy of letter, L. Oswald to [James A. Farley], Nov. 22, 1934, attached to James A. Farley to Louis McHenry Howe, Dec. 19, 1934, ibid., OF 93.

[12] Mrs. J. M. Payne to Franklin D. Roosevelt, Dec. 30, 1934, ibid.

[13] For news reports of such activities, see, e.g., *Georgia Woman's World*, Jan. 1, Feb. 6, Mar. 20, 1936, Robert C. Weaver Papers, Box 8, Schomburg Center for Research in Black Culture; "Black on Blacks," *Time*, Apr. 27, 1936, pp. 10-11; "Elks & Equality," *Time*, Aug. 12, 1935, pp. 9-10. For reactions, see, e.g., letter to the editor from K.L.B. of New York, Jan. 25, 1936, *Georgia Woman's World*, Feb. 6, 1936, Weaver Papers, Box 8; Finley Moore to Franklin D. Roosevelt, Apr. 15, 1936, FDR Papers, OF 93.

You kiss the niggers,
I'll kiss the Jews.
We'll stay in the White House
As long as we choose.[14]

Charges that the Roosevelts were out to revolutionize race relations were patently absurd, but their validity was beside the point. At the hands of reactionary Southerners, any symbolic gestures toward blacks were easily exaggerated into explosive racial propaganda. Such propaganda became the staple of a vituperative anti-Roosevelt campaign among Democrats in the South in anticipation of the 1936 election. The campaign took shape in an abortive bid for the Democratic presidential nomination on the part of the governor of Georgia, Eugene Talmadge. The Talmadge effort was funded by John J. Raskob, Pierre S. du Pont, and other industrialists who strongly opposed the economic and social policies of the New Deal. Race was a relatively minor complaint on their agenda, but it had great potential as a rallying cry.[15] As *Time* magazine pointed out, portraying the Roosevelts as proponents of social equality for blacks was just the "kind of political dynamite [that] could blow larger holes in the Solid South than any other single campaign issue."[16] The Talmadge forces were quick to exploit its potential. "Stop It, Mr. Roosevelt, Stop It!!!" exhorted a banner headline in their campaign organ, the *Georgia Woman's World*. "Stop—and stop quickly—THE EFFORTS OF THE DEMOCRATIC PARTY TO FOIST THE NEGRO AND SOCIAL EQUALITY UPON THE WHITE PEOPLE OF THE SOUTH."[17] "Social equality," like communism, was the kind of charge that could be hurled at the New Deal without much specific evidence but with the certainty that it would inflame popular passions and rally a body of support.[18] "It just makes my blood boil when I read how the President and his wife are acting," one

[14] Quoted in Elliott Roosevelt and James Brough, *A Rendezvous with Destiny: The Roosevelts of the White House* (1975; reprint ed., New York, 1976), p. 146.

[15] *New York Times*, Jan. 30, 1936, p. 1; Apr. 16, 1936, p. 2; "Black on Blacks," p. 11; Allan A. Michie and Frank Ryhlick, *Dixie Demagogues* (New York, 1939), pp. 185-87.

[16] "Black on Blacks," p. 10. On the same theme, see Cole L. Blease to Harold Ickes, Mar. 2, 1936. Department of the Interior Papers, Office of the Secretary, Central Classified Files, File 1-280, pt. 2, Record Group 48, National Archives.

[17] *Georgia Woman's World*, Jan. 1, 1936, Weaver Papers, Box 8.

[18] Sometimes critics used both epithets in the same breath—see, e.g., letter to the editor dated Dec. 15, 1935, *Georgia Woman's World*, Jan. 1, 1936, ibid.

Georgia woman declared. "Let [the Negro] stay in his place."[19] "Mr President," another Georgian summed up, "we southern people dont believe in no such stuff as social equality with the negroes as you are doing."[20]

With millions still out of work, the Supreme Court threatening the very foundations of the New Deal, and an election in the offing, Roosevelt did not need that kind of trouble. It was one thing to risk political repercussions when the issue was important. It was another thing to risk them over something so trivial that could so easily be avoided. It was no wonder that Early and the others were intent on protecting their boss.

The racial climate of the 1930s helps to make more comprehensible the administration's unwillingness to become identified with attempts to enact legislation directed specifically at racial concerns. The experience of the Seventy-fourth Congress shows that, even when racial protection was of tangential significance to a piece of legislation, it was virtually impossible to get any positive action.

While the Seventy-fourth Congress resisted action on lynching, the legislative floodgates opened wide in other areas. After a sluggish start, by the end of the summer of 1935, Congress had enacted what James MacGregor Burns has called "some of the most significant measures of Roosevelt's first term." First came nearly $5 billion for work relief, then the Wagner Labor Relations Act, and then the Social Security Act. "Banking and Tennessee Valley legislation were strengthened. The AAA was modified in an attempt to protect it against judicial veto. The holding company bill . . .

[19] Letter to the editor from Mrs. R. L. Shirley of Ranger, Georgia, Jan. 27, 1936, *Georgia Woman's World*, Feb. 6, 1936, ibid. For nearly identical sentiments, see a letter to the editor in the same issue from Mrs. L. H. of Cairo, Georgia, Jan. 27, 1936.

[20] Homer Bell to Franklin D. Roosevelt, Jan. 9, 1936, FDR Papers, OF 93. For other indictments of the Roosevelts as proponents of social equality, see letters to the editor from Mrs. A. S. of Cohutta, Georgia, Jan. 21, 1936, Mrs. M. V. of Dallas, Georgia, Jan. 28, 1936, J.P.P. of Haylow, Georgia, Jan. 24, 1936, and Mrs. P.O.L. of Abbeville, Georgia, Jan. 26, 1936, all in *Georgia Woman's World*, Feb. 6, 1936, Weaver Papers, Box 8. From Walter White's point of view, the administration was too sensitive to the views of people like Talmadge (*New York Herald Tribune*, Dec. 8, 1935, clipping in Roosevelt Administration Scrapbooks, vol. I, microfilm reel 16, Schomburg Center for Research in Black Culture). White Southerners, on the other hand, believed that the Democratic party was all too sensitive to the urgings of "Walter White and his crowd" (editorial, *Charleston News and Courier*, June 12, 1936, in *The Attitude of the Southern White Press toward Negro Suffrage, 1932-1940*, ed. Rayford W. Logan [Washington, D.C., 1940], p. 62).

went through under intensified administration pressure." And new tax legislation added inheritance taxes and gift taxes to the nation's revenue-producing machinery.[21] To many observers, the legislation of the Second Hundred Days confirmed the President's shift toward a more liberal—some called it radical—program.

If the New Deal was moving leftward, would it act any more decisively to meet the needs of black Americans? There were some early tests, as organizations for racial advancement tried to build some protection for blacks into the centerpieces of the Second Hundred Days—the Wagner Act and the Social Security Act.

By guaranteeing the right to bargain collectively, the National Labor Relations Act of 1935 promised a real "new deal" for American labor. But the labor movement had long been stubbornly hostile to the interests of black workers. Unions excluded blacks through outright constitutional prohibitions against Negro membership, or through subtler devices such as tacit agreements, entrance examinations, and ritual pledges binding members to propose only white workmen for admission to the union. Regardless of the means, the discrimination yielded a uniform end: the underrepresentation of blacks in organized labor. The American Federation of Labor was committed in principle from its earliest years to the organization of all workers, regardless of race, creed, or color. In fact, it tolerated racial exclusion on the part of its member unions, and it had long permitted the issuance of separate charters for unions composed entirely of blacks. Since the 1910s, prominent black unionists and organizations for racial advancement had worked unceasingly to commit the AFL to accord black workers the same rights and treatment as whites. But, despite the concerted efforts of A. Philip Randolph and the National Urban League, among others, the AFL in the mid-1930s remained unwilling to move against racial discrimination in its ranks.[22]

The New Deal's boost to the labor movement threatened to lend official sanction to such practices. The Wagner bill promised to enhance the power and influence of organized labor, and yet it made no mention of the "intolerant anti-Negro policies" which unions typically pursued. To the National Urban League, the omission made the bill less a panacea than a serious "threat to the job security of Negro workers." Unless the bill were amended

[21] James MacGregor Burns, *Roosevelt: The Lion and the Fox* (New York, 1956), pp. 220, 224.

[22] Nancy J. Weiss, *The National Urban League, 1910-1940* (New York, 1974), pp. 204-215, 273, 287-90.

to protect the rights of black workers, it might easily be assumed that racial discrimination carried congressional approval.[23]

As usual, Walter White maneuvered to bring pressure to bear on Congress. Who would be the best senator to introduce amendments to protect black workers? he asked Senator Wagner's secretary, Leon Keyserling, in March 1934. Then White wrote Wagner himself to ask his advice on the best strategy: should proponents of the amendments present the facts about the situation of black workers at the hearings, or was it better to wait for the bill to reach the Senate floor?[24]

White talked to Keyserling and learned why the bill had been drafted in the form the racial advancement organizations considered to be so dangerous. Originally, Wagner had included a provision making the closed shop legal "only when there were no restrictions upon members in the labor union to which the majority of the workers belonged." But he had not reckoned with the reaction of the AFL, which "fought bitterly" to eliminate the clause; "much against his will," Wagner had "had to consent to elimination in order to prevent scuttling of the entire bill." As for strategy, the best course seemed to be to move for the inclusion of such a clause when the bill came up for debate on the floor. It was important not to give labor notice of the effort, for they would surely line up votes against any proposed changes.[25]

The National Urban League took the tack of trying to amend the bill in committee. In April, T. Arnold Hill, now acting as executive secretary of the organization, conferred with Wagner about the League's concerns and then testified before the Senate Committee on Education and Labor, which was holding hearings on the proposed legislation. He told the committee how the AFL discriminated against black workers and explained what was wrong with the bill as drafted. It permitted unions to exclude blacks from membership "and from employment in occupations under their jurisdiction." It denied to black strikebreakers "the status of 'employees' " even in cases where they were "prohibited from joining the striking union." It failed to protect black workers

[23] National Urban League memorandum to Franklin D. Roosevelt, "The Negro Working Population and National Recovery," Jan. 4, 1937, p. 16, National Association for the Advancement of Colored People Papers, Manuscript Division, Library of Congress (hereafter cited as the NAACP Papers). See also T. Arnold Hill, "Labor Marches On," *Opportunity* XII (Apr. 1934):120-21.
[24] Walter White to Leon Keyserling, Mar. 22, 1934; White to Robert F. Wagner, Mar. 28, 1934, NAACP Papers, Box C-257.
[25] Walter White to William H. Hastie, Mar. 28, 1934, ibid.

"from practices of racial discrimination by labor unions." And it permitted unions to establish separate locals composed exclusively of blacks, which were denied the rights and privileges granted to locals composed of whites. The Urban League had prepared amendments to remedy the problems. With respect to the bill's stipulation that strikebreakers would immediately lose their status as "employees" (and thus lose the protections that the bill offered), the League urged that a specific exception be made for strikebreakers who had been barred by "discriminatory policies" from joining the striking union. To deal with the problem of dual locals, it recommended qualifying the definition of "labor organization" to exclude those that discriminated on grounds of "race, color, or creed." As for the larger issue of racial discrimination, the League suggested an amendment which stated, "It shall be an unfair labor practice for a labor union to deny the right of membership and/or in any way to interfere with full participation of any employee otherwise eligible on account of race, color, or creed." In short, no union that persisted in discriminating against blacks could enjoy the protection of the Wagner Act.[26]

Hill rallied his board members and local Urban League officials to write Wagner and the members of the Committee on Education and Labor in support of the proposed amendments.[27] Later that month, the editor of *Opportunity*, Elmer A. Carter, traveled to Washington to confer with the committee members. Carter pronounced himself "convinced" that "a definite majority" were "committed to the position that the Negro worker must be given the same rights under the Act as other workers," and he said that there was "no question" that the bill would be revised.[28]

[26] National Urban League press release, "Hill Consults Wagner on Labor Bill," Apr. 2, 1934, National Urban League Papers, Department of Public Relations files, Manuscript Division, Library of Congress; T. Arnold Hill to Robert F. Wagner, Apr. 2, 1934, in National Urban League, Department of Industrial Relations, 1934 Report; "A Statement of Opinion on Senate Bill S. 2926 . . . by the National Urban League for Social Service among Negroes to the Committee on Education and Labor of the Senate of the United States," Apr. 6, 1934, National Urban League Papers, Department of Industrial Relations files; National Labor Relations Board, *Legislative History of the National Labor Relations Act, 1935*, 2 vols. (Washington, D.C., 1949), I:1058-60. For similar amendments suggested by the Washington, D.C., branch of the NAACP, see ibid., pp. 1035-36.

[27] T. Arnold Hill to "Dear Co-Worker," Apr. 3, 1934; Hill to "Dear Friend," Apr. 16, 1934, National Urban League Papers, Department of Industrial Relations files.

[28] National Urban League press release, "Wagner 'Labor Disputes Act' Will be Revised," Apr. 26, 1934, National Urban League Papers, Department of Public Relations files.

Carter's optimism proved to be ill-founded. Senators listened politely to him and to Hill, but no one in Congress took up the amendments that the Urban League and others proposed. The failure of the racial spokesmen to enlist congressional allies reflected the complicated political circumstances surrounding the Wagner bill. The bill's proposed guarantees for organized labor were extremely controversial; and, since it lacked the official backing of the Roosevelt administration, it faced a rough reception in Congress. In such circumstances, the bill's sponsors needed all the support that they could get, and they could not afford to risk alienating powerful Southerners by including a controversial antidiscrimination clause. Given the racial climate of the time, it is little wonder that they were reluctant to imperil their long-sought labor legislation by fighting to protect black workers. Nor is it surprising that the wishes of the well-organized and increasingly powerful labor movement, which opposed such a clause, should have weighed more heavily than the desires of the loosely organized and less influential black movement.

The Urban League and the NAACP joined in a similarly unsuccessful effort to amend the Social Security Act. When Senate hearings on the bill began in January 1935, Walter White asked the bill's sponsor, Robert F. Wagner, whether it contained "adequate safeguards" against racial discrimination. Wagner assured White that it did.[29] But the senator could not have anticipated the Roosevelt administration's effort to make the bill more palatable to Congress by trimming its costs. As it finally emerged, the Social Security program excluded agricultural and domestic employees from its provisions for unemployment compensation and old-age insurance. This exclusion, the NAACP's legal counsel asserted, was a "direct blow at Negro workers," for two-thirds of gainfully employed blacks worked in precisely those agricultural and domestic service occupations that the Social Security program failed to cover.[30] The more the NAACP "studied the bill the more holes appeared, until from a Negro's point of view it look[ed] like a sieve with the holes just big enough for the majority of Negroes to fall through." The bill "guarantees [the Negro] precisely nothing," the *Crisis* told its readers. "It may be a bitter pill for trusting

[29] Telegram, Walter White to Robert F. Wagner, Jan. 22, 1935; telegram, Wagner to White, Jan. 29, 1935, NAACP Papers, Box C-257.
[30] Roy Wilkins memorandum to Walter White, Feb. 2, 1935; telegram, White to Robert F. Wagner, Feb. 4, 1935; telegram, Charles H. Houston to White, Feb. 6, 1935 (source of the quotation), ibid.; Weiss, *The National Urban League*, Table 12.1, p. 194.

Negroes to swallow . . . but they ought to realize by now that the powers-that-be in the Roosevelt administration have nothing for them." Indeed, warned Abraham Epstein, the executive secretary of the American Association for Old Age Security, blacks stood "to lose a great deal by the unemployment and old age insurance systems provided in the Social Security act."[31]

Not only did the bill exclude the very occupations in which blacks were most heavily concentrated. It also contained no specific prohibitions against discrimination in any of the areas that it did cover. Nor could blacks take much satisfaction from the fact that the old-age pension system was to be administered by the states. There was ample evidence in the handling of other federal monies—for education and relief—that state administration invited racial discrimination.[32]

The Urban League and the NAACP urged the administration not to permit the exclusion of agricultural and domestic workers from coverage.[33] They appealed to the White House to back an amendment that would include the neglected workers under the bill, or to create a voluntary insurance plan to provide them with federal subsidies. Their efforts to reshape the legislation began while it was still in committee and continued long after it had been enacted into law. Again, the effort to amend the act failed to win any political support.[34] Again, too, the failure is scarcely surprising. As Abraham Epstein explained in a candid discussion with Roy Wilkins, "the old age security advocates were not seeking to solve the race problem and did not draw a bill with the idea in mind of speeding the solution of the race problem." What they *were* interested in was "securing old age legislation and . . . antagonizing as few persons in the process as possible."[35] Social security itself was sufficiently controversial; its proponents had no interest in further complicating the delicate effort to win sup-

[31] Statement of Charles H. Houston, representing the NAACP, in U. S. Congress, Senate, Committee on Finance, *Economic Security Act, Hearings . . .* , 74th Cong., 1st sess. (Washington, D. C., 1935), pp. 640-41; "Social Security—for White Folk," *Crisis* XLII (Mar. 1935):80; Abraham Epstein, "The Social Security Act," ibid. (Nov. 1935):347.

[32] National Urban League, Memo to FDR (1937), pp. 15, 20; George Edmund Haynes, "Lily-White Social Security," *Crisis* XLII (Mar. 1935):85.

[33] Walter White to Frances Perkins, Feb. 6, 1935, NAACP Papers, Box C-406; White telegram to Franklin D. Roosevelt, Feb. 6, 1935, ibid., Box C-78.

[34] National Urban League, Memo to FDR (1937), pp. 15, 20; T. Arnold Hill to Executive Secretaries of Affiliated Branches of National Urban League, Mar. 18, 1935, National Urban League Papers, Southern Regional Office files, Series A.

[35] NAACP board minutes, Mar. 11, 1935, p. 4, NAACP Papers, Box A-10.

port for the program by adding provisions certain to raise southern hackles. There was ample evidence that Southerners strongly opposed any provisions susceptible of interpretation as providing an instrumentality for federal meddling in race relations.[36] No wonder, then, that proponents of the legislation shied away from explicit protections for blacks that seemed certain to sabotage the entire program.

The failure of the attempts to amend the Wagner and Social Security bills proved a familiar point: blacks were unable effectively to counteract the influence of stronger, better-organized interest groups. When protection for blacks required an affirmative move on the part of Congress, it invariably failed in the 1930s. When blacks asked for explicit assistance, they were usually unsuccessful. The New Deal simply was not going to go out of its way to benefit the race. But it would go out of its way to assist poor people; and insofar as the legislation of the Second Hundred Days extended the capacity of the federal government to help those who were suffering, it also extended the New Deal's effect on the fortunes of blacks.

To black Americans, the single most important event of the Second Hundred Days—indeed, perhaps of the whole New Deal— was the creation in May 1935 of the Works Progress Administration. The relief program literally became the salvation of millions of unemployed Americans. Blacks were no exception. The WPA put people to work as manual and skilled laborers on construction projects: waterworks, sewage systems, irrigation ditches, hospitals, recreational facilities, power lines, streetcar tracks, airports, and roads. It employed black professionals: architects, accountants, and engineers were hired for construction projects; and writers, musicians, artists, and actors were given vehicles through which to pursue their craft. It put unskilled women to work on sewing projects. It brought new facilities to black neighborhoods: schools, community centers, athletic fields, and swimming pools. It offered important educational, recreational, and vocational

[36] George Martin, *Madam Secretary: Frances Perkins* (Boston, 1976), p. 354, describes a successful effort by Virginia Senator Harry Byrd to delete a provision concerning old-age assistance which would have required each state "to furnish sufficient assistance 'when added to the income of the aged recipient' in order to provide 'a reasonable subsistence compatible with decency and health.' " "It quickly became apparent," Martin writes, "that many Southern legislators feared the provision would allow the federal government to interfere with the manner in which the southern states treated Negroes."

7. A WPA adult education class in Louisiana

8. A 105-year-old former slave learning to write his name in a WPA literacy class at the Godman Guild Settlement House, Columbus, Ohio

9. A WPA adult education typewriting class

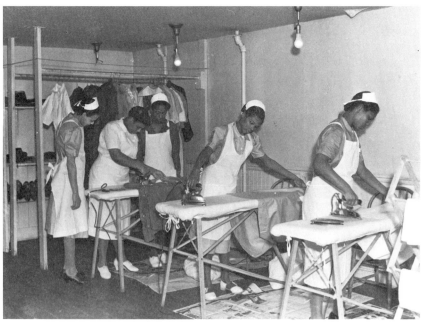

10. An ironing class, part of a WPA household training project in Baltimore

11. Youths working on an NYA construction project

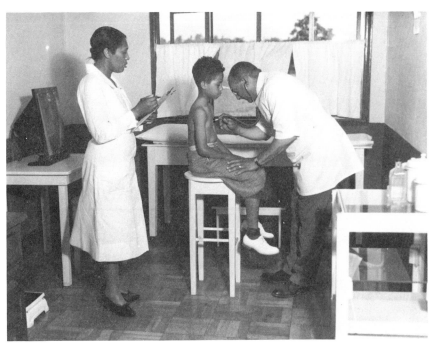

12. The Slossfield Health Center in Birmingham, a clinic constructed
and staffed by the WPA

13. Children learning to salute the flag at a WPA nursery school in New York City
14. A student sculptor at work in the Harlem Community Art Center, a division of the New York City WPA Art Project

services: classes in reading and writing for illiterate adults; instruction in dozens of academic subjects; clubs in dramatics, music, arts, and crafts; courses in home nursing, parenting, health care, and leadership development; and nursery programs for children.[37] One of its subsidiaries, the National Youth Administration, provided part-time employment for high school and college students and put unemployed youths who were not in school to work in a variety of pursuits.[38]

Because of the vigilance of the NYA administrator, Aubrey Williams, and the influence of Mary McLeod Bethune, who directed its Division of Negro Affairs, the Youth Administration "achieved a well-deserved reputation as the most racially enlightened agency in the government."[39] The WPA, on the other hand, was often plagued by discrimination. Left to their own devices, local relief administrators followed their own conservative instincts. Blacks documented the results. From Baton Rouge: "White men work at their trades and all of the Negros work comon labor." From Skipperville, Alabama: "We Por colod people . . . cant get on the releaf." From Salt Lake City: "We are hardly able to get a pick and shovel job." From Chicago: "It seems that the relief here don't employ colored engineers." From Savannah: "They have all white painters working and no colored."[40] North as well as South,

---

[37] In the Works Progress Administration Papers, Division of Information, Record Group 69, National Archives, see: *Interesting Facts about the Negro and the WPA*, n.d. [probably 1936]; Excerpt from Kansas Narrative Report, Aug. 20, 1936; Excerpt from Maryland "Bulletin," June 1936, all in Box 89; Excerpt from W. Va. Narrative Report, Dec. 20, 1936; Excerpt from Ohio Narrative Report, May 20, 1936, both in Box 90; see also *WPA and the Negro*, n.d. [Oct. 1936], Interior Department Papers, File 1-280, pt. 2; "We Work Again," Record Group 69, Motion Picture Collection, National Archives; *New York Times*, Sept. 16, 1935, p. 1, Sept. 17, 1935, p. 8; Rolla A. Southworth to Ellen S. Woodward, May 22, 1936, and L. G. Blackus to Southworth, May 4, 1936, Eleanor Roosevelt Papers, Box 704, Franklin D. Roosevelt Library (hereafter cited as the ER Papers).

[38] Morton Sosna, *In Search of the Silent South: Southern Liberals and the Race Issue* (New York, 1977), pp. 71-72; Elaine M. Smith, "Mary McLeod Bethune and the National Youth Administration" (Paper delivered at the National Archives Conference on Women's History, Apr. 23, 1976, Washington, D.C.); B. Joyce Ross, "Mary McLeod Bethune and the National Youth Administration: A Case Study of Power Relationships in the Black Cabinet of Franklin D. Roosevelt," *Journal of Negro History* LX (Jan. 1975):1-28; Michael S. Holmes, "The New Deal and Georgia's Black Youth," *Journal of Southern History* XXXVIII (Aug. 1972):443-60.

[39] Sosna, *In Search of the Silent South*, p. 71.

[40] Thomas L. Martin to Franklin D. Roosevelt, Sept. 24, 1935, Works Progress Administration Papers, Box 2, Manuscript Division, Moorland-Spingarn Research Center, Howard University (hereafter cited as the WPA Papers); Chat Reese to Franklin D. Roosevelt, Apr. 12, 1935; George C. Gray to Harry L. Hopkins, June 1, 1935, ibid., Box 1; Clarence Lymore to Honorable President, July 18, 1935; George Brown to Harry L. Hopkins, Dec. 16, 1935, ibid., Box 2.

there were disturbing patterns: qualified Negroes denied employment in skilled and white-collar positions; Negroes automatically
classified as unskilled laborers or domestic servants, no matter
what their training; whites put to work and blacks fired or left
unemployed.[41] Complaints to state or local relief officials were
likely to evoke sharp responses. "If you complain," a WPA worker
in Detroit confided, "they say we are running this job—Roosevelt
and Hopkins haven't anything to do with it." A black man in
Baton Rouge protested to a state relief official "that the President
promised all a fair deal." "He told me Dam the President and said
he did not care any dam more for the President than he did for a
dam nigger, and not as much. And said he was running the office
down here and not the dam President or no one else."[42] With
intercession from Washington, it was frequently possible to remedy the problems. But it was impossible to monitor every local
relief office, and "that Monster Predjudice" too often ran "ramp-
ant throughout W.P.A."[43]

It was the old story: significant aid and unmistakable discrimination. From the perspective of the administration, the participation of blacks in the relief and recovery programs of the 1930s
marked a real New Deal for a race ordinarily excluded from the
beneficence of the federal government. To the chairman of the
National Urban League's Emergency Advisory Councils, eager for
some affirmation of administration policy, Roosevelt declared his
confidence in the "equity and fairness" with which blacks were
being treated. The administration intended "the entire recovery
program" to provide "necessary assistance . . . for all persons without regard to race," and there was good evidence that it was
working as planned. "Negroes," Roosevelt wrote in July 1935,
"have shared in the benefits of the unemployment relief program

41 Alfred Edgar Smith, "1935 Report—Summary: Negro Clients of Federal Unemployment Relief," Dec. 31, 1935, Records of the Federal Emergency Relief
Administration, Box 116, Record Group 69, National Archives; Lovie D. Moore
to Harry Hopkins, May 8, 1936; Floyd P. Rice to Hopkins, May 11, 1936; Martha
E. Warren to Hopkins, Apr. 28, 1936; Alexander Williams to Hopkins, Mar. 13,
1936; Robert Goins to Hopkins, Oct. 13, 1935; Anonymous to Hopkins, Oct. 3,
1936; Elobie Woods to Hopkins, Oct. 3, 1936; William Harper to Hopkins, Dec.
21, 1936, all in WPA Papers, Box 2; Pinkie Pilcher to Franklin D. Roosevelt, Dec.
23, 1936, ibid., Box 1; Chester K. Gillispie to Walter White, Nov. 25, 1936, NAACP
Papers, Box C-286.
42 Raymond Randall to Dear Sir, Jan. 6, 1936, WPA Papers, Box 2; Thomas LeRoy
Martin to Franklin D. Roosevelt, n.d. [after Apr. 10, 1935], ibid., Box 1. See also
Citizens Welfare Committee to Director of Emergency Relief, July 5, 1935, ibid.
43 W. F. Davis to Franklin D. Roosevelt, Aug. 22, 1936, ibid.

in a greater proportion to the population than have either white persons or persons of other races."[44] "There has been no drawing of a color line," Secretary Ickes declared in a speech to the Chicago Urban League early in 1936. "This Administration has regarded its obligation to feed and clothe and give shelter to the Negro as no less pressing than its duty to the white man."[45] In a speech a few months later at the annual conference of the NAACP, Ickes elaborated the case: what a dramatic change in federal attitude the administration's "vigorous policy of justice toward Negroes" signified. Since Roosevelt's inauguration, the black American had enjoyed "the greatest advance since the Civil War toward assuring the Negro that degree of justice to which he is entitled and that equality of opportunity under the law which is implicit in his American citizenship."[46] Truly, the New Deal had brought "the dawning of a new day for the American Negro."[47]

Not everyone evaluated the New Deal's racial record in such glowing terms. With "that monster color prejudice ... abroad almost everywhere in Washington and elsewhere," it was hard to recognize the new day that Ickes described.[48] Ordinary blacks reported time and again that local relief administrators refused to hire them or, if they were lucky enough to be included, to pay them on the same basis as whites. Black spokesmen worried over the discrepancy between promise and performance. Distressed by widespread discrimination in New Deal programs, the NAACP tried unsuccessfully at mid-decade to mount a congressional "investigation of the economic plight of the Negro under the New Deal." The idea was Charles Houston's. Walter White thought it was "superb." He could easily envision the spectacle: sharecroppers, "victims of the NRA codes, FERA, AAA, HOLC and other agencies where the Negro has met discrimination" would be brought to Washington "to build up a thorough exposé of the plight of the Negro." Perhaps the Association could persuade Harold Ickes and Harry Hopkins to testify about their difficulty in enforcing an-

[44] Franklin D. Roosevelt to C. C. Spaulding, July 5, 1935, FDR Papers, PPF 2667. See also Spaulding to Roosevelt, June 20, July 30, 1935, ibid. Roosevelt could not be serious that blacks were getting more than their share, the *Afro-American* chastised; where was an appropriate "apology for the prejudice and intolerance ... which gives every white person ... a job before we can get one." Editorial, Aug. 3, 1935.

[45] See, e.g., Harold L. Ickes, speech to Chicago Urban League, Feb. 26, 1936, speech #99, Ickes Papers, Box 279.

[46] Harold L. Ickes, "The Negro as a Citizen," ibid., Box 281.

[47] Ickes, speech to Chicago Urban League, Feb. 26, 1936.

[48] Melvin J. Chisum to Eleanor Roosevelt, Sept. 24, 1934, ER Papers, Box 1325.

tidiscrimination orders in the face of intransigence on the part of local relief administrators and state governments in the South. "Nothing has excited me in a long time so much as this," White wrote to Houston. "Here is a fundamental exposé which cannot help but have profound effect."[49]

At first the reactions of other persons seemed to bear out White's optimism. Congressman William P. Connery, chairman of the House Labor Committee, promised to hold the hearings if the NAACP could find someone to introduce the resolution.[50] Senator Wagner, the Association's ever-faithful ally on Capitol Hill, thought the investigation would be all to the good—"As a general principle I am always in favor of turning the searchlight on the wrong existant."[51] Wagner thought that the proposed investigation would be compatible with the NAACP's major concern—the effort to pass the antilynching bill; "it would show up the injustice done to a number of our citizens just because of their color." But another ally of the NAACP, Edward P. Costigan of Colorado, disagreed; he refused to back a resolution for an investigation for fear that it would boomerang against the antilynching fight, since opponents would interpret it as evidence of "persistent personal hostility to [the] South."[52]

The difficulty of lining up even its staunchest allies was one of the main obstacles to the proposed investigation. The other was more basic: the NAACP could not raise enough money for preliminary clerical and administrative work to get the investigation organized.[53] Walter White proposed an alternate plan to Eleanor Roosevelt: a private meeting between the President and a small committee to discuss "the situation with regard to the Negro." The antilynching impasse, discrimination in jobs and relief, and "the generally wretched conditions in which so many Negroes find themselves" would comprise the principal agenda. Despite Roosevelt's promise to his wife "that he would do his best" to arrange an appointment when the press of business slackened, the opportunity never arose.[54]

[49] NAACP, *26th Annual Report* (1935), p. 5; Walter White to Charles H. Houston, Mar. 9, 1935, NAACP Papers, Box C-78.
[50] NAACP board minutes, Mar. 11, 1935, p. 1, NAACP Papers, Box A-10.
[51] Robert F. Wagner to Walter White, Mar. 29, 1935, ibid., Box C-278.
[52] E. P. Costigan telegram to Walter White, Mar. 29, 1935, ibid.
[53] NAACP, *26th Annual Report*, p. 5. It was not as though the Association was asking for big money. In a typical appeal for funds, it estimated its costs at $2,500. See, e.g., NAACP Application to the Maurice and Laura Falk Foundation, Apr. 8, 1935, NAACP Papers, Box C-278.
[54] Walter White to Eleanor Roosevelt, Sept. 12, 1935; Eleanor Roosevelt to White, Sept. 16, 1935, ER Papers, Box 1362.

Both privately and publicly, NAACP officials lamented the injustices accorded blacks by New Deal agencies.[55] "There is hardly a phase of the New Deal program," Roy Wilkins wrote in a candid letter to Mrs. Roosevelt, "which has not brought some hardship and disillusionment to colored people."[56] White told her privately of the "very widespread disappointment among Negroes in connection with . . . the discrimination . . . in the matter of jobs and relief." He also warned at the NAACP's annual conference in June 1935: "Unless justice is given the Negro, he may be driven by desperation to the use of force."[57]

Other critics were less restrained. At the National Conference on the Economic Crisis and the Negro, cosponsored by the Joint Committee on National Recovery and the Social Science Division of Howard University in May 1935, speaker after speaker indicted the New Deal for its treatment of blacks. "The fact is," the acting executive secretary of the National Urban League, T. Arnold Hill, declared, "the Negro remains that most forgotten man in a program planned to deal new cards to the millions of workers neglected and exploited in the shuffle between capital and labor. The cold fact is that state and national programs of relief, of work relief, and of private reemployment have utterly failed to relieve the exploitation which has characterized Negro labor from its early beginning down to the present day." "The Negro worker," Hill summed up, "has good reason to feel that his government has betrayed him under the New Deal." The Howard University political scientist, Ralph J. Bunche, was more caustic: the New Deal, with its ideology "illogical, inconsistent, vague, and confused" and its program "composed of a mass of self-contradictory experimentation," had accomplished little. For blacks, it meant "the same thing, but more of it." At best, it could "only fix the disadvantages, the differentials, the discriminations, under which the Negro population has labored all along." The import of the conference, a scholarly journal summed up, was "that as far as the Negro is concerned, New Deal social planning generally has availed him little either because of its underlying philosophy, or because its administration has been delegated to local officials

[55] See, for instance, Walter White to J. H. Harmon, Jr., May 24, 1935, NAACP Papers, Box C-383; NAACP press release, "Negro Desperate, Says Walter White, May Use Force If Denied Rights," June 30, 1935, ibid., Box B-11.
[56] Roy Wilkins to Eleanor Roosevelt, May 20, 1935, ibid., Box C-80.
[57] Walter White to Eleanor Roosevelt, Sept. 12, 1935, ER Papers, Box 1362; NAACP press release, "Negro Desperate, Says Walter White. . . ."

who reflect the unenlightened mores of their respective communities."[58]

The problem was not simply that blacks were, as usual, suffering the indignities and hardships of racial discrimination. Black leaders worried that the New Deal would leave the race in worse straits than before. Francis E. Rivers, a Republican lawyer in Harlem, warned of the creation of a permanent class of black reliefers, no longer employable in private industry. William Lloyd Imes, a Harlem minister, expressed concern that "the Negro is rapidly having his status as an underprivileged and last-to-be-thought-of man absolutely crystallized in federal practice."[59] John P. Davis, executive secretary of the Joint Committee on National Recovery, sounded similar notes in his public speeches. "The total effect of the government's social experiments" had been "to plan for permanent poverty." So far as blacks were concerned, those experiments had been conceived "in terms of ghetto planning, in terms of keeping the Negro in an inferior status and in a segregated existence." "None" of the New Deal recovery measures had "benefited the Negro"; in fact, "most of them have had a detrimental effect upon his economic status." "We have waited too long for reforms which never come," Davis asserted. "Now we should know reform was never intended."[60]

The indictment of the New Deal was not a parochial black complaint. Sympathetic whites affirmed that the New Deal had been something less than a fair deal for black Americans. The reporter, Bruce Bliven, recorded that the distribution of federal money in the South had been "excessively inequitable, especially among the Negroes."[61] Mary White Ovington, traveling through the South for the NAACP, reported pessimistically that "the distribution of relief and work, put in the hands of local white people as it is, is usually that the white gets the apple and the Negro the

[58] T. Arnold Hill, "The Plight of the Negro Industrial Worker," *Journal of Negro Education* V (Jan. 1936):40; Ralph J. Bunche, "A Critique of New Deal Social Planning As It Affects Negroes," ibid., pp. 59, 62; "The National Conference on the Economic Crisis and the Negro," ibid., p. 1.

[59] *New York Herald Tribune*, Dec. 8, 1935, clipping in Roosevelt Administration Scrapbooks, vol. I, microfilm reel 16, Schomburg Center for Research in Black Culture.

[60] John P. Davis speech to NAACP Annual Conference, St. Louis, June, 1935; Davis speech to National Conference of Social Work, Atlantic City, May 25, 1936, National Negro Congress Papers, Box 2 (microfilm reel 2), Schomburg Center for Research in Black Culture; NAACP press release, "Charges New Deal Reenslaves Negro; 4 Million on Relief," July 1, 1935, NAACP Papers, Box B-11.

[61] Bruce Bliven, "In the Land of Cotton," *New Republic*, Mar. 21, 1934, p. 152.

core."[62] Inside the administration, honest officials admitted that the picture painted by critics was essentially true. As the relief programs were being administered, Aubrey Williams confessed to Harry Hopkins, "The Negroes don't get a fair deal. I don't know how to secure one for them."[63] "It is very difficult to stop discrimination," Williams told concerned blacks. The administration had made real strides to help them, but their condition was still "pitiable."[64] Even the optimistic Ickes conceded that "the prejudices that have been fostered and built up for 60 years cannot be done away with over night."[65]

What are we to make, then, of the way in which New Deal programs treated blacks? Should the New Deal be praised for extending important benefits to blacks in dire economic distress? Or should it be castigated for failing to avoid discrimination and for perpetuating and perhaps solidifying the inferior status of blacks in the United States? Should one credit official pronouncements of the New Deal's evenhandedness with respect to race? Or should one listen more closely to critics who documented the shortcomings in New Deal racial practices?

There is merit in both sides of the case. The New Deal did help suffering blacks in important ways. But it too rarely escaped the racism typical of American society in the 1930s, and discrimination plagued even most of its best-intentioned programs. Some New Deal programs were responsible for making the situation of blacks in the 1930s even worse; and some programs that aided blacks in the short run may have contributed in the long run to the relegation of blacks to an economically marginal ghetto existence.

Which weighed more heavily with black Americans? The fact that federal programs and federal dollars brought some measure of improvement to the lives of many blacks? Or the failures of the administration to live up to its official commitment to a fair share for blacks without discrimination? The balance sheet was to be struck not by the organizations for racial advancement, not by the press, but by each black man and woman at the polls in the election of 1936.

[62] Mary White Ovington to Arthur B. Spingarn, Mar. 9, 1934, Arthur B. Spingarn Papers, Box 6, Manuscript Division, Library of Congress. On the same theme, see Ovington to Roy Wilkins, Feb. 19, 1934, NAACP Papers, Box C-70.

[63] Aubrey Williams memorandum to Harry Hopkins, Nov. 30, 1934, FERA Papers, Box 19.

[64] Quoted in *Afro-American*, Sept. 21, 1935.

[65] Harold L. Ickes, "The Negro as a Citizen," Ickes Papers, Box 281.

CHAPTER IX ▪ *The Election of 1936*

The election of 1936 brought black Americans decisively into the Roosevelt coalition. Four years earlier, neither Republicans nor Democrats had made much effort to court blacks; and, although black voters disenchanted with Herbert Hoover had begun to break free from their Republican allegiance, deep-rooted wariness of the Democratic party had kept most blacks at least tentatively in the Republican camp. In 1936, with the political choices more clear-cut, blacks joined the massive migration to the Democratic party.

Proponents of splitting the black vote had argued in 1932 that a show of some independence and unpredictability on the part of the black electorate would make the major parties start bidding for black support. Nineteen thirty-six proved the point. For the first time, the black vote became part of the political story in the national press. Between the conventions and the election, the *New York Herald Tribune* assigned the black reporter, Earl Brown, to write a series of articles about it.[1] "In no national election since 1860 have politicians been so Negro-minded," *Time* reported. *Newsweek* remarked on "the new spectacle of national campaigners vying for Negro votes."[2] The phenomenon was so unusual that it was easy to exaggerate its significance; it was "obvious," the *New York Times* correspondent, John Temple Graves, wrote, "that the Negro has become a tremendously important factor in national elections and that the parties from now on may be expected to vie in offers for his support."[3] The black press declared

[1] Interview with Earl Brown, June 29, 1977, New York City. Brown reported on the black vote in Pennsylvania, Illinois, Missouri, Maryland, Delaware, and New Jersey. See *New York Herald Tribune*, July 15, 1936, p. 11; July 16, 1936, p. 7; July 17, 1936, p. 4; Aug. 5, 1936, p. 7; Aug. 6, 1936, p. 8; Aug. 7, 1936, p. 7; Aug. 8, 1936, p. 2; Aug. 26, 1936, p. 11; Aug. 27, 1936, p. 7; Aug. 28, 1936, p. 4; Aug. 29, 1936, p. 5.

[2] "Black Game," *Time*, Aug. 17, 1936, p. 10; "Negroes," *Newsweek*, Sept. 12, 1936, p. 19.

[3] *New York Times*, Oct. 25, 1936, section IV, p. 7. Prominent columnists who speculated about the black vote in the 1936 election included Mark Sullivan, Dorothy Thompson, and Frank R. Kent. See, for example, Sullivan's columns in *New York Herald Tribune*, Aug. 23, 1936, section II, p. 4; Aug. 26, 1936, p. 21; Thompson, "On the Record," ibid., Aug. 11, 1936, p. 17; Kent, "The Swing of the Negroes," *Baltimore Sun*, Nov. 12, 1936, p. 1.

that the black vote would constitute the balance of power in a number of critical states. As the *Pittsburgh Courier* boasted, "Not as Maine goes, but as the Negro goes, will go the 1936 Presidential election!"[4]

These accounts clearly exaggerated the importance of the black vote—after all, blacks were disfranchised in the South and comprised only a small percentage of the eligible electorate in the North. Still, that percentage had grown significantly since 1930. The economic emergency further stimulated the migration of blacks from the South that had begun with the Great Migration of World War I and had continued in the 1920s. The Bureau of the Census estimated that 400,000 blacks left the South between 1930 and 1940. At the same time, there was an increase of 291,600 in the black population of eight northern states—Illinois, Indiana, Michigan, Missouri, New Jersey, New York, Ohio, and Pennsylvania—which accounted for 202 of the 523 electoral votes in 1936.[5] As Table IX.1 shows, blacks comprised a sufficient proportion of the population in these states, and especially in their major cities, to make the black vote worth some attention.

Accordingly, blacks attracted the attention of the major parties in 1936 in ways that had not been the case before. Neither party had satisfied the hopes of organizations for racial advancement, which had pressed for explicit stands on such issues as lynching, disfranchisement, and discrimination in federal programs.[6] The Republican platform gave its plank on the Negro less prominence than in 1932. It squeezed it in as part of the "Furthermore," expressed the party's support for "equal opportunity for our col-

[4] *Pittsburgh Courier*, Oct. 10, 1936. The white press, too, took up the idea of the black vote as the balance of power. See, e.g., *New York Herald Tribune*, Sept. 26, 1936, p. 7.

[5] U.S. Department of Commerce, Bureau of the Census, *Historical Statistics of the United States: Colonial Times to 1957* (Washington, D.C., 1960), pp. 46-47; Richard M. Scammon, comp. and ed., *America at the Polls: A Handbook of American Presidential Election Statistics, 1920-1964* (1965; reprint ed., New York, 1976), p. 9.

[6] On the NAACP's efforts to commit the parties on racial issues, see Walter White, draft of letter to GOP candidates, Mar. 5, 1936, National Association for the Advancement of Colored People Papers, Box C-392, Manuscript Division, Library of Congress (hereafter cited as the NAACP Papers); NAACP board minutes, Apr. 13, 1936, p. 4, and May 11, 1936, p. 3, ibid., Box A-10; "Statement to the Republican National Convention," June 9, 1936, ibid., Box C-392; "To the Democratic National Convention," June 23, 1936, attached to Walter White to Eleanor Roosevelt, June 19, 1936, Eleanor Roosevelt Papers, Box 1411, Franklin D. Roosevelt Library (hereafter cited as the ER Papers). On similar efforts by the National Negro Congress, see [?] to Henry Fletcher, June 1936, National Negro Congress Papers, Box 5 (microfilm reel 3), Schomburg Center for Research in Black Culture.

TABLE IX.1
Black Population, Selected Northern States and Major Cities, 1930 and 1940

| | 1930 | | | 1940 | | |
	Total Population	Black Population	Percent Black	Total Population	Black Population	Percent Black
Illinois	7,630,654	328,972	4.3	7,897,241	387,446	4.9
Chicago	3,376,438	233,903	6.9	3,396,808	277,731	8.2
Indiana	3,238,503	111,982	3.5	3,427,796	121,916	3.6
Indianapolis	364,161	43,967	12.1	386,972	51,142	13.2
Michigan	4,842,325	169,453	3.5	5,256,106	208,345	4.0
Detroit	1,568,662	120,066	7.7	1,623,452	149,119	9.2
Missouri	3,629,367	223,840	6.2	3,784,664	244,386	6.5
Kansas City	399,746	38,574	9.6	399,178	41,574	10.4
St. Louis	821,960	93,580	11.4	816,048	108,765	13.3

New Jersey	4,041,334	208,828	5.2	4,160,165	226,973	5.5
Newark	442,337	38,880	8.8	429,760	45,760	10.6
New York	12,588,066	412,814	3.3	13,479,142	571,221	4.2
New York City	6,930,446	327,706	4.7	7,454,995	458,444	6.1
(Manhattan Borough)	(1,867,312)	(224,670)	(12.0)	(1,889,924)	(298,365)	(15.8)
Ohio	6,646,697	309,304	4.7	6,907,612	339,461	4.9
Cincinnati	451,160	47,818	10.6	455,610	55,593	12.2
Cleveland	900,429	71,899	8.0	878,336	84,504	9.6
Pennsylvania	9,631,350	431,257	4.5	9,900,180	470,172	4.7
Philadelphia	1,950,961	219,599	11.3	1,931,334	250,880	13.0
Pittsburgh	669,817	54,983	8.2	671,659	62,216	9.3

SOURCES: U.S. Department of Commerce, Bureau of Census, Fifteenth Census of the United States: 1930, Population, vol. III: Reports by States (Washington, D.C., 1932), pt. 1, pp. 591, 676, 683, 744, 1115, 1183, 1319, 1388; pt. 2, pp. 177, 223, 259, 326-27, 457, 535, 651, 750-51; Sixteenth Census of the United States: 1940, Population, vol. II: Characteristics of the Population (Washington, D.C., 1943), pt. 2, pp. 476, 640, 676, 814, pt. 3, pp. 760, 892; pt. 4, pp. 312, 449, 456, 812, 925; pt. 5, pp. 14, 157, 178, 542, 703, 710; pt. 6, pp. 14, 211, 218.

ored citizens," and promised its "protection of their economic status and personal safety."[7] It was "a vague statement," "the weakest" in the history of the party, black spokesmen said.[8] "The weakness of the Republican plank" seemed to Walter White to offer the Democrats "a great opportunity."[9] But the authors of the Democratic platform chose not to seize it. "If the Republicans said little of significance on the Negro in their platform," the *Crisis* commented, "the Democrats went them one better by saying nothing."[10] The Democratic platform's failure to make any mention of blacks was a "grave disappointment" to the NAACP and others who had hoped for a forthright statement on pressing racial concerns.[11]

However, the reluctance to confront serious racial issues had to be counterbalanced against other kinds of evidence. First was the abrogation of the Democratic party's century-old two-thirds rule, under which the support of two-thirds of the convention delegates had been required for nomination. In recent years, the rule had become an annoying obstruction; in 1924, in the most flagrant case, the convention balloting had dragged on for 103 ballots before a candidate had managed to secure the necessary votes. Not only was the rule cumbersome, but it clearly shaped the balance of power in the party, for it gave the South a veto power over the convention's choice. Roosevelt had pushed unsuccessfully for repeal of the rule in 1932; now, with his renomination certain, repeal was possible to accomplish. Reducing the necessary margin to a simple majority of the convention delegates was a way of modernizing the Democratic party. Although it was not conceived as a slap at the South, it inevitably reduced the influence of that section in the nominating convention. Proponents of repeal had no thought of thereby enhancing the political power of blacks. But insofar as repeal helped to make the Democrats, in *Opportunity*'s words, a "truly national" party, blacks could not help but benefit.[12]

[7] Kirk H. Porter and Donald Bruce Johnson, comps., *National Party Platforms, 1840-1960*, 2nd ed. (Urbana, Ill., 1961), p. 369.

[8] NAACP press release, "G.O.P. Platform Does Not Mention Lynching," June 12, 1936, NAACP Papers, Box C-392; editorial, *Pittsburgh Courier*, June 20, 1936.

[9] Walter White to Robert F. Wagner, June 17, 1936, NAACP Papers, Box C-392.

[10] "The Democrats Speak," *Crisis* XLIII (Aug. 1936):241.

[11] Porter and Johnson, comps., *National Party Platforms*, pp. 360-63; Walter White telegram to Franklin D. Roosevelt, June 26, 1936, NAACP Papers, Box C-392.

[12] "The Democratic Convention," *Opportunity* XIV (July 1936):197. On repeal

The second positive sign was an obvious willingness on the part of the Democrats to make some overtures to black voters.[13] The Republicans had certainly not done so in their nominating convention. The GOP refused the request of the *Pittsburgh Courier* for a seat at the convention's press tables, perhaps because the *Courier* had led the flight from the party of Lincoln in 1932; perhaps, too, the paper speculated, because "the fight of the Lily Whites to bar Negroes from the convention" would "make spicy news."[14] Credentials fights between lily-white and black-and-tan delegations, who vied to represent certain southern states, *did* make news, and the party chose so often to seat the lily-whites that it "caused a widespread stir among Negroes in the North as well as in the South."[15]

The Democrats, on the other hand, seated ten black delegates and twenty-two alternates from twelve states—the first time the party had accredited blacks as delegates as well as alternates. What a marked contrast it provided to the segregation of the handful of Negro alternates behind chicken wire at the convention in Houston in 1928! For the first time, too, black reporters took seats in the regular press box, and the party scheduled a press conference for black newspapers.[16]

In another first, a black clergyman, Marshall L. Shepard, pastor of Mt. Olivet Tabernacle Baptist Church in Philadelphia and a member of the Pennsylvania legislature, delivered the invocation at a convention session—followed immediately, as if to remedy the damage, by the singing of "Dixie."[17] Shepard's appearance on the podium prompted a widely-publicized walkout by Senator "Cotton Ed" Smith of South Carolina. "By God, he's as black as

---

of the rule, see Arthur M. Schlesinger, Jr., *The Politics of Upheaval* (Boston, 1960), pp. 580-81.

[13] This point is underscored in an editorial in *Chicago Defender*, July 11, 1936.

[14] *Pittsburgh Courier*, June 13, 1936.

[15] *New York Times*, June 4, 1936, p. 2; June 7, 1936, p. 32; June 10, 1936, p. 15 (source of the quotation); June 11, 1936, p. 18; "The G.O.P. Speaks," *Crisis* XLIII (July 1936):209.

[16] *Chicago Defender*, June 27, 1936; *Pittsburgh Courier*, July 4, 1936; William E. Leuchtenburg, "Election of 1936," in *History of American Presidential Elections, 1789-1968*, ed. Arthur M. Schlesinger, Jr. and Fred L. Israel, 4 vols. (New York, 1971), III:2832.

[17] *New York Times*, June 25, 1936, p. 12; *Pittsburgh Courier*, July 4, 1936; Stanley High, "Black Omens," *Saturday Evening Post*, June 4, 1938, p. 40; Program, Democratic National Committee, typescript, n.d., James A. Farley Papers, Box 35, Manuscript Division, Library of Congress. A black minister—in this instance, Bishop James W. Brown of New Mother African Methodist Episcopal Church in Harlem—also delivered the opening prayer at a session of the Republican National Convention. See *New York Times*, June 12, 1936, p. 11.

melted midnight!" Smith declared. "Get outa my way. This mongrel meeting ain't no place for a white man!" "I am not opposed to any Negro praying for me," he subsequently explained, "but I don't want any blue-gummed, slew-footed Senegambian praying for me politically!"[18] When Congressman Arthur W. Mitchell delivered one of the speeches seconding Roosevelt's renomination—the first time that a black person had spoken from the floor of a Democratic convention—Smith walked out again and declared that the convention's "acceptance of the Negro on terms of political equality" had "humiliated the South."[19] The South Carolina delegation unanimously adopted a resolution protesting against the presence of blacks on the convention program.[20]

Even the delegation to notify Vice-President Garner of his renomination included a black man.[21] In view of the Democratic party's reluctance to commit itself on issues of substance such as lynching, disfranchisement, and discrimination, its sudden show of token representation looked to some like a cynical effort to appeal to black voters on the most superficial grounds. Walter White recognized the political trade-offs; as he wrote to Roy Wilkins, the opportunity for Mitchell to speak at the convention came about precisely because Chairman Farley "knew he could not get the planks into the platform which we [the NAACP] asked."[22] But many blacks saw the convention differently. When the custom had been for blacks to be ignored and excluded, even token representation "marked an epoch in the political life of the Negro."[23]

The campaign, like the Democratic convention, showed that the black vote was, for the first time, something to be reckoned with. The Republican National Committee announced "plans for the most intensive campaign among the Negro race ever waged by the Republican party."[24] The Democrats, seeking to capitalize

[18] Quoted in Allan A. Michie and Frank Ryhlick, *Dixie Demagogues* (New York, 1939), pp. 266, 281.

[19] *New York Times*, June 26, 1936, p. 15; *Pittsburgh Courier*, July 4, 1936.

[20] *New York Times*, June 27, 1936, p. 8. While South Carolina made the most noise on the subject, its objections were not idiosyncratic. In Florida, for example, the abolition of the two-thirds rule and the recognition of blacks at the convention caused "real resentment." See George B. Hillis to J. B. Hodges, July 20, 1936, Democratic National Committee Papers, Box 1093, Franklin D. Roosevelt Library.

[21] *Chicago Defender*, June 27, 1936.

[22] Walter White to Roy Wilkins, Aug. 4, 1936, NAACP Papers, Box C-392.

[23] "The Democratic Convention," p. 197.

[24] Republican National Committee press release, Aug. 3, 1936, Claude A. Barnett Papers, Box P3, Chicago Historical Society.

on the electoral trend that had begun in 1932, embarked on what a political analyst for the *Nation* described as "elaborate and unprecedented efforts to woo the colored gentry away from the G.O.P."[25] In the process, the party might lose the South, white southern Democrats worried.[26] Some Southerners put the case more strongly: in the words of the *Charleston News and Observer*, "the Northern Democrats and President Roosevelt . . . are sacrificing the South for the votes of negroes in a dozen Northern cities."[27]

Both parties for the first time advertised extensively in the black press and took full-page advertisements in newspapers and magazines to extol the virtues of their candidates. Sometimes such advertisements were placed in explicit trade for an editorial endorsement.[28] J. Raymond Jones described "a deal" between the Democratic party and the *New York Amsterdam News*, in which the party gave "money . . . for . . . advertising" in exchange "for the newspaper's support" in the election. Farley had also instructed Jones to offer the editor of the *Amsterdam News*, C. B. Powell, the leadership of the Roosevelt campaign in Harlem in an effort to gain the paper's support.[29] Other media offered opportunities as well: the Democrats, as will be discussed shortly, made their own movie about the benefits to blacks under the WPA; Republicans blanketed Negro theaters with three-minute films. Some showed prominent blacks, such as the president of the Negro Elks, speaking in Landon's behalf; some featured black entertainers, such as Mamie Smith and the Beale Street Boys, who sang "Oh, Susannah" and made a pitch for the GOP.[30]

Republicans and Democrats alike competed for endorsements from blacks of note—a wooing process in which each party tried

[25] Paul W. Ward, "Wooing the Negro Vote," *Nation*, Aug. 1, 1936, p. 119.

[26] See, e.g., William L. Grayson to Harllee Branch, July 1, 1936, and Branch to Marvin H. McIntyre, July 3, 1936, Franklin D. Roosevelt Papers, Official File (OF) 300, Box 30, Franklin D. Roosevelt Library (hereafter cited as the FDR Papers).

[27] Editorial, June 28, 1936, in *The Attitude of the Southern White Press toward Negro Suffrage, 1932-1940*, ed. Rayford W. Logan (Washington, D.C., 1940), pp. 65-66.

[28] *Opportunity* XIV (Oct., Nov. 1936):318, 320, 350, 352. For a typical newspaper ad, see *Afro-American*, Oct. 31, 1936. On political advertising in the black press, see also Andrew Buni, *The Negro in Virginia Politics, 1902-1965* (Charlottesville, Va., 1967), p. 115.

[29] Hilton B. Clark interview with J. Raymond Jones, pt. 10, July 13, 1974, pp. 10, 27. The quotations are on p. 10.

[30] On the Democrats' movie, see below, p. 199. On the Republican efforts, see Ralph D. Casey, "Republican Propaganda in the 1936 Campaign," *Public Opinion Quarterly* I (Apr. 1937):35.

Re-Elect ROOSEVELT

Not Promise But Performance

*Read
What He
Has Done - -*

*VOTE FOR
HIS RE-
ELECTION!*

PRESIDENT FRANKLIN D. ROOSEVELT

● **UNEMPLOYMENT RELIEF**
 inaugurated by the Roosevelt Administration saved millions of Negro men, women and children from extreme want by direct relief, WPA and PWA. No racial discrimination permitted by the Federal Government.

● **THE SOCIAL SECURITY LAW**
 passed by the Administration provides for old age pensions and unemployment insurance.

● **THE CIVILIAN CONSERVATION CORPS (CCC)**
 started in 1933 by President Roosevelt has given employment to over 150,000 young Negro men.

● **THE NATIONAL YOUTH ADMINISTRATION (NYA)**
 put in operation by the Roosevelt Administration gives direct educational and economic benefits to over 50,000 young Negro men and women.

● **NEGRO APPOINTMENTS**
 to key government positions in Washington and throughout the country by the Roosevelt Administration exceed any such number in history.

● **THE REGULATION OF BANKING AND INVESTMENTS**
 by the Administration's reforms protects small depositors by insuring bank savings up to $5,000. The Securities and Exchange Act protects the small investor from fraud and misrepresentation.

● **AGAINST ECONOMIC MALADJUSTMENT**
 the Roosevelt Administration stands as a symbol of national revolt against the economic maladjustments sponsored by twelve years of Republican misrule.

15. A Democratic campaign advertisement in *Opportunity*, October 1936

DISTRESS
Knows No Color Line

When the great Depression struck America, it hit high and low, black and white, foreign-born and native, farmer and city dweller alike.

Anxiety, uncertainty, fear, hunger, and tragedy stalked the land.

Distress knows no color line. It hurts just as much to starve if one is black as it does if one is white. It is just as tragic for the life savings of a struggling colored family to be swept away as it is for those of white families to be wiped out.

The great human suffering of millions of Americans called for a man to bring relief from hunger; to provide jobs; to save property and lives; to banish fear and restore hope; to devise a plan for a more abundant life for *all* Americans.

Franklin D. Roosevelt proved to be such a man. A man who realized at once that rescue, like distress, must know no color line. As far as was humanly possible he brought relief to all the people, irrespective of section, occupation, race, color or religion.

Look back to the dark, bitter winter of 1932-33. Then look about you today. Everything is not perfectly adjusted as all would have it, but we are on our way out—*all of us together.*

If we throw out all the shouting back and forth, all the political ballyhoo, and all the involved "arguments," there remains one shining, unanswerable truth:

> Franklin D. Roosevelt put us back on our feet, made it possible for us to hold up our chins and march forward—and he did it for high and low, black and white, foreign-born and native, farmer and city dweller.

Colored Americans and their white fellow citizens can well forget everything else on November 3 and remember that truth.

Vote for . . . .
ROOSEVELT

This is a political advertisement authorized by the Democratic National Committee to be paid for at the regular political rates.

16. A Democratic campaign advertisement in *Opportunity*, November 1936

VOTE FOR
LANDON and KNOX

REPUBLICAN NOMINEES FOR PRESIDENT AND VICE PRESIDENT

THE ELECTION OF ALFRED M. LANDON AND COL. FRANK KNOX MEANS:

The abolition of the horrible discrimination established in such agencies as Unemployment Relief, Social Security Law, the Civilian Conservation Corps (CCC), the National Youth Administration (NYA) and other emergency agencies by the Southern-controlled, Roosevelt New Deal Democratic Administration.

THE ELECTION OF LANDON AND KNOX MEANS:

The termination of the Southern-controlled Roosevelt New Deal Democratic Administration's program to eliminate the Negro from the gainfully employed life of the Nation. This New Deal program proposes to make the Negro a permanent ward of the Nation, permanently unemployed, permanently on relief. The New Deal proposes to confine employment in gainful labor solely to white persons.

THE CONTINUATION OF THE NEW DEAL MEANS:

THE GHETTO, THE RESERVATION, THE JIM CROW, SERFDOM AND EXTINCTION FOR THE NEGRO.

IT MEANS FURTHER THAT THE NEW DEAL HAS CLOSED TO THE NEGRO THE DOOR OF HOPE FOR AN HONORABLE CAREER IN THE FEDERAL SERVICE.

VOTE AGAINST THE RE-ELECTION OF ROOSEVELT BECAUSE:

(a) The New Deal National Recovery Administration (NRA) means government-directed destruction of Negro employment.

(b) The New Deal Agricultural Adjustment Administration (AAA) means government-created destruction of Negro farming.

(c) The New Deal Civilian Conservation Corp (CCC) means peace time segregation for Negro youths.

(d) The New Deal National Youth Administration (NYA) is a mockery of Negro youth.

(e) The New Deal Works Progress Administration (WPA) is killing the skill of Negro workers.

(f) The New Deal National Re-employment Service (NRS) shows constructively the determination of the New Deal to use the government to eliminate the Negro from private employment and confine him permanently to relief.

(g) The Reconstruction Finance Corporation, under the administration of the New Deal, has proved a helper of white American business but a destroyer of Negro business.

(h) The New Deal administration of Relief has prostituted an intended institution of Salvation and made it a modern Reservation for Negroes.

THEREFORE NO THOUGHTFUL AMERICAN NEGRO SHOULD CAST A VOTE FOR THE DEMOCRATIC PARTY.

COLORED VOTERS SHOULD SHOW THEIR RESENTMENT AGAINST PRESIDENT FRANKLIN D. ROOSEVELT'S SILENCE ON THE ANTI-LYNCHING BILL BY VOTING AGAINST HIM.

COLORED VOTERS MUST HELP DEFEND THE CONSTITUTION AND THE SUPREME COURT AGAINST DESTRUCTION BY THE DEMOCRATIC PARTY.

COLORED VOTERS MUST SHOW THEIR RESENTMENT AGAINST THE NEW DEAL DEMOCRATIC ADMINISTRATION'S BRUTAL INDIFFERENCE TO THE RAPE OF ETHIOPIA.

The Republican National Convention in its platform and Gov. Landon in public statements, have pledged the Negro a Square Deal. The Democratic Convention does not mention the Negro in its platform and the Democratic Candidate is silent as to his stand on anti-lynching legislation.

ALL NEGROES WHO SHARE IN FEELING THE WRONGS SUFFERED BY ANY OTHER ONE OF THEIR GROUP HAVE BUT ONE CHOICE ON ELECTION DAY TO HELP ACHIEVE THEIR GOAL: THE SUPPORT OF THE REPUBLICAN PARTY AND ITS STANDARD BEARERS—ALFRED M. LANDON AND FRANK KNOX.

17. A Republican campaign advertisement in *Opportunity*, November 1936

to outdo the other, sometimes with amusing results. At a time when there were so few authentic black heroes, the Republicans were particularly proud of winning the support of the Olympic track star, Jesse Owens. As soon as Owens won his medals in Berlin, the Democrats sent Robert L. Vann, then traveling in Europe, to seek his support for Roosevelt. When Owens arrived in New York aboard the *Queen Mary*, the Democratic emissaries, Jack Dempsey and Bill "Bojangles" Robinson, were there to meet the ship. But Republican agents had reached Owens in Berlin even before Vann, and Owens announced his support for Landon at a well-publicized press conference at Republican headquarters in New York. The party later sent him on a national tour.[31]

Both national committees geared up more elaborate "colored divisions" to organize the campaign among blacks. The New York lawyer, Francis E. Rivers, and the Chicago clergyman, Lacey K. Williams, ran the Republican effort. The Boston lawyer, Julian D. Rainey, and Congressman Arthur W. Mitchell took charge of the Democratic colored divisions.[32] Within weeks of the Democratic convention, Eleanor Roosevelt had urged James Farley to make plans for the campaign among blacks. Farley, in turn, had looked to Will Alexander for advice on how to proceed,[33] but his selection of Mitchell was something of a gaffe. In giving Mitchell "so prom-

[31] *New York Times*, Sept. 3, 1936, p. 10; "Negroes," pp. 18-19; Leuchtenburg, "Election of 1936," p. 2818. For a description of one Owens campaign appearance, see Robert Austin Warner, *New Haven Negroes: A Social History* (New Haven, 1940), pp. 293-94. Newspaper accounts suggested (and Owens did not deny) that Owens was liberally remunerated for his services. *Afro-American*, Nov. 7, 1936.

[32] On the personnel and organization of the parties' campaigns among blacks, see: *New York Herald Tribune*, July 30, 1936, p. 6; Aug. 15, 1936, p. 5; Sept. 26, 1936, p. 7; *New York Times*, Aug. 1, 1936, p. 11; Aug. 7, 1936, p. 8; *Chicago Defender*, *Pittsburgh Courier*, and *Afro-American*, Aug. 8, 1936; "Negroes," p. 19; Thomas T. Spencer, "The Good Neighbor League Colored Committee and the 1936 Democratic Presidential Campaign," *Journal of Negro History* LXIII (Fall 1978):308. For examples of Mitchell's work as head of the Democratic party's western division, see Arthur W. Mitchell to Mrs. G. W. Cummings, Sept. 4, 1936, Arthur W. Mitchell Papers, Box 21, Chicago Historical Society; Mitchell to Eugene V. Gowin, Sept. 21, 1936; Mitchell to W. F. Reden, Sept. 22, 1936; Mitchell to Edna Peoples, Sept. 24, 1936; Mitchell to James A. Farley, Sept. 24, 1936; Mitchell to J. E. Mitchell, Oct. 5, 1936, all in ibid., Box 22; Mitchell to Gertrude Bryant, Oct. 31, 1936, ibid., Box 23; Farley to Mitchell, Aug. 25, 1936, Democratic National Committee Papers, Box 1096. On the activities of the Democratic party's eastern division, see, for example, Report of Roger M. Yancey, Chairman, First Voters Division, Eastern Division of Colored Voters, Sept. 14–Oct. 31, 1936, and Report of William L. Houston, Chairman of the Speakers Bureau, Eastern Division of Colored Voters, Oct. 22, 1936–Nov. 2, 1936, Carrie Burton Overton Papers, Box 6, Archives of Labor History and Urban Affairs, Wayne State University.

[33] Eleanor Roosevelt memorandum to the President, Mr. Farley et al., July 16, 1936; James A. Farley to Eleanor Roosevelt, July 25, 1936, Farley Papers, Box 4.

inent a part in the campaign," Farley misjudged the congressman's standing among black leaders. The NAACP, embroiled in a feud with Mitchell over (among other things) his role in the antilynching fight, judged him to be "a knave and a fool." "The irony of the situation," Walter White commented privately, "is that Farley ... thinks that honors to Mitchell as a colored man will be pleasing to the N.A.A.C.P." Featuring Mitchell so prominently struck White as a way "to drive intelligent Negroes away from Roosevelt."[34]

Whereas in previous years colored divisions had often been window dressing, this year the parties meant business. The colored divisions provided speakers and publicity, sponsored rallies, secured endorsements of their presidential candidates from well-known blacks, and encouraged voter registration. The Democrats profited from the advantages of incumbency and recognized the black vote as a prize ripe for capture, and they made the more impressive effort. Scores of black preachers, educators, editors, and others went on the party's payroll. Farley made judicious use of patronage to rally black support. Some 150 choice governmental jobs went to blacks in major cities. Nearly every state Democratic headquarters had its own Negro division.[35] In a tour of the Midwest, Turner Catledge of the *New York Times* found "the Democratic Negroes ... better organized, down to precinct workers, than the whites."[36]

Allied political groups joined the official colored Democratic divisions. The most notable of these was the Good Neighbor League, a national organization with headquarters in New York City, which argued the case for the New Deal to blacks, labor, and religious groups. Although the league was financed in part by the Democratic National Committee, its official status as an independent, nonpartisan political group made it a useful vehicle

[34] Walter White to Roy Wilkins, Aug. 4, 1936, NAACP Papers, Box C-392.

[35] Joseph F. Guffey, *Seventy Years on the Red-Fire Wagon* (n.p., 1952), p. 171; Eugene A. Hatfield, "The Impact of the New Deal on Black Politics in Pennsylvania, 1928-1936" (Ph.D. diss., University of North Carolina at Chapel Hill, 1979), pp. 222-27; Earl Brown, "How the Negro Voted in the Presidential Election," *Opportunity* XIV (Dec. 1936):360; Joseph Alsop and Robert Kintner, "The Guffey: Biography of a Boss, New Style," *Saturday Evening Post*, Mar. 26, 1938, p. 6. When he wrote his political autobiography in the 1940s, Farley made no mention of any of this (James A. Farley, *Jim Farley's Story: The Roosevelt Years* [New York, 1948]). And, years later, he could not recall making any special effort to court the black vote. (Interview with James A. Farley, Oct. 3, 1974, New York City.)

[36] *New York Times*, Oct. 26, 1936, p. 2.

to reach voters who might support Roosevelt but who might not identify themselves with the Democratic party.[37]

The Good Neighbor League boasted a National Colored Committee of forty clergymen, educators, and professional and business people—nearly all former Republicans—under the chairmanship of Bishop R. R. Wright, Jr., of the African Methodist Episcopal Church. Adam Clayton Powell, Sr., pastor of the Abyssinian Baptist Church in Harlem, served initially as co-chairman but he resigned in a dispute with Wright.[38] The Colored Committee swung into action in September by asserting its intention to make blacks "stop voting for Lincoln and vote for Roosevelt instead."[39] It distributed hundreds of thousands of pieces of campaign literature which recounted its own activities, described the impact of the New Deal on blacks, or featured a prominent black person's version of the case for Roosevelt. It lobbied among churchmen, arranged Sunday afternoon civic forums on political issues, and launched a drive to organize pro-Roosevelt "good neighbor clubs" in Methodist and Baptist churches around the country.[40]

To mark the seventy-fourth anniversary of the preliminary Emancipation Proclamation, the league organized twenty-five simultaneous mass meetings in northern industrial states. They were capped by a nationally-broadcast extravaganza in Madison Square Garden which drew 16,000 blacks. It was, in the words of the man who conceived it, "the biggest Negro political rally ever held." The league lost no opportunity to capitalize on the Lincoln connection; advance publicity for the rallies on September 21

[37] Donald R. McCoy, "The Good Neighbor League and the Presidential Campaign of 1936," *Western Political Quarterly* XIII (Dec. 1960):1011; Spencer, "The Good Neighbor League Colored Committee," pp. 308, 313.

[38] On the activities and funding of the Good Neighbor League, see Finding Aid, Good Neighbor League Papers, Franklin D. Roosevelt Library (hereafter cited as the GNL Papers); Stanley High to Charles E. Edison, Apr. 1, 1936, ibid., Box 1; Good Neighbor League press release, "Conference of National Colored Committee of Good Neighbor League Reveals Strong Support for President Roosevelt," n.d., ibid., Box 10; *New York Times*, Sept. 3, 1936, p. 10; Sept. 4, 1936, p. 2; Sept. 22, 1936, p. 4; Harry Slattery to J. Chester Allen, Sept. 3, 1936, Department of the Interior Papers, Office of the Secretary, Central Classified Files, File 1-280, pt. 2, Record Group 48, National Archives; High, "Black Omens," p. 14; Heads of Dept. Meeting, Sept. 1, 1936, Farley Papers, Box 51; Spencer, "The Good Neighbor League Colored Committee," pp. 309-313.

[39] Quoted in *New York Times*, Sept. 3, 1936, p. 10.

[40] R. R. Wright, Jr., memorandum to Dr. High, n.d.; "Things to be Done in Connection with the Organizing of Colored Churches under the Auspices of the Good Neighbor League for the Purpose of Promoting the Reelection of Pres. Franklin D. Roosevelt," undated typescript, both in GNL Papers, Box 1.

FREE! To Everyone! Come Join In This Monster Tribute!

74th Anniversary Celebration of

Negro Progress

A Dramatic Spectacle Extolling The Negro and His Achievments

•

Monday Sept. 21st at 8 P. M.

at Madison Square Garden

EIGHTH AVENUE at 50th STREET   -   -   NEW YORK CITY

•

. . . SPEAKERS . . .

U. S. SENATOR	CONGRESSWOMAN
Robert F. Wagner	*Caroline G. O'Day*
BISHOP	ELDER
R. C. Ransom	*S. L. Michaux*

Donald R. Richberg Former Head of N R A

•

. . . SPECIAL FEATURES . . .

Cab Calloway and His Cotton Club Orchestra

Elder Michaux's "HAPPY AM I" CHOIR
40-Piece Monarch Elks Band

Sponsored by Colored Committee of

The Good Neighbor League

The Arlain Press — 112

18. A flyer announcing a political rally celebrating the anniversary of the preliminary Emancipation Proclamation, sponsored by the Colored Committee of the Good Neighbor League, September 1936

promised a new Emancipation Proclamation "setting forth current strivings for social and economic betterment of Negroes," and the Colored Committee hailed Roosevelt as the second emancipator.[41] Using as its text Wright's keynote address, "The Second Emancipation," the Madison Square Garden meeting adopted a resolution that called for emancipation "from mere party names and party shibboleths." Blacks, the rally declared, should "not be shackled by the slavery of dead issues of a day long past." They should, rather, "carry forward the real spirit of Abraham Lincoln by supporting the social and economic programs of our great President, Franklin D. Roosevelt."[42] The climax of the rally, as the director of the Good Neighbor League later recounted it, came when the Colored Committee unveiled "a colossal painting of The Second Emancipation—with Franklin D. Roosevelt standing, to a height of twenty feet, his hands outstretched in benediction over a kneeling group of Negroes and with the Spirit of Abraham Lincoln hovering . . . in the shadows of the background."[43]

The themes of the campaign were sharply drawn. Landon proclaimed his "belief in the absolute equality of all American citizens." He condemned lynching and called without specificity for "some legal means" to end it. He made general pronouncements against intolerance and bigotry.[44] These official statements on racial issues were correct, if vague. Caught off guard, however, Landon proved to be less careful. In July, when the candidate was vacationing at Estes Park, Colorado, an *Afro-American* reporter asked him at a press conference what he would do as President about lynching, relief, and the requirement of photographs for civil service applications. Landon refused to comment. As the *Afro-American* told the story, his "face turned red. It was just like a bolt of lightning out of [a] clear blue sky." Landon's press secretary "told the AFRO reporter after the conference that the questions should not have been asked publicly; that they embarrassed the Governor. He also tried to justify Governor Landon's

[41] High, "Black Omens," p. 14 ("biggest . . . rally"); *New York Times*, Sept. 4, 1936, p. 2 ("current strivings"); Good Neighbor League press release, "Negroes Plan Nationwide Series of Meetings for Roosevelt," Sept. 4, [1936], GNL Papers, Box 10.
[42] Quoted in *New York Times*, Sept. 22, 1936, p. 4. For the text of Wright's speech, see R. R. Wright, Jr., "The Second Emancipation," Sept. 21, 1936, GNL Papers, Box 1.
[43] High, "Black Omens," p. 14.
[44] Quoted in *New York Times*, Sept. 3, 1936, p. 10, and Oct. 6, 1936, p. 1. See also ibid., Sept. 27, 1936, p. 30; Oct. 2, 1936, p. 7; and *Chicago Defender*, July 18, 25, 1936.

evasions and refusals by asking if President Roosevelt had been asked similar questions." The *Afro-American* later made much of the separate meals, housing, and headquarters for blacks at the Landon notification ceremonies in Topeka. The Jim Crow arrangements were "said by many [blacks] to be the worst ever witnessed. Some declared that they would have received much better treatment in Alabama or Mississippi."[45]

The Republican appeal to blacks in 1936 consisted essentially of two thrusts: the argument from tradition, and an attack on the New Deal. Remember Lincoln and the Thirteenth and Fourteenth Amendments, Landon reminded blacks. The Democratic party was dominated by anti-black Southerners. In contrast, in the Republican party, the black voter was "in the house of his friends": "The history of the Republican party and that of our colored citizens are so interwoven that it is impossible to think of freedom and the remarkable progress of colored Americans without recalling the origin of our party."[46]

To some voters, it was comforting to hear "the good old doctrines which . . . redeemed [the Republic] in the sixties," and the fact that "the Republicans gave our people the ballot" seemed reason enough to vote for Landon.[47] But most blacks, tired of "ancient ruses" and "oratorical pilgrimages to the tomb of Lincoln," wanted more than to be reminded of "the labors of the Republican Party for this people in their darkest hour."[48] "American people expect you to discuss the issues of the campaign; instead you discuss history," a black Democrat chided Francis E. Rivers.[49] The *Afro-American* made the point succinctly: "ABRAHAM LINCOLN IS NOT A CANDIDATE IN THE PRESIDENTIAL CAMPAIGN."[50]

What was at stake in the campaign, as the AMEZ *Star of Zion* pointed out, was "the present economic adjustment, social jus-

[45] *Afro-American*, July 11, Aug. 1, 1936. See also editorial, July 18, 1936.
[46] Quoted in *New York Times*, Oct. 11, 1936, p. 46, and Sept. 3, 1936, p. 10.
[47] J. Finley Wilson to Mary Church Terrell, Apr. 15, 1936, Mary Church Terrell Papers, Box 8, Manuscript Division, Library of Congress; letter to the editor from Mrs. Thad Miller of Chicago, *Chicago Metropolitan News*, Oct. 10, 1936, Mitchell Papers, Box 22.
[48] Editorial, *Star of Zion*, Oct. 1, 1936 ("ancient ruses"); Joseph L. McLemore to Francis E. Rivers, Oct. 10, 1936, Mitchell Papers, Box 22 ("oratorical pilgrimages"); Landon quoted in Francis E. Rivers, "The Negro Should Support Landon," *Crisis* XLIII (Oct. 1936):297 ("the labors of the Republican Party").
[49] Joseph L. McLemore to Francis E. Rivers, Oct. 10, 1936, Mitchell Papers, Box 22.
[50] *Afro-American*, Oct. 17, 1936.

tice, labor equality, better housing and meat and bread and education."[51] On that terrain, of course, Republican spokesmen denounced the New Deal. They argued that New Deal policies were based on the assumption of a permanent and large reservoir of the unemployed, which would include most blacks; that, as a result of New Deal programs, blacks would be permanently excluded from productive gainful employment; and that the New Deal relief rolls functioned as modern reservations to which blacks would be confined as wards of the federal government.[52] It was a sophisticated argument, but there was no way it could appeal successfully to the majority of blacks in the 1930s. If you were out of work and the New Deal put you on relief, was it a way to exclude you from productive employment and to make you a permanent ward of the government? Or was it a way to extend lifesaving assistance? Given the reality of some immediate relief from economic privation, it was nearly impossible to expect a beneficiary of the New Deal to step back in 1936 and take the long view of the Republican argument.

The Democrats, in contrast, capitalized on the very assistance that the Republicans found so insidious. Speakers read testimonials from blacks who had been helped by federal relief. They recited the litany of New Deal programs and, borrowing Biblical references, reminded their audiences of their debt to the President: "He clothed us when we were naked, gave us drink when we thirsted, fed us when we were hungry and gave us shelter when we were out in the cold."[53] The literature of the Democratic National Committee's Colored Division spelled out the participation of blacks in the programs of the alphabet agencies.[54]

The Democrats' greatest selling point was the WPA, and they used it to maximum advantage. Alfred Edgar Smith got the mes-

[51] Editorial, *Star of Zion*, Oct. 1, 1936.

[52] Republican National Committee, "Negro Balance of Power Should Support Alf M. Landon . . . Frank Knox . . . ," n.d. [1936], Harold L. Ickes Papers, Box 213, Manuscript Division, Library of Congress; Landon quoted in *New York Times*, Oct. 6, 1936, p. 11; Rivers, "The Negro Should Support Landon," p. 296; *New York Herald Tribune*, Aug. 7, 1936, p. 7, Aug. 15, 1936, p. 5.

[53] Warner, *New Haven Negroes*, p. 293 (source of the quotation); James Erroll Miller, "The Negro in Present Day Politics with Special Reference to Philadelphia since 1932" (Ph.D. diss., University of Pennsylvania, 1945), p. 301; Lawrence Hamm interview with Russell Bingham, July 10, 1979, Newark, N.J.

[54] *Take Your Choice*, n.d. [1936], Colored Division, Democratic National Committee pamphlet, NRA/NYA blue box, vertical file, Moorland-Spingarn Research Center, Howard University; "Summons to: Colored Voters," n.d. [1936], Farley Papers, Box 172. Sympathetic black newspapers printed DNC press releases verbatim—see, e.g., *Afro-American*, Oct. 10, 17, 1936.

TAKE YOUR CHOICE

—Reprint New York Amsterdam News
Issued By
The Colored Division of the
Democratic National Campaign Committee

19. A campaign pamphlet
published by the
Colored Division of the
Democratic National
Committee during the
election of 1936

sage from the White House: "Do what you have to do to get
[Roosevelt] reelected."[55] Smith spewed forth publicity about the
participation of blacks in the WPA: weekly news releases for the
black press, glossy pamphlets, articles for general-circulation
magazines, and a biweekly letter to twenty blacks who headed
important organizations.[56] Smith was careful to see that films
which depicted activities of the WPA in the various cities and
states "contained at least one shot of Negro subjects."[57] "A Better
Pennsylvania," for example, showed a black man teaching a black

[55] Interview with Alfred Edgar Smith, May 24, 1977, Washington, D.C.
[56] Alfred Edgar Smith, "Negro Project Workers: 1936 Annual Report," Jan. 1937,
p. 17, Works Progress Administration Papers, Box 10, Manuscript Division, Moorland-Spingarn Research Center, Howard University (hereafter cited as the WPA
Papers).
[57] Alfred Edgar Smith, "Report of Information Service Duties," Sept. 1936, ibid.

child about electronics, a black woman in a WPA sewing room, and blacks working on construction projects. "A Better New York City" showed black WPA construction workers and a black child in a WPA nursery group.[58]

Smith's major effort was a film of his own—"We Work Again," a sixteen-minute sound movie which dramatically portrayed the positive impact of WPA programs on blacks in need. "Only a few years ago, we were a discouraged people," the narration began. "We were the first to lose our jobs when the Depression came along and the last to get them back." "Anxiously we waited, waited for some sign of better days. Then came the Federal Government's work program. One by one it took us out of the bread line. It gave us a new chance to take a normal place in the life of our community. It made us self-supporting. It changed the haggard, hopeless faces of the bread lines into faces filled with hope and happiness, for now we work again!" No one could miss the pointed contrasts: on the one hand, dejected and frightened blacks who lounged on stoops, scanned want ads, lined up at employment agencies, and lived in shantytowns; on the other hand, smiling, smartly dressed men and women, hard at work on a wide variety of WPA projects.[59]

It was not necessary to make a direct pitch for votes. To the blacks who saw "We Work Again" in movie houses or Urban League meetings, the message was unmistakable.[60]

The administration took maximum possible advantage of its control of relief money. To critics, that meant the widespread abuses of venality and intimidation: Democrats bought the black vote by pouring relief money into strategic areas; Democrats made political fealty a condition of WPA employment; Democrats threatened persons on relief that their aid would be cut off if they voted for Landon.[61] In fact, it would have been remarkable if the

[58] For other examples, see "A Better Ohio," "A Better New Jersey," "A Better Michigan," "A Better Chicago." The films are all in Record Group 69, Motion Picture Collection, National Archives.

[59] "We Work Again," ibid.

[60] "A Pioneer's Pioneer: Al Smith," *Oracle* LVII (Summer 1974):6. The film was distributed in late October; Smith reported in January that it had "been showing since in Negro Theatres throughout the country." Alfred Edgar Smith, "Negro Project Workers: 1936 Annual Report," Jan. 1937, p. 17, WPA Papers, Box 10.

[61] *New York Times*, Oct. 28, 1936, p. 15; Hatfield, "The Impact of the New Deal on Black Politics in Pennsylvania," pp. 253, 273-74; Frank Daniels to H. A. Hopkins, Aug. 7, 1936, WPA Papers, Box 1; Mark Sullivan columns, *New York Herald Tribune*, Aug. 23, 1936, section II, p. 4, Aug. 26, 1936, p. 21; Dorothy

party had not attempted to reap political benefits from agencies such as the WPA. Was Smith under orders to use the WPA to enlist black support for the Democrats? He later testified that he had been "flatly" ordered to produce the film. Otherwise, the political potentialities of his job were left implicit. He understood that he should have sense enough to know that he would not have a job at the WPA if he failed to do what he could to advance the political fortunes of the administration.[62]

It was not necessary to use corrupt methods in capitalizing on relief. It often simply meant using clever methods. It was hardly an accident, for instance, that the establishment of the first CCC camp commanded entirely by black officers came in August 1936.[63] It was doubtless not an accident, either, that the dedication of the new chemistry building at Howard University, a PWA project, was set for October 26, in time for front-page coverage in the black press just before voters went to the polls.[64] The administration pulled out all the stops: Ickes spoke first, about the benefits that blacks had received from the New Deal. Next, in his first real address to a black audience, Roosevelt himself dedicated the building and asserted that it was the policy of his administration "that among American citizens there should be no forgotten men and no forgotten races."[65] The entire proceedings were broadcast nationally on radio. To P. B. Young, Jr., the editor of the *Norfolk Journal and Guide*, Roosevelt's speech at Howard was an act of political courage, taken despite the "political risks" of appearing "at this crucial time at an essentially Negro affair and before an overwhelmingly Negro audience."[66] But Young missed the point. The appearance at Howard of Roosevelt and Ickes was a carefully calculated effort to win black votes. And it apparently achieved its objective. An informed observer from Los Angeles,

Thompson, "On the Record," ibid., Aug. 11, 1936, p. 17; Earl Brown articles, ibid., July 15, 1936, p. 11, Aug. 5, 1936, p. 7, Aug. 26, 1936, p. 11, Aug. 27, 1936, p. 7, Aug. 28, 1936, p. 4; Archibald Rutledge, "The Negro and the New Deal," *South Atlantic Quarterly* XXXIX (July 1940):281. Ralph J. Bunche found some evidence to suggest that some local WPA officials in the South pressured WPA employees "to 'vote right.' " See *The Political Status of the Negro in the Age of FDR*, ed. Dewey W. Grantham (Chicago, 1973), p. 58. David Lawrence found a clear correlation between New Deal expenditures and votes for Roosevelt. See "The New Politics," *Saturday Evening Post*, Oct. 22, 1938, pp. 23, 91, 93, 94.

[62] Smith interview.

[63] See Charles Johnson, "The Army, the Negro and the Civilian Conservation Corps: 1933-1942," *Military Affairs* XXXVI (Oct. 1972):86.

[64] See, e.g., *Norfolk Journal and Guide*, Oct. 24, 31, 1936.

[65] Quoted in *New York Times*, Oct. 27, 1936, p. 14. See also p. 1.

[66] *Norfolk Journal and Guide*, Oct. 31, 1936.

for example, reported a week later that there had been a "tre-mendous swing for Roosevelt of [the] Negro vote in southern California since the Secretary's broadcast at Howard University."[67]

Another Democratic appeal was the recognition that the Roosevelt administration had extended to blacks. When the Democratic National Committee distributed more than a million photographs of Mrs. Roosevelt in the company of blacks at Howard University, the implicit message was easy to discern: in this administration no one is afraid to be photographed with blacks. ("I think the thing that helps us more with their vote," Farley told a press conference in August, "is when they pass that picture around of Mrs. Roosevelt.")[68] When the Roosevelts' maid, Lizzie McDuffie, went out on the campaign trail, she conveyed to her audiences a sense not only of the President as a human being, but also of his personal relationship with his black employees. "But I don't know anything about politics, Mr. President," she protested when he asked her to speak for him. "All you have to do is talk Roosevelt," he replied. "Just tell them what we are trying to do here."[69] (In a notable contrast, Landon's black employees confided to a black reporter that they were underpaid, and his cook declared her support for Roosevelt on the grounds that he would do more for the race than her employer would!)[70] When Mary McLeod Bethune delivered a tribute to the President on CBS radio in late October, she was persuasive not only as a respected black woman making the case for Roosevelt, but also because she held a significant position in his administration.[71]

Sending members of the Black Cabinet out on the stump paid

[67] Telegram, Paul R. Williams to Robert C. Weaver, Nov. 3, 1936, Robert C. Weaver Papers, Box 6, Schomburg Center for Research in Black Culture.

[68] Samuel Lubell, *White and Black: Test of a Nation,* 2nd ed., rev. (New York, 1966), p. 60; Alsop and Kintner, "The Guffey," p. 6; press conference, Aug. 18, 1936, Farley Papers, Box 51.

[69] On Mrs. McDuffie's campaigning, see *Afro-American,* Oct. 31, Nov. 14, 1936; *New Bern* (N.C.) *World,* [?] 1936; *St. Louis Post-Dispatch,* Oct. 17, 1936, clippings in McDuffie Papers, Box 1, Negro Collection, Trevor Arnett Library, Atlanta University; Frank Harriott, "Three Who Saw FDR Die," *Negro Digest* IX (May 1951):25; Elizabeth McDuffie, "FDR Was My Boss," *Ebony* VII (Apr. 1952):82. The quotations are from the latter two sources.

[70] *Afro-American,* July 18, 1936. See also ibid., Sept. 5 (editorial), 26, Oct. 3, 1936, and *Pittsburgh Courier,* Oct. 3, 1936, for negative comments about Landon from blacks in Kansas.

[71] "Annual Report of the Division of Negro Affairs (July 1, 1936–June 30, 1937)," June 30, 1937, Records of the National Youth Administration, Series 115, Box 1, Record Group 119, National Archives.

real political dividends. "I am sure your speeches helped a whole lot" in swinging blacks behind Roosevelt, a black lawyer in Topeka wrote to Lawrence Oxley after Oxley's preelection speaking tour in Kansas. "Just a line to congratulate you on saving the nation for the Democratic Party," a correspondent wrote to Robert Weaver after the returns were in. "You did a swell job."[72]

The message to vote Democratic reached blacks through a variety of vehicles. Churchmen, traditionally active in Republican politics, appeared prominently in the Democratic campaign.[73] Ministers embedded political messages in Sunday sermons and made their pulpits available to political candidates. Doubtless there was some truth to the popular allegation that black clergymen could be bought by the highest bidder,[74] but there were certainly enlightened ministers who cared deeply about economic and social issues and used their pulpits to preach in what they considered to be the best interests of the race. Sometimes the message was indirect—a passage from the Scriptures depicting the prophets warring with the rich. Sometimes it was explicit—"Let Jesus lead you and Roosevelt feed you!" Churches held meetings on election eve to advise parishioners on how to vote.[75] On

[72] R. J. Reynolds to Lawrence A. Oxley, Nov. 10, 1936, Lawrence A. Oxley Papers, Box 1380, Record of the United States Employment Service, Record Group 183, National Archives; Paul R. Williams to Robert C. Weaver, Nov. 16, 1936, Weaver Papers, Box 6.

[73] On some political activities of black clergy in behalf of both parties, see, e.g., E. Franklin Frazier, *The Negro Church in America* (New York, 1963), p. 51; *Norfolk Journal and Guide*, Sept. 26, 1936; *Savannah Tribune*, Oct. 1, 1936; *New York Times*, Oct. 12, 1936, p. 18, Oct. 16, 1936, p. 19; Reverdy C. Ransom, *The Negro: The Hope or the Despair of Christianity* (Boston, 1935), p. 26; *Star of Zion*, Oct. 22, 1936; Percy Walden Marshall to James A. Farley, Oct. 13, 1936, and Julian D. Rainey to Marshall, Oct. 16, 1936, Overton Papers, Box 6; William M. Welty, "Black Shepherds: A Study of the Leading Negro Clergymen in New York City, 1900-1940" (Ph.D. diss., New York University, 1969), pp. 320-21, 325-26; Harold F. Gosnell, *Negro Politicians: The Rise of Negro Politics in Chicago* (1935; reprint ed., Chicago, 1969), pp. 94-100.

[74] James E. Allen, "The Negro and the 1940 Presidential Election" (Master's thesis, Howard University, 1943), p. 68; interviews with Sterling Tucker and John Conyers, Jr., Mar. 23, 1977, and George L.-P. Weaver, May 23, 1977, Washington, D.C.; Miller, "The Negro in Pennsylvania Politics," p. 343; V. O. Key, Jr., *Southern Politics in State and Nation* (New York, 1949), p. 654; Ralph J. Bunche, "A Brief and Tentative Analysis of Negro Leadership" (Research memorandum prepared for Carnegie-Myrdal study, Sept. 1940), p. 125, Schomburg Center for Research in Black Culture; Thomas Ralph Solomon, "Participation of Negroes in Detroit Elections" (Ph.D. diss., University of Michigan, 1939), pp. 62-66; Taylor Merrill, "Lynching the Anti-Lynching Bill," *Christian Century*, Feb. 23, 1938, p. 240; Kelly Miller column, "Negro Ministers Dabbling in Politics," *Star of Zion*, Nov. 10, 1936.

[75] Welty, "Black Shepherds," pp. 320-31, 325-26; interviews with William Holmes

election day, the experience of the Golden Leaf Baptist Church in Memphis must have been replicated many times over. A member of the congregation described it to Roosevelt. The pastor, wearing "a big badge with ROOSEVELT on it," led "375 of us to the polls and we voted for you, everyone of us."[76]

Labor unions, too, got out the black vote for the Democratic party. Although the American Federation of Labor had traditionally discriminated against blacks, the new industrial unions worked aggressively to organize them. When the CIO rallied votes for the Democrats, blacks were among the groups that they mobilized.[77]

The black press helped importantly to influence political attitudes. Some black newspapers—the *Chicago Defender, Cleveland Gazette,* and *New York Age* among them—came out for Landon,[78] but the majority—the *Pittsburgh Courier, Atlanta World, Norfolk Journal and Guide, New York Amsterdam News, St. Louis Argus, Chicago Metropolitan News,* and many others—endorsed Roosevelt.[79]

Even the NAACP seemed to have climbed aboard the Democratic bandwagon. Its president, Joel E. Spingarn, announced that

---

Borders, June 10, 1977, Atlanta; Benjamin E. Mays, June 10, 1977, Atlanta; Clarence M. Mitchell, Jr., Oct. 29, 1976, Washington, D.C.; Bryant George, Sept. 24, 1976, New York City; Elmer W. Henderson, Mar. 24, 1977, Washington, D.C.; G. L.-P. Weaver; Bishop Reverdy Ransom quoted in George A. Singleton, *The Romance of African Methodism: A Study of the African Methodist Episcopal Church* (New York, 1952), pp. 151-53; "Daddy" Grace quoted in *Philadelphia Independent,* Oct. 25, 1936, in Miller, "The Negro in Pennsylvania Politics," p. 364, n. 184; St. Clair Drake and Horace R. Cayton, *Black Metropolis: A Study of Negro Life in a Northern City,* rev. ed., 2 vols. (New York, 1962), I:354 (source of the quotation).

[76] Liza Young to Franklin D. Roosevelt, Nov. 7, 1936, WPA Papers, Box 2.

[77] G. L.-P. Weaver interview; Mitchell interview; interviews with Louis E. Martin, May 13, 1977, Chicago, and Robert C. Weaver, Nov. 12, 1976, New York City; Harold F. Gosnell, "The Negro Vote in Northern Cities," *National Municipal Review* XXX (May 1941):278; Harvard Sitkoff, *A New Deal for Blacks: The Emergence of Civil Rights as a National Issue,* vol. I: *The Depression Decade* (New York, 1978), chap. 7.

[78] Editorials, *Chicago Defender,* June 20, Oct. 10, 31, 1936; editorial, *Cleveland Gazette,* Oct. 31, 1936; editorials, *New York Age,* Oct. 17, 24, 31, 1936. See also editorial, *Star of Zion,* Oct. 29, 1936.

[79] Editorials, *Pittsburgh Courier,* Jan. 11, Aug. 29, Oct. 31, 1936; editorial, *Norfolk Journal and Guide,* Oct. 31, 1936; Charles B. McMillan, "Introduction to an Era: A Study of the Political Development of the Negro in New York City, 1917-36" (Senior thesis, Princeton University, 1967), p. 81; J. E. Mitchell to Ambrose O'Connell, Sept. 26, 1936; Arthur W. Mitchell to James A. Farley, Sept. 24, 1936; editorial, *St. Louis Argus,* Sept. 24, 1936, all in Mitchell Papers, Box 22; C. A. Scott interview, Jan. 25, 1968, p. 4, Civil Rights Documentation Project, Ralph J. Bunche Oral History Collection, Moorland-Spingarn Research Center, Howard University.

he was breaking from lifelong Republicanism to support Roosevelt.[80] Endorsements of the President by individuals who were also officials of the staunchly nonpartisan organization gave the impression, to the consternation of some branch officials, "that the national office has gone for Roosevelt."[81]

Black voters were clearly listening. Letters poured in to newspapers, to Democratic campaign headquarters, and to the White House itself: "I am . . . pulling and pushing, shoving and lifting for your return to the White House"; "Record my name for Roosevelt"; "I am for Roosevelt a million times!"; "Roosevelt is the best president we have ever had."[82] When the Gallup Poll asked blacks at the end of August which presidential candidate they preferred, 69 percent named Roosevelt.[83] Black Democratic rallies outdrew Republican gatherings in the same location, sometimes by margins of more than two to one. The President's motorcades drew large and enthusiastic crowds in black neighborhoods. On one occasion when Roosevelt drove through the Bronx on the way to the Polo Grounds for the World Series, Harold Ickes, who joined him, recorded in his diary, "Senator Wagner remarked to me afterward that in former times Negroes would not turn out to see any Democratic candidate." For Roosevelt, though, "there were thousands of them and they displayed great enthusiasm."[84] When Jesse Owens visited Indianapolis on a Republican campaign swing, four vehicles in the nine-car parade sported Roosevelt stickers. Roosevelt banners were prominently displayed in Negro neighborhoods; "Mr. Roosevelt, Our Savior," proclaimed one stretched across a street in Indianapolis. Turner Catledge found "Roosevelt pictures . . . in shop and house windows in the black belts of every Midwest city of any size."[85] Black campaigners for the Democratic ticket were delighted and even "dumbfounded" at finding a "tre-

[80] *New York Times*, Oct. 19, 1936, p. 2; typed copy of Joel E. Spingarn telegram to Franklin D. Roosevelt, Nov. 4, 1936, NAACP Papers, Box C-392; NAACP press release, "Head of N.A.A.C.P. to Make 8 Speeches for Roosevelt," Oct. 10, 1936, NAACP Papers, Box C-392.

[81] Chester K. Gillispie telegram to Walter White, Oct. 17, 1936, NAACP Papers, Box C-392. See also Pearl Mitchell telegram to White, Oct. 17, 1936, ibid.

[82] John Henry Adams to Franklin D. Roosevelt, Oct. 24, 1936, FDR Papers, OF 93; letters to the editor from Ruth Jenkins, Mrs. L. Benson, Norah Scales, *Chicago Metropolitan News*, Oct. 10, 1936, Mitchell Papers, Box 22.

[83] Gallup Poll, Oct. 11, 1936, in George H. Gallup, *The Gallup Poll: Public Opinion, 1935-1971*, 3 vols. (New York, 1972), I:36.

[84] *Pittsburgh Courier*, Oct. 31, 1926; diary entry, Oct. 4, 1936, in Harold L. Ickes, *The Secret Diary of Harold L. Ickes*, vol. I: *The First Thousand Days, 1933-1936* (New York, 1953), p. 689.

[85] *New York Times*, Oct. 26, 1936, p. 2.

mendous ovation" for the party, a "great volume of Roosevelt sentiment."[86] Blacks were reported to be registering Democratic in large numbers. State and regional directors of the Democratic campaign among blacks forecast a Roosevelt vote ranging from 60 to 85 percent in their respective areas. Nationally, the *New York Times* predicted a black Democratic vote of 60 to 66 percent.[87]

Election day brought a stunning Democratic victory. Roosevelt polled 27,757,333 votes to 16,684,231 for Landon, the largest popular plurality—60.8 percent—in history.[88] Roosevelt's showing among blacks substantially exceeded his nationwide average, for he won 81 percent of the black vote in Harlem, 75 percent in black neighborhoods in Pittsburgh, 69 percent in Philadelphia, 66 percent in Detroit, 65 percent in Cincinnati, 60 percent in Cleveland, and 49 percent in Chicago. To the well-known political columnist, Frank R. Kent, that made the electoral behavior of black Americans "the real political sensation of the time."[89] The magnitude of the Roosevelt landslide made moot the oft-repeated contentions of black spokesmen that the black vote would constitute the balance of power in the crucial industrial states in the election of 1936.[90] But there had been a dramatic change in black voting patterns between 1932 and 1936. As Table IX.2 shows, Roosevelt won anywhere from 60 to 250 percent more votes in black neighborhoods in major cities in 1936 than in 1932. In 1932, his performance in black neighborhoods had lagged substantially

[86] Emory B. Smith to W. Forbes Morgan, Oct. 26, 1936; Ross D. Brown to Arthur W. Mitchell, Oct. 11, 1936, Mitchell Papers, Box 23. See also Mitchell to James A. Farley, Oct. 14, 1936, and Mitchell to Edgar G. Brown, Oct. 15, 1936, ibid., as well as Emory B. Smith to James A. Farley, Oct. 26, 1936, Overton Papers, Box 6.

[87] Ross D. Brown to Arthur W. Mitchell, Oct. 11, 1936; Summary of Reports of State Directors, n.d. [Oct. 1936]; F. B. Ransom to Mitchell, Oct. 13, 1936; Colored Democrats of Colorado Springs to Mitchell, postmarked Oct. 13, 1936; Mitchell to James A. Farley, Oct. 14, 22, 1936; O. B. Jefferson to Farley, Oct. 14, 1936; Percy D. Jones memorandum to Mitchell, Oct. 16, 1936, all in ibid.; Mitchell to Farley, Oct. 7, 1936, ibid., Box 22; Julian D. Rainey to Bernard F. Dickmann, Sept. 28, 1936, Overton Papers, Box 7; *New York Times*, Aug. 23, 1936, section II, p. 6; Oct. 26, 1936, p. 2; Nov. 1, 1936, section IV, p. 5.

[88] Scammon, comp. and ed., *America at the Polls*, p. 9.

[89] Frank R. Kent, "The Swing of the Negroes," *Baltimore Sun*, Nov. 12, 1936, p. 1.

[90] Even Democratic National Chairman Farley adopted the balance-of-power formula. See press conference, Aug. 1, 1936, Farley Papers, Box 51. The balance-of-power argument did apply in the election of 1944, when the black vote for Roosevelt in critical northern states exceeded the number needed to shift them into the Republican column. Henry Lee Moon, *Balance of Power: The Negro Vote* (Garden City, N.Y., 1948), pp. 35-36, 198.

TABLE IX.2
Presidential Vote in Black Districts, 1932 and 1936

	1932		1936		% Increase in Demo-cratic Vote, 1932-1936
City	% Repub-lican	% Demo-cratic	% Repub-lican	% Demo-cratic	
Chicago	75.1	21.0	50.5	48.8	132
Cincinnati	71.2	28.8	34.9	65.1	126
Cleveland	82.0	17.3	38.2	60.5	250
Detroit	67.0	31.0	31.8	66.2	114
Knoxville	70.2	29.8	43.8	56.2	89
New York	46.0	50.8	17.1	81.3	60
Philadelphia	70.5	26.7	29.7	68.7	157
Pittsburgh	56.2	41.3	23.5	74.7	81

SOURCES: The figures for Chicago are drawn from the Records of the Board of Election Commissioners of the City of Chicago, which are available on microfiche at the Municipal Reference Library in Chicago; the appropriate precincts were chosen by matching census tracts which were at least 90 percent black by 1940—identified in Ernest W. Burgess and Charles Newcomb, eds., *Census Data of the City of Chicago, 1930* (Chicago, 1933), and U.S. Department of Commerce, Bureau of the Census, *Sixteenth Census of the United States: 1940, Population and Housing: Statistics for Census Tracts and Community Areas: Chicago, Ill.* (Washington, D.C., 1943)—with ward maps which are held by the Board of Election Commissioners in Chicago. The figures for Cincinnati come from Ernest M. Collins, "Cincinnati Negroes and Presidential Politics," *Journal of Negro History* XLI (Apr. 1956):133. The figures for Cleveland are drawn from the Records of the Board of Elections of Cuyahoga County, which are held at the Board of Elections in Cleveland; the appropriate precincts were chosen by matching census tracts which were at least 90 percent black by 1940—identified in Kenneth L. Kusmer, *A Ghetto Takes Shape: Black Cleveland, 1870-1930* (Urbana, Ill., 1976), p. 284, Table 25, and U.S. Department of Commerce, Bureau of the Census, *Sixteenth Census of the United States: 1940, Population and Housing: Statistics for Census Tracts: Cleveland, Ohio and Adjacent Area* (Washington, D.C., 1942)—with ward maps and the Board of Elections of Cuyahoga County's *Register of Voters*, both deposited in the Cuyahoga County Archives in Cleveland. The figures for Detroit are drawn from the Board of County Canvassers' Statement of Returns, on microfilm at the Wayne County Election Commission in Detroit; the appropriate precincts were chosen by matching census tracts which were at least 90 percent black by 1940—identified in Detroit Bureau of Governmental Research, *Population (1930 Census) and Other Social Data for Detroit by Census Tracts* (Schools of Public Affairs and Social Work of Wayne University, Report No. 7 [Detroit, March 1937]), Table 1, and U.S. Department of Commerce, Bureau of the Census, *Sixteenth Census of the United States: 1940, Population and Housing: Statistics for Census Tracts: Detroit, Mich., and Adjacent Area* (Washington, D.C., 1942)—with ward maps held at the Detroit Election Commission. The figures for Knoxville come from Larry W. Dunn, "Knoxville Negro Voting and the Roosevelt Revolution, 1928-1936," *East Tennessee Historical Society's Publications*, no. 43 (1971), p. 89. The figures for New York are drawn from "Official Canvass of the Votes Cast . . . at the Election Held Nov. 3, 1936," *City Record*, Dec. 19, 1936. Those blocks in

TABLE IX.3

Roosevelt Vote, Black Districts and Citywide Returns,
1932 and 1936

	1932		1936	
City	*% in Black Districts*	*% Citywide*	*% in Black Districts*	*% Citywide*
Chicago	21.0	57.3	48.8	65.0
Cincinnati	28.8	51.2	65.1	59.2
Cleveland	17.3	55.6	60.5	70.2
Detroit	31.0	57.7	66.2	65.4
Knoxville	29.8	53.4	56.2	68.2
New York	50.8	66.9	81.3	72.7
Philadelphia	26.7	42.9	68.7	60.4
Pittsburgh	41.3	56.1	74.4	67.5

SOURCES: For the vote in black districts, see Table IX.2. For the citywide returns for Chicago, Cincinnati, Cleveland, Detroit, New York, Philadelphia, and Pittsburgh, see ibid. The Knoxville citywide returns come from the *Knoxville Journal*, Nov. 10, 1932, p. 7, and Nov. 5, 1936, p. 11, courtesy of the Lawson McGee Library, Knoxville.

Harlem which were at least 90 percent black were identified from map no. 3 in Gilbert Osofsky, *Harlem: The Making of a Ghetto; Negro New York, 1890-1930*, 2nd ed. (New York, 1971), p. xvii, and Welfare Council of New York City, *Census Tract Data on Population and Housing: New York City: 1940* (New York, 1942), p. 171; the appropriate election units were chosen with the assistance of assembly district maps which are available on slides at the Municipal Reference and Research Center, New York City. The figures for Philadelphia are drawn from Registration Commission for the City of Philadelphia, *Thirty-first Annual Report, Dec. 31, 1936* (Philadelphia, 1937); the analysis is based on election divisions where the voter registration was at least 90 percent black. The figures for Pittsburgh are drawn from *The Pennsylvania Manual, 1937* (Harrisburg, 1938), pp. 204-12; the appropriate precincts were chosen by matching census tracts identified in U.S. Department of Commerce, Bureau of the Census, *Sixteenth Census of the United States: 1940, Population and Housing: Statistics for Census Tracts: Pittsburgh, Pa.* (Washington, D.C., 1942)—with ward maps provided by the University of Pittsburgh Library. For similar patterns in other cities, see: Larry H. Grothaus, "The Negro in Missouri Politics, 1890-1941" (Ph.D. diss., University of Missouri, 1970), pp. 151-52; William Wayne Giffin, "The Negro in Ohio, 1914-1939" (Ph.D. diss., The Ohio State University, 1968), p. 420; Buni, *The Negro in Virginia Politics*, p. 116; Richard J. Meister, "A History of Gary, Indiana, 1930-1940" (Ph.D. diss., University of Notre Dame, 1967), p. 295; Peirce F. Lewis, "Impact of Negro Migration on the Electoral Geography of Flint, Michigan, 1932-1962: A Cartographic Analysis," *Annals of the Association of American Geographers* LV (Mar. 1965):8; James Braddie Morris, Jr., "Voting Behavior in Four Negro Precincts in Iowa since 1924" (Master's thesis, University of Iowa, 1946), p. 64.

behind his overall showing in each city; in 1936, as Table IX.3 illustrates, black voting corresponded much more closely to general city returns. In Kent's judgment, "The Swing of the Negroes" was the startling news of the 1936 election: "Nothing of more far-reaching significance has happened in politics for a good many years."[91]

"Isn't it perfectly amazing how overwhelming the President's triumph has been?" Walter White wrote Eleanor Roosevelt. This time, blacks, too, had climbed aboard the New Deal bandwagon.[92]

[91] Kent, "The Swing of the Negroes."
[92] Walter White to Eleanor Roosevelt, Nov. 4, 1936, NAACP Papers, Box C-79.

CHAPTER X ▪ *Why Blacks Became Democrats*

Perceptive observers recognized the paradox in the outpouring of black support for the New Deal in the election of 1936. One need not be a diehard Republican to wonder at the marriage between a black electorate and a Democratic party that seemed purposefully to evade any important issue that smacked of race. How could a President who sidestepped on antilynching legislation, seemed outwardly unperturbed by disfranchisement and segregation, and presided over relief programs rife with discrimination, win an overwhelming majority of black votes, and, in so doing, transform the political habits of black Americans for decades to come?

New Deal racial attitudes and discriminatory practices certainly mattered. Black spokesmen—publicists, politicians, leaders of the organizations for racial advancement, and others—protested vigorously against them. But that protest related more to the ritual of black leadership than it did to actual expectations about realizable progress. Positions of national leadership among blacks were few and thus hotly contested; since the late nineteenth century, competition for them had turned on different approaches to racial advancement. For black spokesmen not to have articulated and fought for a racial agenda would have been unthinkable. No newspaper with any pretensions of speaking for the race could have failed to flay the Roosevelt administration for its shortcomings on racial issues. No leader could keep any standing among his colleagues or constituency if he failed to set forth prescriptions for remedying the impact on blacks of racial violence, disfranchisement, and discrimination.

But to read the rhetoric of black spokesmen on racial issues as a predictor of black electoral behavior in 1936 is to misunderstand the process by which most blacks made their political choices. In making sense of those choices, one needs to remember two essential points. First, the racial expectations of most blacks fell considerably short of the protest voiced by black spokesmen. And second, the key to black electoral behavior lay in economics rather than· race.

It is hard to know whether black leaders in the 1930s honestly expected the Roosevelt administration to do more than it did to move toward racial justice. They certainly *hoped* that the administration would do better, but if there was a gap between their public assertions and their private expectations, it has not been recorded. Most ordinary blacks, however, did not expect great strides toward racial advancement. There was no reason for them to—the federal government had not done anything significant for the particular benefit of blacks for as long as most of them could remember. Racial expectations and racial consciousness were considerably more limited then than they became in the postwar era.[1] Robert Carter doubtless spoke for many blacks when he reflected on his own attitudes in the 1930s: "I shut out of my mind the fact of Roosevelt's personal racism—his views—never looked at them, and I think few blacks did. Maybe at that time we weren't as aware and weren't as demanding of white conduct."[2]

Far from being surprised at the failure of the New Deal to embrace a racial agenda, most blacks in the 1930s remarked on how much attention the Roosevelt administration seemed to be paying to them. The administration made unprecedented gestures toward the race. Although trivial, perhaps, in comparison to inaction on lynching, disfranchisement, and discrimination in relief, such gestures struck a responsive chord. In the judgment of Rayford W. Logan, who cast his first vote for Roosevelt in 1936: "Negroes had been so depressed, so frustrated, almost having given up hope, that nearly anything would have created substantial support . . . . The outlook was so bleak . . . that little things counted a great deal. . . . Apart from questions of policy, treating Negroes as human beings was a very significant factor."[3] Despite the fact that Roosevelt had done very little for blacks as a racial minority, he had managed to convey to them that they counted and belonged. In the light of inattention from previous administrations,

[1] Interview with Pauli Murray, July 1, 1977, Alexandria, Va. See also interviews with Kenneth B. Clark, May 17, 1977, New York City; Earl Brown, June 29, 1977, New York City; Bayard Rustin, Nov. 15, 1976, New York City; telephone interview with Barrington D. Parker, Oct. 28, 1976, Washington, D.C.

[2] Interview with Robert A. Carter, Nov. 15, 1976, New York City. George L.-P. Weaver commented, too, on the almost blind acceptance of Roosevelt while he was in office. "At the time, I was as enamored of FDR as most of my generation. I began to look at FDR objectively, I think, more after he passed." Interview, May 23, 1977, Washington, D.C.

[3] Interview with Rayford W. Logan, Nov. 29, 1976, Washington, D.C.

even the limited racial recognition of the New Deal seemed to many black Americans to be a token of hope.[4] As Percy Sutton put it, "When you're on the outside, just being spoken to is substantive rather than symbolic." Or, in the words of Clarence Mitchell, "when you start from a position of zero, even if you move up to the point of two on a scale of twelve, it looks like a big improvement."[5]

The same kind of logic applied to discrimination in New Deal programs. No one condoned it. Most black people knew that they were getting less economic assistance than whites, and most of them needed more than they got. But the point was that they got something, and that kept many families from starving. The simple reality that blacks were not excluded from the economic benefits of the New Deal was a sufficient departure from past practice to make Roosevelt look like a benefactor of the race. "Discrimination or not, *we were participating,*" insisted Charles Matthews, who became one of the first black Democratic ward chairmen in Newark. "We were a part of the economic and social fabric of the community. We started working."[6] The Reverend Samuel Proctor spoke to the same point. The CCC may have been segregated, he said, but blacks could get into CCC camps. The WPA may have been discriminatory, "but before that blacks had no bread. Black folk have never been so crazy as to wait for things to be perfect."[7]

As this testimony illustrates, racial concerns were not para-

---

[4] Interviews with Martin Luther King, Sr., June 10, 1977, Atlanta; W. J. Trent, Jr., Dec. 8, 1976, New York City; Eddie Williams, Oct. 20, 1976, Washington, D.C.; Franklin H. Williams, Oct. 25, 1976, New York City; Ivy Graves, May 4, 1977, New York City; Joseph P. Lash, May 5, 1977, New York City; A. Leon Higginbotham, Jr., Jan. 21, 1981, Philadelphia. As a retired factory worker in Detroit put it in response to a *Newsweek* survey in 1963, "He brought light to us so that we would know we were human beings." William Brink and Louis Harris, *The Negro Revolution in America* (New York, 1963), p. 90.

[5] Interviews with Percy E. Sutton, Nov. 8, 1976, New York City; Clarence M. Mitchell, Jr., Oct. 29, 1976, Washington, D.C.

[6] Lawrence Hamm interview with Charles Matthews, July 17, 1979, Newark, N.J.

[7] Interview with Samuel Proctor, Nov. 10, 1976, New York City. See also Higginbotham interview; interview with Earl B. Dickerson, Aug. 16, 1974, Chicago. Contemporaries made the same point. "I am grateful for the WPA and relief administration," a Chicagoan on relief told Elmer Henderson in the summer of 1938. "Possibly it may not be everything it should be, but it has prevented many from starving." Quoted in Elmer William Henderson, "A Study of the Basic Factors Involved in the Change in the Party Alignment of Negroes in Chicago, 1932-1938" (Master's thesis, University of Chicago, 1939), p. 57. "Sir, we have been used to hard times down here all of our lives until recently," an elderly southern black woman told Will Rogers. "This is the first time we had enough to eat and wear." Quoted in A. Clayton Powell, Sr., *Against the Tide: An Autobiography* (New York, 1938), p. 8. See also editorial, *Pittsburgh Courier*, Apr. 20, 1935.

mount in shaping the response of blacks to the New Deal. Symbolic racial gestures did not cause the shift of blacks to the Democratic party in 1936. Nor did the limitations in the New Deal's record on race significantly retard that shift. In voting Democratic in 1936, blacks did not vote for reasons of racial advantage. Rather, they behaved like most other poor people in the United States.[8] In short, they responded to the New Deal on economic rather than racial grounds.

To black intellectuals and activists who sought to comprehend the "Negro problem" and to devise effective strategies for racial progress, the relative importance of race and class was perhaps the central question of the 1930s.[9] In their behavior at the polls, the masses of black Americans made clear where they stood on the race-class debate. The New Deal had failed to act on the racial agenda of the 1930s. But racial concerns had to be fitted into a scale of priorities, and there was overwhelming agreement among most blacks that economic problems were even more pressing than specifically racial concerns. The struggle to survive took precedence over the struggle for equality. And in the struggle to survive, many New Deal programs made a critical difference.[10]

Blacks in the 1930s spoke eloquently to the point. "I know me and my children would have starved this winter if it was not for the Presendent," wrote a woman in Memphis.[11] "Me and my people have been able to live through the depression with food shoes clothing and fuel all through the kindheartness thoughtfulness and sane leadership of Roosevelt," wrote a mother of ten in Columbus, Ohio.[12] "He is the greatest man I ever saw in the White [House]," declared "A Converted Roosevelt voter" in Ken-

[8] As *Opportunity* predicted before the election, "the Negroes' votes will be divided very much as will the white votes, the Jewish votes, the German votes, the Scandinavian votes, the Italian votes—and for pretty much the same reasons." "The Negro Vote," XIV (Sept. 1936):261. See also interview with Ernest Rice McKinney, Nov. 11, 1976, New York City; Earl Brown, "How the Negro Voted in the Presidential Election," *Opportunity* XIV (Dec. 1936):361.

[9] The race-class debate is a major theme of John B. Kirby's thoughtful book, *Black Americans in the Roosevelt Era: Liberalism and Race* (Knoxville, Tenn., 1980). See also James O. Young, *Black Writers of the Thirties* (Baton Rouge, 1973).

[10] On the primacy of economic over racial concerns, see interviews with Brown, Clark, Higginbotham, Matthews, Murray; interviews with John H. Murphy III, Apr. 28, 1977, Baltimore; Louis E. Martin, May 23, 1977, Chicago; Carl B. Stokes, Aug. 22, 1979, New York City; E. E. Lewis, "The Economic Position of the American Negro: A Brief Summary," *Journal of Negro Education* VIII (July 1939):446.

[11] Cleo Moultry to Eleanor Roosevelt, May 9, 1934, Records of the Federal Emergency Relief Administration, Box 19, Record Group 69, National Archives.

[12] Lena Ohey to the National Demarcrat Headquarter, Sept. 12, 1936, Arthur W. Mitchell Papers, Box 21, Chicago Historical Society.

tucky, whose home had been saved from foreclosure. "Has done moore for the poor people than any President in my time."[13] "You see dis new house," an elderly former slave told an interviewer, "de flower pots, de dog out yonder, de cat in de sun lyin' in de chair on de porch, de seven tubs under de shed, de two big wash pots, you see de pictures hangin' round de wall, de nice beds, all dese things is de blessin's of de Lord through President Roosevelt."[14] A popular song summed up the case:

> Roosevelt! You're my man!
> When the time come
> I ain't got a cent,
> You buy my groceries
> And pay my rent.
> Mr. Roosevelt, you're my man![15]

It was no wonder that such economic assistance paid large political dividends to the Democratic party. An election board official in Columbia, South Carolina, reported that every Negro that he had registered so far had said that he would vote for Roosevelt, because "Roosevelt saved them from starvation [and] gave them aid when they were in distress."[16] A black leader in

[13] W. T. Hodgins to Harry Hopkins, Dec. 4, 1936, Works Progress Administration Papers, Box 4, Manuscript Division, Moorland-Spingarn Research Center, Howard University (hereafter cited as the WPA Papers). On Roosevelt as the poor man's friend, see also: Ozie W. Gammill to WPA, Feb. 19, 1936; Percy Douglass to Franklin D. Roosevelt, Dec. 8, 1934; Mr. and Mrs. Jack Goble to Franklin D. Roosevelt, Dec. 22, 1934; Ben Owens to Franklin D. Roosevelt, May 5, 1935; Edward Jenkins to Franklin D. Roosevelt, July 9, 1936; Jeremiah Wyche to Franklin D. Roosevelt, May 6, 1936, all in ibid., Box 1; Lula Cross to Franklin D. Roosevelt, June 3, 1937, ibid., Box 3; Frisby Thomas to Harry Hopkins and Franklin D. Roosevelt, Oct. 18, 1936; Fred Coleman to Franklin D. Roosevelt, Nov. 4, 1936; Griggs Wilson to Eleanor Roosevelt, Feb. 5, 1938; Steven B. Lewis to Franklin D. Roosevelt, Oct. 8, 1938, all in ibid., Box 4; *Afro-American* street-corner polls, Oct. 10, 17, 24, 1936; interviews with Thomas E. Mitchell, Rothwell Smith, Curtis Payne, Central Harlem Senior Citizens Coalition, Apr. 18, 1977, New York City; interview with Ethel Sarauw, Manhattanville Senior Center, May 4, 1977, New York City; Jacqueline Harris to Nancy J. Weiss, July 29, 1975.

[14] Interview with Louisa Davis, Winnsboro, S.C., n.d., in *The American Slave: A Composite Autobiography*, ed. George P. Rawick, 19 vols. (Westport, Conn. 1972), vol. II, South Carolina, pt. 1, p. 302. See also interview with Phillip Evans, Winnsboro, S.C., n.d., in ibid., vol. II, pt. 2, p. 35.

[15] Quoted in Anzia Yezierska, *Red Ribbon on a White Horse* (New York, 1950), p. 162. Another song, recorded in 1936, implored the President, "Don't Take Away My P.W.A." The lyrics can be found in Paul Oliver, *Blues Fell This Morning: The Meaning of the Blues* (New York, 1960), p. 38. A third song, "Relief Blues," recorded in 1938, identified the President himself as the source of the relief assistance on which blacks depended. See ibid., p. 281.

[16] Quoted in *New York Times*, Aug. 23, 1936, section II, p. 6.

Chicago said the same thing: "Mr. Roosevelt gave us work and bread. Our people will respond by giving Mr. Roosevelt most of their votes."[17] As a woman at a Baltimore political meeting expressed it, "Yes, I'm gonna vote for Roosevelt, because when I was slipping and sliding in the mirey clay Franklin Roosevelt put my feet on the solid rock of the WPA."[18] From Springfield, Ohio, a WPA worker wrote, "I was suffering when you took your seat, but now I eat and live so much better that I am intising everybody I can to vote for you. . . . I . . . don't think it is fair, to eat Roosevelt bread and meat and vote for Gov. Landon."[19]

Even blacks who were not themselves beneficiaries of New Deal projects could not help but be impressed by the difference that they made. When Bishop William J. Walls, a leading figure in the African Methodist Episcopal Zion Church and a lifelong Republican, announced his switch to the Democratic party, he made the case in economic terms. Roosevelt, he said, had "kept the faith with the common people." By "reaching for the 'forgotten man' with the arm of government," he had "kept millions of people from starving." As a result, blacks were better off by the fall of 1936 than they had been "at any time since the beginning

---

[17] Quoted in ibid., Oct. [?] 1936, clipping in Roosevelt Administration scrapbooks, vol. II, microfilm reel 16, Schomburg Center for Research in Black Culture. For other contemporary testimony explaining a vote for Roosevelt in terms of the economic benefits of the New Deal, see, for example, Alice McDowell to Franklin D. Roosevelt, n.d. [Christmas season], attached to Alfred E. Smith to Jacob Baker, Jan. 16, 1936; Jerry Lewis to Franklin D. Roosevelt, Oct. 8, 1937, WPA Papers, Box 1; Eva Wright to Franklin D. Roosevelt, June 19, 1937; Mary McKinney to Franklin D. Roosevelt, July 8, 1937, ibid., Box 3; William Ross to Franklin D. Roosevelt, Oct. 28, 1936, ibid., Box 4; Jo Trent to James A. Farley, July 16, 1936, Carrie Burton Overton Papers, Box 6, Archives of Labor History and Urban Affairs, Wayne State University; Joseph S. Sickler to James A. Farley, Oct. 28, 1936, ibid., Box 7; *New York Herald Tribune*, Oct. 11, 1936, section II, p. 2. Analysts at the time understood the phenomenon in the same way. See, for example, David Ward Howe, "The Observation Post," *Chicago Defender*, Aug. 12, 1939; Henry Lee Moon, "How the Negroes Voted," *Nation*, Nov. 25, 1944, p. 640; John Temple Graves article in *Arkansas Democrat* (Little Rock), Nov. 22, 1936, in *The Attitude of the Southern White Press toward Negro Suffrage, 1932-1940*, ed. Rayford W. Logan (Washington, D.C., 1940), p. 11; Frank R. Kent, "The Great Game of Politics," unidentified clipping, 1936, in Claude A. Barnett Papers, Box P7, Chicago Historical Society; Kent, "The Swing of the Negroes," *Baltimore Sun*, Nov. 12, 1936, p. 1; *Cleveland Call and Post*, Nov. 5, 1936, quoted in Christopher Gray Wye, "Midwest Ghetto: Patterns of Negro Life and Thought in Cleveland, Ohio, 1929-1945" (Ph.D. diss., Kent State University, 1973), pp. 370-71; Lawrence Sullivan, "The Negro Vote," *Atlantic Monthly* CLXVI (Oct. 1940):478. See also Thomas E. Mitchell interview.

[18] Clarence Mitchell interview.

[19] George W. Harris to Franklin D. Roosevelt, Oct. 30, 1936, WPA Papers, Box 4.

*Kain't choose, huh! An' dare you is wid WPA an'
me wid releef groceries!*

20-21. Cartoons in the
Pittsburgh Courier and
the New York Amsterdam
News in October 1936
make clear the economic
basis for black support for
the Democratic party

of the depression."[20] The administration, in the words of the *Pittsburgh Courier*, may not have been doing enough for blacks, but it had made long strides toward meeting the needs of the "average Negro": "a means of getting bread and shelter."[21]

Blacks looking back on the 1930s gave the same kind of explanation for the attraction of blacks to the Democrats. In the words of the president of the Phelps-Stokes Fund, Franklin Williams, "It was not civil rights, it was jobs" that brought blacks into the Democratic party.[22] Blacks became Democrats because the "Democrats had a program that was going to help the underprivileged, or the poor, more than the Republican party," said the Harlem political leader, Lloyd Dickens.[23] Countless blacks echoed the sentiments of the Washington taxicab driver who explained that he voted Democratic because the Democrats "favor the little man, and I've been a little man all my life."[24]

All of this testimony speaks to an important point: if the economic benefits of the New Deal attracted black voters, it follows that the economic status of those voters influenced, even determined, their support for the Democratic party. To put it simply, blacks who were suffering the most from the Depression had the least to lose in leaving the Republican party. And they stood to gain the most from the tangible assistance of the New Deal. Of

[20] Quoted in *Pittsburgh Courier*, Oct. 3, 1936.

[21] Editorials, ibid., Jan. 11, Aug. 29 (source of the quotations), 1936.

[22] Franklin H. Williams interview. Basil Paterson: "You have to say the economics was the key" (interview, Dec. 1, 1976, New York City). Vernon Jordan: "FDR did nothing on segregation, but important things on economics" (interview, Oct. 26, 1976, New York City). Charles Rangel: "It was a question of economics—an identification with party *in spite* of race (interview, Nov. 3, 1976, New York City). Robert Carter: "The Democrats got the blacks by trying to improve the condition of the working class; it seemed that the benefits generally for everyone would filter down to blacks" (interview). See also interviews with Brown; John Conyers, Jr., Mar. 23, 1977, Washington, D.C.; Dickerson; Benjamin E. Mays, June 10, 1977, Atlanta; Martin; Ralph H. Metcalfe, Mar. 24, 1977, Washington, D.C.; Clarence Mitchell; Murphy; Stokes; G. L.-P. Weaver; Lawrence Hamm interview with Russell Bingham, July 10, 1979, Newark, N.J.; Samuel J. Battle, *Reminiscences* (Columbia University Oral History Collection, 1960), p. 49.

[23] Lloyd E. Dickens interview, Nov. 15, 1976, New York City. Or, as Samuel Proctor expressed it, because the government was "the prime mover in ameliorating conditions of the poor," Proctor interview. See also Matthews interview; Lawrence Hamm interview with Julia Gee, July 31, 1979, East Orange, N.J.

[24] Interview with Zack S. Williams, Aug. 14, 1975, Washington, D.C. For similar equations of the Democratic party as the party of the little man or of the poor, see the manuscript questionnaires at the Center for Political Studies, Institute for Social Research, University of Michigan: from their 1968 survey, #s 0109, 0545, 0593, 1410, 1681, 2068, 2080, 2110; from their 1972 survey, #s 0073, 0190, 1657.

course, most blacks felt the effects of the Depression; few of them in the 1930s were really well-to-do. But insofar as one can draw meaningful distinctions of economic condition within the mass of lower and lower-middle class blacks, a consistent pattern appears: Democratic voting grew faster in the poorer black neighborhoods (see Table X.1).

This same point—that the highest-status blacks were the most reluctant to embrace the Democratic party—also shows up clearly when one examines what people said about their political allegiances. The first national survey to document party identification among blacks, conducted in 1937, revealed that 44 percent of those questioned thought of themselves as Democrats. But the pattern was strikingly different among the black elite: 71 percent of the professionals, businessmen, civic leaders, and others who were included in a leading biographical encyclopedia, published in the same year, still called themselves Republicans.[25]

In light of all of this evidence, the black embrace of the Democratic party in 1936 becomes comprehensible as a pragmatic political response. At a time when the Republican party offered

TABLE X.1
Democratic Vote in Black Districts, by Class,
1932 and 1936
(in percentages)

	1932		1936	
City	*Lower-Middle-Class Districts*	*Lower-Class Districts*	*Lower-Middle-Class Districts*	*Lower-Class Districts*
Chicago	17.5	21.3	41.0	49.3
Cleveland	17.6	18.3	55.9	65.3
Detroit	25.5	39.0	62.5	71.8
New York	50.3	54.4	n.a.	n.a.

SOURCES: For the voting returns themselves, see the sources cited above for Table IX.2. For identification of the districts and enumeration of the socioeconomic indices which determined their classification, see the Appendix.

[25] Everett Carll Ladd, Jr., with Charles D. Hadley, *Transformations of the American Party System: Political Coalitions from the New Deal to the 1970s*, 2nd ed. (New York, 1978), p. 60, Table 1.3; *Who's Who in Colored America*, 4th ed. (Brooklyn, N.Y., 1937).

no more than rhetoric and tradition, the Democrats were delivering tangible economic assistance. No matter that it came through no special concern for the plight of blacks—blacks could still benefit as part of the one-third of a nation ill-housed, ill-clad, and ill-nourished that the New Deal was designed to assist. Call it what you will—"a 'bread and butter' vote,"[26] a pragmatic vote, a vote for the lesser of two evils—blacks in 1936 marked Democratic ballots in spite of the party's record on race, in trade for the economic benefits that came their way under the New Deal.

And yet, for some blacks there was more to it than a pragmatic political calculation. Earl Brown, the black reporter who covered the campaign for the *New York Herald Tribune*, understood what was happening. "It was a kind of a religion to vote for Roosevelt in '36," he reflected; "—this was no longer politics." In New York City, Brown saw black voters lining up at the polls at 9:30 on the night before the election, "standing in that line to vote for Roosevelt."[27] At campaign rallies, the display of Roosevelt's photograph or the mention of his name "was sufficient to evoke wild cheers and applause."[28]

In short, blacks not only voted for Franklin Roosevelt—they idolized him as well. They hung his picture—often a full-page campaign photograph cut out of a newspaper—beside that of Christ or Lincoln on the walls of their homes. "Every black home you went into, you saw a picture of Franklin Roosevelt, *framed*," Basil Paterson remembered. "It was the damnedest thing."[29] "I have the President's picture in a light," a woman in Philadelphia explained; "every time it lights up [my son] knows it is the man that is good and helping us to live."[30] Black people named their children for the President. Harlem Hospital welcomed Franklin Delano Wilford, Franklin Delano Kulscar, Donald Roosevelt Evans, Roosevelt Little, and dozens of Eleanors, Franklins, and Del-

[26] Ralph J. Bunche, "Report on the Needs of the Negro (for the Republican Program Committee)," July 1, 1939, Schomburg Center for Research in Black Culture.

[27] Brown interview.

[28] James Erroll Miller, "The Negro in Pennsylvania Politics with Special Reference to Philadelphia since 1932" (Ph.D. diss., University of Pennsylvania, 1945), p. 301.

[29] Paterson interview. See also Jordan interview; diary entry of Sept. 8, 1936, in Harold L. Ickes, *The Secret Diary of Harold L. Ickes*, vol. I: *The First Thousand Days, 1933-1936* (New York, 1953), p. 673.

[30] Harriett Turner to Eleanor Roosevelt, Feb. 25, 1935, WPA Papers, Box 1.

anos besides.[31] Harold Rome captured the phenomenon in "F.D.R. Jones," a song he wrote for a Broadway revue in 1938, *Sing Out the News*:

> Come right in Benjamin Franklin Brown!
> Abraham Lincoln Smith, set yourself right down!
> There's a new hero here,
> He's the man of the year,
> Mr. Franklin D. Roosevelt Jones!

"I wrote the number," Rome later recalled, "because we wanted to say Hurrah for F.D.R. . . . Since blacks seemed to name their children for famous men they admired, this was a good way to do it. . . . During the run of the show, I received quite a few birth announcements of new F.D.R.s."[32]

So many black Americans loved Franklin Roosevelt. They told him so in the handwritten letters penciled on scraps of lined paper that poured into the White House. The grammar and spelling were often very poor, but the message was clear. "You must be a God Sent man," a black Mississippian wrote in 1934. "You have made a great change since you have ben President. . . . You ben Bread for the hungry and clothes for the naked. . . . God Save the President."[33] Or, as a woman in Texas put it in 1935, "It seem lak we got a unseen Eye watchin' an' studyin' our troubles an' lookin' after 'em. . . . I feels lak he's jes' another Moses God has done sent to head His chillun. . . . I'se restin' easy case I know he's got his han' on de throttle an' his eye on de rail."[34] Letters to newspaper editors told the same story: Roosevelt was "the greatest man living today," "the greatest President America has ever had."[35]

---

[31] These babies were born in Harlem Hospital on Nov. 30, 1933, Apr. 23, 1934, Mar. 2, 1938, and Sept. 23, 1938, respectively. Their births, and those of the dozens of others mentioned in the text, can be found in the hospital's birth records. Parents wrote to Roosevelt to tell him that they had named children for him. See, for example, Estelle E. Howard to Franklin D. Roosevelt, Sept. 18, 1934, WPA Papers, Box 2; Ethel Grant to Roosevelt, June 5, 1937, ibid., Box 1; Nettie B. Alexander to Roosevelt, Sept. 26, 1938, ibid., Box 4; English Bagby to Roosevelt, Mar. 7, 1937, Franklin D. Roosevelt Papers, President's Personal File (PPF) 50-B, Franklin D. Roosevelt Library (hereafter cited as the FDR Papers). See also Eleanor James to Nancy J. Weiss, Aug. 29, 1975; Roosevelt Thompkins to Weiss, postmarked Sept. 6, 1975; A. J. Levin to Weiss, June 6, 1976.

[32] Harold Rome to Nancy J. Weiss, Nov. 6, 1978.

[33] S. M. Cotton to Franklin D. Rasenvelt, Dec. 28, 1934, FDR Papers, PPF 30.

[34] Gladys Carroll to Franklin D. Roosevelt, Dec. 9, 1935, ibid., PPF 3056.

[35] Letter to the editor from John of Minneapolis, *Chicago Defender*, Dec. 21, 1935; letter to the editor from "An American Citizen," *Pittsburgh Courier*, Oct. 20, 1934.

To these people, Roosevelt was a man larger than life, one vested with superhuman qualities and capable of outsized accomplishments. He was "a man of brain, common sense and 'guts,' " "endowed with Natural Abilities . . . unfathomable experiences . . . and superior qualities," "a big man, in the biggest job this country has ever had . . . the skipper of the greatest ship that has ever traveled this old ocean."[36] He had "tackled the depression, . . . kicked the wheels of industry into renewed life, . . . bucked the strength of powerful figures and . . . run the gauntlet of public criticism." He was "the all-American President, qualifications—triple threat."[37]

The images recurred again and again: paternity, royalty, and deity. Roosevelt was a father figure, a king, a messiah, "America's Salvation," "a God sent man."[38] "You are to us as Jesus is to the rightous"; "I think Mr. Lincoln was raised up by de Lord, just like Moses, to free a 'culiar people. I think Mr. Roosevelt is de Joshua dat come after him."[39] To many blacks, Roosevelt's re-

[36] Letter to the editor from W.E.T., *Philadelphia Tribune*, Mar. 23, 1933; Resolution, Young Negro Democratic Organization of Tulsa, June 6, 1936, FDR Papers, PPF 23-Y; K. David Cammack to Franklin D. Roosevelt, July 3, 1933, ibid., OF 93.

[37] Edwin L. Best to Franklin D. Roosevelt, Oct. 31, 1933, FDR Papers, OF 93.

[38] On Roosevelt as father figure and king, see Billy McClain to Franklin D. Roosevelt, Dec. 4, 1934, ibid.; interview with Ned Walker, White Oak, S.C., in *The American Slave*, ed. Rawick, vol. III, South Carolina, pt. 4, p. 178; W. G. Mosely to Franklin D. Roosevelt, May 17, 1934, FDR Papers, OF 93. On Roosevelt as savior, see Wilkins interview; George interview; Brown, "How the Negro Voted in the Presidential Election," p. 361; Brink and Harris, *The Negro Revolution in America*, p. 90; Oliver, *Blues Fell This Morning*, p. 281. The quotations are from "Roosevelt America's Salvation," n.d. [Oct. 1936], and telegram, Daniel J. Reed to the President, Oct. 22, 1936, both in Mitchell Papers, Box 23. See also Cora Williams to Franklin D. Roosevelt, Oct. 22, 1936, WPA Papers, Box 2; B. W. Jackson to Eleanor Roosevelt, Jan. 29, 1935; Ruben Clayton to Franklin D. Roosevelt, Dec. 12, 1936; Jeremiah Wyche to Franklin D. Roosevelt, May 6, 1936; Elizabeth Hines to Franklin D. Roosevelt, Sept. 15, 1936, ibid., Box 1; Maggie Cater to Franklin D. Roosevelt, July 23, 1937, ibid., Box 3; Steven B. Lewis to Franklin D. Roosevelt, Oct. 8, 1938; George W. Harris to Franklin D. Roosevelt, Oct. 30, 1936, ibid., Box 4; Lorena Hickok to Harry L. Hopkins, Jan. 16, 1934, Lorena Hickok Papers, Box 11, Franklin D. Roosevelt Library; William Jennifer to James A. Farley, July 29, 1936, Overton Papers, Box 6; interviews with George Briggs, Union, S.C., July 12, 1937, Thomas Dixon, Winnsboro, S.C., n.d., and Jane Johnson, Columbia, S.C., n.d., in *The American Slave*, ed. Rawick, vol. II, South Carolina, pt. 1, pp. 91 and 325, and vol. III, South Carolina, pt. 3, p. 51. Working-class whites used the same religious imagery to describe the President. See Robert S. McElvaine, "Thunder without Lightning: Working-Class Discontent in the United States, 1929-1937" (Ph.D. diss., SUNY-Binghamton, 1974), pp. 74-75.

[39] Aileen Byron to Franklin D. Roosevelt, Oct. 9, 1936, Mitchell Papers, Box 22; interview with Reuben Rosborough, Ridgeway, S.C., in *The American Slave*, ed. Rawick, vol. III, South Carolina, pt. 4, p. 47. On Roosevelt as "the modern Joshua,"

election was "a matter of religious principle," for he had been "a Savior to our race."[40]

Millions of white Americans were also captivated by Roosevelt and shared the perception of him as omnipotent leader and savior of a country in terrible distress. But the adulation on the part of blacks is worth remarking for two reasons. Not only were black Americans singling out a white President as their personal hero; many of them were also doing so in plain defiance of the facts of where he stood on race.

The hero-worship is easily comprehended. In part it reflected the novelty of attention from the White House. W. J. Trent, Jr., put it this way: "It was the first time in our lives that the Great White Father was concerned about us—or doing something to aid us." In part, as Clarence Mitchell grasped, it reflected the nature of the assistance Roosevelt had rendered: "When you've struggled all of your life to keep a little patch of land that's a farm or buy a house and a Depression comes so that you're going to lose it, necessarily a person who leads you out of that difficulty is some- one that you not only cherish yourself but that you pass on to your children and their children as an example of greatness."[41] In part, too, it signified a sophisticated understanding of the relative priorities of economics and race. "It was an indication of the folk wisdom on the part of Negroes that they worshipped the Roo- sevelts in spite of the fact that FDR never clearly defined civil rights goals," Kenneth Clark said. "This might be a reflection of their intuitive understanding that problems of racial equality had their roots in economic problems, and that, once the political

---

see also the comment of an unidentified black minister in "The Democratic Party as a Beacon Light for Political and Economical Emancipation of the Negro," type- script of speech, n.d. [1936], Good Neighbor League Papers, Box 1, Franklin D. Roosevelt Library.

[40] Hattie Mosely, quoted in Arthur W. Aleshire to Arthur W. Mitchell, Oct. 26, 1936, Mitchell Papers, Box 23. For other examples of religious imagery in blacks' perception of Roosevelt, see, e.g., interview with Phillip Evans, Winnsboro, S.C. in *The American Slave*, ed. Rawick, vol. II, South Carolina, pt. 2, p. 35; T. Bernard Blue to Franklin D. Roosevelt, Oct. 24, 1936; National Committee of Negro Americans to Franklin D. Roosevelt, [Oct. 24, 1936], FDR Papers, OF 93; interview with Peter Clifton, Winnsboro, S.C., in *The American Slave*, ed. Rawick, vol. II, South Carolina, pt. 1, p. 209; resolutions attached to letter to Franklin D. Roosevelt from a committee of blacks in Jackson, Miss., Dec. 2, 1933, Records of the Civil Works Administration, Box 83, Record Group 69, National Archives.

[41] Trent interview; Clarence Mitchell interview. Carl Stokes explained the hero worship this way: "When you take any oppressed group of people, when any ray of light shines down upon them, they respond to it gratefully, gratefully because of the first impact of it, and secondly because they hope it will continue" (Stokes interview).

power of the federal government had been harnessed for the attainment of economic equity, its use for the attainment of racial justice became inevitable."[42]

But the adulation also reflected the paucity of black heroes. "You have to understand that [blacks] had no other symbol," Ralph Metcalfe—himself something of a symbol at the time as an Olympic runner—explained; "as a result, they naturally supported [Roosevelt] because he came forth with programs for their benefit."[43] "Till relatively recently all our heroes were white anyway," Basil Paterson reflected. At a time when "there were very few [black] heroes to be found," it was no wonder that blacks shared the heroes of white America.[44]

But to perceive that hero as a special friend of blacks took a real leap of faith. Those blacks with the best perspective on the President knew better. Walter White saw him clearly: perhaps Roosevelt was free of the prejudice that afflicted some of his close advisers, surely he was eager "to secure . . . the full fruits and benefits of democracy" for everyone, blacks included. However, he was never willing to take political risks in behalf of the race. White's colleague, Roy Wilkins, put it succinctly: "Mr. Roosevelt was no friend of the Negro. He wasn't an enemy, but he wasn't a friend."[45]

But for those not close to Roosevelt, it was easy to form different perceptions. Blacks, like other Americans, were susceptible to the "almost mystical" effect of the Roosevelt personality, and the President often came out looking "above any kind of fault so far as blacks [were] concerned."[46] Not only was he without fault, but he was a friend, a beneficent protector, affirmatively and person-

[42] Kenneth B. Clark, "The Dilemma of Power," in *The Negro American*, ed. Kenneth B. Clark and Talcott Parsons (Boston, 1966), p. xiii.

[43] Interview with Ralph H. Metcalfe, Mar. 24, 1977, Washington, D.C. On the same theme, see interview with John Conyers, Jr., Mar 23, 1977, Washington, D.C. Metcalfe's comment is all the more interesting in view of the fact that, as an Olympic track star in the 1930s, he, along with Jesse Owens and Joe Louis, was one of the few symbols with whom blacks identified.

[44] Interview with Basil Paterson, Dec. 1, 1976, New York City.

[45] For White's views, see White column in *Chicago Defender*, Apr. 21, 1945 (source of the quotation); Allan Morrison, "The Secret Papers of FDR," *Negro Digest* IX (Jan. 1951), in *The Negro in Depression and War: Prelude to Revolution, 1930-1945*, ed. Bernard Sternsher (Chicago, 1969), p. 72. For Wilkins, Wilkins interview. For similar assessments, see Franklin H. Williams, Sutton, Robert Weaver interviews. These views are consistent with Frank Freidel's perceptive assessment of Roosevelt as someone who neither blocked those seeking "greater civil rights for Negroes" nor fought "in their behalf"—"at the most, his was a position of benevolent neutrality." *F.D.R. and the South* (Baton Rouge, 1965), p. 97.

[46] Clarence Mitchell interview.

ally concerned with the welfare of the race.[47] These attitudes closely mirrored those of unemployed whites. E. Wight Bakke, who studied the unemployed in New Haven in the 1930s, found "a growing conviction that Roosevelt honestly has the interest of the workers at the basis of his policies." As Roy Rosenzweig pointed out, even though "the substance of the New Deal was often meager for many of the poor and out-of-work, its programs and rhetoric persuaded many to look to Roosevelt to resolve their problems."[48]

The inconsistency between the image that blacks held of Roosevelt's beneficence and the reality of the treatment that blacks experienced during his administration posed no logical problems. The slights, the injustices, and the rank discrimination in the administration of relief were surely the products of less well intentioned underlings who acted in contravention of the President's wishes. If Roosevelt knew how badly blacks were being treated, correspondent after correspondent insisted, he would surely set things to rights.[49] Again, precisely the same attitude was characteristic of working-class whites, who, Robert S. McElvaine has

[47] See, for example, Ophelia Franklin Green to Franklin D. Roosevelt, Sept. 26, 1935; Lewis J. Morgan to Franklin D. Roosevelt, Dec. 16, 1935, WPA Papers, Box 1; W. B. Goodrich to Franklin D. Roosevelt, Feb. 9, 1936; James Bowser to Franklin D. Roosevelt, Mar. 8, 1936; John C. Daniels to Franklin Roosevelt, Sept. 11, 1936; Eva Neal to Franklin D. Roosevelt, Dec. 28, 1936, all in FDR Papers, OF 93; Harvey Henderson to James Roosevelt, June 17, 1936, NAACP Papers, Box C-418; letter to the editor from Talitha S. Saunders of Knoxville, *Pittsburgh Courier*, Apr. 11, 1936; Arthur Thomas to Arthur W. Mitchell, Oct. 15, 1936, Mitchell Papers, Box 23; letter to the editor from H. A. Clarke of Washington, D.C., *Norfolk Journal and Guide*, Oct. 24, 1936; Tom Davis to Harry L. Hopkins, Aug. 17, 1938, WPA Papers, Box 4; "F.D.R. Blues," a song recorded in 1946, in Oliver, *Blues Fell This Morning*, p. 283.

[48] Bakke, *Citizens without Work* (New Haven, 1940), p. 53, quoted in Rosenzweig, " 'Socialism in Our Time': The Socialist Party and the Unemployed, 1929-1936" (unpublished manuscript), pp. 20-21. The Rosenzweig quote is from p. 21 of his essay.

[49] See, e.g., unsigned letter to Franklin D. Roosevelt from a committee of blacks in Jackson, Miss., Dec. 2, 1933, and U.S. Government Subjects, Lincoln County, Oklahoma, to Clark Foreman, Jan. 6, 1934, both in CWA Papers, Box 83; letter to the editor from Kelly Miller, published as "Black Streaks on the Blue Eagle," *Christian Century*, Nov. 8, 1933, p. 1413; letter to the editor from E. W. Dandridge of Wilkinsburg, Pa., *Pittsburgh Courier*, Sept. 23, 1933; Melvin J. Chisum to Eleanor Roosevelt, Sept. 24, 1934, ER Papers, Box 1325; Arthur W. Mitchell, quoted in *Kansas City Star*, Dec. 4, 1934, Mitchell Papers, Box 3; editorial, *Chicago Defender*, May 26, 1934; editorial, *Pittsburgh Courier*, Oct. 14, 1933; Mr. and Mrs. Jack Goble to Franklin D. Roosevelt, Dec. 22, 1934; Milton M. Brown to H. M. [*sic*] McIntyre, June 19, 1937; Lula B. Jackson to Franklin D. Roosevelt, Dec. 4, 1934; Charles Griffen to Franklin D. Roosevelt, Sept. 9, 1934, WPA Papers, Box 1; A. J. White to Frank Harrington, Sept. 6, 1940; Mrs. Little Bell to President Roosevelt, May 6, 1935; Genera B. Adams to Harry L. Hopkins, n.d., ibid., Box 2.

found, "sincerely believed that the president was a friend of the masses and that he was trying to assist them" and accordingly "tended to blame all their problems on Roosevelt's subordinates, who were charged with failing to carry out the president's good intentions."[50]

Distance was one of the factors that gave Roosevelt such a favorable image in the eyes of blacks. The other main ingredient that made Roosevelt a hero was his wife. Up close or at a distance, the First Lady's image stayed constant: here was a genuine friend of blacks. Her sympathetic ear in the heart of the administration made the critical difference in conveying a sense of caring; and her racial involvements made many blacks believe that the President was more interested in racial justice than he actually was.[51] Roosevelt was "the front man," she was "the doer," Roy Wilkins observed; "the personal touches and the personal fight against discrimination were Mrs. Roosevelt's; that attached to Roosevelt also—he couldn't hardly get away from it—and he reaped the political benefit of it."[52] "I used to say," Pauli Murray summed up, "that there were two presidents in that White House, and that Roosevelt was so successful because people were voting for Eleanor as well as they were voting for FDR."[53]

The combination was nearly irresistible: real economic assistance, Eleanor's genuine concern, the President's magical personality—no wonder Roosevelt came out a hero. As if to seal the legitimacy of the judgment, blacks transferred to Roosevelt the adulation that had previously been reserved for Abraham Lincoln. The imagery was familiar: Lincoln, too, had been widely perceived by blacks as a hero, a father figure, a savior, and a messiah. No matter that emancipation had been declared as a war measure and that Lincoln had explicitly stated that he would maintain slavery if he could thereby save the Union. To blacks, he was the Great Emancipator, enshrined ever afterward as the special cham-

---

[50] McElvaine, "Thunder without Lightning," p. 70. See also pp. 77-78.
[51] There is repeated testimony to what Rayford Logan described as Mrs. Roosevelt's role "as a major factor in winning support for President Roosevelt and the New Deal." Logan interview. See also Carter, Gee, Higginbotham, Jordan, Mays, Clarence Mitchell, Paterson, Sutton, Trent interviews; telephone interview with Marjorie Parker, Oct. 28, 1976, Washington, D.C.; *Afro-American*, Nov. 17, 1962; Walter White in *Richmond Times Dispatch*, June 30, 1939, clipping in Aubrey Williams Papers, Box 5, Franklin D. Roosevelt Library.
[52] Wilkins interview ("front man," "doer"); Wilkins, *Reminiscences*, p. 100.
[53] Murray interview.

pion of the race.[54] A similar disjunction between perception and reality operated in the case of Roosevelt. No matter what his racial intent, Lincoln was the father of emancipation; no matter what *his* racial biases, Roosevelt was the father of the New Deal. That made him the second emancipator, the inheritor of Lincoln's mantle, "the best friend the Negro American has had in the White House since Abraham Lincoln," "the Modern Abe Lincoln of the race."[55] That the economic emancipation of the New Deal may have been as flawed as the freedom accomplished through the Thirteenth Amendment somehow escaped comment.

Identification with the President played an important part in the politicization of black Americans. Roosevelt was a magnetic symbol of political authority, one who drew those who identified with him into a positive identification with the larger political system.

[54] On black views of Lincoln, see Benjamin Quarles, *Lincoln and the Negro* (New York, 1962); James M. McPherson, *The Negro's Civil War: How American Negroes Felt and Acted during the War for the Union* (New York, 1965), pp. 43-44, 49-52, 301-308.

[55] The quotations are from Albert L. Hinton column, *Norfolk Journal and Guide*, Apr. 21, 1945; William H. Bolden to Franklin D. Roosevelt, Oct. 4, 1936, FDR Papers, OF 93. The Lincoln association is developed in numerous sources. See, for example, Alton Wright to Franklin D. Roosevelt, Oct. 25, 1934, ibid.; Wright to Roosevelt, Jan. 19, 1935, Lawrence A. Oxley Papers, Box 1390, Records of the United States Employment Service, Record Group 183, National Archives; Thomas M. Brown to Frances Perkins, June 27, 1935, ibid., Box 1392; B.N.T. Gray statement, Aug. 10, 1936, Good Neighbor League Papers, Box 1; W. F. Davis to Franklin D. Roosevelt, Aug. 22, 1936, WPA Papers, Box 1; Mary W. Dewson to Florence Summers, Sept. 2, 1936, Papers of the Women's Division, Democratic National Committee, Box 5, Franklin D. Roosevelt Library; W. F. Reden to Arthur W. Mitchell, Sept. 24, 1936, Mitchell Papers, Box 22; "Roosevelt, the Humanitarian," *Crisis* XLIII (Oct. 1936):299; Lizzie McDuffie, quoted in *New Bern* (N.C.) *World*, [?] 1936, McDuffie Papers, Box 1, Negro Collection, Trevor Arnett Library, Atlanta University; Arthur Thomas to Arthur W. Mitchell, Oct. 15, 1936, Mitchell Papers, Box 23; Eugene Davidson in readers' column, *Afro-American*, Oct. 24, 1936; Joel E. Spingarn, quoted in *New York Times*, Oct. 19, 1936, p. 2; Earl Dickerson, quoted in *Afro-American*, Oct. 31, 1936; interview with Mattie Logan, West Tulsa, Okla., in *The American Slave*, ed. Rawick, vol. VII, Oklahoma, p. 191; interview with Ella Kelly, Winnsboro, S.C. in ibid., vol. III, South Carolina, pt. 3, p. 82; Farrar Matthews to Franklin D. Roosevelt, Apr. 15, 1938; Maggie Johnson to Franklin D. Roosevelt, Jan. 20, 1938, WPA Papers, Box 4; Curley Johnson to Franklin D. Roosevelt, May 15, 1939, ibid., Box 5; Miller, "The Negro in Pennsylvania Politics," p. 190, n. 18; editorial, *Chicago Defender*, Apr. 21, 1945; L. D. Reddick, "Negro People Mourn Loss of Roosevelt," Schomburg Library press release, Apr. 13, 1945, and W.E.B. Du Bois, "What He Meant to the Negro," *PM*, Apr. 24, 1945, both in Franklin D. Roosevelt folder, vertical file, Schomburg Center for Research in Black Culture. Blacks were not alone in perceiving Roosevelt as the inheritor of Lincoln's mantle. On more general efforts by New Dealers to locate themselves in the Lincoln tradition, see David Donald, "Getting Right with Lincoln," *Lincoln Reconsidered: Essays on the Civil War Era*, 2nd ed. (New York, 1956), pp. 13-15.

The South Carolina woman who wrote, "I don't know what Republician or Democrat means but I know one thing true I never get any where untill you taken your seat," spoke to an important point.[56] Identification with Roosevelt was a way station on the road to greater political awareness. That awareness grew because he personified a government that impinged directly on the lives of ordinary people in unprecedented ways.

Most blacks knew the story of Sylvester Harris, the Mississippi farmer who called the White House in distress over the prospect of losing his farm. Somehow, he got the President on the wire. "These white folks down here is gwine take my farm," he told Roosevelt, according to a popular version of the conversation. "I hear you wouldn't let them do it if I asked you." Roosevelt promised to look into the situation, and a government loan saved Harris's property.[57] The uniqueness of Roosevelt's personal intervention in the Harris case was really beside the point. What mattered was the habit of looking to the White House to solve the problems of ordinary people.

By repeatedly appealing to the President for assistance, blacks unconsciously exemplified the new relationship that was emerging between the government and the American people. "Mr. President give us some place where we can make us a living"; "I am asking for help help help, please help I am in need"; "Please Sir get me in shape to farm"; "President Roosevelt, Honored Sir . . . I appeal to you for help in the name of the Lord."[58] No matter that Roosevelt himself rarely answered. By responding to those appeals, at least in many cases, with significant assistance, the New Deal began to change popular perceptions of the possibilities of federal power. The remark of an elderly former slave summed up the transformation. "I gits along pretty good," she said. Her family lived nearby and helped to care for her. But now there was

[56] Ada E. West to Franklin D. Roosevelt, Mar. 3, 1936, WPA Papers, Box 2. For contemporary testimony to Roosevelt's role in awakening interest in politics, see the responses to the *Afro-American*'s street-corner polls, Oct. 17, 1936.

[57] The account of the conversation is in "Roosevelt, the Humanitarian," p. 298. See also *New York Age*, Mar. 10, 1934; *New York Sun*, [Oct. 30, 1934?], and unidentified Associated Press dispatch, Apr. 30, [1935?], clippings in Roosevelt Administration Scrapbooks, vol. I, microfilm reel 16, Schomburg Center for Research in Black Culture. On the pervasiveness of the story, see, for example, interview with Ida Wood, Oct. 25, 1976, New York City.

[58] Letter from "A group of old Negroes" in Dossville, Miss., addressed to Washington Bureau To the Dept. 310, Nov. 5, 1934; A. L. Lloyd to Franklin D. Roosevelt, Dec. 3, 1934; Comer Woods to Franklin D. Roosevelt, Feb. 16, 1935; Cynthia Summers to Franklin D. Roosevelt, Mar. 9, 1935, WPA Papers, Box 1.

something new: "De government helps me out. It sure is a blessing, too—to have sech a good government!"[59] Government became immediate, its impact tangible, its activities relevant. Blacks,
especially, had been shut out of national politics—disfranchised,
discriminated against, their racial concerns unheeded, and their
needs far removed from the issues that held center stage in Washington. The New Deal changed all that: now what happened in
Washington vitally affected the lives of blacks as it did other
Americans. As a result, blacks, like other Americans, found themselves drawn into the political process.[60]

The shift to the Democratic party, therefore, was part of the
larger process of politicization that was changing the political
habits of black Americans. The New Deal not only changed the
political affiliation of the black electorate; it also increased black
interest in political participation. In part the change was one of
attitude. A black laborer captured the transformation in the making. His fellow workers, he said, had "talked more politics since
Mistuh Roosevelt been in than ever befo'."[61] But attitudinal change
was only a small aspect of the politicization that was occurring.
The New Deal brought out new black voters at the same time
that it swung blacks who were already voting away from the
Republican party.[62] Hence the experience of blacks fits both of

[59] Interview with Eliza Scantling, Scotia, S.C., in *The American Slave*, ed. Rawick, vol. III, South Carolina, pt. 4, p. 78.
[60] See, for instance, "Roosevelt, the Humanitarian," p. 299; Brown interview;
Lawrence Hamm interview with Wilnora Holman, July 3, 1979, Newark, N.J.;
Earl Brown, "Negro Vote," Aug. 1940, Claude A. Barnett Papers, Box P3, Chicago
Historical Society; Crystal Bird Fauset, in *Philadelphia Tribune*, Oct. 10, 1940.
[61] Quoted in Ralph J. Bunche, *The Political Status of the Negro in the Age of
FDR*, ed. Dewey W. Grantham (Chicago, 1973), p. 429.
[62] There is ample contemporary evidence on both points. For black Republicans
who shifted to the Democratic party because of Roosevelt, see, for example, DeReath
Beausey to Eleanor Roosevelt, Oct. 16, 1935, Women's Division Papers, Box 5;
untitled typed statement by A. Clayton Powell, Sr., attached to Stanley High to
Reverend A. Clayton Powell, Aug. 1, 1936, Good Neighbor League Papers, Box 1;
John H. Vives to James A. Farley, Aug. 19, 1936, Mitchell Papers, Box 21; Frisby
Thomas to Harry Hopkins and Franklin D. Roosevelt, Oct. 18, 1936; Fred Coleman
to Franklin D. Roosevelt, Nov. 4, 1936; W. T. Hodgins to Harry Hopkins, Dec. 4,
1936, WPA Papers, Box 4; interview with Campbell Davis, Karnack, Texas, n.d.
[1937?], in *The American Slave*, ed. Rawick, vol. IV, Texas, pt. 1, p. 287; Tom
Davis to Harry L. Hopkins, Aug. 17, 1938; Steven B. Lewis to Franklin D. Roosevelt, Oct. 8, 1938, WPA Papers, Box 4; Trent interview; Logan interview; Gee
interview. For blacks who cast their first votes for Roosevelt, see, for example,
Estelle Hall to Franklin D. Roosevelt, July 17, 1936, WPA Papers, Box 4; Clarence
Mitchell interview; G. L.-P. Weaver interview. V. O. Key, Jr., noted that the new
Democratic voters were "more important numerically" than those who shifted
from the Republican party. *Southern Politics*, p. 290.

the models which political scientists use to explain the New Deal realignment: the conversion of previously Republican voters to the Democrats, and the mobilization of "previously apolitical citizens," who simultaneously entered "the political arena and acquire[d] a party identification."[63]

Registration figures tell part of the story of the mobilization of blacks in the 1930s. Some 69,000 blacks were registered to vote in Philadelphia in 1932; in 1936, more than 121,000 blacks were on the voting rolls; by 1940, the number was just short of 135,000.[64] That meant an increase from just over 46 percent of the blacks who could have registered in 1932—those who were at least twenty-one years old—to more than 82 percent in 1940.[65] In Knoxville, somewhat more than a quarter of twenty-one-year-olds in two predominantly black wards were registered to vote in 1928; more than 40 percent were registered by 1936.[66] The voting rolls in Harlem's Nineteenth and Twenty-first Assembly Districts numbered nearly 43,000 in 1930 and nearly 70,000 a decade later. Over the decade of the 1920s, registration had stayed virtually static.[67]

Voter turnout provides more conclusive evidence. In Chicago, the percentage of the potential electorate (those who were at least twenty-one years old) in black districts who went to the polls grew from 61.1 in 1932 to 68.8 in 1940. In Cleveland, it increased from 51.8 in 1932 to 63.6 in 1940. In Detroit, it grew from 41.1 percent to 58.3 percent in the same period. In Harlem, 29.1 percent

[63] On the argument for mobilizing new voters, see, for example, Angus Campbell, Phillip E. Converse, Warren E. Miller, and Donald E. Stokes, *The American Voter* (New York, 1960), especially pp. 153-54; on the argument for the primacy of party-switching, see, for example, James L. Sundquist, *Dynamics of the Party System: Alignment and Realignment of Political Parties in the United States* (Washington, D.C., 1973), especially p. 200. For a good summary of the literature and an analysis which emphasizes mobilization, see Kristi Anderson, *The Creation of a Democratic Majority, 1928-1936* (Chicago, 1979). The quotation is from Anderson, p. xii.

[64] Registration Commission for the City of Philadelphia, *Twenty-seventh Annual Report, December 31, 1932* (Philadelphia, 1933), p. 18; *Thirty-first Annual Report, December 31, 1936* (Philadelphia, 1937), p. 18; *Thirty-fifth Annual Report, December 31, 1940* (Philadelphia, 1941), p. 18.

[65] Derived from U. S. Department of Commerce, Bureau of the Census, *Fifteenth Census of the United States, 1930, Population*, vol. III: *Reports by States* (Washington, D.C., 1932), pt. 2, p. 671, and *Sixteenth Census of the United States, 1940, Population and Housing: Statistics for Census Tracts: Philadelphia, Pa.* (Washington, D.C., 1942), p. 6. The percentage for 1932 is estimated on the basis of the black population twenty-one years of age and older in 1930.

[66] Larry W. Dunn, "Knoxville Negro Voting and the Roosevelt Revolution, 1928-1936," *East Tennessee Historical Society's Publications*, no. 43 (1971), p. 87.

[67] John Albert Morsell, "The Political Behavior of Negroes in New York City" (Ph.D. diss., Columbia University, 1951), pp. 56, 57, 62.

of the potential electorate voted in 1932, 52.8 percent in 1940. To put it another way, the number of people who went to the polls in black districts in Cleveland increased by 14 percent between 1932 and 1940. In Chicago, the increase was almost 26 percent; in Detroit over 30 percent. In Harlem, it reached a staggering 78 percent (see Table X.2). At a time when the size of the potential electorate in these areas remained relatively stable, so significant a change in the size of the actual electorate carried an unmistakable message: national politics had assumed a new, more immediate relevance for black Americans.

Part of the new black electorate came from men and women newly concerned about politics, people who were of age but who simply had not voted before. Part of it came from blacks who were just coming of age in the 1930s. It was more difficult for older blacks, who either remembered slavery and Reconstruction/ Redemption themselves or were the children of people who did, to support the Democratic party (see Tables X.3, X.4, X.5). A

TABLE X.2
Potential Electorate and Voter Turnout in Black Districts,
1932-1940

City	Population 21 and Over		Voter Turnout		
	1930	1940	1932	1936	1940
Chicago	142,545	159,131	87,137	106,838	109,433
Cleveland	22,033*	22,941	12,798	13,901	14,582
Detroit	29,956	27,588	12,326	11,946	16,077
New York	83,104	81,657	24,178	38,474	43,116

SOURCES: For population, see Ernest W. Burgess and Charles Newcomb, eds., *Census Data of the City of Chicago, 1930* (Chicago, 1933), pp. 306, 309, 312; Louis Wirth and Eleanor H. Bernert, eds., *Local Community Fact Book of Chicago* (Chicago, 1949); U.S. Department of Commerce, Bureau of the Census, *Sixteenth Census of the United States: 1940, Population and Housing: Statistics for Census Tracts and Community Areas: Chicago, Ill.* (Washington, D.C., 1943), pp. 59-174; Howard Whipple Green, *Population Characteristics by Census Tracts: Cleveland, Ohio, 1930* (Cleveland, 1931), pp. 73-113; U.S. Department of Commerce, Bureau of the Census, *Sixteenth Census of the United States: 1940, Population and Housing: Statistics for Census Tracts: Cleveland, Ohio, and Adjacent Area* (Washington, D.C., 1942), pp. 7-32; ibid., *Detroit, Mich., and Adjacent Area* (Washington, D.C., 1942), pp. 8-68; Walter Laidlaw, comp. and ed., *Population of the City of New York, 1890-1930* (New York, 1932), pp. 88-89; Welfare Council of New York City, *Census Tract Data on Population and Housing: New York City: 1940* (New York, 1942), p. 147. For voter turnout, see the sources cited above for Table IX.2.
* 20 and over.

TABLE X.3
Party Affiliation, by Age
Professionals, Businessmen, and Civic Leaders
1933

Decade of Birth	% Republican	% Democratic	% Independent
Before 1850 [N = 6]	100.0	—	—
1850s [N = 37]	91.9	—	8.1
1860s [N = 132]	82.6	3.8	13.6
1870s [N = 281]	78.3	5.0	16.7
1880s [N = 397]	76.1	8.0	15.9
1890s [N = 369]	65.6	13.0	21.4
1900s [N = 61]	65.6	16.4	18.0
All decades [N = 1,283]	74.3	8.4	17.3

SOURCE: *Who's Who in Colored America*, 3rd ed. (Brooklyn, N.Y., 1933).

TABLE X.4
Party Affiliation, by Age
Professionals, Businessmen, and Civic Leaders
1937

Decade of Birth	% Republican	% Democratic	% Independent	% Other
Before 1850 [N = 5]	100.0	—	—	—
1850s [N = 36]	88.9	—	8.3	2.8
1860s [N = 121]	80.2	2.5	15.7	1.6
1870s [N = 285]	77.2	16.0	16.1	.7
1880s [N = 406]	72.4	8.4	16.7	2.5
1890s [N = 382]	62.3	13.6	23.3	.8
1900s [N = 74]	59.5	18.9	20.3	1.3
1910s [N = 1]	—	—	100.0	—
All decades [N = 1,310]	71.0	9.2	18.4	1.4

SOURCE: *Who's Who in Colored America*, 4th ed. (Brooklyn, N.Y., 1937).

former slave told the Virginia Writers' Project that she had been sold at auction as a nurse, and "That's why I ain't no Democrat."[68] To another former slave, the Democratic party conjured up images of Jefferson Davis and other Confederates, "And if these young Negroes don't quit messing with the democratic bunch they are

[68] Interview with Melinda Ann Ruffin, Waynesboro, Va., n.d., in *Weevils in the Wheat: Interviews with Virginia Ex-Slaves*, ed. Charles L. Perdue, Jr., Thomas E. Barden, and Robert K. Phillips (Charlottesville, Va., 1976), p. 243.

TABLE X.5
Party Affiliation, by Age
Professionals, Businessmen, and Civic Leaders
1942

Decade of Birth	% Repub- lican	% Demo- cratic	% Inde- pendent	% Other
Before 1860 [N = 32]	87.5	—	12.5	—
1860s [N = 101]	80.2	3.0	14.8	2.0
1870s [N = 264]	75.8	16.9	17.0	0.3
1880s [N = 387]	74.4	9.6	14.7	1.3
1890s [N = 401]	60.6	15.7	23.2	0.5
1900s [N = 88]	56.8	21.6	20.5	0.1
1910s [N = 7]	28.6	42.8	28.6	—
All decades [N = 1,280]	69.7	11.2	18.3	0.8

SOURCE: *Who's Who in Colored America*, 6th ed. (Brooklyn, N.Y., 1942).

going to be right back where we started from."[69] To blacks in the South or fresh from the South, it was hard to identify with the Democrats who had disfranchised or discriminated against them.[70] As John R. Lynch, a lawyer in Chicago who had been elected to Congress from Mississippi during Reconstruction, summed up: "The colored voters cannot help but feel that in voting the Democratic ticket in national elections they will be voting to give their indorsement and their approval to every wrong of which they are victims, every right of which they are deprived, and every injustice of which they suffer."[71]

[69] Interview with Octavia George, Oklahoma City, n.d., in *The American Slave*, ed. Rawick, vol. VII, Oklahoma, p. 114. Another former slave, commenting on the "changes[s] for de worse" among "de Negroes of today," emphasized, "dey don't b'lieve in de Republican no mo at all. I know a lot of good ole colored folks dat would turn over in dey graves if dey knew de young colored folks was ackin dis away." Interview with Matilda Carter, Hampton, Va., Jan. 4, 1937, in *Weevils in the Wheat*, ed. Perdue et al., p. 70.

[70] In their interviews with black nonvoters in Chicago in the 1920s, Charles Edward Merriam and Harold Foote Gosnell found intense opposition to Democrats among blacks who had come from the South. An Alabamian "said that he could never vote for a Democrat as long as he kept his memory," because "the Democrats he knew in Alabama were the 'imps of Satan.' " A woman from Georgia identified the Democrats as " 'the party [that] keeps its foot on the black man.' " *Non-Voting: Causes and Methods of Control* (Chicago, 1924), p. 139. In a poll of Harlem voters in 1944, Paul N. Lazarsfeld found "much the largest amount of Republican sentiment . . . among Negroes born in the South who never went beyond grade school and are now forty-five years of age or older." "Polls, Propaganda, Politics: The Negro Vote," *Nation*, Sept. 30, 1944, p. 379.

[71] Quoted in Harold F. Gosnell, *Negro Politicians: The Rise of Negro Politics in Chicago* (1935; reprint ed., Chicago, 1969), pp. 24-25.

For younger blacks, though, especially those in the North, and more especially the children of the Great Migration who came to political maturity during the Depression, it was much easier to perceive the Democrats as a viable political alternative and much less persuasive when the Republicans invoked the rhetoric of Lincoln and emancipation. These young people proved especially susceptible to the appeal of Franklin Roosevelt. Black college students were typical of their age group in their enthusiasm for Roosevelt. The admiration was shared "even among the left-wing," recalled Kenneth Clark, then a student at Columbia University. Doyle L. Sumner, in the 1930s a Sierra Leonean studying at Hampton Institute, remembered the student body listening attentively to radios during Fireside Chats, the campus devoid of other activity. Forty years later, Sumner could still feel the Roosevelt magic: "If you told me that I'd meet Roosevelt in heaven," he said, "I'd go—he'd do so much good there." Louis Martin reflected that as a student at the University of Michigan in the 1930s, he was "among those young kids who were just absolutely mesmerized by Roosevelt."[72] Less shackled than their elders by ties of sentimentality and tradition, this "new generation" of blacks was freer to vote on the basis of issues and merit.[73] Thus such cities as Chicago, Cleveland, Detroit, Philadelphia, Pittsburgh, and New York, where two-fifths of the potential black electorate in 1940 had reached voting age during the Depression, were political gold mines for the Democratic party.[74]

[72] Interviews with Clark, Martin, and with Doyle L. Sumner, Oct. 25, 1976, New York City. See also interview with Elmer W. Henderson, Mar. 24, 1977, Washington, D.C.

[73] Letter to the editor from Aubrey C. Carpenter, Washington, D.C., *Afro-American*, May 9, 1936; Claude A. Barnett to Elbert Lee Tatum, Oct. 14, 1945, in Tatum, *The Changed Political Thought of the Negro, 1915-1940* (New York, 1951), Appendix 5, p. 193. On generational distinctions in black support for the Democratic party, see also ibid., pp. 111-12; Eugene A. Hatfield, "The Impact of the New Deal on Black Politics in Pennsylvania, 1928-1936" (Ph.D. diss., University of North Carolina at Chapel Hill, 1979), pp. 107, 115-16; F. B. Ransom to Walter White, Nov. 10, 1932, NAACP Papers, Box C-391; Ransom quoted in James A. Farley to Arthur W. Mitchell, Oct. 5, 1936, Mitchell Papers, Box 22; Bruce M. Stave, *The New Deal and the Last Hurrah: Pittsburgh Machine Politics* (Pittsburgh, 1970), p. 34; Irvin C. Mollison to Walter White, Nov. 7, 1936, NAACP Papers, Box C-392; Kelly Miller in *Pittsburgh Courier*, Oct. 31, 1936; Miller column, "Miller Tells Why Younger Generations Favor F.D.R.," *Afro-American*, Oct. 10, 1936.

[74] Derived from U.S. Department of Commerce, Bureau of the Census, *Sixteenth Census of the United States: 1940, Population and Housing: Statistics for Census Tracts and Community Areas: Chicago, Ill.* (Washington, D.C., 1943), p. 6; ibid., *Statistics for Census Tracts: Cleveland, Ohio, and Adjacent Area* (Washington,

Disfranchisement makes it difficult to use conversion or mobilization as meaningful indices of the politicization of blacks in the South. Even there, however, blacks shared in the increased political activity and interest that came with the New Deal. In communities throughout the region in the 1930s, black citizens began to organize to claim their franchise. New groups emerged to promote voter registration, urge payment of the poll tax, and encourage blacks to go to the polls. North Carolina blacks established a Committee on Negro Affairs, with branches in Charlotte, Greensboro, Winston-Salem, Raleigh, and Durham. Blacks in Georgia created a Civic and Political League in Atlanta and a Young Men's Civic Club in Savannah. In Virginia, blacks set up the Hampton County Civic League, Petersburg League of Negro Voters, Portsmouth Civic and Welfare Club, and the Newport News Young Men's Democratic Club. In Alabama, the Tuscaloosa Civic League, Huntsville Negro Voter's Club, and the Montgomery Negro Civic and Improvement League, Inc., served the same purposes. The obstacles were formidable: complicated registration requirements, poll taxes, white primaries, and outright intimidation kept blacks from registering or attempting to vote. Still, the efforts showed some results: the number of registered blacks in Atlanta grew from less than 1,000 in 1936 to 2,100 in 1939; in Miami, where only 50 blacks were on the voting rolls through most of the 1920s and 1930s, 2,000 had qualified by 1940; in Tampa, where barely 100 blacks had voted in 1934, 2,500 were registered by the time of the general election in 1940.[75]

No one mistook the politics of the new voters. The registrar of Macon County, Georgia, who did his best to block blacks from voting, observed that blacks in his area had turned Democratic "since Roosevelt became Santa Claus."[76] "Every nigger is another vote for Roosevelt," declared a justice of the peace in Greene County, Georgia.[77] "You ask any nigger on the street who's the greatest man in the world," exclaimed the secretary-treasurer of the Greene County Democratic committee. "Nine out of ten will

D.C., 1942), p. 6; ibid., *Detroit, Mich., and Adjacent Area* (Washington, D.C., 1942), p. 8; ibid., *Philadelphia, Pa.* (Washington, D.C., 1942), p. 6; and Welfare Council of New York City, *Census Tract Data on Population and Housing: New York City: 1940* (New York, 1942), p. 147.

[75] Bunche, *The Political Status of the Negro*, pp. 273-74, 284-87, 300-301, 307, 311, 315, 324-26.

[76] Quoted in ibid., p. 410.

[77] Quoted in ibid., p. 412. For similar views on the part of white Republicans in the South, see pp. 519, 527, 531.

tell you Franklin D. Roosevelt. Roosevelt's greatest strength is with the lower element. That's why I think he is so dangerous."[78]

Those blacks who were barred from the polls also made clear their political sentiments. "No one out here ever tried to vote," a farm worker in South Carolina told an interviewer. "Eff'n we cud vote, we wouldn't vote for anybody else but Mistuh Roosevelt."[79] The election of 1936 elicited expressions of support for the President from disfranchised blacks throughout the South. "I could not vote but I sure did sweat my rabbit foot for you," one man wrote to Roosevelt.[80] "I could not vote for you but I sure did talk for you to my white people," announced another.[81] A black man in New Orleans explained the logic that lay behind such declarations: "I would vote for President Roosevelt a hundred times, if that were possible," he wrote. "When President Hoover was in, I was walking the streets about to starve or commit a crime, but today I am working on a government project, originated by President Roosevelt."[82]

The economic benefits of the New Deal attracted southern blacks to the Democratic party. Later, one New Deal agency helped to politicize them by giving them experience in voting. Beginning in 1938, the Agricultural Adjustment Administration brought black farmers to the polls to participate in cotton-marketing quota referenda. For many blacks, the referenda meant the first chance that they had ever had to cast ballots. Not only were they allowed to vote, free from intimidation, but they could do so on an equal footing with whites. Ralph J. Bunche appraised the participation of blacks in the AAA referenda as an important stage in the political education of blacks and whites, a development "of the utmost social significance in the South."[83] Some whites saw it differently. "This AAA voting is giving them ideas they can become regular voters," the sheriff of Dallas County, Alabama, objected. "I think it's dangerous."[84]

One cannot help but wonder whether those whites who objected to the politicization of blacks in the 1930s fully imagined the array of "dangers" that politicization eventually brought. The

[78] Quoted in ibid., p. 206.
[79] Quoted in ibid., p. 428.
[80] Luther Gaines to Franklin D. Roosevelt, Nov. 6, 1936, WPA Papers, Box 4.
[81] William Hicks to Franklin D. Roosevelt, Nov. 16, 1936, ibid.
[82] Letter to the editor from Fred A. Cannon of New Orleans, *Pittsburgh Courier*, Oct. 17, 1936 (issue is misdated—actually Oct. 24).
[83] Bunche, *The Political Status of the Negro*, p. 76.
[84] Quoted in ibid., p. 390.

growing interest of blacks in politics, their involvement in the Democratic party, and their new sense that the political process could be responsive to their needs became essential underpinnings of the drive for civil rights. The political habits established during the New Deal had repercussions far beyond their immediate consequences in the 1930s.

But those repercussions lay years, even decades, in the future. What would be the more immediate results of the political transformation effected in 1936? The New Deal had brought blacks into the political process; it had given them a political hero; and it had tied them firmly to the Democratic party. Blacks had enlisted in the New Deal coalition; now what would the Roosevelt administration do for them in return?

CHAPTER XI ▪ *Race in the Second Roosevelt Administration*

The real payoff for blacks, of course, came in precisely the same currency in which black votes had been tendered. Blacks had responded to the economic benefits of the New Deal; in the second Roosevelt administration, continued economic assistance would be their most tangible reward.

Addressing the annual conference of the NAACP in 1937, the Black Cabinet leader, Robert Weaver, reminded his audience of some of the administration's accomplishments: in 1937 alone, 390,000 blacks were employed on WPA projects, nearly 20 percent of the WPA work force; 10,000 black children were cared for daily in WPA nursery schools; more than 35,000 black students were attending high schools and colleges thanks to NYA assistance; some 5,000 black teachers were on the federal payroll to teach black adults to read and write; and black youths represented about 10 percent of the enrollment in CCC camps. In the four years of its existence, the PWA had built more than $7 million worth of black elementary and secondary schools in the South. PWA housing projects provided homes for needy black families at low rents, and black workers shared handsomely in the payrolls as the projects were being constructed. All told, close to a third of such federally-funded housing units were earmarked for black residents.[1]

Statistics fail adequately to convey the significance of these benefits. Compared to the magnitude of the need, the numbers of blacks whom these programs assisted may not have been large. But for the people whose lives were touched, the effect was often

[1] Robert C. Weaver, "The Negro and the Federal Government," address to NAACP annual conference, June 30, 1937, National Association for the Advancement of Colored People Papers, Box B-14, Manuscript Division, Library of Congress (hereafter cited as the NAACP Papers). On housing, see also John P. Murchison, "The Negro and Low-Rent Housing" *Crisis* XLII (July 1935):199-200, 210; *New York Amsterdam News*, Apr. 20, 1940; Robert C. Weaver, "Racial Policy in Public Housing," *Phylon* I (Second Quarter, 1940):149-56, 161; Weaver, *The Negro Ghetto* (New York, 1948), pp. 73-74; Gunnar Myrdal, *An American Dilemma*, 2 vols. (1944; 20th anniv. ed., New York, 1964), I:350.

dramatic. The low-rent housing projects are a case in point. Vernon Jordan remembered growing up in University Homes in Atlanta, the first black public housing project in the country. The complex may have been segregated, but it was clean and warm, and the blacks who moved in were "ecstatic" at their good fortune.[2] In Cleveland, Carl and Louis Stokes lived with their mother, who worked as a domestic servant, "in a rickety old two-family house." "We covered the rat holes with the tops of tin cans," Carl recalled. "The front steps always needed fixing. . . . The coal stove kept the living room warm; we used heated bricks and an old flatiron wrapped in flannel to keep warm in the bedroom. The three of us shared one bed." In 1938, when Carl was eleven, the family moved into an apartment in a new public housing project. "The day we moved was pure wonder," he later wrote. "A sink with hot and cold running water, a place where you could wash clothes with a washing machine, an actual refrigerator. And we learned what it was to live in dependable warmth. For the first time, we had two bedrooms and two beds. My mother for the first time had a room and a bed of her own."[3]

Experiences like these made other New Deal programs lifesavers for the blacks who were fortunate enough to be affected by them. The black families of Gee's Bend, Alabama, showed the impact of the New Deal's rural rehabilitation and resettlement projects. Gee's Bend was a community of 115 black families living on the 7,200-acre Pettway plantation south of Selma. These tenant farmers, descendants of the slaves who had worked the old cotton plantation, had lost their crops, livestock, and equipment in 1931 in the liquidation of the estate of the merchant-landlord to whom they were indebted. The Red Cross intervened with emergency food and clothing; then various state and federal agencies provided temporary relief and employment. In 1935, the federal government's rural rehabilitation program for cotton tenants brought farming equipment, seed, and groceries. In 1936, the Resettlement Administration moved in. Under its direction, and later under that of the Farm Security Administration, the farmers of Gee's Bend succeeded in producing a cotton crop and began once again to raise livestock on their land. The FSA then bought up the old

---

[2] Interview with Vernon E. Jordan, Jr., Oct. 26, 1976, New York City. On the same theme, see interview with A. Leon Higginbotham, Jr., Jan. 21, 1981, Philadelphia.

[3] Carl B. Stokes, *Promises of Power: A Political Autobiography* (New York, 1973), pp. 23-25.

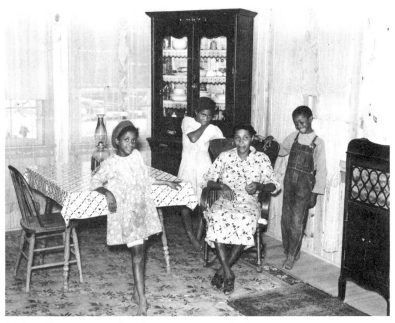

22-23. Sharecropper families in New Madrid County, Missouri, in May 1938. At the top, two children in the kitchen of their home, typical of those in which many families lived before the advent of the rural rehabilitation program. At the bottom, a family in a new pre-fabricated house on the FSA's La Forge project for the rehabilitation of farm labor

plantation and adjacent tracts of land, divided it into individual farms, built new homesteads and outbuildings, and began to re-settle the Gee's Bend families on the new farms. The historian of the experiment recounted the results:

> The Gee's Bend families occupied the units on lease-and-pur-chase contracts; after a five-year trial period, they entered into a sales contract with the government for purchasing their farm-steads over forty years at three percent interest. Regional offi-cials organized the project families into the Gee's Bend Coop-erative Association, a legal device which enabled them to finance and operate a gin, general merchandise store, blacksmith shop, grist mill, and heavy equipment service. The association also cooperatively marketed the cotton grown at Gee's Bend. A med-ical cooperative retained the services of two local physicians and a public health nurse. Finally, the FSA built a community center and a school. By 1940, when construction came to an end, Gee's Bend was a revitalized farm community of about seven hundred people.[4]

Worlds away from Gee's Bend, black artists and writers found employment and a major stimulus for their creative talent in the Federal Theatre and the Federal Writers' Project. The Federal The-atre's sponsorship of Negro theater units in major cities, willing-ness to integrate productions staged by other units, receptivity to plays with racial themes, and determination to bring drama to the masses, offered black playwrights, actors, and directors im-portant opportunities for their professional development.[5] The Writers' Project benefited blacks in two significant ways: it en-gaged black researchers and writers in the reconstruction and documentation of a little-known black past, and it stimulated the development of major black literary talent. The project put blacks to work interviewing ex-slaves, collecting Negro folklore and spir-ituals, preparing detailed studies of specific aspects of black life

[4] Donald Holley, "The Negro in the New Deal Resettlement Program," *Agri-cultural History* XLV (July 1971):184-87 (quotation is from p. 186); Allen Francis Kifer, "The Negro under the New Deal, 1933-1941" (Ph.D. diss., University of Wisconsin, 1961), pp. 191-201; Renwick C. Kennedy, "Rehabilitation: Alabama Version," *Christian Century*, Nov. 14, 1934, pp. 1455-57; Kennedy, "Life at Gee's Bend," ibid., Sept. 1, 1937, pp. 1072-75; John Temple Graves II, "The Big World at Last Reaches Gee's Bend," *New York Times Magazine*, Aug. 22, 1937, pp. 12, 15.

[5] Ronald Ross, "The Role of Blacks in the Federal Theatre, 1935-1939," *Journal of Negro History* LIX (Jan. 1974):38-50; Jane DeHart Mathews, *The Federal The-atre, 1935-1939: Plays, Relief, and Politics* (Princeton, 1967), pp. 298-99.

(they would become major resources for scholars and journalists), and doing research for and writing sections on blacks for city and state guidebooks.[6] In the process, writers such as Zora Neale Hurston, Claude McKay, Arna Bontemps, Ralph Ellison, and Richard Wright found the means, psychological support, and creative strength to develop their art. Wright first worked for the Writers' Project in Illinois; in 1937, he joined the staff in New York, where he worked on the Harlem sections of *New York Panorama* and the *New York City Guide*. He told a project colleague that his employment by the Writers' Project was "the biggest break" he ever had. "For the first time the government is giving us bread and meat." But the sustenance was only part of the project's significance to him. "The President has given us Negroes a chance at last," he declared, "and I tell you I mean to make the most of it. I've had all kinds of jobs. I've shined shoes, washed dishes, I've been a Pullman porter. I've scrubbed floors, cleaned toilets. Those are nigger jobs. Some folks think that's all we're fit for—art is only for white folks." The first Writers' Project payday was "the greatest day" of his life. He was "just rarin' to go." Federal employment gave Wright the chance to publish a number of short pieces and then to complete the novel, *Native Son*, that established his reputation as a major writer.[7]

Employment by the Writers' Project, FSA resettlement projects, PWA construction projects, CCC camps, the chance to go to school through the NYA, access to better housing—these were the kinds of advantages that had led blacks to vote Democratic in 1936. But, while black support for the Democrats in 1936 had turned more on economics than on race, the outcome of that election suggested that race might loom as a larger factor in subsequent political calculations. To Walter White and others, the newly demonstrated mobility and independence of the black vote prom-

[6] Jerre Mangione, *The Dream and the Deal: The Federal Writers' Project, 1935-1943* (Boston, 1972), pp. 123-27, 257-69; memoranda, correspondence, and press releases of the Office on Negro Affairs, Records of the Federal Writers' Project, Box 200, Record Group 69, National Archives; Works Progress Administration press releases in vertical file, Moorland-Spingarn Research Center, Howard University.

[7] On Wright and the Federal Writers' Project, see Constance Webb, *Richard Wright: A Biography* (New York, 1968), pp. 113, 166; Keneth Kinnamon, *The Emergence of Richard Wright: A Study in Literature and Society* (Urbana, Ill., 1972), pp. 14, 66-68, 73. Wright is quoted in Anzia Yezierska, *Red Ribbon on a White Horse* (New York, 1950), pp. 157, 162.

ised to make it "a more potent factor."[8] The parties would do well to heed "the demands of the colored voters."[9] That suggested an explicit return on a massive political investment. Blacks had given their votes to Franklin Roosevelt; now it was time for the New Deal to pay some attention to exclusively racial concerns.

The antilynching bill provided the test case. When the Seventy-fifth Congress opened, it was introduced in the House by Joseph A. Gavagan of New York and in the Senate by Robert F. Wagner and Frederick Van Nuys of Indiana. Gavagan, who represented Harlem, had assumed a central role in the antilynching fight out of political advantage as well as personal conviction. He had been the chief sponsor of antilynching legislation in the House since 1935. Wagner, of course, had given his name to the antilynching bill from the time the NAACP had revived its crusade for the legislation in 1933. His cosponsor, Edward P. Costigan, had been forced to relinquish his office in 1936 because of nervous exhaustion. Van Nuys was a logical substitute for Costigan. He had chaired the subcommittee of the Senate Judiciary Committee that had made a thorough investigation of antilynching proposals and had endorsed the original Costigan-Wagner bill in 1934; in 1936, he had sponsored the resolution calling for a Senate investigation of lynching.[10]

The Wagner-Van Nuys-Gavagan bill closely resembled its predecessors. There had been some revisions—the bill now excluded violence involving gangsters or racketeers and riots that occurred in the course of labor disputes, and it tried to broaden the Lindbergh Kidnapping Act so that it would apply to cases like Claude Neal's.[11] But the basic thrust of the proposed legislation remained the same. Now, observers thought, the bill seemed to stand "a fighting chance."[12] The "public conscience" was clearly "more sensitive" to "the evil of lynching."[13] A Gallup Poll in January 1937 found that 70 percent of those questioned supported anti-

[8] Walter White to Rep. Chester C. Bolton, Nov. 5, 1936, NAACP Papers, Box C-392.

[9] Editorial, *Afro-American*, Nov. 14, 1936.

[10] On Gavagan, see Joseph A. Gavagan, *Reminiscences* (Columbia University Oral History Collection, 1950); on Costigan, *Dictionary of American Biography*, Supplement Two (New York, 1958), p. 124; on Van Nuys, *National Cyclopaedia of American Biography*, vol. XLIV (New York, 1962), pp. 490-91.

[11] Robert L. Zangrando, *The NAACP Crusade Against Lynching, 1909-1950* (Philadelphia, 1980), p. 140.

[12] "Lynch Law," *Literary Digest*, Mar. 20, 1937, p. 8.

[13] "Lynching Must Be Stopped," *Christian Century*, Apr. 28, 1937, p. 545.

lynching legislation. Even Southerners divided 65-35 percent in favor of a federal law.[14]

The bill first came to a test in the House, where, predictably, it encountered "all manner of trickery and opposition."[15] With the Gavagan bill caught in the Rules Committee, the chairman of the Judiciary Committee, Hatton W. Sumners of Texas—no friend of antilynching legislation—reported out a much weaker bill which had been introduced by Arthur W. Mitchell, the black congressman from Chicago.[16] Sumners's diversionary tactic was clear.[17] The Mitchell bill was so "emasculated," in Walter White's words, that it would hardly stop lynching, and ardent supporters of antilynching legislation argued that it was better to have no bill at all than to permit such an ineffective measure to be enacted into law.[18] The NAACP rounded up the necessary signatures for a discharge petition to release the Gavagan bill from the Rules Committee, and it was that bill, instead of Mitchell's (which the House refused to consider), that came to the floor for a vote. A double lynching at Duck Hill, Mississippi, which was reported to the House in the midst of the floor debate, underscored the urgency of the legislation. On April 15, the Gavagan bill passed by a vote of 277 to 120. The split came largely along sectional lines; Speaker Bankhead of Alabama and Majority Leader Rayburn of Texas were among the prominent Democrats recorded in opposition.[19]

As the position of the House leadership suggests, the admin-

[14] Gallup Poll, Jan. 31, 1937, in George H. Gallup, *The Gallup Poll: Public Opinion, 1935-1971*, 3 vols. (New York, 1972), I:48.

[15] Walter White to Eleanor Roosevelt, Apr. 9, 1937, Eleanor Roosevelt Papers, Box 1446, Franklin D. Roosevelt Library (hereafter cited as the ER Papers).

[16] Zangrando succinctly conveys the difference between the Mitchell and Gavagan proposals: "The Mitchell bill applied only to victims seized from official custody; the Gavagan bill covered all instances of mob violence against life and person. For officials found guilty of conspiring or cooperating with the mob, the Mitchell bill proposed imprisonment from two to ten years; the Gavagan bill carried a term of from five to twenty-five years. While Mitchell's bill remained silent about initial federal jurisdiction, Gavagan's invoked action by the United States District Court thirty days after the crime, if state and local officials had failed to respond. The Mitchell bill provided only for a $2,000 to $10,000 fine on the county of death; Gavagan's version held both the county of abduction and the county of death liable. Finally, unlike Mitchell's the Gavagan bill explicitly exempted from creditors' claims any damages assessed against the county(s) on behalf of the victim's survivors." *The NAACP Crusade*, pp. 141-42.

[17] Ibid., p. 141.

[18] Quoted in *Chicago Defender*, Apr. 10, 1937.

[19] NAACP, *28th Annual Report*, pp. 4-6; *New York Times*, Apr. 16, 1937, pp. 1, 8; *Congressional Record*, 75th Cong., 1st sess., Apr. 15, 1937, p. 3563; Zangrando, *The NAACP Crusade*, p. 143.

istration played little role in the passage of the bill. Gavagan later recalled that he had received "very little support from the White House" in any of his efforts in behalf of the antilynching bill. "This apparent disinterestedness on the part of the White House in legislation of this type always puzzled me," he explained, "and although I attempted on several occasions to procure an answer to the query, I was unsuccessful. I finally gave up the attempt, convinced that perhaps after all, President Roosevelt was taking first things first and felt that the more demanding questions were more vital to the nation at that particular time than any equal rights legislation."[20]

Gavagan's analysis was on the mark. No matter that blacks had voted overwhelmingly Democratic in 1936. Even in the second term, as the pace of recovery legislation slowed, Roosevelt and his aides faced matters that they judged to be of greater importance than questions of race. Tommy Corcoran spoke aptly to the question of priorities: "We had first of all the court fight, and then we had the purge fight, and then we had the third-term fight, and then we had Hitler and the war." For "a practical person" like Roosevelt, that left "only a little niche" for racial issues.[21]

When the Wagner-Van Nuys bill was reported favorably by the Senate Judiciary Committee in June 1937, Roosevelt was busy trying to pack the Supreme Court. The court fight further complicated the tortuous course that usually awaited an antilynching bill. It made support from the White House—never willingly tendered—that much more difficult to secure. It preoccupied Roosevelt with a major legislative battle that was peculiarly of his own making; an issue such as antilynching, which at other times might have been considered a diversion of low priority, now became more annoying than inconsequential. The old argument—that the President could not afford to alienate southern support by coming out for antilynching legislation—was never more true than in the court-packing fight, when Roosevelt would have to hold the southern wing of his party in order to pass his highly controversial plan. Antilynching was the kind of issue that opponents of the court bill welcomed. A protracted filibuster might satisfy a range of needs: those Southerners who were reluctant to break openly with Roosevelt on the court plan could divert their constituents

[20] Gavagan, *Reminiscences*, pp. 46-47.
[21] Interview with Thomas G. Corcoran, May 23, 1977, Washington, D.C.

with a show of strong resistance on antilynching;[22] those who were angriest about the court plan could use the filibuster to tie up the Senate and embarrass the administration. From every perspective, it was to the administration's advantage to keep the Wagner-Van Nuys bill off the floor.

Proponents of the antilynching bill tried to bring it to the floor before the court reorganization plan came up for debate,[23] but it was only after the court fight had ended in late July that the Senate turned its attention to other measures. The atmosphere was strained at best: Roosevelt had lost, for all intents and purposes, but there were no victors; and a wrangle over the successor to Majority Leader Joseph T. Robinson of Arkansas, who had dropped dead at the height of the battle, only exacerbated the tensions.

A full agenda awaited congressional action: wages-and-hours legislation, a low-cost housing program, executive reorganization, a major farm bill, and regional development. To the administration, all of the pending proposals took precedence over antilynching legislation, and the new majority leader, Alben W. Barkley of Kentucky, was determined to prevent consideration of the antilynching bill until the more important administration bills were out of the way. Proponents of the antilynching legislation tried some unorthodox tactics to outmaneuver him. They first introduced it as a surprise amendment to a bill to limit the length of freight trains; they next attempted to attach it as a rider to the wages-and-hours bill. Then Wagner took advantage of a parliamentary situation to move consideration of his bill. The Senate was increasingly restive and eager to adjourn, and the prospect of long debate over antilynching was simply insupportable. Accordingly, it voted the next day to postpone consideration of the Wagner-Van Nuys bill until the next session.[24]

The bill came up at the special session of Congress which Roosevelt called for November and immediately provoked a filibuster. When the next regular session convened in January 1938, it was the same story: opponents of the legislation immediately began a filibuster which lasted for six weeks, despite repeated parliamentary maneuvers against it. The filibuster ended only when the Senate agreed in late February to set the antilynching bill

[22] For speculation on this theme, see "Lynch & Anti-lynch," *Time*, Apr. 26, 1937, p. 17.

[23] Walter White to Eleanor Roosevelt, June 10, 24, 1937, ER Papers, Box 1446.

[24] James MacGregor Burns, *Roosevelt: The Lion and the Fox* (New York, 1956), pp. 310-11; *New York Times*, July 27, 1937, p. 1; Aug. 1, 1937, p. 2; Aug. 12, 1937, p. 1; Aug. 13, 1937, p. 6.

aside in order to take up the relief bill.[25] Again Roosevelt was frustratingly silent. At his press conference on January 14 during the early stages of the filibuster, a reporter asked Roosevelt if he favored the bill. As usual, he dodged the issue: "I should say there was enough discussion going on in the Senate."[26] A national magazine later described the President's stance as one of "benevolent neutrality," but to those who cared about the antilynching bill, neutrality was not particularly helpful.[27] Blacks were waiting for some statement from the White House against lynching, James Weldon Johnson wired. Would Roosevelt not "speak a word which will hearten the forces that are striving to rid America of this blackest blot upon her name and silence those who are striving to defeat their effort"?[28] Lizzie McDuffie went to Roosevelt with the same request from Walter White: would he not speak out in support of the measure? He would if it would help, he told her, but it would more likely turn " 'too many valuable people' " against him. " 'Can't people read between the lines?' " he asked. " 'Mrs. Roosevelt would not be sitting in congressional galleries listening to the Anti-lynch deliberations if I didn't favor the bill.' "[29] But reading between the lines provided scant comfort to those who were looking for presidential intervention to help to break the filibuster. It began to look to angry blacks as though the filibuster was continuing "with the blessing of the White House." Roy Wilkins charged that there was "a sort of gentlemen's agreement between the filibusterers and the supporters"—most of whom, he said, "really did not want this bill but would have to vote for it if it came up"—to let the bill be talked to death.[30] To the *Afro-*

[25] *New York Times*, Nov. 15, 1937, pp. 1, 10; Nov. 16, 1937, p. 1; Nov. 17, 1937, pp. 1, 16; Nov. 18, 1937, pp. 1, 14; Nov. 19, 1937, pp. 1, 5, 6; Nov. 20, 1937, pp. 1, 2; Nov. 21, 1937, section IV, p. 7; Nov. 23, 1937, p. 5; Nov. 26, 1937, p. 12; Dec. 21, 1937, pp. 1, 6; Jan. 7, 1938, p. 5; Jan. 8, 1938, p. 3; Jan. 9, 1938, p. 1; Jan. 12, 1938, p. 2; Jan. 13, 1938, p. 8; Jan. 16, 1938, p. 6; Jan. 24, 1938, p. 1; Jan. 26, 1938, p. 1; Jan. 27, 1938, p. 6; Jan. 28, 1938, pp. 6, 20; Jan. 29, 1938, p. 3; Jan. 31, 1938, p. 1; Feb. 5, 1938, p. 7; Feb. 8, 1938, p. 1; Feb. 17, 1938, p. 12; Feb. 22, 1938, p. 1. See also J. Joseph Huthmacher, *Senator Robert F. Wagner and the Rise of Urban Liberalism* (New York, 1968), pp. 238-42.

[26] Press conference no. 425, Jan. 14, 1938, in *Complete Presidential Press Conferences of Franklin D. Roosevelt*, 25 vols. (New York, 1972), 11:88.

[27] "Delicate Aspect," *Time*, Sept. 19, 1938, p. 12.

[28] James Weldon Johnson telegram to Franklin D. Roosevelt, Jan. 24, 1938, James Weldon Johnson Papers, Folder 410, Beinecke Library, Yale University.

[29] Mrs. McDuffie's account of her conversation with Roosevelt is reported in Frank Harriott, "Three Who Saw FDR Die," *Negro Digest* IX (May 1951):25. She and White had known each other during his school days in Atlanta.

[30] Roy Wilkins to Charles Edward Russell, Feb. 1, 1938, NAACP Papers, Box C-80.

American, the failure to break the filibuster showed "that the colored voters have been double-crossed by the White House, by the Republican Senators, and by some Democratic Senators, including a sponsor of the bill." In the judgment of the *Pittsburgh Courier,* the Democratic leadership had "failed utterly."[31]

Publicly, the signals from the President seemed to spell retreat. Perhaps there were alternatives to the antilynching bill, Roosevelt responded to an inquiry at a press conference in March. Congress might empower the attorney general to investigate and publicize the facts about incidents involving mob violence; or it could establish a congressional committee for the same purpose.[32]

Wagner and Van Nuys twice tried to force a vote on the antilynching bill by securing cloture; twice their efforts failed. Finally, even they agreed that the Senate had to attend to other matters.[33]

Blacks may have been exasperated at Roosevelt's failure to help move the antilynching bill through the Senate, but it was no longer clear that he *could* have been of much assistance even if he had been disposed to try. The special session of Congress in the autumn of 1937 had been "a shambles," and when Congress adjourned a few days before Christmas, it had passed not one of the four proposals that Roosevelt had put before it. In 1938, the only really important piece of New Deal legislation (the new Agricultural Adjustment Act aside) to emerge from Congress was the Fair Labor Standards Act. Crippled by the court fight, the coalition that had sustained Roosevelt's first-term triumphs was clearly breaking apart.[34] The President had lost a large measure of influence with Congress—influence which, had he been disposed to exercise it, might have eased the antilynching bill's passage. With Congress openly at odds with the White House and an election close at hand, presidential intervention in behalf of an explosive issue was bad politics from any perspective.

Roosevelt recognized these dangers, but he was also a canny enough politician to understand that the filibuster could alienate black voters. Thus he made a gesture that might counter some

[31] Editorials, Feb. 5, 1938.

[32] Press conference no. 444, Mar. 22, 1938, in *Complete Presidential Press Conferences of Franklin D. Roosevelt,* 11:245-46.

[33] Zangrando, *The NAACP Crusade,* pp. 151-53.

[34] Burns, *Roosevelt: The Lion and the Fox,* pp. 311, 321 (source of the quotation); James T. Patterson, *Congressional Conservatism and the New Deal: The Growth of the Conservative Coalition in Congress, 1933-1939* (Lexington, Ky., 1967). The four proposals were for a farm bill, wage-and-hour legislation, administrative reorganization, and regional planning.

of the political damage. In April, well after the filibuster had ended, Walter White asked to bring a delegation of blacks to the White House to talk about the antilynching bill. Instead of the usual brushoff, his telegram brought an immediate phone call from Marvin McIntyre to set up the appointment.[35] But the gesture was the only concession the delegation won. Roosevelt explained to them that his silence had been in the bill's best interest. Although he favored the legislation, his endorsement, he told them, would have permitted senators who were also opposed to the wages-and-hours bill and other measures to "exploit the situation to gain re-election on a campaign of racial prejudice."[36] The likely result would be the inflammation of racial tensions and the further hamstringing of the progressive thrusts of the New Deal. When White asked for a message to take to black Americans about the administration's attitude on the antilynching bill, Roosevelt responded, "Keep up the fight."[37] Unspoken was the important corollary: keep it up without aid from the White House.

Roosevelt's account of his motives may have been self-justificatory, but it described quite accurately the complicated politics that made federal action against lynching so difficult to accomplish. The President's performance impressed members of the delegation who were less accustomed to dealing with him than White was. They were convinced, White told a colleague, of Roosevelt's "sincerity of interest in the antilynching bill despite the fact that I had warned them before we went to the White House that they were not to be taken in by the charm." To White, "the chief value of taking the delegation there" had been as a "visual reminder of the Negro vote in the 1938 and 1940 elections."[38]

The fortunes of the Wagner-Van Nuys bill told an important story. No matter that blacks had become enthusiastic Democrats; their power was still too limited to move the Democratic party to positive action on racial concerns. Lynching was simply the

[35] Zangrando, *The NAACP Crusade*, p. 155.

[36] The delegation consisted of Walter White; George Edmund Haynes, Department of Race Relations, Federal Council of Churches; Charlotte Hawkins Brown, Palmer Memorial Institute; Frances Williams, YWCA; Carl Murphy, *Baltimore Afro-American* (White House Usher's Diary, Apr. 12, 1938, Franklin D. Roosevelt Library). The quotation is from Robert Lewis Zangrando, "The Efforts of the National Association for the Advancement of Colored People to Secure Passage of a Federal Anti-Lynching Law, 1920-1940" (Ph.D. diss., University of Pennsylvania, 1963), p. 394.

[37] Quoted in *Afro-American*, Apr. 16, 1938.

[38] Walter White to William H. Hastie, Apr. 15, 1938, NAACP Papers, Box C-79.

most visible issue, but the pattern was much more widespread. The Roosevelt administration's record on race in the second term was not much different from what it had been in the first. Blacks had always prophesied that an independent black vote would make the political parties pay heed to a racial agenda. In the late 1930s, the Democrats were not yet paying attention.

The constraints against such positive attention were much the same as they had been in the first term: other priorities and the need to pacify Southerners in Congress. Racial conservatives still dominated much of the day-to-day decision-making in the administration, and they maintained a remarkably tight rein.

The antilynching bill came up again in the Seventy-sixth Congress, but by then any chance for its proponents to exert leverage in its behalf had long passed. Congress was increasingly preoccupied with the war in Europe and the nation's defenses and restive after Roosevelt's abortive purge of conservative Democrats in the congressional elections of 1938. Also, Congress was in no mood to innovate. In January 1939, the Gavagan bill was introduced in the House and the Wagner-Van Nuys bill in the Senate. For the first time, Eleanor Roosevelt made a public statement in support of the legislation—the most unmistakable commitment in her long years of behind-the-scenes support. But neither bill reached the floor before the session was out. The next year, the Gavagan bill passed the House, but, although the Wagner-Van Nuys bill was reported favorably, supporters were unable to get it on the floor before Congress adjourned.[39] Majority Leader Barkley summed up the obstacles: "In the midst of our international situation, our defense program," given the certainty of a filibuster, it was "impractical . . . to make a futile effort to obtain a vote on the bill."[40] Walter White made the ritual protests. In terms of black votes, burying the bill was "likely to be an expensive thing" for the Democrats to do. Barkley's unwillingness to bring it to the floor was a "blow at the patriotism of twelve million Negro citizens."[41] But who was listening and what was the urgency? There had been only three lynchings in 1939; according to pollsters, public support for antilynching legislation, as high as 70

[39] NAACP, *30th Annual Report* (1939), pp. 4-5; "New Anti-Lynch Bill in Senate" and "Mrs. F.D.R. Supports Anti-Lynch Bill," *Crisis* XLVI (Feb. 1939):54; NAACP, *Annual Report* (1940), pp. 11-12.

[40] Quoted in *Pittsburgh Courier*, Oct. 19, 1940.

[41] Walter White to Arthur B. Spingarn, Apr. 23, 1940, Arthur B. Spingarn Papers, Box 9, Manuscript Division, Library of Congress; White telegram to Franklin D. Roosevelt, Oct. 10, 1940, quoted in *Pittsburgh Courier*, Oct. 19, 1940.

percent in 1937, had dropped to 55 percent in 1940.[42] Even the members of the administration most sympathetic to racial concerns recognized the difficulty of gaining attention for them. In the late summer of 1939, when White wanted to see Roosevelt, Aubrey Williams advised against trying, in light of the European situation.[43] France had fallen to Hitler; the Low Countries had been overrun. England badly needed American assistance. The administration, like the nation, had its priorities.

The antilynching battle did not mark the Roosevelt administration as particularly villainous or particularly insensitive to blacks. Despite persistent efforts by the NAACP and others, Congress never passed an antilynching bill. The closest it came was in the Civil Rights Act of 1968, which established fines and jail terms for those who injured or killed persons seeking to exercise their civil rights.[44] The unsuccessful efforts to secure antilynching legislation in the late 1930s simply illustrated that the political transformation of 1936 was insufficient to move the Roosevelt administration to a more positive stance on racial matters. Political calculation, colored by prejudice, usually molded the administration's responses. On the big issues, as antilynching shows, avoidance was still the rule.

Disfranchisement is another case in point. The legal battle of the NAACP against the white primary, which was to culminate in victory in *Smith v. Allwright* in 1944, went forward without benefit of encouragement from the White House or tangible assistance from the Department of Justice.[45] Despite the urgings of the NAACP, Attorney General Homer Cummings declined to institute criminal proceedings against election officials in Texas who barred blacks from voting in Democratic primary elections. Such an action would have infuriated the white South. As Assistant Attorney General Joseph Keenan told the NAACP, suffrage prosecution was "loaded with political dynamite."[46] Neither *Grovey v. Townsend* (1935) nor *Smith v. Allwright* elicited an *amicus*

[42] "At the Store," *Time*, Jan. 22, 1940, pp. 18-19; Gallup Poll, Feb. 19, 1940, in Gallup, *The Gallup Poll*, I:209.

[43] Aubrey Williams to Walter White, Sept. 1, 1939, Aubrey Williams Papers, Box 5, Franklin D. Roosevelt Library.

[44] Zangrando, *The NAACP Crusade*, p. 19.

[45] Steven F. Lawson, *Black Ballots: Voting Rights in the South, 1944-1969* (New York, 1976), pp. 23-54.

[46] Joseph Keenan to Walter White, Dec. 28, 1934, NAACP Papers, quoted in ibid., p. 33.

curiae brief from the Department of Justice. As Solicitor General Charles Fahy reasoned with respect to *Smith v. Allwright*, the federal government was not a party to the case; why make a gesture that could not "fail to offend many others, in Texas and the South generally"?[47]

The campaign to abolish the poll tax—which disfranchised poor whites as well as blacks—briefly engaged Roosevelt's interest, for it presented a means of striking at the conservative southern Democrats whom he was eager to purge from the party.[48] At first he ventured encouraging statements. "The right to vote," he declared, "must be open to all our citizens irrespective of race, color, or creed—without tax or artificial restriction of any kind. The sooner we get to that basis of political equality, the better it will be for the country as a whole."[49] The movement for repeal in Florida in 1937 won the President's endorsement.[50] So, at first, did the campaign for repeal in Arizona in 1938. Roosevelt wrote privately to Democratic National Committeeman Brooks Hays about his pleasure at the prospect of abolishing the tax, which he described as "inevitably contrary to the fundamental democracy . . . in which we believe."[51] Questioned about the poll tax at a press conference in September, Roosevelt denounced it "as a relic of the Revolutionary era," but he made it plain that he was not referring to disfranchisement of blacks—"they . . . were a problem to be handled separately."[52]

When Roosevelt's efforts to purge conservative Democrats failed in primary elections in Georgia and South Carolina, he backpedaled from open advocacy of repeal and tried to mollify southern politicians who were angry about his meddling in the politics of the region.[53] When Senator Pat Harrison of Mississippi chastised him for endorsing repeal in Arizona, Roosevelt assured him that he had only been expressing a personal opinion: "At no time and in no manner did I ever suggest federal legislation of any kind to deprive states of their rights directly or indirectly to impose the

[47] Charles Fahy memorandum to Francis Biddle, Oct. 29, 1943, Roosevelt Papers, quoted in ibid., p. 42.

[48] Ibid., pp. 56-58.

[49] Quoted in Stetson Kennedy, *Southern Exposure* (Garden City, N.Y., 1946), p. 359.

[50] Harvard Sitkoff, *A New Deal for Blacks: The Emergence of Civil Rights as a National Issue*, vol. I: *The Depression Decade* (New York, 1978), p. 134.

[51] Quoted in Frank Freidel, *F.D.R. and the South* (Baton Rouge, 1965), p. 98.

[52] "Delicate Aspect," p. 12.

[53] Lawson, *Black Ballots*, p. 57.

poll tax."[54] In 1939, when repeal advocates in Tennessee asked for the President's support, he declined to intervene "in campaigns of state issues."[55]

A conversation with Aubrey Williams revealed once again the way political instincts determined Roosevelt's response on racial issues. Williams was one of the few New Dealers who anguished over disfranchisement, and he would have liked Roosevelt to support legislation repealing the poll tax. He raised the issue with the President during a train trip from Warm Springs back to Washington. As the train moved toward Atlanta, Williams recalled,

> people had gathered on the banks of the rail road hoping to get a glimpse of him—most of them Negroes. I thought it would be a good time to broach the subject, ... feeling that no man could fail to be moved by the sight of mile after mile of people—most of whom were denied the simplest elementary right of participating in their government.

But Roosevelt responded in terms of expediency instead of morality: " 'Politics is the art of the possible,' " he told Williams. The administration had other bills before Congress. " 'At the present time the passage of a law abolishing the poll tax is impossible and effort to do so would weaken our chances of getting these things—I do not believe in attempting something for the purpose of one's image—I believe you should never undertake anything unless you have evidence that you have at least a 50-50 chance of winning.' "[56] Roosevelt's caution accurately foreshadowed the impossibility of getting a bill to abolish the poll tax through Congress. It was not until the ratification of the Twenty-fourth Amendment in 1964 that the poll tax was outlawed as a requirement for voting in national elections.[57]

On racial issues of lesser moment, the response of the Roosevelt administration depended on who was in charge. Roosevelt's closest aides continued to resist even the most tangential White House association with racial causes. Jonathan Daniels, who joined the staff during the war, described the men around Roosevelt as "almost reactionary in the matter" of race. "There wasn't much color

---

[54] Quoted in Freidel, *F.D.R. and the South*, p. 98.

[55] Stephen Early to Mrs. Carl Stafford, Feb. 3, 1939, Roosevelt Papers, quoted in Lawson, *Black Ballots*, p. 57.

[56] Quoted in John Salmond, " 'Aubrey Williams Remembers': A Note on Franklin D. Roosevelt's Attitude toward Negro Rights," *Alabama Review* XXV (Jan. 1972):68-69.

[57] Lawson, *Black Ballots*, pp. 58-82.

24. While Mrs. Roosevelt was frequently photographed in the company of black people, such photographs of the President are rare. Here he meets the distinguished scientist, George Washington Carver, during a visit to Tuskegee Institute in 1939

*un*consciousness; they were *all* conscious of color, and they didn't want to stir up the rats on a thing like this."[58] It was one thing for the President to make an occasional public appearance with blacks—as, for example, when he dedicated the Eleanor Roosevelt School House, a school for black children at Warm Springs, in 1937, or when he visited Tuskegee Institute and met the famous scientist, George Washington Carver, in 1939.[59] But these were isolated instances, and they occurred in the blandest possible racial contexts. The Warm Springs school was for vocational train-

[58] Jonathan Daniels interview, Nov. 16, 1979, p. 19, Eleanor Roosevelt Oral History Project, Franklin D. Roosevelt Library.

[59] On the Warm Springs school, see *New York Times*, Mar. 19, 1937, p. 17, and Ruth Stevens, *"Hi-Ya Neighbor"* (New York, 1947), pp. 53, 55-57; on the visit to Tuskegee, *New York Times*, Mar. 31, 1939, p. 16.

ing, and it was safely segregated; Tuskegee, which had been founded by Booker T. Washington, was a vocational institution in the most conservative tradition of black education.

It was another thing to implicate Roosevelt in racial matters that might smack of support for racial justice. The matter of presidential greetings to the organizations for racial advancement, which had been construed as politically explosive during the first administration, was handled the same way in the second. As a rule, the White House was willing to send "cordial greetings" and messages of "goodwill," but Roosevelt and his advisers scrupulously avoided even the slightest mention of "controversial issues" such as lynching and disfranchisement on the ground that they were "entirely too dangerous" to talk about.[60] In the case of the NAACP, the caution of the staff reflected Roosevelt's own views. A draft of a presidential testimonial to Walter White on the occasion of the twenty-fifth anniversary of White's work in behalf of blacks came back with the notation, "Miss Tully brought this. . . . Says the President doesn't think too much of this organization—not to be to [sic] fullsome—tone it down a bit."[61]

It was not only the NAACP that raised White House hackles. Even the most innocent requests from more conservative quarters often failed to produce results. When the National Negro Business League asked for a few words from Roosevelt for its annual meeting in 1939, the request was referred to the Department of Commerce, which "advised the White House not to send any message." By the time that anyone realized that a mistake had been made, "the convention was over and members of the Business League were very much upset."[62] When T. Arnold Hill asked the President for "a word of greeting" in conjunction with the National Urban League's Vocational Opportunity Campaign in 1938, Stephen Early told him that Roosevelt would be unable to find the time to send it because of "very heavy pressure in connection

[60] Walter White to Franklin D. Roosevelt, June 5, 1939; William D. Hassett, Memorandum for the Commissioner of Education, June 6, 1939; [Marvin H.] McIntyre, memorandum to Mr. Hassett, June 23, 1938 ("cordial greetings," "controversial issues"); Hassett, Memorandum for Mr. David Niles, June 24, 1938 ("entirely too dangerous," "goodwill"), all in Franklin D. Roosevelt Papers, President's Personal File (PPF) 1336, Franklin D. Roosevelt Library (hereafter cited as the FDR Papers).
[61] Note attached to draft of Franklin D. Roosevelt to Arthur B. Spingarn, Sept. 28, 1943, ibid.
[62] Sam Bledsoe memorandum to the Secretary of Agriculture, Aug. 22, 1940, ibid., PPF 6815. The oversight was remedied the following year. See Franklin D. Roosevelt telegram to J. E. Walker, Aug. 23, 1940, ibid.

with the public business."[63] But Hill had also asked Mrs. Roosevelt for assistance in persuading her husband to write a letter of encouragement, and her intercession did the trick. "I did not know of Mrs. Roosevelt's interest in the National Urban League," one of the President's staff members confessed to Early. "I wish you all success in your efforts to be helpful to others," Roosevelt finally wrote.[64] But what a round of correspondence and negotiation it had required to obtain even that innocuous message!

Bending over backwards to protect the President from venturing too far into the racial thicket may, as Roy Wilkins described it, have been "typical" of the way a White House staff shields any chief executive from unnecessary controversy. But it shows how narrowly the staff men closest to Roosevelt defined the bounds of "safe" utterances when it came to race. "They were scared," Robert Weaver reflected; they saw racial questions as "political dynamite," and their automatic response was: "Don't touch it."[65] The result was further to constrict the White House field of vision in such a way as to militate against positive attention to matters of race.

Where aides like Stephen Early controlled the terrain, the administration's response on racial issues was invariably cautious. Where there was room for maneuvering on the part of Eleanor Roosevelt or Harold Ickes, the outcome was appreciably different.

In the second administration, as in the first, Eleanor Roosevelt functioned as a self-designated ambassador to black Americans. Again and again, she addressed black audiences. The circumstances varied considerably: a gathering in behalf of the *Crisis* in a black church in Harlem; the annual meeting of the National Council of Negro Women; a National Negro Congress-sponsored celebration of the seventy-fifth anniversary of the Emancipation Proclamation; the anniversary of the founding of Hampton Institute; a symposium on household employment; a dinner to mark National Sharecropper Week; a visit to Bethune-Cookman College. The constants were the First Lady's concern, the sincerity of her remarks, the enthusiastic response of her listeners, and the

[63] T. Arnold Hill to Franklin D. Roosevelt, Feb. 18, 1938; Stephen Early to Hill, Feb. 23, 1938, ibid., PPF 902.

[64] T. Arnold Hill to Eleanor Roosevelt, Feb. 18, 1938; Memorandum, W[illiam] D. H[assett] to Mr. [Stephen] Early, Feb. 24, 1938; Franklin D. Roosevelt to Hill, Feb. 24, 1938, ibid.

[65] Interviews with Roy Wilkins, Aug. 17, 1976, New York City; Robert C. Weaver, Nov. 12, 1976, New York City.

public notice that such appearances drew.[66] On occasion, there were unexpected twists that served as special reminders of her racial egalitarianism. When, for example, Mary McLeod Bethune's voice cracked during her speech at a benefit for Bethune-Cookman College, Mrs. Roosevelt got up to get her a glass of water. "This is democracy in action," a black policeman who witnessed the event said, "the wife of the President of the United States pouring a glass of ice-water for a Negro woman who's real black—she's black as a black shoe—and handing it to her and she was drinking it."[67]

Probably the most celebrated of Mrs. Roosevelt's appearances occurred at the founding meeting of the Southern Conference on Human Welfare in Birmingham in November 1938. In two dramatic gestures, she captured public attention. The first came when Mrs. Bethune entered the meeting hall. Mrs. Roosevelt greeted her warmly, "almost [taking] her in her arms." "There wasn't a sound" in the room, an observer later reported; "they were so shocked."[68] The second incident arose when the Birmingham police discovered that the conferees had been holding integrated sessions and insisted that they comply with a city ordinance that required segregated seating. Mrs. Roosevelt would have none of that, and she and Aubrey Williams deliberately sat on the colored side. "Rather than give in" when the police told her that she was violating the law, she asked that chairs be placed for them in the middle of the stage, "facing the whole group."[69]

Although Mrs. Roosevelt refused to acquiesce in the segregated

[66] *New York Times*, Oct. 23, 1937, p. 3; Dec. 19, 1937, p. 28; Feb. 11, 1938, p. 16; Apr. 22, 1938, p. 7; National Council of Negro Women minutes, Dec. 18, 1937, National Council of Negro Women Papers, Series 2, Box 1, Folder 3, National Archives for Black Women's History, Washington, D.C. (hereafter cited as the NCNW Papers); NCNW Executive Secretary's Report, 1939-40, ibid., Series 2, Box 1, Folder 8; *New York Amsterdam News*, Mar. 9, 1940; Joseph P. Lash, *Eleanor Roosevelt: A Friend's Memoir* (Garden City, N.Y., 1964), p. 81; Roy Wilkins with Tom Mathews, *Standing Fast: The Autobiography of Roy Wilkins* (New York, 1982), pp. 130-31.

[67] Samuel J. Battle, *Reminiscences* (Columbia University Oral History Collection, 1960), pp. 51-52; Mary McLeod Bethune, "My Secret Talks with FDR," *Ebony* IV (Apr. 1949), in *The Negro in Depression and War: Prelude to Revolution, 1930-1945*, ed. Bernard Sternsher (Chicago, 1969), p. 62.

[68] Mrs. John Hope, quoted in NCNW minutes, Nov. 26, 1938, NCNW Papers, Series 2, Box 1, Folder 4.

[69] The quotation is from Eleanor Roosevelt, *This I Remember* (New York, 1949), pp. 173-74. See also W. T. Couch, "Southerners Inspect the South," *New Republic*, Dec. 14, 1938, pp. 168-69; Morton Sosna, *In Search of the Silent South: Southern Liberals and the Race Issue* (New York, 1977), pp. 94-95.

seating, she stopped short of directly attacking segregation in her public address to the gathering. She had ample opportunity to do so, for a reporter in the audience asked her views of the Alabama segregation law. She sidestepped the issue by observing that "this was a matter for Alabama" to deal with. Some liberals criticized her for her caution. There were many helpful things that she might have said, a reporter for the *New Republic* admonished. She could have explained that a conference was different from a social gathering; she could have pointed out that there were "many kinds and degrees of segregation, some good, some bad, some indifferent." She should have done *something* to help clarify the question that had long been "the South's worst bugaboo."[70]

To most blacks, however, what was important was what Mrs. Roosevelt did, not what she did not do. The *Afro-American* put it plainly: "sometimes actions speak louder than words."[71] "You would have to have lived in that era to know . . . what kind of an impact this had on the Negro population," Pauli Murray reflected. "It was immediately the cause of comment. . . . These kinds of symbolic gestures that Mrs. Roosevelt made were so significant to a group of people who were literally just coming out of the nadir, so to speak, of humiliation and degradation."[72]

Secretary Ickes, too, continued through generous racial gestures to embody the New Deal's moral conscience. Like Mrs. Roosevelt, he made frequent speeches to black groups—for example, at the dedication of a PWA hospital for blacks in St. Louis; at a meeting of the National Negro Congress; and at the seventy-first anniversary celebration of Howard University, carried over a nationwide radio hookup.[73] His strong recommendation prompted the President's appointment in 1937 of William H. Hastie as district judge for the Virgin Islands—the first black man to sit on the federal bench. Hastie had a reputation as a brilliant legal analyst and strategist. A Phi Beta Kappa graduate of Amherst College, he had earned his law degree in 1930 at Harvard and had served as an editor of the law review. He had gone home to Washington to join the law firm of Houston and Houston, which his cousin, Charles, had just left to become dean of the Howard University

---

[70] Couch, "Southerners Inspect the South," pp. 168-69. See also Tamara K. Hareven, *Eleanor Roosevelt: An American Conscience* (Chicago, 1968), p. 118.

[71] Editorial, *Afro-American*, Dec. 17, 1938.

[72] Interview with Pauli Murray, July 1, 1977, Alexandria, Va.

[73] See Ickes speech #143, Feb. 22, 1937, Harold L. Ickes Papers, Box 289, Manuscript Division, Library of Congress; speech #187, Oct. 7, 1938, Box 305; speech #178, Mar. 2, 1938, Box 302.

School of Law. Hastie taught at Howard, too, and helped Houston build it into a training ground for the black lawyers who waged the legal battle for civil rights.[74] When Ickes, eager "to do something on the affirmative side for the Negro race," decided in 1933 to look for a black person who might qualify as an assistant solicitor in the Department of the Interior, Hastie won the job. He "more than made good," in Ickes's estimation, and the secretary began to push him for the Virgin Islands judgeship. Ickes spoke to the President about Hastie's qualifications, and Roosevelt promised to consider the appointment. Attorney General Homer Cummings objected on the ground that the Negroes of the Virgin Islands would oppose the appointment of a Negro from the continental United States. Cummings held the nomination up for several months, but Roosevelt, heeding Ickes's urgings, sent it to the Senate in February 1937. When the nomination encountered resistance from Millard E. Tydings, the Maryland Democrat who chaired the Territories and Insular Affairs Committee, Ickes orchestrated enough pressure on Tydings from blacks in Maryland to get Hastie confirmed in March.[75]

The most dramatic evidence of the difference Ickes made on racial matters came in an incident that also involved Mrs. Roosevelt: the celebrated case of Marian Anderson.

In 1939, as it had for several years, the Howard University School of Music scheduled an appearance by Marian Anderson as part of its regular concert series. When Miss Anderson sang, it was no ordinary event. "A voice like yours is heard once in a hundred years," Arturo Toscanini told her after a concert in 1935.[76] The famous contralto was known worldwide as a distinguished artist. In 1936 and 1937, Howard's Anderson concert had been held in a black high school auditorium. But the facility was too small to raise enough money to cover the costs of sponsoring so celebrated a performer. In 1938, Howard rented the Rialto Theatre, but it was in receivership in 1939, so the Music School asked the Daughters of the American Revolution for permission to hold the

---

[74] Richard Kluger, *Simple Justice: The History of Brown v. Board of Education and Black America's Struggle for Equality* (New York, 1975), pp. 158, 194-95; *Current Biography*, 1944, p. 277.

[75] Harold L. Ickes, "My Twelve Years with F.D.R.," *Saturday Evening Post*, June 26, 1948, pp. 79 (source of the quotations), 81. See also diary entry, Aug. 13, 1935, in Harold L. Ickes, *The Secret Diary of Harold L. Ickes*, vol. I: *The First Thousand Days, 1933-1936* (New York, 1953), p. 416; *Pittsburgh Courier*, Feb. 13, 1937; "All at One Table," *Time*, Feb. 15, 1937, p. 15; editorial, *New York Age*, Feb. 20, 1937.

[76] Quoted in S. Hurok, *Impresario: A Memoir* (New York, 1946) p. 240.

concert on Easter Sunday in Constitution Hall. When the DAR refused on the ground of race, the Music School turned again to the District public schools, but this time it asked for a white high school auditorium with a capacity 65 percent larger than the one it had used two years before.[77]

At every level, it ran into a stone wall. The director of the community center department said no. The superintendent of schools backed her up. On February 16, the board of education upheld the superintendent's decision. Neither a black artist nor an interracial audience would be permitted to occupy a white high school auditorium.[78] "I am shocked beyond words," Miss Anderson said, "to be barred from the capital of my own country after having appeared almost in every other capital in the world."[79]

Outraged at the board's action, black leaders organized the Marian Anderson Citizens Committee to fight the decision.[80] Superficially, it was an independent coalition of clergymen, labor leaders, teachers, and representatives of civic and fraternal organizations. Actually, the committee's chairman was the NAACP's chief legal strategist, Charles H. Houston, and it cleared its activities with Walter White and his staff at the Association's headquarters in New York.[81]

In time, the Citizens Committee took on the DAR in an attempt to change the policy of racial exclusion at Constitution Hall.[82] But its immediate concern was the board of education. The request for Central High School was no challenge to the District's dual school system: the concert would take place outside school hours, when the auditorium was a public facility available for community use. Surely the decision could not be allowed to stand. The board would have to be made to reconsider. Relying on time-honored tactics—mass meetings, petitions, letters of support from prominent artists and political figures, and protests from the NAACP—the Citizens Committee succeeded in reopening the issue.[83]

[77] Charles C. Cohen et al., Memorandum to the Board of Education, Feb. 15, 1939, Marian Anderson Collection, Box 1, Moorland-Spingarn Research Center, Howard University (hereafter cited as MAC).
[78] NAACP press release, Feb. 17, 1939, MAC, Box 2.
[79] Quoted in *New York Times*, Feb. 28, 1939, p. 5.
[80] Marian Anderson Citizens Committee press release, Feb. 20, 1939, MAC, Box 2.
[81] See, for example, Charles H. Houston memorandum for Walter [White] and Hubert [Delany], Mar. 4, 1939; White to Houston, Mar. 6, 13, 1939, ibid., Box 1.
[82] For a fascinating account of a May meeting between the DAR and the Citizens Committee, see John Lovell, Jr. to Charles H. Houston, June 1, 1939, ibid.
[83] NAACP press release, Feb. 17, 1939; petition, The Citizens Committee for

Under intense public pressure, the board reversed its decision. The concert could be held at Central High School. But the board set a troubling condition: the event would be a one-time-only exception; the dual school system would be reaffirmed; and Houston and the others would have to promise never again to request the use of a white facility for an interracial audience. Houston wavered briefly: most blacks favored refusing the board's terms; most of his white allies, on the other hand, favored going ahead with the concert in order to set a precedent. Houston himself "wanted Marian Anderson to sing in Central, but not at the cost of my dignity and self-respect."[84]

To Walter White and his fellow NAACP strategists in New York, there was no issue: the school board's terms were unacceptable, and the auditorium would have to be refused unequivocally.[85]

The Citizens Committee went back to the board again. Reconsider, it urged, let us hold the concert at Central "without the impossible and humiliating conditions now imposed."[86] By this point, however, the negotiations with the board had more to do with principle than with the practical issue of the setting for the concert. The next board meeting would not take place until April 5, so there would be too little time, no matter what the board's decision, to get ready for April 9. While the negotiations continued, Sol Hurok, Marian Anderson's manager, came up with an alternate plan: why not stage the concert outdoors, free of charge, as a "rebuke" to those who had snubbed the singer. Walter White thought that Hurok's proposal was "exciting" and suggested the Lincoln Memorial as "the most logical place" for the concert.[87]

Miss Anderson herself had some reluctance about the idea. "I

Protesting the Exclusion of Marian Anderson to the Board of Education of the District of Columbia, Feb. 18, 25, 1939; Marian Anderson Citizens Committee press release, Feb. 25, 1939, ibid., Box 2; Charles H. Houston, "Statement on Request for Use of Central High School . . . ," Extract from Stenographic Record at Meeting of the Board of Education held Mar. 1, 1939; Arthur Capper to Charles H. Houston, Mar. 2, 1939; William E. Borah telegram to Houston, Mar. 3, 1939; Fiorello La Guardia to John Lovell, Jr., Feb. 27, 1939; H. B. Lansburgh to Lovell, Mar. 6, 1939, ibid., Box 1.

[84] Report of the Committee of the Board of Education on the Community Use of Buildings, Mar. 3, 1939; Charles H. Houston memorandum for Walter [White] and Hubert [Delany], Mar. 4, 1939, ibid., Box 1. For the views of the man in the street, see *Afro-American*, Mar. 11, 1939.

[85] Walter White to Charles H. Houston, Mar. 6, 13, 1939, MAC, Box 1.

[86] [Charles H. Houston] to Nadia Boulanger, Mar. 28, 1939, ibid.

[87] Hurok quoted in *New York Times*, Mar. 21, 1939, p. 27; White quoted in Walter White, *A Man Called White: The Autobiography of Walter White* (New York, 1948), p. 181.

don't like a lot of show," she later wrote, "and one could not tell in advance what direction the affair would take." After Hurok presented the plan, though, she gave it some thought. "I studied my conscience," she recalled; even though the idea of an outdoor concert made her uncomfortable "as an individual," she recognized that, "in principle," it was "sound." "As I thought further, I could see that my significance as an individual was small in this affair. I had become, whether I liked it or not, a symbol, representing my people. I had to appear."[88] White took the proposal to Oscar Chapman, the assistant secretary of the interior, who was "enormously enthusiastic" and went at once to Secretary Ickes. Ickes, "equally excited over the prospect of such a demonstration of democracy," hurried to the White House to secure the President's approval.[89] "Tell Oscar," Roosevelt reportedly said, "he has my permission to have Marian sing from the top of the Washington Monument if he wants it."[90] By the time Howard University made the official request to the Department of the Interior,[91] the plans were already in place: Marian Anderson would sing from the steps of the Memorial, and the concert would be broadcast across the nation.

Surely Mrs. Roosevelt must have had a hand in the decision, but the written record yields little evidence about the nature of her participation.[92] Since she was out of town for most of March and early April, it is especially difficult to pinpoint her intervention.[93] Certainly she felt strongly about the issue. Marian Anderson had sung for the Roosevelts at the White House before,[94] and in the midst of the controversy, the White House announced that she would sing there again when the King and Queen of

[88] Marian Anderson, *My Lord, What a Morning: An Autobiography* (New York, 1956), p. 189.

[89] White, *A Man Called White*, pp. 181-82. Roosevelt left for Warm Springs on March 29. Whether he and Ickes discussed the matter at their regular Tuesday lunch on March 28 or at a special meeting cannot be determined. See White House Usher's Diary, March 1939.

[90] Quoted in Harry McAlpin, "Silver Lining," *Chicago Defender*, Jan. 30, 1943.

[91] V. D. Johnston to Oscar L. Chapman, Mar. 30, 1939, MAC, Box 1.

[92] W. J. Trent, Jr., a racial adviser on Ickes's staff, thought that Mrs. Roosevelt called the issue to Ickes's attention. Trent interview, Dec. 8, 1976, New York City.

[93] White House Usher's Diary, March and April 1939.

[94] Ibid., Feb. 19, 1936. Lizzie McDuffie claimed credit for arranging the appearance. Lizzie McDuffie, "I Swept the King's Carpet," draft chapter, Lizzie McDuffie Memoirs, Franklin D. Roosevelt Memorial Foundation, Record Group 21, Franklin D. Roosevelt Library.

England came to visit in May.[95] In a more dramatic demonstration of support for Miss Anderson, the First Lady had resigned from the DAR in protest against the singer's exclusion from Constitution Hall. Mrs. Roosevelt had explained her action in her newspaper column, "My Day." She had debated the question for some time, she wrote:

> The question is, if you belong to an organization and disapprove of an action which is typical of a policy, shall you resign or is it better to work for a changed point of view within the organization? In the past when I was able to work actively in any organization to which I belonged, I have usually stayed in until I had at least made a fight and been defeated. Even then I have as a rule accepted my defeat and decided either that I was wrong or that I was perhaps a little too far ahead of the thinking of the majority of that time. I have often found that the thing in which I was interested was done some years later. But, in this case I belong to an organization in which I can do no active work. They have taken an action which has been widely talked of in the press. To remain as a member implies approval of that action, and therefore I am resigning.[96]

"I am not surprised at Mrs. Roosevelt's action," Miss Anderson had commented at the time, "because she seems to me to be one who really comprehends the true meaning of democracy."[97] A Gallup Poll published on March 20 revealed that two-thirds of the respondents approved of the First Lady's resignation.[98]

Although Mrs. Roosevelt undoubtedly conferred with Walter White in planning for the concert and may have helped to engage the support of the administration, she declined to take a more public role. She was the obvious choice for the chairmanship of the sponsoring committee, but that would have subjected her to even more intense attack from southern reactionaries who "were already pillorying her for her attitude on the Negro." White, for one, felt that she should not "put herself on the spot." In the end, she decided to remain in Hyde Park for Easter instead of attending the concert.[99]

[95] *Afro-American*, Mar. 18, 1939.
[96] "My Day," Feb. 28, 1939, quoted in Lash, *Eleanor and Franklin*, p. 526.
[97] Quoted in *New York Times*, Feb. 28, 1939, p. 5.
[98] Gallup Poll, Mar. 20, 1939, in Gallup, *The Gallup Poll*, I:142. For typical newspaper reactions, see, for example, editorial, *Afro-American*, Mar. 11, 1939.
[99] White, *A Man Called White*, p. 182; *Afro-American*, Apr. 15, 1939. James

The First Lady's absence in no way diminished the drama of the scene. The crowd had begun assembling four hours before the concert was scheduled to begin. By five o'clock, seventy-five thousand Americans were massed along the reflecting pool, whites shoulder to shoulder with blacks, and cabinet members, Supreme Court justices, senators, and diplomats alongside common laborers. The *Afro-American* called it "one of those rare occasions when caste is forgotten, when dignitaries rub elbows with street urchins, and when milady and her servant meet in the same social sphere."[100] Charles Houston captured the drama perfectly in the statement that he drafted for the radio announcer at the request of Oscar Chapman. It was "the greatest audience ever assembled in Washington in one spot," gathered "in the open air where all races and creeds are welcome," in order "to hear a great artist and give a living testimonial to the spirit of democracy." How "fitting and symbolic" that Miss Anderson "should be singing on Easter Sunday on the steps of the Memorial to the Great Emancipator who struck the shackles of slavery from her people 76 years ago."[101]

In a statement cleared by the White House,[102] Harold Ickes introduced the distinguished artist. "Genius, like justice, is blind," he declared. "For genius has touched with the tip of her wing this woman who, if it had not been for the great mind of Jefferson, if it had not been for the great heart of Lincoln, would not be able to stand among us today a free individual in a free land. Genius draws no color line."[103]

The expectant throng grew still, and Marian Anderson walked to the microphone. The "vast multitude" overwhelmed her. "There seemed to be people as far as the eye could see," she later wrote. "I had a feeling that a great wave of good will poured out from these people, almost engulfing me." The great singer raised her voice in the hymn "America." "I felt for a moment as though I were choking," she remembered. "For a desperate second I thought that the words, well as I know them, would not come."[104]

Then the words poured forth. "My country 'tis of thee, sweet

Roosevelt said that his mother decided not to attend because she did not want to be accused of exploiting the situation. Interview, Feb. 28, 1977, Newport Beach, Calif.

[100] *Afro-American*, Apr. 15, 1939.

[101] Untitled Charles H. Houston memorandum, Apr. 8, 1939, MAC, Box 2.

[102] Michael W. Straus memorandum to the Secretary [Ickes], Mar. 7 [more likely Apr. 7—probably misdated], 1939, Ickes Papers, Folder 249D, Box 315.

[103] "Remarks of Secretary of the Interior Harold L. Ickes in Introducing Marian Anderson . . . Apr. 9, 1939," MAC, Box 2.

[104] Anderson, *My Lord, What a Morning*, p. 191.

25

26

27

land of liberty," she began, and soon came the triumphant affirmation: "From every mountainside, let freedom ring." The peculiar poignance of the phrases could not have been lost on the audience. A Donizetti aria and Schubert's "Ave Maria" followed, and the concert concluded with three Negro spirituals.[105] Miss Anderson stood briefly at the microphone. "I'm not a speaker," she said. "I'm just so overwhelmed today, I cannot express myself. You don't know what you've done for me. The immensity of this affair has done so much to me. I'm not up to giving a nice speech. I thank you from the bottom of my heart."[106] Years later, she described what she had felt as she stood with the statue of Lincoln to her back and faced the thousands assembled below: It "was more than a concert for me. It was a dedication. . . . It seemed that everyone present was a living witness to the ideals of freedom for which President Lincoln died. When I sang that day, I was singing to the entire Nation."[107]

The effect was electric. "Something happened in all of our hearts," a joyful Mary McLeod Bethune wrote to Houston. "I came away almost walking in the air. My hopes for the future were brightened." The concert and "the reverence and the concentration of the throngs . . . told a story of hope for tomorrow—a story of triumph—a story of pulling together—[a] story of splendor and real democracy."[108] In his office on Easter Monday, Secretary Ickes had tears in his eyes as he told a black aide how privileged he felt to have had a role in so extraordinary an event. He called it "the most moving occasion" of his life.[109]

Predictably, some racial reactionaries took offense, and Ickes received his share of angry letters. "Why don't you take Marian Anderson and her group out to your home and set your wife on the platform next to her," one proponent of segregation wrote. "It would make a fine picture." "No doubt some of your ancestors, or relatives were kinky headed," another snapped. The concert

---

[105] Program, Marian Anderson Concert, MAC, Box 2; *Afro-American*, Apr. 15, 1939.

[106] Quoted in *Afro-American*, Apr. 15, 1939.

[107] "Remarks of Marian Anderson on the occasion of the presentation to the Government of the mural depicting the Marian Anderson Lincoln Memorial Concert," Jan. 6, 1943, MAC, Box 2.

[108] Mary McLeod Bethune to Charles H. Houston, Apr. 10, 1939, ibid., Box 1.

[109] Trent interview. "We realize what it meant for you to grant the authorization for the concert in the first place," Houston wrote Ickes. "You have made us all feel more hopeful in the final triumph for justice." Charles H. Houston to Harold L. Ickes, Apr. 11, 1939, Department of the Interior Papers, Office of the Secretary, Central Classified Files, File 1-280, Marian Anderson subfile (hereafter cited as MA), pt. 1, Record Group 48, National Archives.

was "a degrading spectacle," "a ridiculous exhibition"—"You ought to hang your head in shame."[110]

But the recriminations were drowned out by the groundswell of approval. Most dramatic was the reaction from the nation's blacks. To them, the Marian Anderson affair was a *"grand* epoch making event," a "lesson in tolerance," "a demonstration in Democracy of which as Americans we may be justly proud."[111] Tributes and expressions of gratitude poured into Ickes's office; the secretary won lavish praise for his "magnanimity of spirit" and "high statesmanship" in arranging and presiding over the concert.[112]

The Anderson affair told black Americans, in a highly visible, emotionally-charged way, that the Roosevelt administration cared and that it would go out of its way to demonstrate that concern. "You have renewed our hope," a civic association official in Washington wrote Ickes. Or, as a man from Brooklyn put it, "If we had more leaders of the type that you, Sen. Wagner and our beloved President and Mrs. Roosevelt are what a grand and glorious country this really would be [for] the minority groups."[113]

That summer, as if to seal the association, Mrs. Roosevelt presented the Spingarn medal to Miss Anderson at the NAACP's annual conference in Richmond. Undaunted by her racially conservative surroundings, she spoke forthrightly about democracy and equality. "Only a woman of great courage and of unusual foresight could have registered her convictions with such force and persuasion," the *Chicago Defender* commented. "It was a great speech, a great occasion, surpassed only by the greatness of Mrs. Roosevelt."[114]

At first glance it did not make sense. How could the admin-

---

[110] Unsigned letter to Harold L. Ickes, postmarked Apr. 3, 1939, Interior Department Papers, File 1-280, MA, pt. 1; "An admirer of Hugh Johnson" to Ickes, Apr. 15, 1939, Ickes Papers, Folder 249, Box 315; Russell K. Lowry to Ickes, Apr. 11, 1939, ibid., Folder 249A, Box 315.

[111] Mrs. Stanley L. Barnette to Harold Ickes, Apr. 10, 1939, Ickes Papers, Folder 249, Box 315 (*"grand* epoch making event"); Ruth Logan Roberts to Ickes, Apr. 11, 1939, Interior Department Papers, File 1-280, MA, pt. 1. See also A. A. Birch to Ickes, Apr. 17, 1939, Ickes Papers, Folder 249, Box 315.

[112] L. E. Burke to Ickes, Apr. 17, 1939; Rev. C. J. Henderson telegram to Ickes, Apr. 10, 1939, Interior Department Papers, File 1-280, MA, pt. 1. See also Oliver C. Cox to Ickes, Apr. 9, 1939; telegram, Willie E. Brown, Estelle L. Wilson, Mattie L. Hunter to Ickes, Apr. 10, 1939, Ickes Papers, Folder 249, Box 315; and Edward B. Ramsey to Ikes [sic], Apr. 10, 1939, ibid., Folder 249B, Box 315.

[113] Blanche C. Knorl to Harold L. Ickes, Apr. 24, 1939, Ickes Papers, Folder 249A, Box 315; Kenneth Harrison to Ickes, Apr. 9, 1939, Interior Department Papers, File 1-280, MA, pt. 1.

[114] Editorial, *Chicago Defender*, July 8, 1939.

istration resist sending a simple letter of greeting to an organization for racial advancement and at the same time go out of its way to be identified publicly with Marian Anderson, indeed, literally sponsor the Anderson concert at the Lincoln Memorial? In fact, it was easy to understand. The administration was no monolith. Left to their own devices, Stephen Early and his cohorts would invariably follow their own instincts and stay as far as possible from anything that could be construed as a racial issue. Eleanor Roosevelt, Harold Ickes, and a few others took a wholly different point of view, and, where there was room for their sway, the outcome would very likely be different. What made the Anderson affair one of those cases where more progressive racial views could prevail? First, the NAACP went straight to its friends in the administration. Second, the cause of Marian Anderson was not strictly racial. The issue was also that the DAR and the Washington school board had attempted to stifle great talent on extraneous racial grounds. Third, it was possible to sponsor the Lincoln Memorial concert without risk of significant political repercussions. It was different from an issue such as antilynching legislation in that it in no way threatened the established system of race relations in the South; it involved no federal encroachment on state rights; and it entailed no congressional action, hence no need to risk votes that the administration needed for other measures. Finally, as the public endorsement of Mrs. Roosevelt's resignation from the DAR portended, the concert had every chance of winning strong popular approval.

As their racial conservatism revealed, the New Dealers were clever politicians. Tommy Corcoran explained their political calculus. Where it was possible to make a gesture that might appeal to blacks without alienating more important supporters, why not do it? The New Deal had a "humanitarian streak," after all; and besides, they were in the business of winning votes.[115] The Marian Anderson concert was precisely the kind of symbolic gesture that made blacks feel that they counted in the New Deal. How could it fail to pay dividends in the election of 1940?

[115] Corcoran interview.

CHAPTER XII · *The Election of 1940*

As the election of 1940 approached, blacks made clear their hope that Franklin Roosevelt would continue in office. A black Chicagoan wrote to the President in 1938 to say that he and his wife had voted for Roosevelt before; if Roosevelt could "run 2 more times," they would vote for him again.[1] "To hell with any more elections," a black man in Detroit exclaimed, "we're gonna make him king."[2]

Black spokesmen were sure that Roosevelt would hold the Negro vote. If Roosevelt should run again, Walter White predicted at the NAACP's annual conference in the summer of 1939, he would "undoubtedly" win the support of blacks.[3] The executive secretary of the National Negro Congress, John P. Davis, a frequent critic of the New Deal, agreed: "The Negro vote is for Roosevelt and the New Deal all the way."[4] A Gallup Poll in December 1939 revealed that 66 percent of the blacks surveyed favored the Democratic party in the election in the following year.[5]

And yet some analysts foresaw a swing back to the Republican party. Off-year elections had demonstrated significant slippage from the Democratic strength of 1936 (see Table XII.1). The administration had not delivered an antilynching law; it had not acted to enfranchise blacks in the South; and it had not stopped discrimination in New Deal programs. Blacks were still excluded in large numbers from productive employment. There might be a good chance for the Republicans to recapture black allegiance.[6]

[1] Jessie Rose to Franklin D. Roosevelt, Oct. 10, 1938, Works Progress Administration Papers, Box 4, Manuscript Division, Moorland-Spingarn Research Center, Howard University.

[2] Quoted in interview with Louis E. Martin, May 13, 1977, Chicago.

[3] Quoted in *New York Times*, July 1, 1939, p. 4.

[4] Quoted in *Chicago Defender*, July 29, 1939. For a similar appraisal, see letter to the editor from Kelly Miller, *Afro-American*, Mar. 18, 1939.

[5] Gallup Poll, Feb. 5, 1940, in George H. Gallup, *The Gallup Poll: Public Opinion, 1935-1971*, 3 vols. (New York, 1972), I:207.

[6] "Negroes' Swing," *Newsweek*, Apr. 10, 1939, p. 16.

TABLE XII.1
Democratic Vote in Black Districts
Presidential Election, 1936
Senatorial and Gubernatorial Elections, 1938
(in percentages)

City	1936 President	1938 U.S. Senator	1938 Governor
Chicago	48.8	48.4	—
Cleveland	60.5	40.3	42.0
Detroit	66.2	—	64.3*
New York	81.3	74.0	69.4
Philadelphia	68.7	57.2	57.1
Pittsburgh	74.7	69.6	68.4

SOURCES: The returns for the senatorial and gubernatorial elections of 1938 are derived from the following sources: Records of the Board of Election Commissioners of the City of Chicago, available on microfiche at the Municipal Reference Library, Chicago; Records of the Board of Elections of Cuyahoga County, Board of Elections, Cleveland; Board of County Canvassers' Statement of Returns, available on microfilm at the Wayne County Election Commission, Detroit; "Official Canvass of the Votes Cast . . . at the Election Held November 8, 1938," *City Record*, Dec. 17, 1938; Registration Commission for the City of Philadelphia, *Thirty-third Annual Report, December 31, 1938* (Philadelphia, 1939); *The Pennsylvania Manual, 1939* (Harrisburg, 1940). For the vote in 1936 and the sources for the election units studied, see Table IX.2.

* Based on incomplete returns

The sources are silent on Republican perceptions of their purported opportunity. At least at first, the national chairman, John Hamilton, took steps to run a more effective campaign among blacks than the party had been able to muster in the two previous elections. For years the GOP had relied on the same clique of black politicians to mastermind its appeal to the race. As the election of 1940 approached, many blacks believed that the "old Guard" should be supplanted by "more progressive leaders." It appeared, the *Philadelphia Tribune* reported, that Hamilton had decided "to give other elements in the party a chance to show what they could do." The Republican Program Committee, which was charged with writing a statement of Republican principles for the forthcoming election, included some new black faces among its members. In order to provide expert information for the Program Committee, the National Committee hired the Howard University political scientist, Ralph J. Bunche, to prepare a report on the needs and attitudes of black Americans. Another influential black educator, Emmett J. Scott of Tuskegee Institute, joined the party's staff to handle publicity in the Negro press. At the same time, black women launched a new monthly magazine, the *Women's Voice*, "Published in the Interests of Republican Policies."[7]

Bunche submitted a 130-page typescript to the Program Committee in July 1939. His message was blunt: "The Negro is in need of everything that a constructive, humane, American political program can give him—employment, land, housing, relief, health protection, unemployment and old-age insurance, enjoyment of civil rights—all that a twentieth-century American citizen is entitled to. The New Deal has done much to help, unquestionably, but it has fallen far short of meeting adequately the minimal needs of the Negro. It has gotten off on the wrong foot in some instances, gone up blind alleys in others, and has often run afoul of race prejudice."

How might the Republicans turn the needs of black Americans and the shortcomings of the New Deal to the party's political advantage? "The Negro Democratic vote in 1932 and 1936 was a 'bread and butter' vote," Bunche wrote. Blacks had left the Republicans, not for the positive attraction of the Democrats as a party, but because of the tangible economic benefits offered by the New Deal. Nevertheless, the Republican party itself had contributed to their departure by engaging in heavyhanded attempts to win southern white support and by cultivating an old-fashioned, "socially unintelligent, inept and self-seeking" Republican Negro leadership. In order to appeal once again to blacks, the party would have to cultivate new black leadership and replace "the old slogans, the shop-worn dogmas and appeals used so effectively in the past" with "concrete evidence . . . of a determination to fully integrate the Negro in American life."[8]

To the Republican Program Committee, Bunche's proposals were too "impractical," too "revolutionary," and too reflective of the temper of the New Deal. It was clear, according to a member of the committee, that the party did not want to "stick its neck

[7] *Philadelphia Tribune*, Feb. 29, 1940; *New York Age*, Feb. 24, 1940; "Negroes' Swing," p. 16; *New York Times*, July 16, 1939, p. 25. The first issue of the *Women's Voice* appeared in May 1939. There is a long, detailed memorandum in the Claude A. Barnett Papers suggesting strategy for the Republican campaign among blacks. It is not clear, however, to whom it was directed in the party hierarchy, or under what circumstances it was written. See Claude A. Barnett memorandum, May 19, 1939, Barnett Papers, Chicago Historical Society.

[8] Ralph J. Bunche, "Report on the Needs of the Negro (for the Republican Program Committee)," July 1, 1939, pp. 3, 9-12; Schomburg Center for Research in Black Culture.

out on such problems."[9] Accordingly, the report was simply ignored. When the Program Committee released its statement of principles in February 1940, five paragraphs in the 115-page report spoke to the situation of blacks. Instead of Bunche's themes, the document reiterated a familiar indictment of the New Deal. "Enlightened" blacks were beginning to realize, it declared, that the New Deal had encouraged "a progressive shunting of Negroes out of normal productive enterprise into a kind of separate relief economy, leaving them, as it were, on permanent 'reservations' of public relief."[10]

The Program Committee's generalities lent support to the view of the *New York Amsterdam News* that the Bunche report had been "too hot" for the Republicans "to handle" and had accordingly been "ditched" by "the party bosses." Bunche, the paper wrote, was "the most 'forgotten man' '' at the Republican national convention in June 1940.[11] Still, the Republican party's platform of 1940 came closer than the Program Committee's statement of principles to articulating the kinds of specific programmatic commitments that Bunche had recommended. It promised blacks "a square deal in the economic and political life of this nation." Then it continued: "Discrimination in the civil service, the army, navy, and all other branches of the Government must cease. To enjoy the full benefits of life, liberty and the pursuit of happiness universal suffrage must be made effective for the Negro citizen. Mob violence shocks the conscience of the nation and legislation to curb this evil should be enacted."[12]

Black Republicans tried to wax optimistic; in the words of the *Cleveland Gazette*, the plank was "the most satisfactory and inclusive expression which has appeared in a Republican platform for 30 years."[13] Still, it was difficult to muster a great deal of enthusiasm. Even that staunchly Republican newspaper, the *Philadelphia Tribune*, had to acknowledge that there was a wide gap

[9] Rep. Frances E. Bolton, quoted in James E. Allen, "The Negro and the 1940 Presidential Election" (Master's thesis, Howard University, 1943), p. 86. For similar sentiments from the committee's chairman, Glenn Frank, see ibid., p. 83.

[10] "A Program for a Dynamic America: A Statement of Republican Principles," Report of Republican Program Committee Submitted to Republican National Committee, Feb. 16, 1940, pp. 91-92, New Deal Folder, vertical file, Moorland-Spingarn Research Center; *New York Age*, Feb. 24, 1940.

[11] *New York Amsterdam News*, June 29, 1940.

[12] Kirk H. Porter and Donald Bruce Johnson, comps., *National Party Platforms, 1840-1960*, 2nd ed. (Urbana, Ill., 1961), p. 393.

[13] *Cleveland Gazette*, July 6, 1940. For similar opinions see editorials on the same date in *Pittsburgh Courier* and *New York Age*.

between "writing a straightforward plank in the ... platform" and "translating that plank into reality."[14] Roy Wilkins was less charitable. The plank was full of "vague phrase[s]," not explicit promises, he wrote in his weekly newspaper column. Blacks ought not to be misled. There was nothing in the recent history of the party to substantiate the platform's purported concern for the race.[15]

Nor was there much evidence in the personal history of the Republican candidate, Wendell Willkie, to indicate the nature of the party's commitment to blacks. The most notable aspect of that history was the paucity of information that it provided about Willkie's views on race. Critics pointed to the racial conservatism of his hometown, Elwood, Indiana. This small town in central Indiana had no Negro residents and had gained a reputation as "the home of race prejudice." Black newspapers made much of a sign which they claimed had hung there for years: "Nigger," it declared, "don't let the sun go down on you here." It was widely reported that the sign had been taken down the day that Willkie won the Republican nomination. Since Willkie had had no previous political career, he had never been required to take stands on issues of vital concern to blacks. Supporters found encouragement in his efforts in the 1920s, when he had been a Democrat, to put the Democratic party on record in opposition to the Ku Klux Klan. But skeptics saw him as a representative of the public utilities—where discrimination was the rule in employment— and as a big businessman personally unacquainted with blacks and insensitive to their needs.[16]

By his conduct as a candidate, Willkie tried hard to compensate for the deficiencies in his image as it appeared to blacks. To black delegates at the convention, he declared, "IF I AM ELECTED PRESIDENT I WILL SEEK TO REMOVE ALL KINDS OF DIS-CRIMINATION FROM ALL KINDS OF GROUPS." He asked for their support and promised blacks "their fair proportion of appointments [and] their fair representation in policy making"

[14] Editorial, *Philadelphia Tribune*, July 4, 1940. For a similar view, see editorial, *Norfolk Journal and Guide*, July 6, 1940.

[15] Roy Wilkins, "Watchtower," *New York Amsterdam News*, July 6, 1940.

[16] *New York Amsterdam News*, Aug. 24 ("the home of race prejudice"), Sept. 7, 1940; Elbert Lee Tatum, *The Changed Political Thought of the Negro, 1915-1940* (New York, 1951), p. 162 ("Nigger, don't let the sun go down on you here"); *New York Age*, July 13, 1940; Roy Wilkins, "Watchtower," *New York Amsterdam News*, June 22, 1940; Bishop R. R. Wright, Jr., "No Hope for the Race in Willkie Candidacy," *Norfolk Journal and Guide*, Oct. 26, 1940.

whether or not they backed him.[17] "There is no man more opposed to racial discrimination," he told the managing editor of the *Philadelphia Tribune*. Blacks were welcomed to the notification ceremonies in Elwood in August. In campaign speeches to mass audiences in South Side Chicago and Harlem, Willkie committed himself explicitly to end discrimination in relief and in federal employment and to support antilynching legislation.[18]

But all that Willkie could offer blacks were promises, and those promises, as the political scientist, Harold F. Gosnell, pointed out in an analysis of the black vote in the election of 1940, "were less tangible than Roosevelt's record."[19] Once the Democratic party renominated the President and thus disposed of black concerns that it might turn to a conservative like John Nance Garner, the principal campaign issues for blacks became Franklin D. Roosevelt and the New Deal.[20]

The Democratic campaign of 1940 illustrated the ability of the Roosevelt administration to use racial symbolism to political advantage. It also demonstrated how easy it was, whether through inadvertence or because of policy conflicts, for racial issues to become politically explosive.

For the first time, Roosevelt ran on a platform with a specific Negro plank. The NAACP and others had asked for explicit pledges of action to end discrimination in federal employment, in the allocation of federal funds, and in the administration of federal programs; to abolish the poll tax and the white primary; to ban segregation in the armed forces; and to enact antilynching legislation.[21] The plank emphasized the administration's past achievements: "Our Negro citizens have participated actively in the economic and social advances launched by this Administration." It spoke of future racial policies only in the most general language: "We shall continue to strive for complete legislative

[17] Quoted in *Cleveland Gazette*, July 27, 1940.

[18] *Philadelphia Tribune*, July 4 (source of the quotation), Sept. 19, 1940; *Cleveland Gazette*, Aug. 31, Sept. 21, 1940; *New York Amsterdam News*, Oct. 12, 1940. The mimeographed text of the Chicago address, Sept. 13, 1940, is in Mary Church Terrell Papers, Box 9, Manuscript Division, Library of Congress. For Willkie's efforts in behalf of civil rights in the 1940s, see Donald Bruce Johnson, *The Republican Party and Wendell Willkie* (Urbana, Ill., 1960), pp. 228, 286-88, 304-305, 314-17, and Ellsworth Barnard, *Wendell Willkie: Fighter for Freedom* (Marquette, Mich., 1966), pp. 337-38, 340-41, 408-409, 473, 496-97.

[19] Harold F. Gosnell, "The Negro Vote in Northern Cities," *National Municipal Review* XXX (May 1941):266.

[20] On opposition to Garner, see, for example, editorial, *Pittsburgh Courier*, Apr. 15, 1939, and *New York Amsterdam News*, Jan. 20, 1940.

[21] *New York Age*, July 20, 1940.

safeguards against discrimination in government service and benefits, and in the national defense forces. We pledge to uphold due process and the equal protection of the laws for every citizen, regardless of race, creed or color."[22] Disturbingly weak on specifics, it even fell "far short of the promises made Negro voters by the Republican party." Black commentators understood the political calculus: the inclusion of the plank meant that the party was bidding for the black vote; the plank's weakness showed the relative importance to the Democrats of the black voter and the white southern voter. "The moral," the *Pittsburgh Courier* pointed out, was that blacks would "get consideration and concessions in the degree that they control sufficient votes to bring effective pressure to bear on their elected representatives and are intelligently organized for that purpose."[23]

As for the Democratic campaign among blacks, where the stakes were relatively insignificant and the risk of alienating the white South was low, the racial gestures were generous. The Post Office, for example, issued two commemorative postage stamps with racial themes—the Booker T. Washington stamp, in April, was the first one "ever to carry the head of a Negro"; the second stamp, issued in a timely fashion in late October, marked the seventy-fifth anniversary of the ratification of the Thirteenth Amendment. The true anniversary date, Republican critics pointed out, would not have come until December.[24] Eleanor Roosevelt continued to address important black organizations—for example, the convention in September of the Brotherhood of Sleeping Car Porters. Roosevelt's calendar, which rarely included appointments with blacks, showed a half dozen such meetings in 1940. Racial concerns, seldom even mentioned at White House press conferences in the first seven years of the Roosevelt presidency, became the subject of extended discussion at a press conference with representatives of the American Youth Congress in June.[25]

[22] Porter and Johnson, comps., *National Party Platforms*, p. 387.

[23] Editorial, *New York Age*, July 27, 1940; editorial and Ted Poston column, *Pittsburgh Courier*, July 27, 1940. The *Philadelphia Tribune* called the plank "mere verbiage. It says absolutely nothing." Editorial, July 25, 1940.

[24] *Philadelphia Tribune*, Feb. 15, Apr. 4 (source of the quotation), 11, Oct. 3, 24, 1940; *Pittsburgh Courier*, Oct. 26, 1940; Postmaster General to Elder Lightfoot Solomon Michaux, Oct. 1, 1940, Franklin D. Roosevelt Papers, President's Personal File (PPF) 6945, Franklin D. Roosevelt Library (hereafter cited as the FDR Papers).

[25] *New York Amsterdam News*, Sept. 28, 1940; White House Usher's Diary, Jan. 12, Aug. 16, Sept. 12, 27, Oct. 25, Dec. 18, 1940, Franklin D. Roosevelt Library; press conference no. 649-A, June 5, 1940, in *Complete Presidential Press Conferences of Franklin D. Roosevelt*, 25 vols. (New York, 1972), 15:462-63, 467-69, 471-75, 481-84, 523-25.

But where the issue was important and the stakes were high—as in the case of segregation in the armed forces—concessions to blacks were much more difficult to come by. Blacks had begun agitating about the issue of segregation in the armed forces well before the campaign began. They had ample cause for concern, for they were barred completely from the Marine Corps and the Army Air Corps, limited to the messman's branch of the navy, and severely restricted in enlistment opportunities in the army. While their principal preoccupation in the early months of the European war was to secure a fair share of jobs in the nascent defense industries, they regarded full access to the armed forces as an important symbol of their citizenship. Beginning in late 1938, the black press, black organizations, and individual black leaders began to speak out about the importance of full participation for blacks in the armed forces. Blacks and their congressional allies tried repeatedly to amend defense legislation to insure equal opportunities for blacks; either the amendments failed, or the War Department found ways to interpret the legislation to allow the continuation of existing practices. The stalemate made segregation and discrimination in the armed forces a potent political issue in the forthcoming election. To ignore it, black Democrats counseled the White House, might carry a heavy political price.[26]

In the face of mounting criticism over the persistence of discrimination in the armed forces, Walter White asked the First Lady to arrange a meeting between the President and a delegation of black leaders. Roosevelt agreed, and the meeting was set for September 27, 1940.[27] The delegation consisted of White, A. Philip Randolph, the president of the Brotherhood of Sleeping Car Porters, and T. Arnold Hill, who was on leave from the National Urban League as a racial adviser in the National Youth Administration. With Roosevelt were Secretary of the Navy Frank Knox

[26] Richard M. Dalfiume, *Desegregation of the U. S. Armed Forces: Fighting on Two Fronts, 1939-1953* (Columbia, Mo., 1969), pp. 26-36. For the military's own account of blacks and the armed forces in this period, see two sources: Ulysses Lee, *The Employment of Negro Troops* (Washington, D.C., 1966), a volume in the series United States Army in World War II, published by the Office of the Chief of Military History, United States Army; and Morris J. MacGregor, Jr., *Integration of the Armed Forces, 1940-1965* (Washington, D.C., 1981), the first volume in the Defense Studies Series, published by the Center of Military History, United States Army.

[27] S. T. E[arly] confidential memorandum for General [Edwin M.] Watson, Sept. 19, 1940, FDR Papers, Official File (OF) 2538.

and Assistant Secretary of War Robert P. Patterson, who substituted for Secretary Henry L. Stimson.[28]

Randolph made plain the delegation's purpose. "The Negro people ... feel they are not wanted in the armed forces of the country," he said. "They feel they have earned their right to participate in every phase of the government by virtue of their record in past wars since the Revolution." Roosevelt announced that the War Department was ready to involve blacks in all branches of the armed services: "The *main* point to get across is ... that we are not ... [as we did] in the World War, confining the Negro to the noncombat services. We're putting them right *in*, proportionately, into the combat services."[29] White asked what Roosevelt's announcement meant. Did it apply to officers as well as enlisted men? Would blacks be confined to separate units? Did the new policy apply to the navy as well as to the army?

The responses were mixed at best. Patterson said that the army was ready to call black reserve officers to active duty, but at a yet-to-be-determined date. The question of nonsegregated units caught administration officials unaware; it appeared that none of them had thought about the possibility. Insofar as the army was concerned, racial mixing seemed feasible, at least in divisions or regiments from the North, as Knox pointed out to Roosevelt. The President seemed "immediately receptive" and suggested that black regiments and batteries be situated next to white regiments and batteries; in wartime, it would be "the usual procedure" for one to seek replacements from another. That way "the Army could 'back into' the formation of units without segregation."[30]

Knox emphasized that "an army fighting allegedly for democracy should be the last place in which to practice undemocratic segregation." His own navy was another matter. There the problem struck him as "almost insoluble" because of the insurmountable difficulties of mixing blacks and whites in close quarters

[28] The conference is summarized in a typescript entitled "Conference at the White House ... Sept. 27, 1940," Arthur B. Spingarn Papers, Box 9, Manuscript Division, Library of Congress, and in NAACP press release, "Details of White House Conference on Army-Navy-Industry Discrimination Against Negroes Revealed," Oct. 5, 1940, FDR Papers, OF 93, Box 3. According to the White House Usher's Diary (Sept. 27, 1940), it lasted for a half hour.

[29] The quotations come from fragments of a tape recording of the conference, published in "The FDR Tapes: Secret Recordings Made in the Oval Office of the President in the Autumn of 1940," *American Heritage* XXXIII (Feb./Mar. 1982):23-24.

[30] "Conference at the White House ... Sept. 27, 1940."

aboard ship.[31] "If you could have a Northern ship and a Southern ship it would be different," Roosevelt laughed. "But you can't *do* that." Still, the navy was organizing new bands; why not put "a colored band on some of these ships," the President suggested to Knox, "because they're *darned good at it....* Look, to increase the *opportunity*, that's what we're after." Not only that, the presence of black musicians would begin to accustom white sailors to having blacks on board. Roosevelt also suggested that the army and navy have black spokesmen at their headquarters. He himself had had a "colored messenger," a secretarial clerk who was "of very, very great service" to him at the Navy Department in World War I, and he thought a similar arrangement could work effectively now: "get somebody colored [who will act as] the clearinghouse."[32]

The delegation gave the administration officials a memorandum that set forth specific steps toward full integration of blacks into the armed forces. Chief among the demands were the use of Negro officers and enlisted men throughout the services and the elimination of segregated military units. The officials promised to study the memorandum and see what could be done. After consulting with others in the government, Roosevelt said, he would be in touch with the Negro leaders once again.[33]

The consultations never proceeded very far. Knox threatened to resign as secretary if Roosevelt desegregated the navy. Stimson balked at considering any reforms in the racial practices of the army. He resented the attempt by blacks to turn the racial policy of the armed forces into a political issue: "The Negroes," he wrote in his diary, "are taking advantage of this period just before [the] election to try to get everything they can in the way of recognition from the Army." Moreover, defense legislation was pending in Congress, and southern Democrats would surely be unhappy about concessions to blacks.[34]

[31] Ibid.

[32] "The FDR Tapes," p. 24. The editor of the tapes, R.J.C. Butow, suggests that Roosevelt's comments about musicians and spokesmen came from a different meeting, on Oct. 10, but they are summarized in the typescript "Conference at the White House" and thus are likely to have been part of the meeting with the delegation on Sept. 27.

[33] "Conference at the White House . . . Sept. 27, 1940"; Dalfiume, *Desegregation of the U. S. Armed Forces,* p. 38.

[34] Stimson is quoted in Dalfiume, *Desegregation of the U. S. Armed Forces,* p. 42. See also Harvard Sitkoff, *A New Deal for Blacks: The Emergence of Civil Rights as a National Issue,* vol. I: *The Depression Decade* (New York, 1978), pp. 306-307.

Accordingly, Roosevelt approved a statement, prepared by the War Department, setting forth the administration's policy on the participation of blacks in the armed forces.[35] The statement, released on October 9 without the promised further discussion with the Negro leaders, pledged that the War Department would utilize "the services of negroes . . . on a fair and equitable basis." It offered specific commitments in that direction:

1. The strength of the negro personnel of the Army . . . will be maintained on the general basis of proportion of the negro population of the country.

2. Negro organizations will be established in each major branch of the service, combatant as well as non-combatant.

3. Negro Reserve officers eligible for active duty will be assigned to negro units officered by colored personnel.

4. When officer candidate schools are established, opportunities will be given to negroes to qualify for Reserve commissions.

5. Negroes are being given aviation training as pilots, mechanics, and technical specialists. This training will be accelerated. Negro aviation units will be formed as soon as the necessary personnel has been trained.

6. At arsenals and Army posts negro civilians are accorded equal opportunity for employment at work for which they are qualified by ability, education and experience.

Then came the odious disclaimer:

The policy of the War Department is not to intermingle colored and white enlisted personnel in the same regimental organizations. This policy has been proven satisfactory over a long period of years and to make changes would produce situations destructive to morale and detrimental to the preparations for national defense. For similar reasons the Department does not contemplate assigning colored Reserve officers other than those of the Medical Corps and chaplains to existing negro combat units of the Regular Army.[36]

[35] Robert P. Patterson memorandum to the President, Oct. 8, 1940; Stephen Early to Patterson, Oct. 9, 1940, FDR Papers, OF 93, Box 3.
[36] Undated typescript, War Department Policy in Regard to Negroes, FDR Papers, OF 93, Box 3.

Roosevelt saw the War Department policy as "a very substantial advance over what has been the practice in past years."[37] Blacks disagreed violently. Sanctioning Jim Crow was bad enough. To compound the insult, the announcement by the White House press secretary, Stephen Early, made it look as though the new policy came with their approval. The policy had been drafted, Early told the press, "as a result" of Roosevelt's meeting on September 27 with White, Randolph, and Hill.[38]

Blacks were outraged. Early's phraseology was "a 'trick' to give the impression that Negroes had approved of the Army jim crow, and to remove the pressure from President Roosevelt," the NAACP charged. In a telegram to the White House on October 10, the three leaders reminded Roosevelt that, in their written memorandum, they had "specifically repudiated segregation." "We are inexpressibly shocked that a President of the United States at a time of national peril should surrender so completely to enemies of Democracy who would destroy national unity by advocating segregation. Official approval by the Commander-in-Chief . . . of such discrimination and segregation is a stab in the back of Democracy."[39]

Had Early been careless about his phrasing? Or had he attempted "a trick"? The policy remained unchanged, but Early backpedaled from the implication that it had the approval of the black leaders. He certainly had not meant to cause them any embarrassment, he wrote to Walter White. In fact, he said, his announcement had made the distinction clear. He had not said that the specific policy had their approval, but rather that the formation of a policy on Negro participation in national defense had been a consequence of their discussions with the President. What he had meant "was that, in all probability, there would have been no 'statement of policy with regard to negroes in national defense' had it not been for [their] conference."[40]

The White House, caught by surprise by the furor over Early's statement and concerned about holding the black vote, responded

[37] Franklin D. Roosevelt to Walter White, Oct. 25, 1940, ibid., OF 93.
[38] Early's statement to the press is recapitulated in Stephen Early to Walter White, Oct. 25, 1940, ibid.
[39] The telegram is quoted in NAACP press release, "White House Charged with Trickery in Announcing Jim Crow Policy of Army," Oct. 11, 1940, ibid.
[40] Stephen Early to Walter White, Oct. 18, 25 (source of the quotation), 1940, ibid. As an indication of how badly Early misjudged the implications of the incident, see his memorandum to Charlie Michelson, Oct. 9, 1940, ibid., instructing the Democratic National Committee publicity director to use the policy statement "in the colored press and to have it given the widest possible distribution among colored organizations through the country."

with a barrage of symbolic racial gestures to counter some of the damage that had been done in the black community.[41] On October 25, the President announced the promotion to brigadier general of Colonel Benjamin O. Davis, Sr., commander of the 369th National Guard Regiment in New York and the only black colonel and the highest ranking black officer in the United States Army. At the same time, Roosevelt also announced two new appointments of blacks to aid in the defense efforts: William H. Hastie as civilian aide to the secretary of war, and Major Campbell C. Johnson, an instructor at Howard University and the executive secretary of the 12th Street YMCA in Washington, as executive assistant to the director of Selective Service.[42]

It was impossible to miss the political motives behind Roosevelt's actions. Only weeks earlier, when Roosevelt had promoted eighty-four colonels to brigadier general, he had passed Davis by. Black commentators explained the about-face as an effort "to win back the Negro voters," in other words, to repair the political damage done by the announcement of the War Department's Jim Crow policy.[43] White House motives notwithstanding, there was a new black general, and, with war coming on, that was a symbolic statement of no small importance.[44] Roosevelt had little to lose when he made the appointment. Indeed, it would be almost entirely symbolic, for Davis would reach mandatory retirement age the following March. The irony is that the appointment would not have been contemplated if it had not become necessary to put out a political fire.

The timing of the Davis appointment proved useful for other reasons that Roosevelt could not have anticipated. By the time that most Negro weeklies could report the promotion of Davis,

[41] On White House sensitivity to the political consequences, see Dalfiume, *Desegregation of the U. S. Armed Forces*, pp. 40-41; James Rowe, Jr., memoranda for the President, Oct. 18, 31, 1940, FDR Papers, OF 1413-B, OF 93, respectively. Walter White warned repeatedly of the political consequences of administration insensitivity on the matter of armed forces discrimination. See, e.g., White to Jacob Billikopf, Oct. 9, 1940, ibid., OF 2538.

[42] *New York Amsterdam News*, Nov. 2, 1940. On Hastie's role as civilian aide, see Phillip McGuire, "Judge Hastie, World War II, and Army Racism," *Journal of Negro History* LXII (Oct. 1977):351-62.

[43] See, for example, *Philadelphia Tribune*, Oct. 31, 1940; editorial, *New York Age*, Nov. 2, 1940 (source of the quotation).

[44] It was certainly big news in the black press—see, for example, coverage in the *New York Amsterdam News*, Nov. 2, 1940, and the banner headline in the *Norfolk Journal and Guide*, Nov. 2, 1940. An editorial in the *Amsterdam News* of that date discusses the positive importance of the appointment. The *Pittsburgh Courier*, determined in its opposition to Roosevelt, attacked the appointments as "too little and too late"—a "last minute desperate maneuver." Editorial, Nov. 2, 1940.

there was another racial story to cover, and the Davis headlines conveniently overshadowed the reporting of a preelection incident that no candidate could have welcomed.[45] Roosevelt spoke at a major rally in Madison Square Garden in New York on the night of October 28. Afterwards, as the presidential party scrambled to make their train at Pennsylvania Station, Early kicked or kneed a Negro policeman, James Sloan, who was guarding the staircase to the track. There were multiple versions of what actually happened. Had the policemen been doing their duty in following orders to let no one pass, or had they wrongly refused to honor—perhaps even to inspect—the party's credentials? Had Early been calm and reasonable and the police insulting, or was it the other way around? Had Early deliberately assaulted the Negro officer in a typical display of temper, or had he raised his knee in self-defense when the policeman shoved him?[46] It was difficult to determine which version was accurate, but it was perfectly apparent that there was nothing to be gained for Roosevelt from newspaper headlines that proclaimed, in inch-and-a-half type, "Secretary of Pres. Roosevelt Kicks N.Y. Negro Policeman."[47]

Republicans tried to make political capital out of the incident. They printed broadsides that featured a picture of Sloan recuperating in bed, with the admonition, "NEGROES—if you want your President to be surrounded by Southern influences of this kind, vote for Roosevelt. If you want to be treated with respect, vote

[45] The front page of the *New York Amsterdam News* for Nov. 2, 1940, summed up the recent events of the campaign, positive and negative. The "Harlem for FDR" headline beside photographs of the President at a rally at Madison Square Garden shared the page with these stories: "Col. Davis Promoted"; "Name Hastie Aide to War Secretary"; "Kicking of Officer Stirs Wide Storm!"

[46] For Early's own statement, see the transcript of his press conference, Oct. 29, 1940, Stephen T. Early Papers, Box 35, Franklin D. Roosevelt Library. Eyewitness accounts by reporters in the party which corroborate Early's version include statements by Doris Fleeson, Oct. 29, 1940; Bruce Pinter, John Henry, Thomas F. Reynolds, Walter Trohan, and George Durno, all Oct. 30, 1940; Blair Moody, Oct. 31, 1940; Theodore G. Alford, Nov. 1, 1940, all in Sloan Incident Scrapbook, Early Papers. *Time* magazine's account was sharply critical of Early ("Early's Temper," *Time*, Nov. 11, 1940, pp. 17-18; Thomas F. Reynolds et al. to Time Inc., Nov. 8, 1940; Manfred Gottfried to Reynolds, Nov. 15, 1940, all in Early Papers, Box 35); *Editor and Publisher* came to his defense ("White House Corps Defends 'Steve' Early," *Editor and Publisher*, Nov. 16, 1940, p. 4, Early Papers, Box 35). For continuing coverage of the incident in the daily press, see *New York Herald Tribune*, Oct. 30, 1940, p. 11; Oct. 31, 1940, p. 11; Nov. 1, 1940, pp. 1, 11; and clippings in Sloan Incident Scrapbook, Early Papers.

[47] *New York Age*, Nov. 2, 1940.

for WENDELL WILLKIE!"[48] The world heavyweight boxing champion, Joe Louis, who was touring Harlem for Willkie, called it "the foulest blow in the campaign."[49] Worried Democrats assessed the political impact. Black voters were upset—there was no doubt about that; some declared their intention to vote for Willkie because of the incident.[50] Walter White later wrote that his telephone "rang night and day" as friends of the President called to ask "what could be done to repair the damage."[51] Paul Douglas, a professor of political economy at the University of Chicago, wired that "unless something drastic were done," the Democrats could fail to carry his state. Harry Hopkins asked Ickes what to do. Ickes advised that Early should resign, or at least that he should go to the policeman's home to apologize.[52] Early did neither, although he did issue a statement in which he denied any wrongdoing but apologized for having had any part in the "unfortunate altercation."[53] Still eager to contain the political repercussions, administration officials reached for a sure ace in the hole: why not get Marian Anderson to appear at a meeting and sing or issue a statement? Ickes tried unsuccessfully to reach her, but she did finally sing for the Democrats on a national radio broadcast on election eve.[54]

As it happened, despite Republican efforts to play up the incident, its repercussions dissipated of their own accord. When Joe Louis stopped at Sloan's home to be photographed at his bedside, a reporter asked Sloan, "What are your politics?" "I am a Democrat," he replied; "I will vote for Mr. Roosevelt."[55] "It would be

---

[48] "Negro Kicked in Groin by the President's Secretary," broadside, Sloan Incident Scrapbook, Early Papers.

[49] Quoted in Grace Tully, *F.D.R.: My Boss* (New York, 1949), p. 153.

[50] Telegram, A. W. Springs to Stephen T. Early, Nov. 2, 1940; telegram, Randall Toliver to the President, Oct. 30, 1940; telegram, Samuel Richardson to Early, Oct. 30, 1940; telegram, F. S. Wickware to the President, Oct. 30, 1940; C. B. Bourne and H. A. Kelly to Franklin D. Roosevelt, Nov. 16, 1940; Fleming R. Waller to Early, Nov. 13, 1940; Waller to Roosevelt, Nov. 14, 1940; William W. Brainard, Jr. to Early, n.d.; Thomas J. McFarland to Early, Oct. 30, 1940; Kelsie R. Duncan to Early, Oct. 30, 1940; Jessie Finley to Mr. Roosevelt, n.d.; A. C. Ricke to Early, [Nov. 4, 1940]; Robert Jones to Early, Nov. 4, 1940; George Boomer to Early, Nov. 2, 1940, Early Papers, Box 35.

[51] Walter White, *A Man Called White: The Autobiography of Walter White* (New York, 1948), p. 188.

[52] Diary entry, Nov. 5, 1940, in Harold L. Ickes, *The Secret Diary of Harold L. Ickes*, vol. III: *The Lowering Clouds, 1939-1941* (New York, 1954), pp. 361-62.

[53] Untitled Stephen Early press release, Oct. 31, 1940, Early Papers, Box 35; Early to James Sloan, Oct. 31, 1940, Sloan Incident Scrapbook, Early Papers.

[54] Diary entry, Nov. 5, 1940, in Ickes, *Secret Diary*, vol. III, p. 362.

[55] *New York Times*, Nov. 1, 1940, p. 20.

silly to blame the President for something he could not help,"
Sloan explained. "If anybody thinks they can turn me against our
great President who has done so much for my race because of this
thing, they certainly are mistaken."[56]

The Sloan incident illustrated the peripheral place of race in
national politics in 1940. Of course it was unfortunate that the
patrolman had been injured, but the altercation was of minor
importance. With neither party really willing to grapple directly
and specifically with major racial issues of concern to black Americans, minor racial incidents could assume a political life of their
own, out of all proportion to their actual significance.

In fact, it was unlikely that the Davis appointment would buy a
great many votes for Franklin Roosevelt or that the Sloan incident
would cause many blacks to support Wendell Willkie. The real
issues in the election of 1940 were still Franklin D. Roosevelt
and the New Deal. After eight years of the Democratic administration, which mattered more to blacks—economic assistance
or inaction on a racial agenda? Did the Democrats win favor for
aiding blacks with relief, or were they to be castigated for keeping
blacks out of productive employment?

The black press remained divided. Robert L. Vann, piqued at
his treatment by the Democratic administration and concerned
that blacks not become captive to a single party, led the *Pittsburgh
Courier* back to the party of Lincoln. Traditionally Republican
papers like the *New York Age, Philadelphia Tribune,* and *Cleveland Gazette* declared for Willkie. To the *Age,* relief was "de-
stroying initiative and self-confidence in the individual"; the Negro, it concluded, had "actually lost ground under the New Deal."
"It is true that sufficient crumbs have been dropped to keep them
[colored citizens] from starving," the *Tribune* conceded. "But colored people have reached the point where they are entitled to and
are demanding more than crumbs." Whether or not the Republicans would live up to their pledges remained to be seen, but
blacks ought to vote to give Willkie a chance to do what Roosevelt
refused to do or was unable to do: "PUT THE MASSES OF COL-
ORED PEOPLE TO WORK AT DECENT WAGES SO THAT THEY,
WITH OTHER AMERICANS, CAN MAINTAIN THEIR SELF-

[56] *New York Herald Tribune,* Nov. 3, 1940, p. 32. Sloan wrote Early after the
election of his joy at Roosevelt's reelection; the incident, he declared, was "an
accident that happened void of all malice." James M. Sloan to Stephen Early, Nov.
22, 1940, Sloan Incident Scrapbook, Early Papers.

RESPECT." Longtime Roosevelt supporters such as the *Norfolk Journal and Guide* and the *New York Amsterdam News* again declared for the President, while John H. Sengstacke swung the *Chicago Defender* into the Democratic column. Liberated from its traditional Republicanism by the death of its editor, Robert S. Abbott, the *Defender* justified its shift in terms of the economic and social policies of the New Deal: No administration in history had done more "to achieve economic and social democracy," and blacks had shared in the benefits. Roosevelt, Sengstacke declared, was "a great humanitarian and a great champion of the common people"; blacks "should vote en masse for the re-election of the greatest President we have had since Lincoln's time."[57]

How individual voters made their choices depended less on their racial identity than on their economic fortunes. As Ralph Bunche explained in his massive report, "The Political Status of the Negro": "The Negro vote is subject to the same variations in interest as the white vote—there are sectional, class, religious and ideological differences dividing the Negro vote as the white. ... While it is true that the Negro voter must always be a 'race conscious' voter so long as racial division remains typical of American life, it is also true that there are many issues of even more fundamental importance to [his] welfare."[58] In 1940, as was so often the case, those issues were largely economic.

Traveling through the Midwest, Roy Wilkins was struck by the class basis for black people's political preferences. "It has been revealing to note," he wrote in August after a trip to Illinois, Wisconsin, and Minnesota, "that the Negro middle and upper class reacts to the New Deal programs not as Negroes, but as middle class people." They

> complain about federal taxes. They complain about so much spending. They complain about the WPA and the relief program, saying (of all things) that relief is "ruining" Negroes so they

[57] Vann died on Oct. 24, 1940, but the *Courier* remained in the Willkie camp. See, e.g., editorials, *Pittsburgh Courier*, Aug. 24, 31, 1940; editorials, *New York Age*, Feb. 17, Oct. 5 (source of the quotation), 1940; editorials, *Philadelphia Tribune*, July 25 ("sufficient crumbs"), Oct. 17, 1940 ("PUT THE MASSES ... TO WORK"); editorials, *New York Amsterdam News*, Sept. 14, 28, Nov. 2, 1940; editorials, *Chicago Defender*, Oct. 12, 26 (source of the quotation), Nov. 2, 1940; John H. Sengstacke column, "The Way of All Things," ibid., Nov. 2, 1940.

[58] Ralph J. Bunche, "The Political Status of the Negro" (research memorandum prepared for Carnegie-Myrdal study, Sept. 1940), bk. IV, chap. 15, p. 1253, quoted in John Albert Morsell, "The Political Behavior of Negroes in New York City" (Ph.D. diss., Columbia University, 1951), p. 3.

won't work—at the wage scale the complainers think they ought to get. They complain about unemployment insurance and social security. They complain about union labor. . . . They say the Negro wants jobs and not relief and they tell you with a straight face that they think the Republicans, with a big business man like Willkie, will give Negroes jobs. And to cap the climax they complain about "breaking the third term tradition," and say they are afraid of a dictatorship.[59]

In October, he found the same phenomenon in Detroit, Toledo, Cleveland, and Youngstown: "The upper class Negroes are pretty much for Mr. Willkie and the GOP. The working Negroes are for Mr. Roosevelt."[60]

Again and again, "working Negroes" explained their political preference in economic terms. "Any man who works with his hands knows how to vote in this election," a Negro porter told Wilkins.[61] "I am going to vote for the party that will help us the most," a housewife in Philadelphia declared; "although some of us are on relief, we didn't even have that when the Republicans were in office."[62] "Roosevelt has tried to lift a heavy burden from the shoulders of the 'little' man," a Brooklyn woman said, "and we belong in that class."[63] A black Philadelphian, stopped on the street by a reporter after the election, summed up the case: "Roosevelt is the poor man's friend. . . . Being a poor man I cast my vote for FDR."[64]

In 1940, the "poor man" was the typical black American. Of the nearly four and a half million blacks who held regular em-

---

[59] Roy Wilkins, "Watchtower," *New York Amsterdam News*, Aug. 24, 1940. Wilkins reported his findings with some consternation. "I suppose," he wrote, "it is idealistic to expect that middle and upper class Negroes will react any differently than other people of their class. One would think, however, that they would realize what has been done for millions of their less fortunate racial brothers. Of course they have had to help pay for it, but that should be the lot of the more fortunate, the more talented. For the first time in the history of this country government means something to the man farther down."

[60] Ibid., Oct. 12, 1940. For retrospective analyses along the same lines, see Gosnell, "The Negro Vote in Northern Cities," p. 278; interview with A. Leon Higginbotham, Jr., Jan. 21, 1981, Philadelphia.

[61] Roy Wilkins, "Watchtower," *New York Amsterdam News*, Oct. 12, 1940.

[62] Quoted in *Philadelphia Tribune*, July 25, 1940. "Now every Negroes in the United state should case there vote for you," a man in Tampa wrote the President, ". . . for under your administration we wear not left to starve." Eugene J. Smith to Franklin D. Roosevelt, Nov. 2, 1940, WPA Papers, Box 2.

[63] Quoted in *Pittsburgh Courier*, Oct. 26, 1940.

[64] Quoted in *Philadelphia Tribune*, Nov. 7, 1940.

ployment, slightly more than a third worked on farms—most of them as tenants, sharecroppers, or farm laborers. Of the nearly three million employed in nonagricultural occupations, more than four-fifths worked in semiskilled or unskilled positions. Black unemployment stood at 11 percent—a decline attributable to the employment of 319,241 blacks (or 6 percent of the potential black labor force) in emergency work created by the New Deal.[65]

These emergency workers were the men who found employment on governmental construction projects and the women who supported their families and learned a trade in government-sponsored sewing rooms. These were the adults who learned to read and write in government-sponsored literacy classes. These were the families whose children profited from government-sponsored infant care programs, nursery schools, boys and girls clubs, recreational facilities, community centers, school buildings, and college scholarships. These were the people who found apartments in the new public housing projects.[66] Although the programs were

[65] U. S. Department of Commerce, Bureau of the Census, *Sixteenth Census of the United States: 1940, Population*, vol. II: *Characteristics of the Population* (Washington, D.C., 1943), pt. 1, pp. 44-46; Alba M. Edwards, *Comparative Occupational Statistics for the United States, 1870-1940* (Washington, D.C., 1943), p. 189. The precise figures are as follows: 5,389,191 blacks over fourteen in the labor force; 4,479,068 employed (except emergency work); 319,241 employed on emergency work; 590,882 seeking work; 1,556,361 employed on farms. Of the nonagricultural employed workers, 22.7 percent were unskilled laborers, 45.8 percent unskilled servants, and 18.3 percent semiskilled workers. The comparable figures for whites are 9.0, 6.7, 25.8. Three hundred thousand was the average black employment on WPA in 1939 (c. 14 percent of all WPA workers). In 1938, it was 400,000 (13.3 percent); in September 1940, black employment on WPA was estimated to be close to 253,500, or 15 percent of the WPA work force. See Alfred Edgar Smith, "Negro Project Workers: 1938 Annual Report," Jan. 1939, WPA Papers, Box 10; WPA press release, "Widespread Benefits Derived by Negroes from WPA in 1939 Are Reviewed by Staff Adviser," Feb. 2, 1940, Records of the Works Progress Administration, Division of Information, Box 90, Record Group 69, National Archives; and Alfred Edgar Smith, "Report of Activities, Sept. 1-30, 1940," WPA Papers, Box 11.

[66] On federal benefits for blacks in the second Roosevelt Administration, see, for example, the various WPA press releases in Records of the Works Progress Administration, Division of Information, Boxes 89, 90; WPA press releases in WPA Folder, vertical file, Moorland-Spingarn Research Center, Howard University; Alfred Edgar Smith, "Negro Project Workers: 1937 Annual Report," Jan. 1938, Records of the Works Progress Administration, Box 90; press releases, Federal Emergency Administration of Public Works, n.d. [1938], and Sept. 21, 1938; *Jobs for American Workers: The Negro in the Government's Work Program* (May 1, 1940), all in William J. Trent, Jr. Papers, Box 1, Manuscript Division, Moorland-Spingarn Research Center, Howard University; *Why the Colored Citizen Should Help Re-elect President Roosevelt* (1940), FDR Papers, OF 93, Box 3; *Way of Progress: Negro Participation in the Federal Works Agency Program* (1940), John

by no means free of discrimination,[67] federal officials frequently succeeded in adjusting complaints, and in major northern cities, at least, benefits were extended with a relatively even hand.[68]

Critics of the New Deal persisted in charging the Democrats with manipulating relief in order to buy votes. Supporters saw the votes as freely given. No matter what the point of view, however, there was a clear consensus: among blacks, the election turned on economic assistance.[69] "Any time people are out of work, in poverty, have lost their savings," W.E.B. Du Bois explained, "any kind of a 'deal' that helps them is going to be favored. Large numbers of colored people in the United States would have starved to death if it had not been for the Roosevelt policies."[70] The *Iowa Bystander* put it plainly: "The Negro voted not on the basis of race interest, which the Bystander believes is Republican, but on the theory that the Democrats under Roosevelt had provided WPA relief and other gratuities which they feared would be dropped if the Republicans were elected. Nothing else mattered."[71]

It was no wonder, then, that when blacks went to the polls, "the poor man's friend" won the large majority of their votes. In Harlem, where Roosevelt had won 81.3 percent of the votes in

M. Carmody Papers, Box 96, Franklin D. Roosevelt Library; Melvin Reuben Maskin, "Black Education and the New Deal: The Urban Experience" (Ph.D. diss., New York University, 1973).

[67] See, for example, T. Arnold Hill, *The Negro and Economic Reconstruction* (Washington, D.C., 1937), p. 61; W. L. Byrd to Roy Wilkins, Jan. 11, 1937; J. B. Bowden to Dr. M. D. Potter, Mar. 2, 1937, NAACP Papers, Box C-418; Lester B. Granger to the Editor, Aug. 20, 1937, *New York Times*, Aug. 24, 1937, p. 20; H. B. Burdett to Franklin D. Roosevelt, Mar. 7, 1937; Brady Beaumont to Franklin D. Roosevelt, Apr. 5, 1937, WPA Papers, Box 1; Phyllis W. Francis to Alfred Edgar Smith, Aug. 26, 1937; Elizabeth E. Hyde to Lawrence M. Pinckney, Report on the Employment of Negro Women in the Sewing Rooms of Charleston, attached to Pinckney to Ellen S. Woodward, Sept. 27, 1937, ibid., Box 3; Woodward memorandum to Eleanor Roosevelt, Apr. 4, 1938, Eleanor Roosevelt Papers, Box 741, Franklin D. Roosevelt Library; Rev. R. H. Sawyer to NAACP, July 18, 25, 1938, NAACP Papers, Box C-286; Frances Jennings to Mr. and Mrs. Roosevelt, Nov. 8, 1938, WPA Papers, Box 4; O'dell Allen to Dear Sir, Feb. 12, 1939, ibid., Box 5.

[68] Alfred Edgar Smith, "Negro Project Workers: 1937 Annual Report," Jan. 1938, Records of the Works Progress Administration, Division of Information, Box 90; Maskin, "Black Education and the New Deal," pp. 113, 115, 195, 257-58.

[69] Ludlow W. Werner, "Across the Desk," *New York Age*, Nov. 2, 1940; *Pittsburgh Courier*, Nov. 2, 1940; editorial, *Cleveland Gazette*, Nov. 9, 1940; *Atlanta Daily World*, Nov. 9, 1940, quoted in Alfred Edgar Smith, "Report of Activities, Nov. 1-30, 1940," WPA Papers, Box 11.

[70] Quoted in Alfred Edgar Smith, "Report of Activities, Mar. 1-31, 1940," WPA Papers, Box 11.

[71] *Iowa Bystander* (Des Moines), Nov. 23, 1940, quoted in Alfred Edgar Smith, "Report of Activities, Nov. 1-30, 1940," WPA Papers, Box 11.

TABLE XII.2
Presidential Vote in Black Districts, 1940

City	% Republican	% Democratic
Chicago	47.3	52.2
Cincinnati	33.1	66.9
Cleveland	35.3	64.7
Detroit	24.3	74.8
New York	18.6	81.0
Philadelphia	31.2	68.4
Pittsburgh	17.6	82.0

SOURCES: The figures for Chicago are drawn from the records of the Board of Election Commissioners of the City of Chicago, which are available on microfiche at the Municipal Reference Library in Chicago; the appropriate precincts were chosen by matching census tracts which were at least 90 percent black—identified in U.S. Department of Commerce, Bureau of the Census, *Sixteenth Census of the United States: 1940, Population and Housing: Statistics for Census Tracts and Community Areas: Chicago, Ill.* (Washington, D.C., 1943)—with ward maps which are held by the Board of Election Commissioners in Chicago. The figures for Cincinnati come from Ernest M. Collins, "Cincinnati Negroes and Presidential Politics," *Journal of Negro History* XLI (Apr. 1956):133. The figures for Cleveland are drawn from the Records of the Board of Elections of Cuyahoga County, which are held at the Board of Elections in Cleveland; the appropriate precincts were chosen by matching census tracts which were at least 90 percent black—identified in U.S. Department of Commerce, Bureau of the Census, *Sixteenth Census of the United States: 1940, Population and Housing: Statistics for Census Tracts: Cleveland, Ohio and Adjacent Area* (Washington, D.C., 1942)—with ward maps and the Board of Elections of Cuyahoga County's *Register of Voters*, both deposited in the Cuyahoga County Archives in Cleveland. The figures for Detroit are drawn from the Board of County Canvassers' Statement of Returns, on microfilm at the Wayne County Election Commission in Detroit; the appropriate precincts were chosen by matching census tracts which were at least 90 percent black—identified in U.S. Department of Commerce, Bureau of the Census, *Sixteenth Census of the United States: 1940, Population and Housing: Statistics for Census Tracts: Detroit, Mich., and Adjacent Area* (Washington, D.C., 1942)—with ward maps held at the Detroit Election Commission. The figures for New York are drawn from "Official Canvass of the Votes Cast . . . at the Election Held November 5, 1940," *City Record*, Dec. 19, 1940; the appropriate election units were chosen by matching blocks in Harlem identified in Welfare Council of New York City, *Census Tract Data on Population and Housing: New York City: 1940* (New York, 1942), p. 171, and assembly district maps which are available on slides at the Municipal Reference and Research Center, New York City. The figures for Philadelphia are drawn from Registration Commission for the City of Philadelphia, *Thirty-fifth Annual Report, December 31, 1940* (Philadelphia, 1941); the analysis is based on election divisions in which the voter registration was at least 90 percent black. The figures for Pittsburgh are drawn from *The Pennsylvania Manual, 1941* (Harrisburg, 1941), pp. 174-82; the appropriate precincts were chosen by matching census tracts identified in U.S. Department of Commerce, Bureau of the Census, *Sixteenth Census of the United States: 1940, Population and Housing: Statistics for Census Tracts: Pittsburgh, Pa.* (Washington, D.C., 1942) with ward maps provided by the University of Pittsburgh Library.

TABLE XII.3
Democratic Vote in Black Districts, by Class, 1940
(in percentages)

City	Lower-Middle-Class Districts	Lower-Class Districts
Chicago	46.1	52.8
Cleveland	58.7	69.1
Detroit	70.1	79.8
New York	73.9	81.5

SOURCES: For the voting returns themselves, see the sources cited for Table XII.2. For identification of the districts and enumeration of the socioeconomic indices which determined their classification, see Appendix.

1936, he got 81 percent in 1940. In Cincinnati, where he had earned 65.1 percent of the vote in black districts in 1936, he won 66.9 percent. Just over 52 percent of the voters in black districts in Chicago voted for Roosevelt in 1940—a gain of more than 3 percent over 1936. The Democratic margin in black districts in Detroit grew as well—66.2 percent in 1936, 74.8 percent in 1940. In the black precincts of Philadelphia, where Roosevelt had won 68.7 percent in 1936, his vote dropped off by only three-tenths of 1 percent (see Table XII.2). As had been the case in 1936, economic status shaped black political behavior: Roosevelt's showing was the strongest in the poorest black neighborhoods (see Table XII.3).

At a time when the Roosevelt vote among all groups dropped off considerably—he beat Willkie by a margin of 54.7 to 44.8 percent, as compared to his victory of 60.8 to 36.5 percent over Landon in 1936[72]—his support among blacks held up strongly. Nationwide, the President was estimated to be the choice of 67 percent of black Americans in 1940, as compared with 71 percent in 1936.[73] That meant that his slippage among blacks was considerably smaller than the decline in the Democratic vote in the general electorate.[74] Indeed, with the exception of Jews, who favored Roosevelt by margins of 85 percent in 1936 and 84 percent

[72] Richard M. Scammon, comp. and ed., *America at the Polls: A Handbook of American Presidential Election Statistics, 1920-1964* (1965; reprint ed., New York, 1976), pp. 9, 11.

[73] Everett Carll Ladd, Jr., with Charles D. Hadley, *Transformations of the American Party System: Political Coalitions from the New Deal to the 1970s*, 2nd ed. (New York, 1978), p. 60, Table 1.3.

[74] Everett Carll Ladd observes that while the Roosevelt vote "dropped off rather sharply (1936 to 1940) among most segments of the population, among blacks it remained essentially constant." *Transformations of the American Party System*, p. 59.

in 1940, blacks were more enthusiastic about the New Deal than almost any other group of American voters.[75]

Not only did the Roosevelt vote in black districts hold up better than it did in the general electorate, but opinion surveys showed that blacks were even more supportive of the New Deal than poor Americans in general. Polls conducted by *Fortune* magazine in July 1938 showed the dramatic affirmation by blacks of the President:[76]

"Is your present feeling toward President Roosevelt one of general approval—general disapproval?"

	Approve	Disapprove	Undecided
All	54.8%	33.9%	11.3%
Poor	75.1	24.9	
Lower Middle Class	61.6	38.4	
Upper Middle Class	52.5	47.5	
Prosperous	38.7	61.3	
Negroes	84.7	15.3	

"On the whole, do you like or dislike his personality?"

	Like	Dislike	Undecided	Uninformed
All	80.3%	11.7%	4.0%	4.0%
Poor	92.5	7.5		
Lower Middle Class	88.5	11.5		
Upper Middle Class	84.5	15.5		
Prosperous	74.4	25.6		
Negroes	93.0	7.0		

"On the whole, do you like or dislike his general economic objectives?"

	Like	Dislike	Undecided	Uninformed
All	48.1%	29.1%	11.1%	11.7%
Poor	73.9	26.1		
Lower Middle Class	62.2	37.8		
Upper Middle Class	55.2	44.8		
Prosperous	42.2	57.8		
Negroes	87.3	12.7		

[75] Jews, like blacks, had been Republican before the New Deal. See ibid., pp. 61-62.

[76] Hadley Cantril, ed., *Public Opinion, 1935-1946* (Princeton, 1951), pp. 758-59, 979.

"On the whole, do you like or dislike the methods by which he seeks to achieve them?"

	Like	Dislike	Undecided	Uninformed
All	35.5%	40.0%	13.0%	11.5%
Poor	64.9	35.1		
Lower Middle Class	46.6	53.4		
Upper Middle Class	35.9	64.1		
Prosperous	25.9	74.1		
Negroes	78.7	21.3		

"On the whole, do you approve or disapprove of President Roosevelt's attitude toward big business?"

	Like	Dislike	Undecided	Uniformed
All	37.3%	34.0%	11.8%	16.9%
Poor	65.6	34.4		
Lower Middle Class	53.5	46.5		
Upper Middle Class	42.5	57.5		
Prosperous	31.2	68.8		
Negroes	85.2	14.8		

"Do you think that President Roosevelt has concentrated too much power in his own hands?"

	Yes	No	Don't Know
All	45.3%	44.4%	10.3%
Poor	33.7	53.8	12.5
Lower Middle Class	46.5	43.9	9.6
Upper Middle Class	53.6	38.4	8.0
Prosperous	66.9	28.9	4.2
Negroes	19.5	59.2	21.3

Later *Fortune* polls showed the same trend with respect to the New Deal: blacks were more enthusiastic than other groups about the new scope of governmental activity:[77]

June 1939: "Do you think our government should or should not provide for all people who have no other means of subsistence? Be responsible for seeing to it that everyone who wants to work has a job?"

[77] Ibid., pp. 980-81.

Provide Subsistence

	Should	Should Not	Don't Know/ Depends
Prosperous	50.0%	41.6%	8.4%
Upper Middle Class	59.6	31.4	9.0
Lower Middle Class	69.4	22.3	8.3
Poor	77.1	15.0	7.9
Negroes	85.0	7.9	7.1

Provide Jobs

	Should	Should Not	Don't Know/ Depends
Prosperous	39.2%	54.6%	6.2%
Upper Middle Class	50.0	43.7	6.3
Lower Middle Class	60.4	31.7	7.9
Poor	71.4	22.7	5.9
Negroes	83.4	12.9	3.7

March 1940: "Do you think the government should provide for all people who have no other means of obtaining a living?"

	Yes	No	Don't Know
National total	65.1%	27.8%	7.1%
Prosperous	48.2	45.3	6.5
Upper Middle Class	55.7	37.7	6.6
Lower Middle Class	64.5	28.7	6.8
Poor	73.9	18.4	7.7
Negroes	82.8	9.1	8.1

May 1940: "What would you like to see the next administration do about the New Deal?"

	Go further with it	Keep it as it is	Modify it	Repeal most of it	Don't Know
National total	10.0%	14.4%	39.4%	20.6%	15.6%
Prosperous	3.3	6.9	53.2	30.0	6.6
Upper Middle Class	6.8	8.9	48.1	26.5	9.7
Lower Middle Class	10.1	15.2	40.1	18.4	16.2
Poor	13.7	20.3	25.9	16.4	23.7
Negroes	25.5	22.7	25.5	12.7	13.6

The special chemistry of Franklin Roosevelt and the tangible benefits of the New Deal had bred an intensity of commitment that would pay important long-term dividends for the Democratic party.

By registering for a second time their overwhelming support for Roosevelt, black voters raised an interesting question. Had the black vote, as spokesmen like to describe it, become truly independent—an uncertain factor to be bid for by both parties?[78] Or had it begun to lay the groundwork for a political bondage of a different kind? Was it the property of Franklin Roosevelt, or did it belong equally to his party?

A comparison of the Democratic vote in black districts in presidential and off-year elections suggests that blacks became Roosevelt voters before they became Democrats. As Table XII.4 illustrates, the dramatic change in black voting patterns that first manifested itself in the presidential election in 1936 did not carry over into state and local contests. With few exceptions, the Democratic vote in black districts fell off in mayoral, senatorial, and gubernatorial elections in 1937-1939 and then rose significantly when Roosevelt's name again appeared on the ballot in 1940.

Contemporary testimony supports the notion that there was a difference between black support for Roosevelt and the New Deal and black partisan identification with the Democratic party.[79] Blacks who were interviewed in 1936 made the point repeatedly: "I'm not for the Democrats, but I am for the man."[80] As the election of 1940 approached, black spokesmen reiterated the theme. "The Race is more Rooseveltian, 'especially MRS. Rooseveltian,' than Democratic," Walter White declared.[81] The Democrats had "no mortgage on Race voters," a *Chicago Defender* columnist pointed out. "The future of the Democrats in the minds of Race voters is dependent upon the position Mr. Roosevelt will occupy

[78] See, for example, Kelly Miller column in *Chicago Defender*, June 3, 1939; *Defender* editorial, Feb. 24, 1940; editorial, *Pittsburgh Courier*, Nov. 9, 1940.

[79] On this theme, see Henry Lee Moon, *Balance of Power: The Negro Vote* (Garden City, N.Y., 1948), p. 19.

[80] There are several comments to this effect in the *Afro-American*'s street-corner poll, Oct. 31, 1936. See also Ferdinand Q. Morton, "The Colored Voter," *Opportunity* XV (Mar. 1937):87; NAACP press release, "Vote Does Not Mean Race Belongs to Democrats, Says Statement of N.A.A.C.P.," Nov. 6, 1936, NAACP Papers, Box C-392; "Roosevelt's Opportunity, *Crisis* XLIII (Dec. 1936):369; Bunche, "Report on the Needs of the Negro," p. 10.

[81] Quoted in *Chicago Defender*, Apr. 1, 1939. White made a similar point in private correspondence the following year: "I think," he predicted, "the majority of Negroes will vote for Roosevelt—not for the Democrats." Walter White to Jacob Billikopf, Oct. 9, 1940, FDR Papers, OF 2538.

TABLE XII.4

Democratic Vote in Black Districts in Presidential and Off-Year Elections, 1932-1940

(in percentages)

City	1932 Pres.	1933 Mayor	1934 U.S. Sen.	1934 Gov.	1935 Mayor	1936 Pres.	1937 Mayor	1938 U.S. Sen.	1938 Gov.	1939 Mayor	1940 Pres.
Chicago	21.0	—	—	—	78.3	48.8	—	48.4*	—	57.6	52.2
Cleveland	17.3	12.1	22.5	20.0	11.3	60.5	23.6	40.3	42.0	40.0	64.7
Detroit	31.0	21.6	27.7	28.6	18.6	66.2	29.9	—	64.3*	78.7	74.8
New York	50.8	—	59.6	62.2	—	81.3	—	74.0	69.4	—	81.0
Philadelphia	26.7	—	41.7	—	44.2	68.7	—	57.2	57.3	50.0	68.4
Pittsburgh	41.3	—	44.7	42.6	—	74.7	—	69.6	68.4	—	82.0

SOURCES: In addition to the sources cited for Tables I.1, IX.2, and XII.2, above, see also the *Proceedings of the Board of City Canvassers, City of Detroit,* deposited at the Detroit Election Commission, for mayoral elections in that city; "Official Canvass of the Votes Cast . . . at the Election Held November 6, 1934," *City Record,* Dec. 31, 1934, and "Official Canvass of the Votes Cast . . . at the Election Held November 8, 1938," ibid., Dec. 17, 1938, for off-year elections in New York; Registration Commission for the City of Philadelphia, *Twenty-ninth Annual Report, December 31, 1934* (Philadelphia, 1935), *Thirtieth Annual Report, December 31, 1935* (Philadelphia, 1936), *Thirty-third Annual Report, December 31, 1938* (Philadelphia, 1939), *Thirty-fourth Annual Report, December 31, 1939* (Philadelphia, 1940), and *The Pennsylvania Manual, 1935-36* (Harrisburg, 1936), pp. 563-84, and 1939 (Harrisburg, 1940), pp. 280-301, for Philadelphia; and ibid., 1935-36, pp. 457-65, and 1939, pp. 174-83, for Pittsburgh.

* Based on incomplete returns

in the affairs of the party."[82] Roy Wilkins agreed: "It is the Roosevelts, not the Democratic party, who have helped the race."[83]

Opinion surveys reveal "a massive discrepancy between the partisan self-identification of blacks and their electoral behavior" in this period.[84] While 71 percent of blacks questioned in 1936 declared themselves to be Roosevelt supporters, only 44 percent of those surveyed the following year identified themselves as Democrats. In 1940, the discrepancy was equally striking: a 67 percent black Democratic presidential vote, as compared with a 42 percent black Democratic party identification.[85] Partisan allegiance remained squarely rooted in economic circumstances; among middle- and upper-class black professionals, businessmen, and civic leaders, close to 70 percent still called themselves Republicans.[86]

By contrast to the experience of blacks, as Table XII.5 makes

TABLE XII.5
Presidential Vote and Party Identification among Whites, 1940
(in percentages)

	White nonsouthern Catholics	White nonsouthern Protestants	White southern Protestants
Democratic presidential vote	70	39	80
Democratic party identification	62	31	81

SOURCE: Everett Carll Ladd, Jr., with Charles D. Hadley, *Transformations of the American Party System: Political Coalitions from the New Deal to the 1970s,* 2nd ed. (New York, 1978), p. 51, Table 1.1.

[82] David Ward Howe, "The Observation Post," *Chicago Defender,* Aug. 12, 1939.
[83] Roy Wilkins, "Watchtower," *New York Amsterdam News,* July 6, 1940. A student of the 1940 presidential election noted "the judgment of many Negro political observers in the North and Middle West that Mr. Roosevelt got the colored vote as an individual and not as a Democrat." Allen, "The Negro in the 1940 Presidential Election," p. 104.
[84] Ladd, *Transformations of the American Party System,* p. 113.
[85] Ibid., p. 60, Table 1.3. A similar disjunction shows up in the Gallup Poll. When Negro voters were surveyed in December 1939, 82 percent said that they approved of Roosevelt's performance as president, while 66 percent expressed the hope that the Democratic party would win the presidential election in 1940. Gallup Poll, Feb. 5, 1940, in Gallup, *The Gallup Poll,* I:207.
[86] Derived from *Who's Who in Colored America,* 6th ed. (Brooklyn, N.Y., 1942). The figures are based on 1,280 professionals, businessmen, and civic leaders who submitted birthdates and party affiliations.

clear, the correspondence between presidential vote and party identification among whites was much closer. The only group of white voters to resemble blacks in the discrepancy between presidential vote and party identification were Jews. A Gallup Poll in 1940 revealed that 84 percent of Jews surveyed had voted for Roosevelt, but only 45 percent described themselves as Democrats.[87]

In the words of the political scientist, Everett Carll Ladd, blacks presented

> a classic case ... of a group pulled strongly to the national Democratic party; yet so recently propelled away from its historic partisan allegiance that it manifested a major lag in party self-identification. Presumably, if the impulses emanating from national party program were subsequently to have changed—that is if the national Republican party had become the principal proponent of policies supported by black Americans—the potential for a permanent or long-term conversion implied by the [foregoing] data ... need not have been realized. Such a shift did not occur, however, and during the ensuing decades ... a drastic change in the partisan self-perception of blacks occurred, bringing I.D. into correspondence with regular vote preferences.[88]

When Harry S Truman added a commitment to civil rights to the New Deal's promise of economic and social justice, it became plausible for blacks to see themselves as Democrats as well as to vote for the Democratic candidate in presidential elections.[89]

[87] Ladd, *Transformations of the American Party System*, p. 62.

[88] Ibid., p. 60.

[89] The gap between party identification and presidential vote narrowed significantly with the Truman administration. In 1944, 40 percent of the blacks surveyed called themselves Democrats, while 68 percent said that they voted Democratic. In 1948, 56 percent called themselves Democrats, and 77 percent were Democratic voters. In 1952, 66 percent called themselves Democrats, and 76 percent were Democratic voters. See ibid., p. 112, Table 2.3.

Conclusion

"Roosevelt! Roosevelt! All he ever done for the nigger was to put him on relief," exclaimed Harold, a Negro character in Chester Himes's novel, *Lonely Crusade.* "Roosevelt! How he done it I do not know—starve you niggers and made you love 'im."[1]

Harold might have been speaking for a later generation of scholars, who saw the Roosevelt magic as something of a sham. To these historians of the New Left, the embrace of the Democratic party on the part of blacks in the 1930s came in plain defiance of the actual benefits that the New Deal extended to the race. For the most part, Barton J. Bernstein has argued, the New Deal left black Americans, like other "marginal men," "outside the new order": "Perhaps this is one of the crueller ironies of liberal politics, that the marginal men trapped in hopelessness were seduced by rhetoric, by the style and movement, by the symbolism of efforts seldom reaching beyond words."[2]

There is ample evidence to support the view that the New Deal failed to do full justice to the economic needs of black Americans. But as the testimony of contemporaries makes clear, most blacks were not "seduced" by rhetoric, style, and symbolism to the point of being unable to perceive the inequities in the way they were being treated. Black spokesmen in the 1930s understood quite clearly the shortcomings of the New Deal with respect to black Americans; even the beneficiaries of New Deal aid frequently recognized the discrimination in the assistance that they received.

Some blacks in the 1930s foresaw, too, that New Deal aid was not an unmixed blessing. Critics who worried over the creation of a permanent underclass of black reliefers and feared placing the augmented force of the federal government behind segregation

[1] Chester Himes, *Lonely Crusade* (New York, 1947), p. 55.
[2] Barton J. Bernstein, "The Conservative Achievements of Liberal Reform," in *Towards a New Past: Dissenting Essays in American History*, ed. Bernstein (New York, 1967), p. 281.

and ghettoization had an important point.[3] As scholars have shown, for all its short-term benefits, the New Deal did contribute in some respects to a longer-term worsening in the lot of black Americans. The housing program, for example, clearly accelerated the residential segregation of blacks in urban ghettos.[4] And public employment seems actually "to have depressed the Negro job structure by engaging many workers in job categories below those which they had filled in the private sector of the economy before the Depression began."[5]

To assume that such considerations should have kept blacks at arm's length from the New Deal presumes a set of choices that did not exist in the 1930s. To which other political party might blacks have given their support? The party with the best record on race was the American Communist party. But most blacks wanted to get into the American system, not to overturn it, and the emphasis of the Communist party on separatist self-determination in the black belt ran contrary to the aspirations of blacks for legal equality and integration in the larger society. For all the blandishments of the Communists and their deliberate efforts to assimilate blacks into the party hierarchy, communism was simply not a realistic alternative for the vast majority of blacks during the Depression.[6]

[3] For example, John P. Davis speech to NAACP annual conference, quoted in NAACP press release, "Charges New Deal Reenslaves Negro; 4 Million on Relief," July 1, 1935, National Association for the Advancement of Colored People Papers, Box B-11, Manuscript Division, Library of Congress; William Lloyd Imes and Francis E. Rivers, quoted in *New York Herald Tribune*, Dec. 8, 1935, clipping in NRA/NYA blue box, vertical file, Moorland-Spingarn Research Center, Howard University; Lester B. Granger interview, May 22, 1968, pp. 63-65, Civil Rights Documentation Project, Ralph J. Bunche Oral History Collection, Moorland-Spingarn Research Center.

[4] Gunnar Myrdal, *An American Dilemma*, 2 vols. (1944; 20th anniv. ed., New York, 1964), I:349; Robert C. Weaver, *The Negro Ghetto* (New York, 1948), pp. 75-76; Charles Abrams, "The Housing Problem and the Negro," in *The Negro American*, ed. Talcott Parsons and Kenneth B. Clark (Boston, 1966), p. 517; Kenneth T. Jackson, "Uncle Sam and Housing: A Half Century of Suburban Subsidy and Encouragement" (Paper presented at Conference on the Past and Present of New York's Suburban Crisis, Columbia University, Apr. 29, 1977).

[5] Christopher G. Wye, "The New Deal and the Negro Community: Toward a Broader Conceptualization," *Journal of American History* LIX (Dec. 1972):621-39 (the quotation is from 634).

[6] On communism and blacks, see, for example, William A. Nolan, *Communism versus the Negro* (Chicago, 1951); Wilson Record, *The Negro and the Communist Party* (Chapel Hill, 1951); Nell Irvin Painter, *The Narrative of Hosea Hudson: His Life as a Negro Communist in the South* (Cambridge, Mass., 1979); Mark D. Naison, "The Communist Party in Harlem: 1928-1936" (Ph.D. diss., Columbia University, 1975).

Conclusion

In light of the available options, and in the context of what had gone before, the black embrace of the Democratic party stands, not in contravention of the best interests of the race, but as a realistic response to the political circumstances of the 1930s. It may be tragic that it took so little to win black support for the New Deal, but the hard facts are that it was much more than blacks were accustomed to getting. Surely there was more than a little rhetorical excess in assessments such as those of the *Norfolk Journal and Guide*, which wrote that Roosevelt "did more than any other to make our emancipation real, to lift us from the depths of second-class citizenship, to make of us free and equal men in a nation pledged to democracy in fact as well as in theory." Still, such claims cannot be discounted. As the *Crisis* pointed out, for the first time blacks "were included as a component part of the population. . . . It is true that the millenium in race relations did not arrive under Roosevelt. But cynics and scoffers to the contrary, the great body of Negro citizens made progress." As a result, "Mr. Roosevelt created an atmosphere on the race question unmatched by any administration, certainly since the turn of the century." Gunnar Myrdal put it clearly: "The Negro's share may be meager in all this state activity, but he has been given a share. He has been given a broader and more variegated front to defend and from which to push forward. This is the great import of the New Deal to the Negro. For almost the first time in the history of the nation the state has done something substantial in a social way without excluding the Negro."[7]

Meager though the Negro's share may have been, it came in the form of tangible benefits that touched the lives of millions of black Americans. Systematic measurement of the economic impact of the New Deal on blacks is difficult to come by. We have no precise, reliable indices of the economic status of blacks in 1933 and 1940, for example. Nor can we discern much useful information from the data on unemployment in the federal censuses of 1930 and 1940, since census-takers used different categories and concepts in measuring employment in each of these years.[8] But the limited data which is available makes one pattern

[7] Editorial, *Norfolk Journal and Guide*, Apr. 21, 1945; "Franklin D. Roosevelt," *Crisis* LII (May 1945):129; Myrdal, *An American Dilemma*, I:74.

[8] U.S. Department of Commerce, Bureau of the Census, *Sixteenth Census of the United States: 1940, Population: Estimates of Labor Force, Employment, and Unemployment in the United States, 1940 and 1930* (Washington, D.C., 1944) attempts to present the data on a comparable basis, but it is not broken down by race.

abundantly clear: employment on public emergency work accounted for a significant reduction in black unemployment (see Table XIII.1). In turn, as a consequence of the economic assistance that came their way under the New Deal, blacks moved decisively into the Democratic party.

Without the economic crisis of the 1930s, that political migration would not have occurred when or as overwhelmingly as it did. Neither major party was prepared to adopt an affirmative position on important racial issues such as lynching, disfranchisement, segregation, and discrimination. The transcendence of economic over racial concerns during the Depression, indeed the close congruence of race and class for blacks, made it possible for the Democratic party to win black voters by the simple fact of not excluding them from the economic benefits that it brought to suffering Americans generally. To be sure, the New Deal's excursions into racial symbolism helped appreciably to cement the bond, but the essential political tie was forged in the cauldron of economic distress.

That tie proved to be remarkably enduring. A number of circumstances thrust the Democratic party's appeal to black voters into a more explicitly racial context after 1940. Blacks themselves, in the words of Ralph Bunche, developed from the experience of the 1930s "a much keener sense than formerly of the uses to which the ballot can be put." They now knew that the ballot was "negotiable" and that it could "be exchanged for definite social improvements for themselves."[9] Thanks to the politicization stimulated by the New Deal, they moved increasingly to use that ballot as a lever to encourage attention to racial concerns. At the same time, the continued urbanization of blacks, and with it the concentration of large numbers of black voters in northern cities, made the black vote a more significant factor in the Democratic party's calculations. The death of Franklin Roosevelt raised the question of the transference of black political loyalties from the President to his party. The rise of the civil rights movement, the increasing racial consciousness of black Americans as a consequence of World War II, and the diminution of the economic emergency brought racial issues to the fore in the 1940s in ways that had not occurred in the previous decade. Harry S Truman looked to civil rights as a means to transform black Roosevelt

[9] Ralph J. Bunche, "Report on the Needs of the Negro (for the Republican Program Committee)," July 1, 1939, p. 8, Schomburg Center for Research in Black Culture.

TABLE XIII.1

Unemployed Persons and Persons on Public Emergency Work as Percent of Total Labor Force in Selected Cities, 1931 and 1940

City	% Unemployed, Jan. 1931				% Seeking Work, Mar. 1940				% on Public Emergency Work, Mar. 1940			
	MALE		FEMALE		MALE		FEMALE		MALE		FEMALE	
	Negro	White	Negro	White	Non-white	White	Non-white	White	Non-white	White	Non-white	White
New York					19.3	15.0	19.9	14.9	10.6	2.9	3.5	1.2
Bronx	24.6	21.0	18.5	16.7								
Brooklyn	30.5	23.0	28.5	16.7								
Manhattan	25.4	19.4	28.5	11.2								
Philadelphia	42.4	27.3	41.0	20.8	33.7	15.6	22.9	14.2	5.3	2.1	6.5	1.7
Chicago	43.5	29.7	58.5	19.4	16.7	11.1	24.4	9.3	18.6	3.1	11.5	1.7
Detroit	60.2	32.4	75.0	17.4	15.7	9.6	19.2	11.7	17.4	2.7	10.6	2.2

SOURCE: Richard Sterner, *The Negro's Share: A Study of Income, Consumption, Housing and Public Assistance* (New York, 1943), pp. 362-63, Appendix Tables 12-13.

supporters into black Democrats. Later, the explicit commitment of John F. Kennedy and Lyndon B. Johnson to the cause of civil rights converted a healthy black majority into a nearly unanimous black commitment to the Democratic party.

But the Roosevelt legacy endured. Even as late as the 1960s, political clubs in black neighborhoods bore Roosevelt's name. In the election of 1960, in advertisements in black newspapers, John F. Kennedy deliberately cloaked himself in the Roosevelt mantle. As if to seal the connection, he sent Franklin D. Roosevelt, Jr., to campaign for him in the black ghettos of the North.[10] Surveys of black political attitudes continued to elicit references to the New Deal as the source of the respondents' allegiance to the Democratic party.[11] Decades after Franklin Roosevelt first entered the White House, the immediacy of his appeal, the captivating quality of his personality, and the tangible results of his beneficence remained compelling images in the minds of countless black Americans. That continued to translate into votes for the Democratic party.

[10] On the political clubs, see interview with Charles Rangel, Nov. 3, 1976, New York City. For the advertisements, see *Chicago Defender*, Oct. 1, 29, Nov. 5, 1960. In addition to the campaigning he did in black districts, Franklin D. Roosevelt, Jr., campaigned for Kennedy throughout the country. On the continuing usefulness of the Roosevelt association to Democratic politicians seeking the black vote, see interviews with Basil Paterson, Dec. 1, 1976, New York City; John Conyers, Jr., Mar. 23, 1977, Washington, D.C.; and Carl B. Stokes, Aug. 22, 1979, New York City. William J. McKenna notes that Philadelphia Democrats enlisted James Roosevelt to campaign in black areas in the 1963 mayoral election "in recognition of the lasting influence of President Roosevelt among the Negroes." "The Negro Vote in Philadelphia Elections," *Pennsylvania History* XXXII (Oct. 1965):412, n. 18.

[11] See, for example, the following manuscript questionnaires at the Center for Political Studies, Institute for Social Research, University of Michigan: from their 1968 survey, #s 0109, 0774, 1437, 1681, 1718; from their 1972 survey, #s 0073, 0190. For corroborating evidence, see Samuel Lubell, "The Negro and the Democratic Coalition," *Commentary* XXXVIII (Aug. 1964):22, and interview with Rayford W. Logan, Nov. 29, 1976, Washington, D.C. In an editorial just before the 1962 congressional elections, the *Pittsburgh Courier* commented disapprovingly on the tendency of blacks "to vote out of habit and misinformation for a man and an administration that is dead." "The myth of Rooseveltian miracles looms larger as the New Deal recedes farther into the past," the *Courier* went on, "and 30 years after the amiable squire of Hyde Park entered the White House, one still hears ever stronger how he saved the Negro from starvation and want; and this is given as the principal reason why the Democratic party has a priority claim on the Negro vote." Nov. 3, 1962.

Appendix

The tables which follow identify the voting districts in various cities that form the basis for the electoral analysis in this book. They also show the census units that correspond to these political units and list the socioeconomic characteristics that led me to distinguish between lower-middle-class and lower-class voting districts in some of the cities which I studied.

In choosing cities to analyze, I looked for concentrations of black population that would yield a number of census tracts or voting districts that were at least 90 percent black by 1940, and where at least some of them were 90 percent black by 1930. I focused my own analysis on six major northern cities that met this criterion: Chicago, Cleveland, Detroit, New York, Philadelphia, and Pittsburgh. I supplemented the voting data I found with some data developed by other scholars for one ward in Cincinnati and one in Knoxville which also met my criterion for concentration of black population.

When I turned to the analysis of voting by class, I found it necessary to eliminate Pittsburgh and Philadelphia from the list. In Pittsburgh, there were only three census tracts with a sufficient concentration of blacks by 1940, and the socioeconomic characteristics of all three were so similar that it was impossible to distinguish among them. In Philadelphia, the black population was too scattered to make census tracts a useful unit of analysis (there were only two tracts that were 90 percent black by 1940). Thanks to the Philadelphia Registration Commission, which published registration figures by race for each election division, it was easy to determine how blacks voted, but the absence of census data for units as small as election divisions made it impossible to break the voting returns down by class.

The starting point for any attempt to classify census tracts (and thus voting districts) by class in this period are the invaluable reports of statistics for major cities by census tracts which were published in the *Population and Housing* series of the *Sixteenth Census: 1940*. Unfortunately, the Bureau of the Census did not publish similar material for 1930; in some cities, however, local statisticians or census committees did publish census tract data for 1930. Where possible, I used data for 1930 and 1940 in determining the identification of census tracts by class. For Detroit, however, I was unable to locate data on socioeconomic characteristics by tract for 1930, so I used the information for 1940 as the basis for my classification.

There is no accepted method for determining the class of a particular census tract. I selected a number of indices which seemed to provide a good picture of the socioeconomic status of each of the tracts I analyzed. I used no set formula for deciding which tracts were lower-middle class and which were lower class, however. Categories of information changed from census to census; the range within each category was different for different cities. Taking into account all of the characteristics I listed, I formed a judgment about where to draw the line between lower-middle- and lower-class tracts in each city. Everyone would probably agree that the tracts I call lower class deserve that appellation. Those I label lower-middle class are more problematic; for some of them, upper-lower class might be a more apt description. For the sake of simplicity, however, I have used only lower-middle class to describe them. I hope the reader will accept, then, that lower-middle class is less a precise description of socioeconomic status than it is a way of distinguishing those tracts that were somewhat better off than the poorest ones in this period.

The nature of the available data requires a different method for making socioeconomic distinctions among voting districts in New York City. The Bureau of the Census reported its findings for New York City in 1940 in units called health areas. Each health area in Harlem subsumed two or more census tracts. As Table A.7 shows, the size of the health areas and the relative homogeneity of Harlem in this period make it impossible to use published census data of the kind employed for other cities to draw meaningful socioeconomic distinctions among voting districts. Tract data is available in Welfare Council of New York City, *Census Tract Data on Population and Housing: New York City: 1940* (New York, 1942), but it includes no information about employment, and the information provided about dwelling units is insufficient to provide the basis for an analysis of this kind. Walter Laidlaw, comp. and ed., *Population of the City of New York, 1890-1930* (New York, 1932), provides detailed information by census tracts for 1930, but the categories it covers—population density, composition of the population, etc.—do not speak to the question of economic status.

Therefore, I relied on data presented in two other publications— *New York City Market Analysis*, compiled by the *New York Herald Tribune, News,* and *Times* (New York, 1933), and *New York City Market Analysis*, compiled by the *New York News, Times, Daily Mirror,* and *Journal-American* (New York, 1942). These books provide basic socioeconomic data for every section of the city and present color-coded maps which give a block-by-block picture of the economic status of the residents. By correlating those maps with my own election district maps of Harlem, I was able to make some class distinctions among the districts. Two factors determined the color-coding in *New York City Market Analysis*—monthly rents and annual family expenditures. Those districts which I describe as lower-middle class had monthly rents of $50 and above and annual family expenditures of $3,000 or more. (The mean family expenditure reported for Harlem in 1933 was $3,097; for 1942, $2,158.) Those which I call lower class fell below those figures. Since the block-by-block patterns described in the volume published in 1933 (based on the 1930 census) are quite different from those in the volume published in 1942, it seemed inadvisable to make any assumptions about the socio-economic status of election districts in 1936. Therefore, I analyzed the Harlem data by class for 1932 and 1940 only.

TABLE A.1

Census Units, Political Units, and Black Population, Selected Cities, 1928-1940

City	Census Unit	1928	1932	1933	1934	1935	1936	1937	1938	1939	1940	% Black 1930	% Black 1940
Chicago	Community Area 35	W2-Pcts. 1-5, 9, 11-38, 40-42, 46-61; W3-Pcts. 1-6, 8-11	W1-Pcts. 28-31; W2-Pcts. 3-25, 27, 29-35, 38-49, 55, 56, 60-68, 70			Same	W1-Pcts. 13, 15, 16, 28; W2-Pcts. 3-5, 7-17, 19-25, 27, 29-35, 38-49, 55, 56, 60-63, 65-68, 70, 91, 92, 96, 97, 99-102		W1-Pcts. 13, 15, 16, 28; W2-Pcts. 2, 4-17, 19-25, 27, 29-35, 38-49, 55, 62, 63, 65-68, 70, 91, 96-102	Same	Same	88.6	93.8
	Community Area 38	W3-Pcts. 27-48, 50-70, 72-79; W4-Pcts. 12-27, 32-42, 54-57, 60, 61, 63, 64, 69-80, 83; W14-Pcts. 1, 19, 20,	W2-Pcts. 71-95, 97; W3-Pcts. 1-42, 64-69; W4-Pcts. 44-67			W2-Pcts. 18, 28, 64, 72-91; W3-Pcts. 1-39, 41, 42, 57, 64-67; W4-Pcts. 45, 47-69	W2-Pcts. 18, 28, 64, 71-90, 93-95, 104-110; W3-Pcts. 1-39, 41, 42, 57, 64-86, 92; W4-Pcts. 45, 47-69,		W2-Pcts. 3, 18, 28, 54, 56-58, 60, 61, 64, 71-90, 93-95; W3-Pcts. 1-39, 41, 42, 57, 64-72, 74-86, 92; W4-Pcts. 45-69, 71-73, 81, 84-87	Same	Same	94.7	98.1

TABLE A.1 (cont.)

City	Census Unit	Political Units										% Black	
		1928	1932	1933	1934	1935	1936	1937	1938	1939	1940	1930	1940
		22, 23, 26							71-73, 81, 84, 85				
	Community Area 40	W4-Pcts. 28-31, 58, 62, 81, 82; W5-Pcts. 23-43; W14-Pcts. 43-45, 47; W17-Pcts. 1-3, 13, 14, 21-25, 27	W3-Pcts. 43-57, 59-63, 70; W5-Pcts. 62-88			W3-Pcts. 40, 43-51, 53-56, 58-63; W5-Pcts. 62-88	W3-Pcts. 40, 43-51, 53-56, 58-63, 88, 89, 91; W5-Pcts. 62-88, 93,104-107, 110-114		W3-Pcts. 40, 43-51, 53-56, 58-63, 87-91; W5-Pcts. 62-67, 69-88, 93, 104-114	Same	Same	91.9	97.2
	Tracts 385-387	W32-Pcts. 29, 30	W28-Pcts. 32, 35, 37, 40			W28-Pcts. 31, 35, 37, 40	W28-Pcts. 31, 35, 40, 63		Same	Same	Same	92.8	97.8
	Tract 625	W6-Pcts. 50-56, 65-67	W6-Pcts. 12, 13, 15-22			Same	W6-Pcts. 12, 13, 15-22, 82		Same	Same	Same	81.1	92.3
	Tracts 934-935	W19-Pcts. 52, 59, 96	W19-Pcts. 44-46			W19-Pcts. 44-46, 61	Same		Same	Same	Same	90.8	93.2
Cincinnati	Ward 16		Ward 16	Same	Same		Same	Same	Same	Same	Same	78.1	92.2
Cleveland	Tract H-9	W11-Pcts. J-N	Same			Same	Same	Same	Same	Same	Same	88.6	92.9
	Tract I-8	W12-Pcts. K-M	Same	Same	Same	Same	Same	Same	Same	Same	Same	75.7	92.8

Tract M-3	W18-Pcts. I-K, Q	Same	Same	Same	Same	Same	Same	Same	Same	81.0	93.6
Tract M-4	W18-Pcts. L-N, R, S	Same	Same	Same	Same	Same	Same	Same	Same	76.1	90.4
Tract M-6	W19-Pcts. T-Y	Same	Same	Same	Same	Same	Same	Same	Same	81.0	90.8
Tract M-7	W17-Pcts. D-F	Same	Same	Same	Same	Same	Same	Same	Same	90.6	96.1
Tract M-8	W17-Pcts. G-J	Same	Same	Same	Same	Same	Same	Same	Same	78.3	92.4
Detroit Tract 120	W14-Pcts. 21-23; W 16-Pct. 27	Same	Same	Same	Same	Same	Same	Same	Same	79.1	90.0
Tract 509	W7-Pcts. 3-5	Same	Same	Same	Same	Same	Same	Same	Same	89.5	91.8
Tract 511	W9-Pcts. 3-6	Same	Same	Same	Same	Same	Same	Same	Same	86.4	91.5
Tract 528	W5-Pcts. 4-7	Same	Same	Same	Same	Same	Same	Same	Same	94.8	96.2
Tract 529	W3-Pcts. 3-6	Same	Same	Same	Same	Same	Same	Same	Same	95.6	98.6
Tract 534	W3-Pcts. 9-10	Same	Same	Same	W3-Pcts. 9-10A	Same	Same	Same	Same	90.0	93.7
Tract 535	W3-Pcts. 7-8	Same	Same	Same	Same	Same	Same	Same	Same	96.5	99.7
Tract 536	W5-Pcts. 8-9	Same	Same	Same	Same	Same	Same	Same	Same	90.8	96.0
Tract 544	W3-Pcts. 11-15	Same	Same	Same	Same	Same	Same	Same	Same	76.6	97.1

TABLE A.1 (cont.)

City	Census		Political Units									% Black	
		1928	1932	1933 1934	1935	1936	1937	1938	1939	1940	1930	1940	
Knoxville	Ward 5	Ward 5	Ward 5	Same		Same					95.1	94.1
New York	Tracts 208, 210, 212, 214, 224, 226, 228, 230, 232, 234, 236	A.D. 13- E.D. 15-19; A.D. 19- E.D. 16- 26; A.D. 21-E.D. 11-15, 17- 26, 34; A.D. 22- E.D. 30- 32, 34-36	A.D. 13- E.D. 17, 18, 20-23, 42; A.D. 19- E.D. 18-21, 23-29, 31- 34; A.D. 21- E.D. 16-19, 21-31; A.D. 22- E.D. 35-39, 41-43	Same	A.D. 13- E.D. 17, 18, 20-24; A.D. 19-E.D. 17-21, 23- 29, 31-34; A.D. 21- E.D. 16-19, 21-31; A.D. 22-E.D. 34-37, 40-44	A.D. 13- E.D. 15, 16, 18-22; A.D. 19-E.D. 18- 21, 23-29, 31-34; A.D. 21-E.D. 16-19, 21- 31; A.D. 22- E.D. 34-37, 40-44		A.D. 13- E.D. 15-17, 20-22; A.D. 19-E.D. 19- 27, 30-39; A.D. 21-E.D. 16-20, 22- 27, 30-41; A.D. 22- E.D. 38-40, 43-47, 49-51		A.D. 13- E.D. 15- 17, 20-22; A.D. 19- E.D.19-27, 30- 39; A.D. 21- E.D. 16-20, 22-27, 30- 40; A.D. 22- E.D. 38-40, 43-47, 49-51	97.4	99.3
Philadelphia		W4-E.D. 18; W7-E.D. 7, 12, 13, 15, 27; W20-E.D. 32; W30-E.D. 3, 5-9; W32- E.D. 18; W34- E.D. 39; W36- E.D. 1, 2, 9; W44-E.D. 1, 32; W47-E.D.	W7-E.D. 7, 12, 13; W20- E.D. 32; W 29-E.D. 2; W30-E.D. 3, 5-9, 12, 13; W32-E.D. 18; W34-E.D. 37, 39; W36- E.D. 2; W44- E.D. 1, 5, 32;	W4-E.D. 9; W20- E.D. 30; W24-E.D. 27; W29- E.D. 2; W30-E.D. 2-6, 9, 10, W32- E.D. 10, 14; W34-	Same	W4-E.D. 9; W20-E.D. 30; W24-E.D. 27; W29-E.D. 2; W30-E.D. 2-6, 9, 10; W32-E.D. 10, 14; W34- E.D. 13, 15; W36-E.D. 2; W44-E.D. 1;		W4-E.D. 9; W7- E.D. 14; W20-E.D. 27, 30; W24- E.D. 27; W28-E.D. 14; W29- E.D. 2; W 30-E.D.	W4- E.D. 9; W7- E.D. 14; W20- E.D. 27, 30; W28- E.D. 14; W29- E.D.	Same (93.4 percent black registration)		

	22, 26 (92.2 percent black registration)	W47-E.D. 22, 26 (92.9 percent black registration)	E.D. 13, 15; W36-E.D. 2; W44-E.D. 1; W47-E.D. 14, 19	W47-E.D. 14, 19 (93.2 percent black registration)	2-11; W 32-E.D. 9, 10, 14; W34-E.D. 13, 15; W36-E.D. 1, 2; W44-E.D. 1; W47-E.D. 14-16, 18, 19	2; W30-E.D. 2-11; W32-E.D. 9, 10, 14; W34-E.D. 13, 15; W36-E.D. 1, 2; W44-E.D. 1; W47-E.D. 14-16, 18, 19
Pittsburgh	Tracts 5A, 5D, 5E	W5-Pcts. 1, 4, 6, 13, 14	Same	Same	Same	Same	92.6

NOTE: In some cities, the boundaries of political units remained constant during the entire period of this study. In others, redistricting occurred at every possible opportunity. Hence the apparent imbalance in the table above.

KEY: W = ward
  A.D. = assembly district
  E.D. (New York) = election district
  E.D. (Philadelphia) = election division

TABLE A.2

Chicago Community Areas and Census Tracts: Socioeconomic Characteristics, 1930

Census Unit	% Black	% of Families Owning Homes	Median Monthly Rent	% of Families on Relief, 1934	% of Families with Radio
			LOWER CLASS		
Area 35	88.6	10.8	$35.28	63.6	30.9
Area 38	94.7	9.9	$44.46	52.3	46.9
Area 40	91.9	8.1	$57.50	36.1	61.6
Tract 385	87.1	8.8	n.a.	n.a.	19.7
Tract 386	96.3	8.2	n.a.	n.a.	20.8
Tract 387	95.0	9.1	n.a.	n.a.	40.0
			LOWER-MIDDLE CLASS		
Tract 625	81.1	26.6	n.a.	n.a.	65.2
Tract 934	92.6	70.3	n.a.	n.a.	53.2
Tract 935	89.1	67.6	n.a.	n.a.	49.1

SOURCES: Ernest W. Burgess and Charles Newcomb, eds., *Census Data of the City of Chicago, 1930* (Chicago, 1933); Louis Wirth and Margaret Furez, eds., *Local Community Fact Book, 1938* (Chicago, 1938).

TABLE A.3

Chicago Community Areas and Census Tracts: Socioeconomic Characteristics, 1940

Census Unit	% Black	% of Owner-Occupied Dwelling Units	Median Contract or Estimated Monthly Rent	% of Labor Force on Public Emergency Work	% of Labor Force Seeking Work	% of Dwelling Units with Mechanical Refrigeration	% of Dwelling Units with Radios
LOWER CLASS							
Area 35	93.8	6.2	$20.83	21.1	22.0	17.2	86.3
Area 38	98.1	5.6	$26.29	14.9	18.8	37.4	93.0
Area 40	97.2	5.1	$35.27	11.4	16.4	55.8	96.1
Tract 385	94.7	10.8	n.a.	37.4	5.5	5.4	86.5
Tract 386	99.8	5.6	$16.67	42.6	—	6.7	66.9
Tract 387	97.6	4.8	n.a.	11.5	34.4	2.4	78.0
LOWER-MIDDLE CLASS							
Tract 625	92.3	23.3	$36.65	8.9	13.3	66.3	97.0
Tract 934	91.6	54.9	$24.70	15.4	15.0	48.8	88.9
Tract 935	94.6	54.9	$26.64	13.4	18.9	50.5	92.8

SOURCES: U.S. Department of Commerce, Bureau of the Census, *Sixteenth Census of the United States: 1940, Population and Housing: Statistics for Census Tracts and Community Areas: Chicago, Ill.* (Washington, D.C., 1943); Louis Wirth and Eleanor H. Bernert, eds., *Local Community Fact Book of Chicago* (Chicago, 1949).

TABLE A.4

Cleveland Census Tracts: Socioeconomic Characteristics, 1930

Census Tract	% Black	% of Homes Owned	Equivalent Monthly Rent	Number of Gainful Workers Unemployed per 100 Families	% of Families with Radios
			LOWER CLASS		
H-9	88.8	6	$28	21.7	18.8
M-7	90.6	4	$31	16.5	17.3
M-8	78.3	6	$27	20.1	19.0
I-8*	75.7	6	$26	23.2	17.4
			LOWER-MIDDLE CLASS		
M-3	81.0	20	$34	17.1	35.1
M-4	76.1	26	$37	7.4	43.9
M-6	81.0	26	$37	6.0	30.6

SOURCE: Howard Whipple Green, *Population Characteristics by Census Tracts: Cleveland, Ohio, 1930* (Cleveland, 1931).
* Because the socioeconomic status of I-8 shifts between 1930 and 1940, it has not been included in calculations of voting by class.

TABLE A.5
Cleveland Census Tracts: Socioeconomic Characteristics, 1940

Census Tract	% Black	% of Owner-Occupied Dwelling Units	Median Contract or Estimated Monthly Rent	% of Labor Force on Public Emergency Work	% of Labor Force Seeking Work	% of Dwelling Units with Mechanical Refrigeration	% of Dwelling Units with Radios
LOWER CLASS							
H-9	92.9	4.8	$18.69	25.9	22.0	13.4	88.4
M-7	96.1	3.4	$18.93	25.8	22.1	15.9	92.9
M-8	92.4	6.5	$19.06	28.1	24.1	14.2	90.7
LOWER-MIDDLE CLASS							
I-8*	92.8	—	$22.06	9.1	5.0	81.5	98.9
M-3	93.6	16.6	$22.30	18.4	12.1	28.3	94.9
M-4	90.9	19.3	$23.86	12.9	15.3	47.1	96.9
M-6	90.8	22.7	$25.20	13.5	15.0	38.7	95.3

SOURCE: U.S. Department of Commerce, Bureau of the Census, Sixteenth Census of the United States: 1940, Population and Housing: Statistics for Census Tracts: Cleveland, Ohio and Adjacent Area (Washington, D.C., 1942).

* Because the socioeconomic status of I-8 shifts between 1930 and 1940, it has not been included in calculations of voting by class.

TABLE A.6
Detroit Census Tracts: Socioeconomic Characteristics, 1940

Census Tract	% Black	% of Owner-Occupied Dwelling Units	Median Contract or Estimated Monthly Rent	% of Labor Force on Public Emergency Work	% of Labor Force Seeking Work	% of Dwelling Units with Mechanical Refrigeration	% of Dwelling Units with Radios
				LOWER CLASS			
528	96.2	3.0	$24.20	27.7	27.8	9.0	82.9
529	98.6	1.5	$23.84	16.7	21.3	24.6	85.2
534	93.7	9.0	$24.10	19.3	21.2	10.1	90.3
536	96.0	4.6	$22.95	32.0	20.1	6.7	89.1
535*	99.7	1.5	$18.88	13.0	10.7	73.4	95.3
				LOWER-MIDDLE CLASS			
120	90.0	35.0	$33.87	5.4	10.9	67.8	98.8
509	91.8	21.3	$21.32	20.4	18.2	10.8	82.7
511	91.5	16.4	$22.78	21.9	17.4	15.8	90.6
544	97.1	4.3	$34.09	11.8	18.5	35.0	97.2

Source: U.S. Department of Commerce, Bureau of the Census, Sixteenth Census of the United States: 1940, Population and Housing: Statistics for Census Tracts: Detroit, Mich., and Adjacent Area (Washington, D.C., 1942).
* The indicators for Tract 535 are sufficiently ambiguous to make it difficult to categorize in the absence of census data for 1930. Therefore, it has not been included in calculations of voting by class.

TABLE A.7
Harlem Health Areas: Socioeconomic Characteristics, 1940

Health Area	% Black	% of Owner-Occupied Dwelling Units	Median Contract or Estimated Monthly Rent	% of Labor Force on Public Emergency Work	% of Labor Force Seeking Work	% of Dwelling Units with Mechanical Refrigeration	% of Dwelling Units with Radios
8	99.8	0.1	$35.45	8.5	19.5	39.3	98.0
10	99.5	2.7	$40.20	8.9	20.1	37.9	98.0
12	99.5	5.2	$35.02	9.9	17.8	21.7	95.9
13	98.5	1.5	$33.31	11.2	23.1	17.1	97.0

SOURCE: U.S. Department of Commerce, Bureau of the Census, *Sixteenth Census of the United States: 1940, Population and Housing: Statistics for Health Areas: New York City* (Washington, D.C., 1942).

A Note on Sources

Given the abundance of footnotes on the preceding pages, it would serve little purpose to provide a full bibliography of all the materials on which this study is based. This Note on Sources is designed to direct the reader to the most important primary sources in three categories: manuscript collections, newspapers and magazines, and oral history interviews.

Manuscript Collections

The extraordinary resources of the Franklin D. Roosevelt Library in Hyde Park, New York, provide the starting point for anyone who studies the New Deal. Both the Franklin D. Roosevelt Papers and the Eleanor Roosevelt Papers contain voluminous materials which document administration policies toward blacks, the personal attitudes and activities of the President and the First Lady as they relate to race, and the attitudes of blacks toward the Roosevelts. The White House Usher's Diary, 1933-1940, in the Records of the Office of the Chief of Social Entertainments, which lists the business and social activities of Franklin and Eleanor Roosevelt, makes it possible to trace most of their official encounters with black people. The Good Neighbor League Papers include important materials bearing on the role of the League in the election of 1936, and the Stephen T. Early Papers describe the Sloan incident during the campaign of 1940. There are scattered items in a number of other collections at Hyde Park, including the John M. Carmody Papers, the Democratic National Committee Papers, the Papers of the Women's Division of the Democratic National Committee, the Lorena Hickok Papers, the Rexford G. Tugwell Papers, and the Aubrey Williams Papers.

The National Archives houses the records of the cabinet departments and emergency agencies. For the purposes of this study, the most important are: the Records of the Civil Works Administration, the Records of the Federal Emergency Relief Administration, and the Records of the Works Progress Administration, all in Record Group 69; the Records of the National Youth Administration, in Record Group 119; the Records of the Department of the Interior, in Record Group 48; and the Records of the Department of Agriculture, in Record Group 16. The Manuscript Division of the Library of Congress houses the papers of two important administration officials: James A. Farley and Harold L. Ickes. The Federal Bureau of Investigation files on the National Association for the Advancement of Colored People, the National Negro Congress, and the National Urban League, 1933-1945, were made available to me under the Freedom of Information/Privacy Act.

Among the papers of the various organizations for racial advancement, the most important are those of the National Association for the Advancement of Colored People, in the Manuscript Division of the Library of Congress. The collection includes rich and varied materials on such subjects as the battle for antilynching legislation (which should be supplemented by the Edward P. Costigan Papers, Western Historical Collections, Norlin Library, University of Colorado), political activities, and the participation of blacks in the relief and recovery programs of the New Deal. There are some scattered items of interest in the papers of two NAACP officials: James Weldon Johnson, at the Beinecke Library, Yale University; and Arthur B. Spingarn, in the Manuscript Division of the Library of Congress. The National Negro Congress Papers, at the Schomburg Center for Research in Black Culture, New York City, include fragmentary records of the Joint Committee on National Recovery. There are some useful materials in the National Urban League Papers, Manuscript Division, Library of Congress, and the Records of the National Council of Negro Women, National Archives for Black Women's History, Washington, D.C.

The papers of blacks who were involved in politics and government in the 1930s are an invaluable resource. For the Black Cabinet, the following are currently available to scholars: the Lawrence A. Oxley Papers, in the Records of the United States Employment Service, Record Group 183, National Archives; the William J. Trent, Jr. Papers, Manuscript Division, Moorland-Spingarn Research Center, Howard University; the Robert C. Weaver Papers, Schomburg Center for Research in Black Culture; and the Works Progress Administration Papers (actually the papers of Alfred Edgar Smith), Manuscript Division, Moorland-Spingarn Research Center. The Frank S. Horne Papers, Amistad Research Center,

Dillard University, unfortunately contain very little information about his government service in the 1930s. The vast collection of Arthur W. Mitchell Papers, Chicago Historical Society, documents his congressional career as well as his activities in connection with the Colored Division of the Democratic National Committee in the election of 1936. Information about Julian D. Rainey's campaign activities can be found in the papers of Rainey's secretary, Carrie Burton Overton, in the Archives of Labor History and Urban Affairs, Wayne State University. The Mary Church Terrell Papers, Manuscript Division, Library of Congress, include some material relating to Terrell's role in the Republican presidential campaign in 1932. The McDuffie Papers, Negro Collection, Trevor Arnett Library, Atlanta University, provide some evidence of the roles played by Roosevelt's valet and maid, Irvin and Elizabeth McDuffie. There are preliminary drafts of Mrs. McDuffie's memoirs in the Franklin D. Roosevelt Memorial Foundation, Record Group 21, Franklin D. Roosevelt Library.

The papers of the director of the Associated Negro Press, Claude A. Barnett, in the Chicago Historical Society, include correspondence and numerous newspaper clippings bearing on the political activities and attitudes of blacks in this period. The Marian Anderson Collection, Manuscript Division, Moorland-Spingarn Research Center, provides extensive documentation with respect to the Easter Sunday concert in 1939. The Birth Records of Harlem Hospital, 1933-1945, allowed me to identify babies who were named for the Roosevelts.

Two major repositories for materials relating to the history of blacks in the United States—the Schomburg Center for Research in Black Culture and the Moorland-Spingarn Research Center—maintain vertical files which include a variety of clippings, press releases, and other documents pertaining to some of the principal actors and agencies mentioned in this study. Particularly notable are the Roosevelt Administration Scrapbooks at the Schomburg.

NEWSPAPERS AND MAGAZINES

Black newspapers and magazines provide detailed information about the political attitudes and activities of black people, the effect of New Deal programs on blacks, and virtually every other subject covered in this book. I read extensively in the following weekly newspapers: *Afro-American, Chicago Defender, Cleveland Gazette, New York Age, New York Amsterdam News, Nor-*

folk Journal and Guide, Philadelphia Tribune, Pittsburgh Courier, and *Savannah Tribune. Crisis*, the magazine of the National Association for the Advancement of Colored People, and *Opportunity*, the journal of the National Urban League, are both full of relevant material. Other black periodicals, popular as well as scholarly, which I read with some care include: *Ebony, Journal of Negro Education, Journal of Negro History, Negro Digest, Negro History Bulletin*, and *Phylon*.

Among white newspapers, I read extensively in the *New York Times* for the period 1928-1940, and mined the *New York Herald Tribune* for its coverage of the presidential campaigns in 1936 and 1940. The popular magazines that paid the most attention to blacks in this period were *Christian Century, New Republic, Newsweek, Saturday Evening Post*, and *Time*.

ORAL HISTORY INTERVIEWS

This book relies heavily on oral history of two kinds: interviews conducted expressly for this study, and transcripts of interviews deposited in research libraries or held privately.

The following interviews were conducted for this study:

Interviews conducted by Nancy J. Weiss
William Holmes Borders, June 10, 1977, Atlanta
Earl Brown, June 29, 1977, New York City
Theodore E. Brown, Nov. 29, 1976, Washington, D.C.
Herrington Bryce, Oct. 20, 1976, Washington, D.C. (by telephone)
Yvonne Brathwaite Burke, Mar. 24, 1977, Washington, D.C.
Robert A. Carter, Nov. 15, 1976, New York City
Central Harlem Senior Citizens' Coalition, group interviews, April 18, 1977, New York City
Kenneth B. Clark, May 17, 1977, New York City
John Conyers, Jr., Mar. 23, 1977, Washington, D.C.
Thomas G. Corcoran, May 23, 1977, Washington, D.C.
John A. Davis, Nov. 8, 1976, New York City
Lloyd E. Dickens, Nov. 15, 1976, New York City
Earl B. Dickerson, Aug. 16, 1974, Chicago
James A. Farley, Oct. 3, 1974, New York City
Bryant George, Sept. 24, 1976, New York City
David M. Grant, June 22, 1977, St. Louis (by telephone)
Ivy Graves, May 4, 1977, New York City

Elmer W. Henderson, Mar. 24, 1977, Washington, D.C.
Laurence I. Hewes, Jr., Feb. 7, 1977, Santa Barbara
A. Leon Higginbotham, Jr., Jan. 21, 1981, Philadelphia
Graham W. Jackson, June 10, 1977, Atlanta
Vernon E. Jordan, Jr., Oct. 26, 1976, New York City
Ernest L. Kaiser, May 20, 1977, New York City
Martin Luther King, Sr., June 10, 1977, Atlanta
Joseph P. Lash, May 5, 1977, New York City
Rayford W. Logan, Nov. 29, 1976, Washington, D.C.
Manhattanville Senior Center, group interviews, May 4, 1977,
    New York City
Ernest Rice McKinney, Nov. 11, 1976, New York City
Louis E. Martin, May 13, 1977, Chicago
Benjamin E. Mays, June 10, 1977, Atlanta
Ralph H. Metcalfe, Mar. 24, 1977, Washington, D.C.
Clarence M. Mitchell, Jr., Oct. 29, 1976, Dec. 7, 1979, Washington,
    D.C.
E. Frederic Morrow, Apr. 29, 1977, Princeton, N.J.
John H. Murphy III, Apr. 28, 1977, Baltimore
Pauli Murray, July 1, 1977, Alexandria, Va.
Barrington D. Parker, Oct. 28, 1976, Washington, D.C. (by tele-
    phone)
Marjorie Parker, Oct. 28, 1976, Washington, D.C. (by telephone)
Basil Paterson, Dec. 1, 1976, New York City
Samuel D. Proctor, Nov. 10, 1976, New York City
Charles Rangel, Nov. 3, 1976, New York City
William Raspberry, Oct. 20, 1976, Washington, D.C.
James Roosevelt, Feb. 28, 1977, Newport Beach, Calif.
John A. Roosevelt, Mar. 11, 1977, New York City
Bayard Rustin, Nov. 15, 1976, New York City
Alfred Edgar Smith, May 24, 1977, Washington, D.C.
John Sparkman, May 23, 1977, Washington, D.C.
Carl B. Stokes, Aug. 22, 1979, New York City
Doyle L. Sumner, Oct. 25, 27, 1976, New York City
Percy E. Sutton, Nov. 8, 1976, New York City
W. J. Trent, Jr., Dec. 8, 1976, New York City
Sterling Tucker, Mar. 23, 1977, Washington, D.C.
Rexford G. Tugwell, Feb. 7, 1977, Santa Barbara
Harold R. Tyler, Jr., Oct. 29, 1976, Washington, D.C.
George L.-P. Weaver, May 23, 1977, Washington, D.C.
Robert C. Weaver, Nov. 12, 1976, Oct. 12, 1979, New York City
Roy Wilkins, Aug. 17, 1976, New York City
Eddie Williams, Oct. 20, 1976, Washington, D.C.

Franklin H. Williams, Oct. 25, 1976, New York City
Zack S. Williams, Aug. 14, 1975, Washington, D.C.
Ida Wood, Oct. 25, 1976, New York City

Interviews conducted by Lawrence Hamm

Russell Bingham, July 10, 1979, Newark, N.J.
Ernest Bowser, Aug. 14, 1979, East Orange, N.J.
Julia Gee, July 31, 1979, East Orange, N.J.
Wilnora Holman, July 3, 1979, Newark, N.J.
Charles Matthews, July 17, 1979, Newark, N.J.
Harry Van Dyke, Aug. 28, 1979, Newark, N.J.

Transcripts of interviews deposited in research libraries that proved particularly helpful include:

In the Columbia University Oral History Collection, the Reminiscences of

Will Winton Alexander, 1952
Samuel J. Battle, 1960
Joseph A. Gavagan, 1950
Frances Perkins, 1955
George S. Schuyler, 1962
Norman Thomas, 1949-1950
Henry Agard Wallace, 1963
Roy Wilkins, 1960

In the Civil Rights Documentation Project, Ralph J. Bunche Oral History Collection, Moorland-Spingarn Research Center, Howard University, interviews with

Lucille Black, Nov. 1, 1967
Eugene Davidson, June 28, 1968
Lester B. Granger, May 22, 1968
Dorothy Height, Feb. 13, 1970
Frank Smith Horne, Sept. 4, 1968
Ruby Hurley, Jan. 26, 1968
Clarence Mitchell, Jr., Dec. 6, 1968
A. Philip Randolph, Jan. 14, 1969
C. A. Scott, Jan. 25, 1968

In the Eleanor Roosevelt Oral History Project, Franklin D. Roosevelt Library, interviews with

Jonathan Daniels, Nov. 16, 1979
C. R. Smith, 1978

Other

Hilton B. Clark interviews with J. Raymond Jones, 1974-1975, transcripts in the possession of Mr. Clark

Dorothy Height interview, Black Women's Oral History Project, Schlesinger Library, 1977, copy in Columbia University Oral History Collection

Debra Newman interview with Lawrence A. Oxley, Apr. 23, 1973, Records of the United States Employment Service, Box 1385, Record Group 183, National Archives

Robert Weaver oral history interview, Nov. 30, 1973, Labor-Management Documentation Center, New York State School of Industrial and Labor Relations, Cornell University, transcript provided by Mr. Weaver

Rexford G. Tugwell interviews with Eleanor Roosevelt, June 24, 1957, Hyde Park, N.Y.; William, D. Hassett, June 26, 1957, Northfield, Vt.; and Daisy Bonner, July 26, 1957, Warm Springs, Ga., transcripts lent by Frank Freidel

Index

Library of Congress Cataloging in Publication Data

Weiss, Nancy J. (Nancy Joan), 1944-
Farewell to the party of Lincoln.
Bibliography: p.   Includes index.
1. Roosevelt, Franklin D. (Franklin Delano),
1882-1945—Relations with Afro-Americans.
2. Afro-Americans—Politics and suffrage.
3. Voting—United States—History—20th century.
I. Title.
E807.W44   1983   973.917′092′4   83-3247
ISBN 0-691-04703-0
ISBN 0-691-10151-8 (lim. pbk. ed.)

Nancy J. Weiss is Professor of History at Princeton University.
She is the author of *The National Urban League, 1910-1940* (1974)
and is currently writing a biography of Whitney M. Young, Jr.